Legendary
LEADERS
of the Bible

6-24-12

Legendary
LEADERS
of the Bible

15 Stories You
Should Know

Shanna D. Gregor

BARBOUR
PUBLISHING

Our mission is to publish and distribute inspirational products offering exceptional value and biblical encouragement to the masses.

Member of the
Evangelical Christian
Publishers Association

CONTENTS

INTRODUCTION

The lives depicted in the pages of the Bible provide examples—both positive and negative—of relationships with God. The lives of *Legendary Leaders of the Bible* give us beautiful pictures and powerful examples that we can apply to the choices and decisions we make each day. It is my prayer that these practical and biblical examples will give you insight and instruction, as well as encourage you to develop a deeper relationship with the Lord and with those you lead. May you experience His plans and fulfill His purpose in all you do as a modern-day leader, pointing those you come in contact with to a personal relationship with Christ.

SHANNA D. GREGOR

Abraham

THE FATHER OF FAITH

ON A WALK WITH GOD

Abraham's story is far from ordinary. Born in the land of Ur, his parents named him Abram. His people worshipped other gods, yet the one true God spoke to him and asked him to do an extraordinary thing: to trust Him. He requested that Abram leave everything familiar—his extended family, his home—all he had ever known—and take a walk with God. Abram obeyed God, not even knowing where he was going.

Because Abram trusted God and faithfully obeyed Him, God made a covenant with him and promised Abram that he would become the father of many nations, even changing his name to Abraham to reflect this (meaning "father of a multitude"). At the time, Abraham and his wife, Sarah, had no children and were beyond childbearing age. Growing impatient as year after year passed with no child, Abraham questioned God and took matters into his own hands. Abraham was far from perfect, but his life choices are listed as examples for others to follow in Hebrews 11—the Hall of the Faithful. His entire life, from the time that God called him out of the land of Ur, to his very last days, he believed God and walked with Him in faith.

DID YOU KNOW?

In Abraham's day, a caravan traveled approximately twenty miles a day. A trip from Haran, where Abraham lived at the time, to Canaan was a distance of about five hundred miles. Such a trip would take about a month.

LEADERSHIP LESSON #1
OBEY WITHOUT KNOWING

And without faith it is impossible to please God,
because anyone who comes to him must believe that he
exists and that he rewards those who earnestly seek him. . . .
By faith Abraham, when called to go to a place he
would later receive as his inheritance, obeyed and went,
even though he did not know where he was going.
HEBREWS 11:6, 8

Most of Abraham's family and community worshipped false gods. Yet, Abraham believed God and trusted Him enough to follow Him to a better place. Most people want to know details about where they're going and why before making a decision. After all, it's one thing to know where you're going and plan your journey; it's entirely another to just start walking. But all Abraham knew was that God told him to leave his family and start walking to a land that would be revealed to him. In a spectacular display of faith, Abraham obeyed God without demanding answers.

Abraham's decision to trust God with his life and with his family pleased God. It demonstrated that his relationship with God was strong. Has God asked you to do something when you didn't have all the answers? Perhaps it was difficult to commit and follow Him. Most likely your obedience stretched your faith to a new level.

LEADERSHIP LESSON #2
LEAVE A LEGACY

By faith even Sarah, who was past childbearing age,
was enabled to bear children because she considered him
faithful who had made the promise. And so from this one man,
and he as good as dead, came descendants as numerous as the
stars in the sky and as countless as the sand on the seashore.
HEBREWS 11:11–12

Abraham's legacy is one of sustained faith. He trusted God to keep His promise of descendants as numerous as the stars in the sky. Though Abraham wasn't perfect, he genuinely believed God. When Sarah impatiently convinced him to have a child with her handmaiden, God gave him a son, Ishmael. When Sarah finally conceived, she, too, had a son—named Isaac. Ishmael was the product of earthly schemes, and Isaac was the product of God's promise, but each son produced a nation that continues to thrive today.

Abraham's life provides a picture of what it means to walk with God. It's no wonder scripture often refers to God as the God of Abraham. As flawed humans, we can take heart in knowing God always delivers on His promises to the faithful, even if we waver in a moment of weakness. He cares for each of us, taking the good with the bad, and always has the big picture of our future in mind. Isn't that amazing? Reflect today where your walk with God has led you thus far and what kind of legacy you're leaving behind.

LEADERSHIP LESSON #3
LOOK TO THE ETERNAL

And even when he reached the land God promised him,
he lived there by faith—for he was like a foreigner,
living in tents. And so did Isaac and Jacob, who inherited
the same promise. Abraham was confidently looking
forward to a city with eternal foundations,
a city designed and built by God.
HEBREWS 11:9–10 NLT

Abraham's eyes were fixed on something more than the physical land that God had promised him. His heart longed for the eternal home where he would one day see the face of God. Like Abraham, we should live each day mindful of where we are going. While God wants us to enjoy and find fulfillment in the here and now, it's important to keep in mind that our lives on earth are but a small speck in the vast sphere of eternity.

Leaders should look to the eternal, knowing that the decisions they make today have a lasting impact for all time. God gives us standards to live by to ensure we can spend eternity with Him, so we can influence others to choose to spend eternity in a city where we will reign with Jesus and behold the face of God.

LEADERSHIP LESSON #4
PASS THE TEST

*By faith Abraham, when he was tested, offered up Isaac,
and he who had received the promises offered up his only
begotten son, of whom it was said, "In Isaac your seed
shall be called," concluding that God was able to
raise him up, even from the dead, from which
he also received him in a figurative sense.*
HEBREWS 11:17–19 NKJV

God is faithful. Abraham knew that no matter what God asked of him—no matter how unthinkable—he could always trust God to honor His promises and keep his best interests in mind. So when God asked Abraham to sacrifice the very son He had guaranteed him, Abraham believed that God would not forsake him.

There were no testimonies of anyone being raised from the dead. Yet Abraham believed if that was what it took for God to keep His promise, then God would do it. God wouldn't let Isaac die—right? Imagine the doubt Abraham must have battled in his mind. But in the end, he was willing to do as God asked. He passed the test, and God intervened, saving Isaac after all.

Sometimes leadership requires radical obedience, but, as Abraham's example assures us, God will never go back on His Word.

LEADERSHIP LESSON #5
SEE THE BIG PICTURE

[The LORD] took him outside and said, "Now look toward the heavens, and count the stars, if you are able to count them." And He said to him, "So shall your descendants be." Then he believed in the LORD; and He reckoned it to him as righteousness.
GENESIS 15:5–6 NASB

As children we are eager to believe in miracles, but age and cynicism often wear on our perception of reality as we get older. Abraham was an exception. In his old age he hadn't lost his childlike ability to believe in the impossible. God gave him a picture of what it meant when He called him "Father Abraham." His offspring would number more than the stars in the sky and the sands of the sea.

How many times have you had a God-given dream and thought, *What does God's plan for me look like?* Sometimes there are so many distractions clouding the way that you can't clearly see the picture of the life God has given you. Abraham took time to step outside his tent and look at what God wanted him to see. Get quiet, step outside of life's distractions, and let God show you the big picture He has for your life.

LEADERSHIP LESSON #6
WORK WITH GOD

What we read in Scripture is, "Abraham entered into what
God was doing for him, and that was the turning point.
He trusted God to set him right instead of
trying to be right on his own."
ROMANS 4:3 MSG

Henry Blackaby has said, "Find out where God is at work and join Him there." It's good advice, especially considering that God is always at work and longs for our participation in His master plan. In general, Abraham embraced what God was doing in his life and worked with Him by following His lead and doing His will. However, there were a few times when Abraham tried to bring God's plan to fruition on his own terms—like when he conceived a son with his wife's handmaiden. The result was a child—but not the child God had promised.

It can be hard for leaders to relinquish control sometimes—even to God. It's important, though, in working with God, that we acknowledge Him as the foreman. By following His direction and submitting to His timing, it's a lot easier to see His promises fulfilled.

DISCUSSION QUESTIONS

1. Obedience is extremely important to God. When Abraham stepped out in faith, he took his nephew, Lot, with him. Do you think this was partial obedience on Abraham's part?

2. What did the decision to include Lot cost Abraham?

3. Abraham allowed other people to influence his decisions rather than waiting on God to fulfill His promise. Are you often tempted to listen to others?

Daniel

A LIFE TO MODEL

A HEART PURPOSED FOR GOD

Taken from his homeland into captivity as a teenager, Daniel quickly determined in the depth of his soul to keep his commitment to God. When commanded to eat the king's food (which did not follow Jewish dietary restrictions), Daniel refused to violate the laws of his God. He was unwilling to cave to pressure and conform to the new culture of his captors, obeying God no matter the consequences.

Daniel purposed in his heart to put God first in every part of his life, and God granted him favor in the hearts of others. This strong sense of direction and purpose gained him admiration and respect—even in the eyes of the king of his captivity.

From his days as a teenager to late into his life, Daniel refused to compromise his convictions, and God positioned him as a voice to speak God's message to the hearts of the kings. Daniel's life is a model to be followed and confirmation that you can succeed in life without compromising your soul—if you're willing to purpose in your heart to put God first no matter the cost.

CRIME AND PUNISHMENT

At the height of the Babylonian Empire, criminals found guilty of murder, treason, and arson were executed by being torn apart by wild animals, a punishment called *damnatio ad beastie*, or "condemnation to beasts." Those accused of religious crimes—such as being a Christian—could also be sentenced to this punishment. Daniel's sentence to spend the night in the lions' den was not an unusual sentence in his day.

LEADERSHIP LESSON #7
CULTIVATE A HUMBLE HEART

*"And it is not because I am wiser than anyone else
that I know the secret of your dream, but because
God wants you to understand what was in your heart."*
DANIEL 2:30 NLT

Daniel did not seek the approval of a king, but the approval of his God. After interpreting King Nebuchadnezzar's dream, Daniel could have adopted a proud attitude and taken credit for the wisdom God had bestowed on him. Instead, Daniel remained humble. He rightfully gave all the glory to God.

Daniel had asked the others to pray and fast. His willingness to follow God with a humble heart and set a good example saved all the wise men from the king's proclamation of death for those who could not interpret his dream. When God grants you favor among others, where do you point the spotlight? As Daniel demonstrates, it's not only important as a leader to include your team in your success, but also the Source of all success: God.

LEADERSHIP LESSON #8
MAKE A PERSONAL COMMITMENT

*But Daniel resolved not to defile himself with
the royal food and wine, and he asked the chief official
for permission not to defile himself this way.*
DANIEL 1:8

Daniel's personal commitment to God was more important to him than his very life. He was forced to live in a society that that did not honor God, yet he made a personal choice to follow hard after Him anyway. Daniel made his choice in his heart long before he was ever tempted by the Babylonian lifestyle.

No doubt Daniel was perceived as a leader by those around him because of his strong personal commitments and unwavering resolve to do things God's way. Likewise, even though our modern culture does not (for the most part) honor God, when we stick to our personal commitment to Him in the face of temptation, we will find ourselves highly favored—by God and others.

LEADERSHIP LESSON #9
HAVE THE RIGHT MOTIVATION

*"This man Daniel, whom the king named Belteshazzar,
has exceptional ability and is filled with divine knowledge
and understanding. He can interpret dreams,
explain riddles, and solve difficult problems.
Call for Daniel, and he will tell you
what the writing means."*
DANIEL 5:12 NLT

Daniel had earned quite a reputation as a wise man within the courts of the Babylonian and Persian kings. Time and time again he demonstrated his ability to give important and timely feedback to these rulers, but more impressive still was his indifference to bribery and worldly compensation. When the king offered Daniel gifts and great power to explain the writing on the wall, Daniel refused the gifts. It was more important to Daniel that the kings understood that his dream interpretations were not tainted by the king's flattery or material rewards.

As leaders it is important that we are guided by the right motivation. When mere money and power are our only motives, how can we expect to be taken seriously? But if we choose to do something solely because it's the thing God would have us do according to His will, people will recognize our integrity and the impact will be eternal.

LEADERSHIP LESSON #10
GAIN CONFIDENCE
THROUGH GOD'S LOVE

And the man said to me, "Daniel, you are very precious
to God, so listen carefully to what I have to say to you.
Stand up, for I have now been sent to you."
When he said this to me, I stood up, still trembling.
DANIEL 10:11 NLT

Daniel knew he was greatly loved by God. He was relentless in his desire to please Him and obey Him, and God was there every step of the way to encourage Daniel to pray for his people and speak to kings the very words God handed down from the throne of heaven.

There is no greater blessing than to know you are deeply loved by God. The Bible promises that you are loved with an everlasting love. There is nothing you can do to make God stop loving you. That knowledge can give you the confidence needed to stand before kings and officials and proclaim God's Word boldly—even today.

LEADERSHIP LESSON #11
BE DISCIPLINED IN PRAYER

When Daniel knew that the writing was signed,
he went home. And in his upper room, with his windows
open toward Jerusalem, he knelt down on his knees three
times that day, and prayed and gave thanks before his God,
as was his custom since early days.
DANIEL 6:10 NKJV

Daniel believed God was with him every moment of his day. He took time out for conversations with God, and the spiritual disciplines Daniel practiced each day drew him closer to God, allowing him to hear God's instruction. Even when a decree was made that he could be thrown into a den of hungry lions as punishment for praying to God, he refused to let go of that connection that sustained him. And sure enough, God delivered Daniel by shutting the mouths of the lions.

Life today can be hectic. Busy schedules can push into our time with God. Are you disciplined in prayer? Leaders committed to prayer find success in every aspect of life. If God can shut the lions' mouths for Daniel, don't you think He can give you all the time you need to do what's important if you seek Him in prayer first?

LEADERSHIP LESSON #12
DON'T BE AFRAID OF HARD WORK

*Then this Daniel began distinguishing himself among
the commissioners and satraps because he possessed
an extraordinary spirit, and the king planned
to appoint him over the entire kingdom.*
DANIEL 6:3 NASB

Daniel was industrious. He wasn't afraid of hard work. He was a son of the royal family of Judah and could have refused to work with his Babylonian masters. Instead, he demonstrated a great work ethic and became a key adviser to the kings of the Babylonian and the Persian Empires.

Christians lead best when they set an example of diligence, hard work, and productiveness. God wants us to be examples of Him in all we do. When we are willing to go the extra mile, do the best we can do, then God can put His "super" on our "natural" for an outcome that is worth all the effort we can give.

DISCUSSION QUESTIONS

1. Imagine what it must have been like to be of noble blood, finding yourself servant to your enemies. Would you have rebelled a little bit? Would you have been tempted to have a pity party?

2. Daniel knew his strength came from his relationship with God. He was able to do what was before him because of his faith in the one true God. What is standing in your way of success?

3. Do you see a little of Daniel in yourself? What characteristics do you see in the life of Daniel that can help you become the leader God intended you to be?

David

A Heart That Beats for God

ROCKY ASCENT TO ROYALTY

David was the son his father had forgotten. He was left out with the sheep when the prophet Samuel came to his house to anoint the next king of Israel. His own father didn't think he had king potential. Yet God saw his heart instead of his appearance and called David to lead His chosen people.

A warrior for God, as a teenager David stood against a giant "uncircumcised Philistine" that dared mock his God. Appointed as a servant in the house of Saul, he developed a friendship with the king's son, Jonathan. But his warrior spirit and triumphs in battle caused King Saul to become jealous of David's success. David hid the promise from God that he would be king deep in his heart to avoid the full brunt of Saul's wrath. Imagine how difficult it must have been for David to carry his dream in his heart, never knowing when it would become a reality.

Even after he became king, David's passion carried him past the boundaries God set before him and into sin, yet he remained tender toward God and quick to take responsibility and repent.

HIGHS AND LOWS OF KING DAVID'S LIFE

- ↑ Anointed king of Israel (1 Samuel 16)
- ↑ Killed Goliath, the giant Philistine (1 Samuel 17)
- ↓ Ran for his life from King Saul (1 Samuel 18–31)
- ↓ Found Ziklag destroyed and his men want to kill him (1 Samuel 30)
- ↑ Crowned king over Judah and Israel (2 Samuel 12; 15)
- ↓ Chose to commit adultery and murder (2 Samuel 11)
- ↑ Made preparations for God's temple in the city (1 Chronicles 22)

LEADERSHIP LESSON #13
STAY CLOSE TO GOD

God removed [Saul] from office and put King David in his place, with this commendation: "I've searched the land and found this David, son of Jesse. He's a man whose heart beats to my heart, a man who will do what I tell him."
ACTS 13:22 MSG

David had his priorities straight. He spent time developing a relationship with God. He became intimate with Him. In fact, he is described in Acts 13:22 (MSG) as one whose heart beats to the same rhythm as God's, which implies that the desires of David's heart must have been in harmony with God's desires.

Imagine becoming so intimate in your relationship with God that you are totally in sync with Him—knowing exactly what pleases Him and what grieves Him. Such a remarkably sensitive relationship takes time to cultivate, but it's not impossible to achieve. Improving our self-awareness and taking more time out for God can put us in tune with the things God is involved in and our personal motivations. Ask yourself: are you doing things today with a heart that beats with God's heart?

LEADERSHIP LESSON #14
KEEP A TRANSPARENT HEART

Where can I go from Your Spirit? Or where can I flee from
Your presence? If I ascend into heaven, You are there;
if I make my bed in hell, behold, You are there. If I take
the wings of the morning, and dwell in the uttermost
parts of the sea, even there Your hand shall lead me,
and Your right hand shall hold me.
PSALM 139:7–10 NKJV

David wrote seventy-three psalms, unafraid to demonstrate transparency and vulnerability in everything he wrote. He gave his heart fully to the Lord, holding nothing back. He shared his disappointments and his triumphs. When he was tempted to become angry or offended with God about something, he shared his concerns and feelings openly, as if writing to a close friend.

David understood that God was with him, no matter where he went or what he did. He laid his heart open and bare before God, knowing that God knew his every thought and intention anyway. In the same way, God knows you better than you know yourself. It's time to let go and be real with Him. Let Him hear the real you in your prayer time. Allow yourself to become an open book before Him, and God will likewise give you the courage you need to be transparent before those you lead.

LEADERSHIP LESSON #15
KEEP A PLIABLE HEART

"You did it in secret, but I will do this thing in broad daylight before all Israel." Then David said to Nathan, "I have sinned against the LORD." Nathan replied, "The LORD has taken away your sin. You are not going to die. But because by doing this you have shown utter contempt for the LORD, the son born to you will die."

2 SAMUEL 12:12–14

David committed adultery, and when Uriah's wife, Bathsheba, became pregnant with David's child, he attempted to cover the sin by having Uriah killed in battle. Covering one sin with another may have kept other people from finding out, but the adultery and murder were never hidden from God. Through the prophet Nathan, God exposed David's heart. David repented and accepted the consequences of his sin.

David was never perfect, but he was willing to ask God for forgiveness. Leadership requires a heart that is tender toward the Spirit of God and open to correction. Pride can harden the heart of leaders, but tenderness toward God will keep your heart pliable and ready for God to work in you and through you.

LEADERSHIP LESSON #16
RESPECT AUTHORITY

Saul went into a cave to relieve himself. But as it happened,
David and his men were hiding farther back in that very
cave! "Now's your opportunity!" David's men whispered to
him. "Today the LORD is telling you, 'I will certainly put
your enemy into your power, to do with as you wish.'"
Then David crept forward and cut off a piece of the
hem of Saul's robe. But then David's conscience began
bothering him because he had cut Saul's robe.
1 SAMUEL 24:3–5 NLT

David knew that someday he would be king, but for a long season in his life, Saul remained the jealous king who wanted to kill David because of his popularity among the people as a war hero. David's men wanted to help him seize his promise from God—perhaps ahead of the Lord's timing—and although as king, Saul had not followed God, David knew it was not his place to remove him from the throne. David recognized that God had placed Saul there, and it would be God who removed him.

So many times we want to help God keep His promises. Yet leaders who have great respect for those in authority are able to follow God's plan according to God's timing. It's important to see your dream become a reality on God's terms instead of your own. The transition is easier and the reward is greater when you do things God's way.

LEADERSHIP LESSON #17
KNOW YOU BELONG TO GOD

Then David spoke to the men who stood by him,
saying, "What shall be done for the man who kills this
Philistine and takes away the reproach from Israel?
For who is this uncircumcised Philistine,
that he should defy the armies of the living God?"
1 SAMUEL 17:26 NKJV

David knew he belonged to the almighty God, while the Philistine giant served a false god. His passion and fervor to see God honored consumed him. He was unwilling to allow his enemy to speak against his God. His faith to see God deliver His people out of the hand of their enemies gave him courage and boldness to stand strong and deliver the head of the giant to his king.

It was the power of God that infused David with strength to do the supernatural. Goliath, the giant, laughed at David because of his small stature, but David's awesome faith was bigger than anything Goliath could match. When you know you belong to God, you can stand in the face of the giants in your life and return from battle a giant-slayer!

LEADERSHIP LESSON #18
HAVE CONCERN FOR THE THINGS OF GOD

*When David was dwelling in his house, that David said
to Nathan the prophet, "See now, I dwell in a house of
cedar, but the ark of the covenant of the LORD is under tent
curtains." Then Nathan said to David, "Do all that
is in your heart, for God is with you."*
1 CHRONICLES 17:1–2 NKJV

Unlike Saul, who neglected the things of God, David
made them a priority. As David looked around his
palace home, he recognized that his home was nicer than
the tent in which the presence of God—the ark of the
covenant—dwelled. When it came to God, for David, no
detail was too insignificant and no sacrifice was too great.

God knows what you need and when you need it to
bring about your full potential; He's the One who created
you with that potential in the first place. God's dwelling
place today is in the hearts of people. Sometimes we make
choices that defile our hearts and devalue the house in
which He dwells. However, when we become concerned
about the things of God, a God-centered perspective
brings us to a place where we can lead others by our example and point them to a relationship with God.

DISCUSSION QUESTIONS

David had great victories and great failures. His life demonstrates that forgiveness from God does not remove the consequences that result from our sin but provides the grace to walk it off.

1. Is asking God for forgiveness something that is easy for you?

2. Are you willing to lay your heart open and live transparently before God?

3. How do you think you can deepen your relationship with God?

Deborah

Girl Power Takes the Lead

KEEPING THE PEACE

Even today it can be unusual for a woman to lead a nation, but that was especially true for Deborah. She lived in a generation when most of her nation was not taught about God, His miracles, or His laws. She served as the fourth judge of Israel and was the only woman to serve in this vital role. Deborah made herself available to God as a resource to her people, to be placed wherever He desired to send her. Her gifts and talents as an adviser, mediator, and planner demonstrated wisdom and leadership when her people needed it most, and she trusted God to help her utilize her skills wisely.

Deborah's life is an example of how we are to be available to God and to others at all times. She did what needed to be done instead of waiting for someone else to step up, and she encouraged her people to do the same. Her relationship with God gave her confidence and discernment to lead a country to peace for forty years.

DEBORAH'S SONG

Found in Judges chapter 5, Deborah's song gives a poetic account of the victory she and Barak procured for Israel. It could possibly be the first example of Hebrew poetry. In addition to Deborah's contribution to the battle, her song gives credit to the many other fighting women—including Jael, the wife of Heber, a Kenite tent maker. Jael killed Israel's enemy Sisera by driving a tent peg through his temple while he was sleeping.

LEADERSHIP LESSON #19
BE WILLING TO FOLLOW GOD

Now Deborah, a prophetess, the wife of Lappidoth,
was judging Israel at that time. She used to sit under
the palm tree of Deborah between Ramah and Bethel
in the hill country of Ephraim; and the sons
of Israel came up to her for judgment.
JUDGES 4:4–5 NASB

Judges ruled Israel between the time of Joshua's death and the time in which God gave Israel kings. As Israel served foreign gods as a result of allowing their enemies to live, God allowed Israel's enemies to gain power over them and destroy their land. When Israel realized the consequence of its sin, the people cried out to God, and in His grace He rescued them by giving them judges, like Deborah, who would point the way back to God.

Deborah was willing to follow God and remind those she counseled of God's Word for their lives. She provides a historic example that can provide far-reaching insight and direction for leaders who are willing to follow God and walk in His ways in their personal lives.

LEADERSHIP LESSON #20
PROVIDE SUPPORT

Now she sent and summoned Barak the son of Abinoam
from Kedesh-naphtali, and said to him, "Behold, the LORD,
the God of Israel, has commanded, 'Go and march
to Mount Tabor, and take with you ten thousand men from
the sons of Naphtali and from the sons of Zebulun.
I will draw out to you Sisera, the commander of Jabin's
army, with his chariots and his many troops to the river
Kishon, and I will give him into your hand.' " Then Barak
said to her, "If you will go with me, then I will go;
but if you will not go with me, I will not go."
JUDGES 4:6–8 NASB

Barak was the general in charge of the army of Israel, and yet he wanted Deborah to go with him into battle. Deborah's words of encouragement and prophecy for victory were not enough to get Barak to go forward. He needed her physical presence in battle, so she went willingly and gave him the kind of support he needed.

Sometimes leadership requires that you help right alongside your team to accomplish the work at hand. Deborah's flexibility to go into battle and offer her support proved necessary for Israel to achieve a great victory. Part of being a leader involves supporting others in whatever capacity is necessary to ensure success—even if it means stepping out from behind the scenes and playing a more visible role.

LEADERSHIP LESSON #21
FACE ADVERSITY

The People of Israel kept right on doing evil in GOD's
sight. With Ehud dead, GOD sold them off to Jabin king
of Canaan who ruled from Hazor. Sisera, who lived in
Harosheth Haggoyim, was the commander of his army.
The People of Israel cried out to GOD because he had
cruelly oppressed them with his nine hundred
iron chariots for twenty years.
JUDGES 4:1–3 MSG

Over the course of history, heroic leaders have come forward in the most difficult times. Hardships and hard times can be God's catalyst for positive change. Deborah was not power hungry or controlling, but lived her life for God in front of her people. Her passion for a relationship with God brought her front and center to the national stage of Israel. Her willingness to do what was right in the sight of God aligned with the needs of her people.

The truth is that when things are going well and life becomes comfortable, we are tempted to rely less on God. When hardship comes, we need a leader who has lived a life pleasing to God and can lead us to the truth. Leaders who serve as steadfast beacons in an ever-changing world are willing to step forward and do all that God has placed in their hearts for the good of His people.

LEADERSHIP LESSON #22
INFLUENCE OTHERS TO LIVE FOR GOD

Barak told her, "I will go, but only if you go with me."
"Very well," she replied, "I will go with you.
But you will receive no honor in this venture,
for the LORD's victory over Sisera will be at the hands
of a woman." So Deborah went with Barak to Kedesh.
JUDGES 4:8–9 NLT

Deborah was an exception on many levels during her time. She demonstrated faith instead of fear, trust in God instead of trust in man, and courage in the face of opposition. Like many of the judges of Israel, she was known as a charismatic leader, but her popularity never swayed her intention to set a godly example for her people. When her people did what was right in their own eyes, she instructed them in the laws of God. When others chose false gods, she continued to live faithfully for the one true God.

Like the Israelites, people today are looking for a leader who is living life according to God's design. Leaders who do what's right when they don't think anyone is watching influence others to live for God.

LEADERSHIP LESSON #23
GIVE GOD CREDIT

*"Hear, O kings; give ear, O rulers! I—to the LORD,
I will sing, I will sing praise to the LORD, the God of Israel.
LORD, when You went out from Seir, when You marched
from the field of Edom, the earth quaked, the heavens also
dripped, even the clouds dripped water." The mountains
quaked at the presence of the LORD, this Sinai,
at the presence of the LORD, the God of Israel."*

JUDGES 5:3–5 NASB

When praise came Deborah's way, she was quick to give all the honor and glory to God. She remained keenly aware that God was calling the shots in her life. She heard His voice as prophetess for her people and directed them to victory, but she lived her life in many ways similar to Paul when he said, "Follow my example as I follow the example of Christ," giving God glory in all things (1 Corinthians 11:1).

It can be easy to pat ourselves on the back when things go well, but if we live life according to God's direction, then all the praise should go back to Him for blessing our lives with bounty and goodness. When we give God the credit, we point others to Him and encourage them to see God work in their own lives.

LEADERSHIP LESSON #24
FIGHT BATTLES WITH PRAISE

"LORD, may all your enemies die like Sisera!
But may those who love you rise like the sun in all its
power!" Then there was peace in the land for forty years.
JUDGES 5:31 NLT

The striking thing about Deborah entering battle with Barak is that she praised God the whole way. She knew the power of praise. While Israel's army fought with weapons fashioned of earthly materials, she fought with praise—celebrating God for His faithfulness. Once the victory had been won, she continued to sing praises, giving God alone credit for the triumph. Music and singing were vital to her people's culture, and she used both to demonstrate how the Israelites should thank their God.

Praise is a strong weapon in battle, even today. Praise silences the enemy (Psalm 8:2). As we praise God throughout our daily battles, we should give Him credit for working out circumstances in our favor. Like Deborah, through praise, we can lead others to victory each day.

DISCUSSION QUESTIONS

1. Do you believe how you live your life points others to a relationship with God?

2. How has praise played a role in your victories over difficulties in your life?

3. Do you agree that times of difficulty produce amazing leaders?

Esther

From Orphan to Queen

BORN FOR SUCH A TIME AS THIS

Living in exile in the Persian capital, Esther was raised by Mordecai, her older cousin. Much like Daniel and his preparation to serve the king, Esther, chosen for her beauty, was taken to the king's palace and placed in his harem. Mordecai instructed her to hide her true identity because of the discrimination against the Jews.

An evil man named Haman convinced King Xerxes, who was still unaware of Queen Esther's nationality, to issue a decree to annihilate the Jews. Mordecai asked Esther to go to the king and beg him to retract the decree. But a visit to the king without an invitation could mean death.

Esther did not foretell the future like a prophet, teach as an apostle, or lead like a king. Instead, she allowed God to use her beauty and character to influence the king and save God's people from extermination. Often great leaders are positioned behind the scenes until God calls them to take courage and do what they were born to do.

IN ESTHER'S WORDS

- "I will go to the king, which is against the law, and if I perish, I perish!" (Esther 4:16 NKJV).
- "For my people and I have been sold to those who would kill, slaughter, and annihilate us. If we had merely been sold as slaves, I could remain quiet, for that would be too trivial a matter to warrant disturbing the king" (Esther 7:4 NLT).
- "If I have found favor in your eyes, O King, and if it pleases the king, give me my life, and give my people their lives" (Esther 7:3 MSG).

LEADERSHIP LESSON #25
BE PREPARED

*Mordecai had a cousin named Hadassah, whom he had
brought up because she had neither father nor mother.
This young woman, who was also known as Esther,
had a lovely figure and was beautiful. Mordecai had taken
her as his own daughter when her father and mother died.*
ESTHER 2:7

When Esther's story began, she probably had every
reason to think God had abandoned her. She was
an exile in a foreign land, orphaned when her parents
died, and raised by a cousin. Then she was chosen to join
the king's harem because of her beauty. Perhaps Esther
questioned God's purpose and wondered if her life was
even a part of His plan. Yet she continued to love God and
grow in her relationship with Him. Unknown to Esther,
her time of preparation would be used to save the very
lives of her people—God's people.

Every leader has a time of preparation before God
calls them to do His will. Esther continued in the palace
each day preparing for an audience with the king. When
it was time for her to step up, she was ready to do all that
God asked of her.

LEADERSHIP LESSON #26
SEEK WISE COUNSEL

Now when the turn came for Esther the daughter of Abihail the uncle of Mordecai, who had taken her as his daughter, to go in to the king, she requested nothing but what Hegai the king's eunuch, the custodian of the women, advised. And Esther obtained favor in the sight of all who saw her.
ESTHER 2:15 NKJV

Esther had been preparing to meet the king. Her turn to appear before him was vital to her future. She took counsel from her custodian, the man who had trained her. She followed her instructor's direction to the letter with hope of a positive experience during her first visit with the king. Wise leaders learn from others. They seek out and choose counsel from those who have experience in the area in which they need instruction.

Esther listened to Hegai's instruction and followed his advice and was successful as a result. It can be tempting to go our own way once we've gained enough experience to enter into the world, but Esther's life demonstrates the need to adhere to the training and instruction we receive during our time of preparation.

LEADERSHIP LESSON #27
REMEMBER THAT TIMING IS EVERYTHING

So Esther was taken to King Ahasuerus to his royal
palace in the tenth month which is the month Tebeth,
in the seventh year of his reign.
ESTHER 2:16 NASB

Often we can grow impatient during a time of preparation and want to press forward before we're ready. Or we become comfortable with where we're at and are unwilling to move in a different direction when the time is right. Esther, however, was in the right place at precisely the right time. God ordered her steps and brought her into the presence of the king at a season in her life when she could accomplish what He needed of her. God knew when the conditions were right to present her to the king.

Timing is everything when it comes to God's plans for our lives. In order to be in the right place at the right time, we have to listen closely to God and let Him use those around us as catalysts to propel us forward. When we listen to His instruction and follow His lead, we can have the biggest impact on the lives of those around us.

LEADERSHIP LESSON #28
AVOID AN EGO

The king fell in love with Esther far more than with any of his other women or any of the other virgins—he was totally smitten by her. He placed a royal crown on her head and made her queen in place of Vashti.
ESTHER 2:17 MSG

The Bible says that Esther found favor in the eyes of all who looked upon her. She had hidden her ethnicity from those in the palace—even the king. When it came her turn to enter his court, she immediately became his favorite of all the other women. God's favor went before her even before she entered the palace. Most likely that favor opened the door for her to be chosen to enter into the king's harem.

Esther realized her newfound attention was not garnered by anything she had done, but by something the Lord had done on her behalf. Favor is a blessing that comes when you obey God and follow Him. When we choose His will and His way, opportunities will open before us.

LEADERSHIP LESSON #29
ORGANIZE A SUPPORT GROUP

Mordecai sent this reply to Esther: "Don't think for a
moment that because you're in the palace you will escape
when all other Jews are killed. If you keep quiet at a time
like this, deliverance and relief for the Jews will arise from
some other place, but you and your relatives will die.
Who knows if perhaps you were made queen for just such a
time as this?" Then Esther sent this reply to Mordecai:
"Go and gather together all the Jews of Susa and fast for me.
Do not eat or drink for three days, night or day. My maids
and I will do the same. And then, though it is against the
law, I will go in to see the king. If I must die, I must die."
ESTHER 4:13–17 NLT

Although Esther was reluctant at first to go before
the king, the words of her cousin Mordecai set her
straight. She accepted her opportunity to do what was
right, but she didn't leave it at that. She asked her people
to fast for her for three days, and she and her attendants
did the same. They petitioned God to intervene—not just
to spare Esther's life as she defied the law to appear before
the king, but also to make a way for the entire nation of
Jews to be saved from Haman's plot.

Sometimes having a support group makes a big difference. Esther understood the concept of strength in
numbers—especially when it came to spiritual battle—
and she asked her fellow Jews to join her in preparation
for her big moment. When you're faced with a challenge,
don't be afraid to ask others to fast and pray on your behalf. After all, God gave us each other to accomplish great
things!

LEADERSHIP LESSON #30
Settle for a Short-Term Perspective

*Then the king extended the gold scepter to Esther and she
arose and stood before him. "If it pleases the king," she said,
"and if he regards me with favor and thinks it the right thing
to do, and if he is pleased with me, let an order be written
overruling the dispatches that Haman son of Hammedatha,
the Agagite, devised and wrote to destroy the Jews in all the
king's provinces. For how can I bear to see disaster fall on my
people? How can I bear to see the destruction of my family?"
King Xerxes replied to Queen Esther and to Mordecai the Jew,
"Because Haman attacked the Jews, I have given his estate to
Esther, and they have impaled him on the pole he set up.
Now write another decree in the king's name in behalf of the
Jews as seems best to you, and seal it with the king's signet
ring—for no document written in the king's name
and sealed with his ring can be revoked."*
ESTHER 8:4–8

Esther did what she could do and left the rest up to
God. Esther didn't have the book of Esther to study
up on. She didn't know what was going on behind the
scenes that was out of her control. For instance, Esther
was unaware that God was reminding the king about
Mordecai's good deed that had never been paid. She
couldn't know how the king would react to her requests,
but she trusted God would do His part, as she did hers.

We want the big picture as we look to our future. We
think it will help us better understand God's direction and
feel more reassured in our actions, but God reveals just exactly what we need to know. We have to do our part—like
Esther did—and trust that all things work together on
behalf of those who love the Lord and obey Him.

DISCUSSION QUESTIONS

1. Can you remember a time in your life when God was preparing you? What things surprised you as you walked out that season of your life?

2. Has there been a time when you were fearful of someone's response to something God was directing you to do? How did you handle that?

3. Have you ever fasted? What things are important to you when you fast?

Jesus

THE ONE TO FOLLOW

HUMBLE AND HOLY

We are instructed through God's Word to "follow God's example, therefore, as dearly loved children and walk in the way of love, just as Christ loved us and gave himself up for us as a fragrant offering and sacrifice to God" (Ephesians 5:1–2).

Jesus, the Great Teacher, led by example and clearly followed in the way of His Father. We, too, were created to imitate our heavenly Father, and Jesus' life sets high standards for how we are to interact with God and with others. He came to earth and lived as a man to demonstrate to us how we are to live as sons and daughters of the Most High God.

GOD AND MAN

Not a lot is said in the Bible about Jesus' childhood. We can read the details of His birth, and we have one short story in Luke 2 about His teaching in the temple as a twelve-year-old child. From then on, until He begins His ministry, we don't have any details. Luke 2:52 condenses His adolescence and early adulthood into a single verse: "And Jesus grew in wisdom and stature, and in favor with God and man." We can tell by this scripture that He was growing and maturing, physically, mentally, emotionally, as we all do. He was the oldest in a large family and probably worked alongside Joseph at his carpentry. On the outside, He was just like any one of us, but on the inside He was God's Son, prepared to endure human anguish to pave the way for our salvation.

LEADERSHIP LESSON #31
SAY AND DO AS THE FATHER

*Therefore Jesus answered and was saying to them,
"Truly, truly, I say to you, the Son can do nothing of
Himself, unless it is something He sees the Father doing;
for whatever the Father does, these things the Son
also does in like manner."*
JOHN 5:19 NASB

The old adage "Like father, like son" is especially evident in the life of Jesus. He lived as God desired Him to live because of His unity with the Father and His desire to please Him. Jesus' prayer life demonstrated His constant connection with the Father. He prayed for wisdom in all things and spoke as God instructed Him. He knew God through prayer, worship, and scripture.

Many have asked themselves at times of indecision, "What would Jesus do?" But if we are truly serious in our commitment to follow Christ, we should ask instead, as Jesus must have asked, "What would the Father have Me to do?" Jesus fulfilled His God-given mission by saying and doing just what His Father intended.

LEADERSHIP LESSON #32
BE A SERVANT LEADER

*[Jesus] poured water into a basin and began
to wash the disciples' feet, and to wipe them
with the towel with which He was girded.*
JOHN 13:5 NKJV

Jesus said the first shall be last and the last shall be first
(Mark 10:31)—a revolutionary statement that must
have been very confusing to those who heard it. Even
today, our worldly values are just the opposite of Jesus'
words. Individuals generally feel as though they have to
fight to get to the top—stepping on anyone who gets in
the way. We have adopted a "survival of the fittest" men-
tality in defining success in the short term, but Jesus was
referring to the eternal, big picture. In the end, it's servant
leadership that receives the greatest reward.

Great leadership demonstrates a heart of service:
choosing to put others first. Great leaders choose to respond to adversity with humility and gentleness. Jesus
served those He led and challenges us to do the same.

LEADERSHIP LESSON #33
LIVING A BALANCED LIFE

Jesus resumed talking to the people, but now tenderly.
"The Father has given me all these things to do and say.
This is a unique Father-Son operation, coming out of Father
and Son intimacies and knowledge. No one knows the Son
the way the Father does, nor the Father the way the Son
does. But I'm not keeping it to myself; I'm ready to go over
it line by line with anyone willing to listen. Are you tired?
Worn out? Burned out on religion? Come to me. Get away
with me and you'll recover your life. I'll show you how to
take a real rest. Walk with me and work with me—
watch how I do it. Learn the unforced rhythms of grace.
I won't lay anything heavy or ill-fitting on you."
MATTHEW 11:27–29 MSG

It seems life moves faster with each passing year. There are always day-to-day sources of stress and anxiety, and we're burdened with pressure from all sides more than ever. But that's not the life God desires us to have.

Jesus became a bridge between humankind and the heavenly Father. Through the salvation He offers, we can connect to God and live the life He destined for us to experience. God wants us to have healthy, balanced lives. As we experience the unity with God that's described in Matthew 11:27–29, we can discover how to balance our lives and receive direction from God. We can learn to live our lives as He intended, basking in the steady glow of His love.

LEADERSHIP LESSON #34
ESTABLISH THE RIGHT MOTIVES

"For what will it profit a man if he gains the whole world, and loses his own soul?"
MARK 8:36 NKJV

Jesus spoke bluntly about the misguided religious leadership of His day. He condemned them for their abusive, arrogant, and selfish example of leadership. He was clear that true leadership requires the right motives. While the world looks to find pleasure in power, position, and possessions, Jesus reminds us that all these hollow pursuits are temporary.

Effective leaders are filled with ambition to achieve a relationship with God above all else. They demonstrate a pure heart filled with honest intentions. They have learned that a life lived for God is the ultimate treasure. Jesus doesn't require leaders to be perfect—He only requires that they put eternal goals first, making leading others to salvation a priority.

LEADERSHIP LESSON #35
LOVE YOUR ENEMIES

"If all you do is love the lovable, do you expect a bonus?
Anybody can do that. If you simply say hello to those who
greet you, do you expect a medal?
Any run-of-the-mill sinner does that."
MATTHEW 5:46–47 MSG

Jesus commanded some hard things—like "love your enemies" and "do good to those who mistreat you." Rather than condone the Jews' desire for revenge on their oppressive Roman adversaries, Jesus encouraged them to retaliate with love—to make a conscious effort to act in kindness instead of hate.

Our human nature is to pay people back for the harm they've done. We want to see justice served and our enemies suffer. But that is not God's way. Jesus offered forgiveness and love even to those who sent Him to the cross. When we show our enemies the same respect we desire to be treated with, we love them in the same way Christ loved us. We become the outward reflection of God's love.

LEADERSHIP LESSON #36
ASK, SEEK, KNOCK

"And so I tell you, keep on asking, and you will receive
what you ask for. Keep on seeking, and you will find.
Keep on knocking, and the door will be opened to you.
For everyone who asks, receives. Everyone who seeks, finds.
And to everyone who knocks, the door will be opened."
LUKE 11:9–10 NLT

Jesus walked among His disciples, demonstrating a constant pursuit of God the Father through all He did. As we turn the pages of His story in the Bible, He encourages us to passionately continue in our search for a deeper relationship with Him. God has the answers for our lives, but so often the distractions and frantic pace of every day keep us from going the distance in pursuit of those answers.

Any relationship worth having takes work. Marriage requires trust and an exchange of heart. Good working relationships require effective communication. Likewise, knowing God takes attention, effort, commitment, and follow-through. Jesus gives us the assurance that if we don't give up, we will find the answers we are looking for.

DISCUSSION QUESTIONS

1. Is your life a reflection of God? Are you imitating Him by doing and saying what the Father does and says?

2. Do you find it difficult to love your enemies and forgive those who hurt you? What helps you to forgive in spite of their actions?

3. Have your motives ever been questioned? Can you honestly say the intentions of your heart are pure?

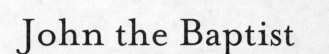

John the Baptist

The Forerunner

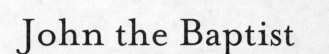

EMBRACING DESTINY

John the Baptist was an extremely unique individual in his day, and he remains a striking and inspiring biblical figure even in our modern era. Isaiah prophesied his birth and an angel announced when he was born. His father, Zechariah, prayed for a son; God answered and told him exactly what to name him. His mother, Elizabeth, and Mary, the mother of Jesus, were cousins. When Mary visited Elizabeth while both were pregnant, John leaped in his mother's womb and Elizabeth was filled with the Holy Spirit (Luke 1:36).

John knew his purpose—perhaps from birth. He was appointed by God to announce Jesus as the Messiah as He stepped into His ministry. He lived to prepare the way of the Lord. He was charismatic in his delivery and bold in his belief, and people would travel out into the desert to hear him speak. He was a fearless leader, unwilling to compromise and bold in confronting people about sin as he pointed them to Jesus.

Fast Facts about John

- He was six months older than Jesus (Luke 1:36).
- John was sustained with locust and honey, and he used camel hair with a leather girdle for clothes (Matthew 3:4).
- John's message attracted many people, and they wondered if he might be the Messiah (John 3:28–30).
- John was beheaded at the hand of Herod before Jesus died (Matthew 14:7–9).

LEADERSHIP LESSON #37
Maintain A Devoted Lifestyle

And [the Pharisees] asked him, saying, "Why then do
you baptize if you are not the Christ, nor Elijah,
nor the Prophet?" John answered them, saying,
"I baptize with water, but there stands One among you whom
you do not know. It is He who, coming after me, is preferred
before me, whose sandal strap I am not worthy to loose."
John 1:25–27 NKJV

John knew the people needed a Savior and that the promised Deliverer of the world was coming. He was the forerunner who came before Jesus declaring the need for repentance and salvation. Evangelist to many, he boldly and unashamedly declared the good news of Jesus Christ. He lived a life devoted to the message of Christ long before Jesus' ministry began.

His message was not popular, especially with the Jewish leaders. But John's devotion and commitment to preparing the way of the Lord was his strength in the face of hardship. It kept him focused and ready until the day Jesus embraced His ministry as the promised One who takes away the sins of the world.

LEADERSHIP LESSON #38
DO WHAT YOU KNOW

*The next day John saw Jesus coming toward him and said,
"Look, the Lamb of God, who takes away the sin of the
world! This is the one I meant when I said, 'A man who
comes after me has surpassed me because he was before me.'
I myself did not know him, but the reason I came baptizing
with water was that he might be revealed to Israel."*

JOHN 1:29–31

John knew Jesus when he saw Him and revealed His
identity to passersby: "Look, the Lamb of God!" John
was doing what he knew he was supposed to do: baptizing
people in water as they came to God, encouraging them
to repent and prepare their heart for the Truth that was
coming.

What are you supposed to be doing as you look forward to Jesus' return? Will He find you faithfully doing
what you know is necessary to prepare His way? Be a leader,
like John, and follow your instincts as you watch and wait
for Jesus' return.

LEADERSHIP LESSON #39
DOUBT YOUR DOUBTS

"Let me tell you what's going on here: No one in history
surpasses John the Baptizer; but in the kingdom he prepared
you for, the lowliest person is ahead of him."
MATTHEW 11:11 MSG

We've all had doubts—even John the Baptist! As John sat in Herod's prison, he must have reflected on all he had done to prepare the people for Jesus' ministry—and then wondered why God would reward him with a prison sentence. He began to doubt what he had believed all his life (Matthew 11:4–6).

But Jesus reassured John's faith by addressing the signs and wonders prophesied about the Messiah that Jesus had fulfilled—healing the lame, deaf, and blind; raising the dead; and preaching to the poor. In Jesus' own words, no one fulfilled his God-given destiny better than John. All leaders experience moments of self-doubt and times when having faith seems futile, but when we are tempted to doubt those things we've believed, we should always look to the Word of God to discover the truth.

LEADERSHIP LESSON #40
SEE YOURSELF IN THE WORD

John replied in the words of the prophet Isaiah:
"I am a voice shouting in the wilderness,
'Clear the way for the LORD's coming!'"
JOHN 1:23 NLT

John's knowledge and understanding of scripture allowed him to see himself in God's Word in Isaiah 40:3. He was born to prepare the way of the Lord. He knew the Messiah was coming, and he wanted the people to be ready to receive Him. John's deliberate exposure of people's life choices gave them no excuse but to acknowledge their sin. And while his words of truth inspired many to repent, those same words also provoked others to resist the truth and resent him.

Let's face it: it can be hard for leaders to guide people down the right path without sounding pushy or judgmental. And that's why John didn't just hold the truth up like a mirror to others—he also held it up to himself, recognizing that his words would sound hollow and insincere if he didn't hold himself to the same high standards he encouraged others to embrace. Helping others recognize themselves as God sees them is just part of being a leader. We must also be able to see ourselves according to God's Word.

LEADERSHIP LESSON #41
LET YOUR LIFE SHINE

"There is another who testifies of Me, and I know that the testimony which He gives about Me is true. You have sent to John, and he has testified to the truth. But the testimony which I receive is not from man, but I say these things so that you may be saved. He was the lamp that was burning and was shining and you were willing to rejoice for a while in his light."

JOHN 5:32–35 NASB

After he was killed, John's disciples buried his body and then located Jesus to tell Him everything that had happened. John's life was bright and drew people to the Truth—to Jesus. John's disciples were heartsick that such a powerful beacon of faith had been snuffed out. They had lost a friend and a leader. Jesus was also grieved at the news of John's death, yet He redirected their despair by reminding them of the great things John had achieved in His name through the power of God.

Like John, we should strive to leave behind a bright legacy that continues to inspire and influence others long after we're gone. That may seem like a tall order, but all that's required is attention to detail. By focusing on the little things, like utilizing scripture as a tool of encouragement and forging honest and sincere relationships, generations to come will rejoice in the light of our lives and come to cherish the saving truth of the gospel.

LEADERSHIP LESSON #42
DECLARE THE TRUTH

*John answered them saying, "I baptize in water,
but among you stands One whom you do not know.
It is He who comes after me, the thong of whose
sandal I am not worthy to untie.". . .
The next day he saw Jesus coming to him
and said, "Behold, the Lamb of God who
takes away the sin of the world!"*
JOHN 1:26–27, 29 NASB

John's mission was to prepare the way of the Lord—a mission he took to heart. He spent all his time telling others to repent and be saved, baptizing them to signify each new beginning and each clean heart. Day in and day out he foretold of the Messiah's coming. He didn't question it—he simply declared it. When Jesus finally made His debut, John knew in his heart that He was the One whom he had been preparing for. He boldly pointed him out—"Behold!" There He is! Imagine John's excitement when the day—that day he had dreamed about for so long—finally came.

What about you? Are you declaring the truth of Jesus' return? As we live each day to bring others into His eternal kingdom, know that someday soon you, too, will be able to declare, "He's finally here!"

DISCUSSION QUESTIONS

1. When doubt comes into your heart, how do you turn things around?

2. In what ways do you let your life shine each day?

3. Are you actively looking for Jesus' return? What can you do to declare that truth each day to point others to an eternal perspective?

Joseph

THE DREAM BELIEVER

HIGHLY FAVORED

Joseph's family history had a big impact on the direction of his life. His father was Jacob, also known as Israel, who worked seven years for his beloved Rachel's hand in marriage. Jacob's father-in-law deceived him, however, and gave him Leah, Rachel's sister, instead. He didn't give up on his desire for Rachel, though, and he worked another seven years to finally earn her as his second wife. But once they were married, Rachel had difficulty conceiving children. So even though Leah gave Jacob many sons, when Rachel finally gave birth to Joseph, he was instantly Jacob's favorite child.

This favoritism infuriated Jacob's other brothers, and they sold him into slavery. This journey from favored son to slave, prisoner to Egypt's second-in-command, ultimately led to provisions for all of Israel during seven years of famine when the nation otherwise would have perished. Jacob's life is a story of how God can take the worst possible circumstances and turn them into a positive outcome for His people.

JOSEPH'S PARALLELS TO JESUS

- Highly favored by their fathers (Genesis 37:3; Matthew 3:17)
- Shepherds to their father's sheep (Genesis 37:2; John 10:11)
- Tempted (Genesis 39:7; Matthew 4:1)
- Sold for the price of a slave (Genesis 37:28; Matthew 26:15)
- Bound with chains (Genesis 39:20; Matthew 27:2)
- Forgave those who harmed them (Genesis 45:1–15; Luke 23:34)
- Saved their nation when God turned what was evil to good (Genesis 50:20; 1 Corinthians 2:7–8)

LEADERSHIP LESSON #43
HARNESS THE POWER OF FORGIVENESS

His brothers came and threw themselves down before Joseph.
"Look, we are your slaves!" they said. But Joseph replied,
"Don't be afraid of me. Am I God that I can punish you?
You intended to harm me, but God intended it all for good.
He brought me to this position so I could save the lives of
many people. No, don't be afraid. I will continue to take
care of you and your children." So he reassured
them by speaking kindly to them.
GENESIS 50:18–21 NLT

Joseph's journey began with the ultimate betrayal. After telling his brothers of a dream in which they all bowed down to him, their jealousy—compounded by their father's obvious favoritism—drove them to sell Joseph into slavery.

All those years that Joseph languished as an Egyptian slave could have been spent plotting revenge on his brothers. He could have easily let his anger turn to hatred, but instead, he chose to forgive them. When he later found himself second-in-command over all of Egypt, his brothers stood before him and he spoke to them kindly, assuring them of his forgiveness. True leaders know that forgiveness frees them from the bondage of past wrongs. They choose to let it go, and like Joseph, respond with love.

LEADERSHIP LESSON #44
PROVE LOYAL AND TRUSTWORTHY

*The LORD was with Joseph so that he prospered, and he lived
in the house of his Egyptian master. When his master saw
that the LORD was with him and that the LORD gave him
success in everything he did, Joseph found favor in his eyes
and became his attendant. Potiphar put him in charge
of his household, and he entrusted to his care
everything he owned.*
GENESIS 39:2–4

Everything that Joseph touched prospered—and his
Egyptian master noticed. He found Joseph loyal and
trustworthy, realizing the Lord was with him, and he consequently put him in charge of his home. Joseph was a
slave, but his upright attitude and passion for God led
him to prosperity. In the midst of seemingly difficult circumstances, the favor of God enriched his life both liter-
ally and figuratively.

Like an effective leader, Joseph demonstrated that every task—no matter how big or small—should be done in
God's honor. Joseph served his master as if he were serving
the Lord and found satisfaction beyond compare.

LEADERSHIP LESSON #45
HAVE PATIENCE IN TOUGH TIMES

*Pharaoh's chief cup-bearer, however, forgot all about Joseph,
never giving him another thought.*
GENESIS 40:23 NLT

It can be extremely disheartening when someone forgets about you—or worse still, forgets a big favor you've done for them. Joseph hoped that his ability to interpret his prison mate's dream would quickly open the prison doors and present an opportunity to then reenter the outside world. But years passed, and the cupbearer resumed his position with the king, putting his memories of prison—and Joseph—behind him.

Patience is important when going through tough times. Joseph could have tried to make things happen on his own, but instead he waited on God to position him in the right place. God reminded the cupbearer of his interaction with Joseph when the king dreamed a dream, and the cupbearer secured him an audience with the king, which quickly led to a lucrative advisory position in the palace.

LEADERSHIP LESSON #46
Use Your Gift to Make a Way

*So Pharaoh said to Joseph, "Since God has informed you of
all this, there is no one so discerning and wise as you are.
You shall be over my house, and according to your command
all my people shall do homage; only in the throne
I will be greater than you." Pharaoh said to Joseph,
"See, I have set you over all the land of Egypt."*
GENESIS 41:39–41 NASB

Joseph had an amazing gift that God used to save Egypt
and the nation of Israel from famine. Joseph's journey
from the day of his brothers' betrayal to the day he stood
before Pharaoh to interpret his dream ultimately resulted
in salvation for Joseph's family. It was the fulfillment of
the dream Joseph had as a boy—the dream that ironically
had angered his brothers enough to sell him into slavery
in the first place.

God created Joseph to dream and then used that gift
to fulfill an amazing purpose through him—proof that
God gives gifts that compliment His plan for our lives.
Great leaders understand that all gifts are worth cultivating and giving thanks for. After all, who knows what
amazing purpose God has in store for you?

LEADERSHIP LESSON #47
MAINTAIN A GODLY REPUTATION

As time went on, his master's wife became infatuated with Joseph and one day said, "Sleep with me." He wouldn't do it. He said to his master's wife, "Look, with me here, my master doesn't give a second thought to anything that goes on here—he's put me in charge of everything he owns. He treats me as an equal. The only thing he hasn't turned over to me is you. You're his wife, after all! How could I violate his trust and sin against God?" She pestered him day after day after day, but he stood his ground. He refused to go to bed with her.

GENESIS 39:7–10 MSG

Joseph was unwilling to compromise his relationship with God. Even though Potiphar's wife tempted Joseph with assurances that her husband would be none the wiser, he knew dishonoring Potiphar was a break in trust with his master and, even more important, a sin against God. Joseph weighed her proposition and made a decision that kept him in right standing with God. Unfortunately for Potiphar, and for Joseph, he believed his wife's false accusations of attempted rape and had Joseph thrown in jail.

In the end, we can't be responsible for the choices others make that affect our lives—only the choices we make. Leadership requires that we live our lives constantly pursuing righteousness in God's eyes, regardless of the unintended consequences.

LEADERSHIP LESSON #48
BE A BLESSING

"I will establish my covenant as an everlasting covenant
between me and you and your descendants after you
for the generations to come, to be your God and
the God of your descendants after you."
GENESIS 17:7

Even in captivity, Joseph found favor in the eyes of those he served and experienced the blessing of the covenant God promised to his great-grandfather, Abraham. In the same way his father, Jacob, served his uncle, Laban, resulting in the prosperity of Laban's household, the households Joseph served were blessed through him as well. This was the direct result of God's promise to Abraham for an everlasting covenant that would extend to all his descendants.

Through Jesus, we, too, have been made sons and daughters of Abraham and have inherited rights to the same blessings he enjoyed. One way to lead others to Christ is to let that blessing flow through us into the lives of others. Like Joseph, when we live our lives according to God's design, we, too, can be blessed to be a blessing.

DISCUSSION QUESTIONS

1. Do you have a dream that God has
    given you? Perhaps you are someone
    whom God has put in leadership
    to encourage the dream of another
    person.

2. Do you believe that God has blessed
    you to be a blessing? In what ways has
    He blessed you?

3. Have you been tempted to compromise
    your right standing with God? What
    has helped you stay the course?

Moses

FREEDOM FIGHTER FOR GOD'S PEOPLE

GOD ON HIS SIDE

From the very beginning, Moses was blessed through divine appointments and miracles. God miraculously saved him from Pharaoh's edict to kill all Hebrew babies, and then through divine appointment he was adopted by Pharaoh's daughter. He grew up in the palace with all the benefits of royalty—yet he never forgot God or his people. As a young man, He rejected his royal heritage and place among Egypt's elect to become a voice for God's chosen race. He escaped to Median after killing an Egyptian to save a Hebrew. Years later, God made himself known to Moses through a burning bush and sent him back to Egypt to demand the release of the Hebrew nation from captivity.

Through Moses' leadership, God's people survived the ten plaques that ultimately compelled Pharaoh to let His people go. And God supernaturally provided for his people as they experienced the parting of the Red Sea and continued sustenance in the desert for forty years—eventually culminating in their arrival at the Promised Land.

THE LAND OF GOSHEN

Goshen was given to Joseph's father, Jacob, and his family when they moved to Egypt to avoid the seven years of famine. It became the Hebrew homeland for four hundred years as his descendants became the nation God delivered through the hand of Moses.

LEADERSHIP LESSON #49
VALUE YOUR EDUCATION

*"At that time Moses was born—a beautiful child in God's
eyes. His parents cared for him at home for three months.
When they had to abandon him, Pharaoh's daughter
adopted him and raised him as her own son.
Moses was taught all the wisdom of the Egyptians,
and he was powerful in both speech and action."*
ACTS 7:20–22 NLT

God gave Moses the foundation necessary to accomplish his destiny. When Pharaoh's daughter found Moses, his sister quickly offered a Hebrew nurse to care for him. Whether Pharaoh's daughter knew it or not, she paid wages for his care to his own mother! Then, when he was old enough, he went to live with Pharaoh's daughter in the palace.

Moses learned his heritage and the truth about the God who had miraculously saved him while at his mother's knee. Then life in the palace included the best education he could have possibly had. He came to intimately know and understand both worlds—Hebrew and Egyptian. It was God's way of preparing Moses for His purpose. The journey of life can often look chaotic, and we may not understand the reason for a certain path—but God prepares us for great things when we embrace the path He chooses.

LEADERSHIP LESSON #50
LEAD BY FAITH

*By faith Moses, when he became of age, refused to be called
the son of Pharaoh's daughter, choosing rather to suffer
affliction with the people of God than to enjoy the passing
pleasures of sin, esteeming the reproach of Christ greater
riches than the treasures in Egypt; for he looked to the
reward. By faith he forsook Egypt, not fearing the wrath of
the king; for he endured as seeing Him who is invisible.*
HEBREWS 11:24–27 NKJV

Faith is the most important requirement for leadership.
It took faith for Moses to reject the house of Pharaoh,
because in doing so, he aligned himself with those oppressed by Pharaoh. He believed that unglamorous service
to God was a greater reward than the pampered riches of
the palace. His faith challenged him to look beyond what
incentives his relationship with Pharaoh might provide
and deeper into what God had planned for him.

Even if a person possesses every other quality of leadership, without faith it is impossible to please God. Faith
gives us the courage to step outside our comfort zones,
just as Moses did, and embrace the person God desires us
to become. When we lead by faith, those who follow reap
the rewards of our faithfulness. Although Moses never set
foot into the Promised Land, his leadership brought the
next generation home.

LEADERSHIP LESSON #51
PRACTICE INTERCESSORY PRAYER

*"So I fell down before the LORD the forty days and nights,
which I did because the LORD had said He would destroy you.
I prayed to the LORD and said, 'O Lord GOD, do not destroy
Your people, even Your inheritance, whom You have redeemed
through Your greatness, whom You have brought out of Egypt
with a mighty hand. Remember Your servants, Abraham,
Isaac, and Jacob; do not look at the stubbornness of this people
or at their wickedness or their sin. Otherwise the land from
which You brought us may say, "Because the LORD was not
able to bring them into the land which He had promised
them and because He hated them He has brought them out
to slay them in the wilderness." Yet they are Your people,
even Your inheritance, whom You have brought out by
Your great power and Your outstretched arm.' "*
DEUTERONOMY 9:25–29 NASB

Moses mediated on behalf of his people many times when they made God angry—from worshipping the golden calf to refusing to possess the land God promised them. Moses had to answer for the people as a whole and for his own family. His brother, Aaron, made a huge mistake in leadership when he allowed the people to create the golden calf for idol worship. His sister, Miriam, spoke out against Moses, and the result of her sin was leprosy. Moses pleaded for their lives and frequently asked God to forgive the nation for their disobedience—even offering his own life for the lives of the people of his nation.

Effective leaders accept their role as negotiator and speak with God on behalf of those they lead. Have you taken time lately to pray for those God has positioned you to lead?

LEADERSHIP LESSON #52
ACT WITH BOLDNESS

"GOD will fight the battle for you. And you? You keep your
mouths shut!" GOD said to Moses: "Why cry out to me?
Speak to the Israelites. Order them to get moving. Hold your
staff high and stretch your hand out over the sea: Split the sea!
The Israelites will walk through the sea on dry ground. . . ."
Then Moses stretched out his hand over the sea and GOD,
with a terrific east wind all night long, made the sea go
back. He made the sea dry ground. The seawaters split.
The Israelites walked through the sea on dry ground
with the waters a wall to the right and to the left.

EXODUS 14:14–16, 21–22 MSG

Moses extended his staff, and the Hebrews watched ten plagues come upon Egypt. Moses acted boldly, and the result was a series of miraculous displays of God's power. Water turned to blood, frogs completely covered the land, gnats swarmed like dust, flies consumed Egyptian livestock; boils erupted on the Egyptians, hailstorms destroyed food and grain supplies, and darkness covered Egypt while there was light in the land of Goshen. The final plague took the life of every firstborn whose home was without the blood of a lamb on its doorpost.

Finally, the Hebrews made their exodus as God held the waters of the Red Sea back so they could walk across dry ground, glancing back to see their enemies destroyed as the water swept the Egyptians away. Moses acted boldly, and God performed mighty works on behalf of His people. In order to see the miraculous, it often takes some bold action on our part.

LEADERSHIP LESSON #53
CONNECT OTHERS WITH GOD

*" 'You yourselves have seen what I did to Egypt,
and how I carried you on eagles' wings and brought you to
myself. Now if you obey me fully and keep my covenant,
then out of all nations you will be my treasured possession.
Although the whole earth is mine, you will be for me a
kingdom of priests and a holy nation.' These are the
words you are to speak to the Israelites."*
EXODUS 19:4–6

Moses talked with God; he had a close personal relationship with Him. The whole reason God brought them out of bondage was so that they could worship Him freely and know Him intimately. They experienced God in a way that no other generation had since Joseph and his family settled in Goshen four hundred years prior.

Moses' passion was to lead others to experience God like he had. He wanted them to know God and hear from Him as he had that day that he encountered the burning bush and received the Ten Commandments. Do you have a hunger to lead others to God? You have a realm of influence that only you can tap into. Let that passion for connecting others with God grow in you and help you win more hearts to Christ.

LEADERSHIP LESSON #54
RELISH RESPONSIBILITY

*"You and Aaron must take the staff and assemble the entire
community. As the people watch, speak to the rock over there,
and it will pour out its water. You will provide enough
water from the rock to satisfy the whole community and
their livestock.". . . Then Moses raised his hand and struck
the rock twice with the staff, and water gushed out.
So the entire community and their livestock drank their fill.
But the LORD said to Moses and Aaron, "Because you did not
trust me enough to demonstrate my holiness to the people of
Israel, you will not lead them into the land I am giving them!"*
NUMBERS 20:8, 11–12 NLT

With great leadership comes great responsibility. God was very specific in His instructions to Moses and the Hebrews, and they understood that obedience to God's commands was often the difference between life and death. Those who did not apply blood to their doorposts, even if they lived in Goshen, lost their firstborn. So when Moses struck the rock twice instead of speaking to the rock as God had told him to do, there were consequences for his disobedience that kept him from entering the Promised Land.

Moses, the leader of the Hebrews, had disobeyed, and God held him accountable—just as He would have held anyone else accountable. When we are leading others, it's important to remember that we must carefully choose our actions and then cope with the consequences—whether they be good or bad.

DISCUSSION QUESTIONS

1. It's difficult to remain patient during times of education and training. What are you learning in your own time of preparation?

2. Knowing when to put action to our faith can be challenging. How do you know when to act boldly as Moses did?

3. Are you dealing with some consequences in your life? How are you being held accountable to God and others?

Nehemiah

SERVANT AND RESTORER

THE PROBLEM SOLVER

Nehemiah carried a deep passion for God, his people, and his homeland. When he heard of the condition of the wall in Jerusalem, his grief overwhelmed him and exploded into a passion to see it restored. As cupbearer to King Artaxerxes, he asked permission from the king to go to Jerusalem and rebuild the wall of his city.

Nehemiah recognized a problem and took the necessary action to influence his countrymen to restore and rebuild Jerusalem's walls. With God on his side and after much prayer and careful consideration, he planned, contributed, inspired, and overcame obstacles until the walls were supernaturally completed in just fifty-two days!

DID YOU KNOW?

City walls may seem insignificant in our modern era, but in Nehemiah's day, they were as vital to life as electricity and running water are to us today. Strong walls provided security and served as protection against outside enemies.

When we read that Nehemiah rebuilt the walls of the city in fifty-two days, the reconstruction sounds like it was a walk in the park, right? But the truth is that it was a miraculous achievement. In order to adequately secure the ninety acres of the city, the wall had to be eight feet thick at the base, twenty to thirty feet high, and almost two miles long. The west and north walls were repairable, but the other walls had to be completely rebuilt. It's no wonder Nehemiah looked to God first in prayer before he ever took action!

LEADERSHIP LESSON #55
START WITH PRAYER

The prayer of a righteous person is powerful and effective.
JAMES 5:16

After Nehemiah received the difficult news that Jerusalem's holy city walls were still in shambles, he immediately turned to prayer. It wasn't a quick prayer, but instead included fasting that lasted for days. He considered God's promises and believed that he himself was a part of the answer—a part of God's plans. He honored God and recognized Him as the only One who could help him and his people. He repented for his countrymen and asked God for favor with the king to grant him permission to go and rebuild.

Nehemiah was a man of action, but he took time to prepare his heart, allowing God room to work according to His will. Do you allow your passion to motivate you to pour your heart out to God in prayer? Effective leadership goes a step further to hear and to do the will of God.

LEADERSHIP LESSON #56
ASK FOR DIRECTION

*"O LORD, I pray, please let Your ear be attentive to the
prayer of Your servant, and to the prayer of Your servants
who desire to fear Your name; and let Your servant prosper
this day, I pray, and grant him mercy in the sight of this
man." For I was the king's cupbearer.*

NEHEMIAH 1:11 NKJV

Nehemiah wasn't afraid to ask for help. He desperately
prayed for direction, eagerly listening for God's response as he plotted a solution for Jerusalem. When the
king noticed his anxiety, he inquired about Nehemiah's
heaviness of heart. It alarmed Nehemiah because it was
dangerous to demonstrate sorrow while in the presence
of the king. But God brought peace to his heart and gave
him the courage to ask the king for permission to go to
Jerusalem.

Life is so busy that it's difficult to hear God sometimes. But when we live our lives with a consistently open
heart and prayerful attitude, we can receive direction from
God as life's circumstances unfold before us.

LEADERSHIP LESSON #57
Take Ownership

*Hanani, one of my brothers, came to visit me with some
other men who had just arrived from Judah. I asked them
about the Jews who had returned there from captivity and
about how things were going in Jerusalem. They said to me,
"Things are not going well for those who returned to the
province of Judah. They are in great trouble and disgrace.
The wall of Jerusalem has been torn down, and the gates
have been destroyed by fire." When I heard this,
I sat down and wept. In fact, for days I mourned,
fasted, and prayed to the God of heaven.*
Nehemiah 1:2–4 NLT

Nehemiah had a prominent role in society as the king's
cupbearer. Often in the presence of the king, he had
opportunity to speak to him, perhaps sometimes even in-
fluencing his decisions. He could have allowed his cushy
job to keep him from feeling responsible for Jerusalem,
convincing himself that it was someone else's responsibility to restore the city. Instead, he allowed himself to be
overcome with a passionate ambition to tackle it himself.
He felt the pain of his holy city and looked to God for
consolation and direction.

Even though Nehemiah didn't live in Jerusalem, he
took ownership of his city—God's city. True leaders are
willing to take responsibility instead of waiting for someone else to act. Is there something God wants you to do?
Ask Him about it today.

LEADERSHIP LESSON #58
HOLD OTHERS ACCOUNTABLE

When I arrived back in Jerusalem, I learned about Eliashib's evil deed in providing Tobiah with a room in the courtyards of the Temple of God. I became very upset and threw all of Tobiah's belongings out of the room. Then I demanded that the rooms be purified, and I brought back the articles for God's Temple, the grain offerings, and the frankincense. I also discovered that the Levites had not been given their proscribed portions of food, so they and the singers who were to conduct the worship services had all returned to work their fields. I immediately confronted the leaders and demanded, "Why has the Temple of God been neglected?" Then I called all the Levites back again and restored them to their proper duties.

NEHEMIAH 13:7–11 NLT

Nehemiah returned to Babylon after twelve years in Jerusalem. Though he was only gone for a short time, he found when he returned to Jerusalem that the Jews had seriously defied God's law. Allowing marriages between foreigners and Jews was the very thing that brought the curse of captivity upon them, and Nehemiah called the people to be accountable. He cleaned house and set the foreigners outside the city, shutting the city gates so people would be unable to work on the Sabbath day. He restored the temple and the priest to their rightful places.

Nehemiah restored order by doing some things that the leadership of the city didn't necessarily like, but it was important that he hold them accountable. Doing what is right isn't always easy or popular, but leadership requires accountability in our personal lives and in the lives of those we lead.

LEADERSHIP LESSON #59
OPPOSE THE OPPOSITION

Furthermore I said to the king, "If it pleases the king,
let letters be given to me for the governors of the region beyond
the River, that they must permit me to pass through till I come
to Judah, and a letter to Asaph the keeper of the king's forest,
that he must give me timber to make beams for the gates of
the citadel which pertains to the temple, for the city wall,
and for the house that I will occupy." And the king granted them
to me according to the good hand of my God upon me. . . .
When Sanballat the Horonite and Tobiah the Ammonite
official heard of it, they were deeply disturbed that a man
had come to seek the well-being of the children of Israel.
NEHEMIAH 2:7–8, 10 NKJV

O   pposition to rebuilding the walls of Jerusalem had been gaining strength for ninety years, spurred on by those who had settled on the Jews' land after they were taken into captivity. That opposition quickly greeted Nehemiah when he arrived on the scene. Leaders from the outskirts of Jerusalem did not take kindly to this not-so-ordinary exile. But Nehemiah was the king's cupbearer and adviser. He arrived with letters from the king giving him the power and authority to rebuild the walls and fortify the city, and he would not be turned away.

When God has given you an assignment, it's vital that you remain determined to succeed no matter what. Nehemiah worked hard and remained dedicated to rebuilding the city in the face of ridicule, always seeking compromise with his opponents.

LEADERSHIP LESSON #60
BE A SPIRITUAL ANCHOR

*And all the people gathered as one man at the square which
was in front of the Water Gate, and they asked Ezra the scribe
to bring the book of the law of Moses which the LORD had
given to Israel. . . Then Nehemiah, who was the governor,
and Ezra the priest and scribe, and the Levites who taught
the people said to all the people, "This day is holy to the LORD
your God; do not mourn or weep." For all the people were
weeping when they heard the words of the law.*
NEHEMIAH 8:1, 9 NASB

Nehemiah was not Jerusalem's religious leader. Although he served as governor, Ezra was the scribe
and religious teacher in Nehemiah's day. Nehemiah was
just so moved by his personal relationship with God that
he dedicated each day of his life to doing God's will. Nehemiah lived the conviction he believed, and working
with Ezra, Nehemiah pointed his people back to God. As
the law of Moses was read, the people grieved when they
began to understand just how far they had moved beyond
what God had instructed them to do.

We need strong leaders to help shape our world. Nehemiah shaped his city for God and led the people by
example to do the right thing according to God's Word.
He lived his life as a spiritual anchor for others that they
could draw strength from in times of spiritual unrest.

DISCUSSION QUESTIONS

1. Most things in life worth having—even a strong relationship with God—require overcoming opposition. What things have you had to fight for, or even stand your ground for, in pursuit of building your relationship with God?

2. Nehemiah's opposition tried to get him to compromise after they saw he would not be stopped. What things have you been tempted to compromise in your walk with God?

3. Nehemiah held fast to the truths of God's Word for himself and his people. What are the words of God you hold fast to for your life?

Noah

Flooded with Passion for God

A STRONG BEACON OF FAITH

Noah's world was taken over by evil, violence, and corruption—in many ways, not unlike our world today. It was so bad that God was sorrowful for what humankind had chosen for themselves, just as parents feel sorrow when their child chooses to do wrong. Noah and his family were the only people left on earth who remained faithful and willing to follow after God and do His will.

God chose Noah and his family to be a remnant of His creation, immune to the harsh judgment He had prepared for those who refused to obey Him and lead godly lives. Noah was a farmer, a shipbuilder, a zookeeper, and the only evangelist. Building the ark was a huge undertaking that required a great deal of faith and obedience. Day after day he built a boat to God's specific standards, fully trusting God wouldn't bring the rain until he, his family, and all the animals were safely on board. In the 120 years it took to build the ark, he continued to preach salvation to the people around him. Unfortunately, only his family believed him and was saved.

ARK FUN FACTS

- The legendary landing place of Noah's ark, Mount Ararat, is in the far eastern portion of the country of Turkey.
- The ark was as high as a five-story building and one and a half football fields in length.
- The ark housed Noah, his family, and all the animals for more than a year.
- God—not Noah—closed the door of the ark.

LEADERSHIP LESSON #61
Obey God

*"I'm setting up my covenant with you that never again
will everything living be destroyed by floodwaters; no,
never again will a flood destroy the Earth." God continued,
"This is the sign of the covenant I am making between me
and you and everything living around you and everyone
living after you. I'm putting my rainbow in the clouds,
a sign of the covenant between me and the Earth."*
GENESIS 9:11–13 MSG

After the rains stopped, Noah sent birds out to see if the earth was dry yet. After spending so much time at sea, everyone on board was probably incredibly anxious to get back on dry land and must have celebrated enthusiastically when God sent the dove back with a sign of life. But even though the ground beneath Noah's feet felt familiar, everything around him had changed. Aside from his family and the animals God had instructed him to save, everything else had been swept from the face of the earth. It was a bittersweet homecoming.

God made a covenant with Noah that day promising never again to allow water to flood the earth and kill all life; that as long as the earth remained there would be seasons, and whenever a rainbow appeared in the sky, it was a sign that God remembered His promise. Even to this day, a rainbow signifies promise to everyone who sees it. As believers, it reminds us of God's faithfulness to those who obey.

LEADERSHIP LESSON #62
STAND STRONG IN THE MINORITY

The LORD said, "I will blot out man whom I have created from the face of the land, from man to animals to creeping things and to birds of the sky; for I am sorry that I have made them." But Noah found favor in the eyes of the LORD.
GENESIS 6:7–8 NASB

As evil and corrupt as Noah's world was, it's easy to imagine the kind of ridicule and scorn he endured on a daily basis as people walked past the boat he was building. They had never even experienced rain, much less the impending flood that Noah told them about.

It's often tempting to relinquish a position when you're in the minority. But Noah stuck to his guns and saw the ark to fruition. Noah was the first to be in the minority, but he wasn't the last. God's people have often been in the minority. Like Noah's admirable example, God expects His children to stand for what is right, even when everyone else may insist they're wrong.

LEADERSHIP LESSON #63
DARE TO BREAK THE MOLD

By faith, Noah built a ship in the middle of dry land.
He was warned about something he couldn't see,
and acted on what he was told. The result? His family was
saved. His act of faith drew a sharp line between the evil
of the unbelieving world and the rightness of the believing
world. As a result, Noah became intimate with God.
HEBREWS 11:7 MSG

Noah's eyes were not fixed on the worldly, evil desires of those around him. Instead, his focus and dedication was on growing in his relationship with God. Doing what God instructed him to do was his highest priority. No doubt he enjoyed his exchanges with God as he spent time with Him, confided in Him, and received instruction from Him. Noah felt his behavior honored God while others regarded him as just plain crazy.

As you live your life pleasing to God, hopefully others will see a difference in you. Don't be afraid to be different. Encouraging others to follow your lead is all a matter of perception. If you act ashamed or embarrassed about your relationship with God, you're misrepresenting joy and purpose that comes from cultivating a connection with Him.

LEADERSHIP LESSON #64
MAKE NO EXCUSES

And Noah did according to all
that the LORD commanded him.
GENESIS 7:5 NKJV

One of the things that set Noah apart from the rest of humankind was his "no excuses" attitude. Though it's not recorded in the Bible, it's very possible that God approached other men and women besides Noah to build the ark. Perhaps they offered God excuses about why they couldn't serve Him. It was too hot outside or they had no carpentry experience. But Noah did everything the Lord asked of him without complaint or question, and very likely he got busy doing it right away.

We may think we can excuse ourselves from God's service because we think it's more convenient for someone else to tackle or there's someone else better educated or better qualified to do the job. But God doesn't ask us to come prepared—He just asks us to come willing to do the work according to His standards.

LEADERSHIP LESSON #65
FINISH WHAT YOU START

*And let endurance have its perfect result, so that you may be
perfect and complete, lacking in nothing.*
JAMES 1:4 NASB

Noah spent day after day, year after year, decade after decade hammering and sawing away until he had worked for more than a century on the ark. It was a ship constructed in response to God's specific instructions and likely the only ship of its kind during that time. No one had ever before built a ship so big that it could hold two of every species of animal. He spent a total of 120 years building it.

Can you imagine the kind of motivation it took to finish such a huge project? (Especially considering that most of us don't stick with our New Year's resolutions past the first month.) But even after the ark was built, the waiting game had only begun. Once inside the ark, Noah and his family waited for the rain to stop—and then to recede. In the end, Noah and his family were left with God's blessing and the promise of a fresh start for all humankind—and that made it all worthwhile.

Feel encouraged today that whatever you're waiting on is worth it when the outcome is the perfect work of God.

LEADERSHIP LESSON #66
HAVE A HEART FOR EVANGELISM

*And God did not spare the ancient world—except for Noah
and the seven others in his family. Noah warned the world
of God's righteous judgment. So God protected Noah when
he destroyed the world of ungodly people with a vast flood.*
2 PETER 2:5 NLT

For over a century, Noah proclaimed the end of the
world to others, extending them an opportunity to
be saved from the impending destruction. He preached a
message of repentance and salvation that was very similar
to the message of today's gospel. It had to be a tough audience. Noah knew God and poured all his passion into
doing God's work, but only his family believed.

Noah knew the truth, proclaimed it, and believed
God. He tried day after day to impress upon others the
truth of God's plan that he knew in his heart. People rejected God and probably rejected Noah, but despite that
rejection, he never gave up. Do you have a heart for evan-
gelism? How passionate are you about leading others to
Jesus?

DISCUSSION QUESTIONS

1. One hundred twenty years is a long time to stand in faith and believe for something to come to pass. Do you have difficulty holding fast to your faith when you don't see answers right away?

2. How do you respond when you find yourself in the minority with regard to your faith?

3. Do you find that your obedience to God shines a light on the disobedience of others? How do you respond to that?

Paul

THE GREAT EVANGELIST

SEEING THE LIGHT

Paul laid his life transparent in a series of epistles to the early church that make up much of what we recognize today as the New Testament, but we first meet Paul as Saul, which was his name before he became a believer. His persecution of those who believed in Jesus as the Messiah is first mentioned in Acts 1:8 at the stoning death of Stephen, the first martyr of the Christian faith. Paul's miraculous conversion occurred on the road to Damascus. A startling light from heaven flashed around him. He fell to the ground and heard a voice say to him, "Saul, Saul, why do you persecute me?" "Who are you, Lord?" Saul asked. "I am Jesus, whom you are persecuting," He replied (Acts 9:3–5). From that moment on, Paul's life transformed into a ministry of gratitude for God's mercy and grace.

CAUGHT IN THE MIDDLE

Paul was caught in the middle once he became a Christian. Those he had persecuted still feared him and didn't trust him at first. The Jews were confused and angry, and they felt betrayed when Paul switched sides.

LEADERSHIP LESSON #67
TRUST GOD TO GIVE YOU
WHAT IT TAKES

But the Lord said, "Go, for Saul is my chosen instrument
to take my message to the Gentiles and to kings,
as well as to the people of Israel."
ACTS 9:15 NLT

God chose Paul to take the message of Jesus Christ to all people, and He gave him everything he needed to accomplish his purpose. Paul was groomed in the Jewish faith by a highly respected rabbi. The words of scripture were imprinted on his heart, and he was fluent in Hebrew, Greek, and Aramaic, so he could communicate well with many people. Plus, as a citizen of Rome, he traveled freely.

The revelation of Jesus Christ exploded into his heart and provided the most important thing he needed to become all that God destined him to be. Refuse the lie that you don't have what it takes. Everything it takes to do what God destined you to do is already within you through the power of Christ Jesus.

LEADERSHIP LESSON #68
KNOW THAT GOD CAN REACH ANYONE

But He [Jesus], because He continues forever,
has an unchangeable priesthood. Therefore He is also able to
save to the uttermost those who come to God through Him,
since He always lives to make intercession for them.
HEBREWS 7:24–25 NKJV

Through Jesus Christ, every single person on the earth can have a second chance—or even a third or fourth. Paul's story is one of great transformation from his participation in the stoning of the first Christian martyr to his legacy as a powerful evangelist for Christ. His story spoke to people in his day and continues to inspire others through the pages of the Bible that he penned. Like Paul, no matter what sins we've committed, no matter what story our past has to tell, we are brand new when we come to know Christ Jesus.

There is no sin too deep that God can't reach us. No matter where we go, God can bring us back to where we should be in Him and use us for His glory in a mighty way. Paul's life is a shining example of all God can do if and when we're willing to give ourselves and others another chance.

LEADERSHIP LESSON #69
EXPRESS TRUE HUMILITY

And when they had come to him, he said to them,
"You yourselves know, from the first day that I set foot in
Asia, how I was with you the whole time, serving the Lord
with all humility and with tears and with trials which
came upon me through the plots of the Jews."
ACTS 20:18–19 NASB

Paul accomplished great things, but he consistently gave all the credit to God. He counted it all as a result of the grace of God in his life. He humbled himself under the mighty hand of God and allowed himself to be molded into the image of Christ. Paul knew it was not about him at all; not about where he had been or what he knew—but only about the One he had come to know—Christ Jesus.

With true humility he expressed his passion to know God and for others to know Him. It's easy to get lost in all that we've done, and it can be so exciting when God works through us to accomplish His will. However, as a leader, it's vital to remain focused and humble with our eyes on God instead of ourselves. It is only by His grace that we achieve success.

LEADERSHIP LESSON #70
BE DETERMINED TO WIN

Alive, I'm Christ's messenger; dead, I'm his bounty.
Life versus even more life! I can't lose.
PHILIPPIANS 1:21 MSG

Paul endured some unthinkable hardships—beatings, prison, shipwrecks—and still he remained determined to win. He kept his heart right and his attitude in check. No matter what came his way—even the threat of death—he was steadfast in sharing the message of Christ Jesus. Thanks to the freedom of speech we enjoy in the United States, we don't experience the likes of Christian persecution that occurred in Paul's day—or even that occurs in other countries across our world.

Paul was unshakable in his determination to live for Christ, and he did so boldly and without compromise. He allowed his light to shine in every circumstance. How about you? When things get difficult, do you remain determined to win for Christ no matter the cost?

LEADERSHIP LESSON #71
HAVE GREAT RESPECT FOR THE TRUTH

*I am not ashamed of the gospel, because it is the power
of God that brings salvation to everyone who believes:
first to the Jew, then to the Gentile.*
ROMANS 1:16

Paul was not ashamed of the gospel, because it was the
real thing. He knew what the truth of God's Word
could achieve, and he had witnessed its life-changing
power in the hearts of all who received it. Whatever
people needed, he knew the message of the gospel held
the answer. His desire wasn't for people to be merely im-
pressed with his words or delivery when he spoke. Instead,
he wanted them to experience the power of God in a real
way and discover how it could empower them to live a
transformed life.

When leading others, it's important to demonstrate
how the message of Christ has empowered you. What witness of Christ do you give to others through the lifestyle
you lead and the words that you say? Is the life-changing
power of God living and active in you to the point that
others realize something is different about you?

LEADERSHIP LESSON #72
NEVER LIMIT THE MESSAGE

When I first came to you, dear brothers and sisters,
I didn't use lofty words and impressive wisdom to tell you
God's secret plan. For I decided that while I was with you I
would forget everything except Jesus Christ, the one who was
crucified. I came to you in weakness—timid and trembling.
And my message and my preaching were very plain.
Rather than using clever and persuasive speeches, I relied
only on the power of the Holy Spirit. I did this so you would
trust not in human wisdom but in the power of God.
1 CORINTHIANS 2:1–5 NLT

When Paul spoke, it was vitally important to him that his listeners experienced the full message of Christ. He was well aware it wasn't all about impressive words or how he performed in front of his audience. He spoke what he felt the Lord would have him to say and trusted that the Holy Spirit would move in the hearts of his listeners to lead them to a greater spiritual understanding. He held nothing back, never watering down the message of Christ.

Perhaps you've had an opportunity to share the message of Christ with someone but doubted your own ability to share with them fully. Paul knew that the message wasn't limited to his delivery. If you have the opportunity to speak to someone about your Lord and Savior, take Paul's approach. He spoke what was necessary and trusted God to do the work in the hearts of those he spoke to.

DISCUSSION QUESTIONS

1. Paul's heart beat to see everyone know Christ Jesus, and that made him an amazing evangelist. How do you rate your level of passion to tell others about Christ?

2. Paul was persecuted and spent time in jail for expressing his beliefs. What type of persecution do you face as a Christian, and how do you deal with it?

3. Paul had an amazing conversion story. Do you feel comfortable sharing your story with others?

Peter

THE UNSTOPPABLE APOSTLE

TRANSFORMED THROUGH FAITH

Peter was a leader of leaders and often functioned as the spokesperson of the twelve original apostles. His name appears first in the list of apostles for a reason (Matthew 10:2; Mark 3:16; Luke 6:14; Acts 1:13). He was outspoken, impetuous, and passionate in his desire to follow Christ and lead others in His way. He stepped out in faith, walked on water, and learned never to take his eyes off Jesus.

Perhaps one of the reasons Peter was so out-of-the-box was because he had a great desire to grow spiritually, to know Jesus, and to understand His spiritual truths. He was quick to act, even if the action resulted in discipline. Once Peter experienced the death, burial, and resurrection of Jesus, he became mature. He was transformed and became even more passionate about the truth of the Gospel.

IT'S RELEVANT

The story of Peter's miraculous escape from prison appears in Acts 12. The church was praying for him, and when Peter knocked on the door, they didn't let him in. They didn't believe it was him, but believed instead that it was his angel. Peter kept knocking, and when they finally opened the door, the Bible says "they were astonished"—demonstrating that sometimes when God answers our prayers, we're so surprised we can't see the answer standing in front of us.

LEADERSHIP LESSON #73
PREPARE FOR OPPOSITION

They seized Peter and John and, because it was
evening, they put them in jail until the next day.
But many who heard the message believed;
so the number of men grew to about five thousand.
ACTS 4:3–4

The religious leaders of Jesus' day had hoped His death would silence the Jesus movement. They were deeply concerned when the disciples continued to preach in Jesus' name. A crowd gathered after Peter and John healed a crippled man. They seized the opportunity to spread the gospel and give credit to Jesus and were consequently jailed.

Sometimes people think after they choose to live for God that life gets easier. That is far from the truth. Peter was probably not surprised by his imprisonment because he had heard Jesus' warning: "But before all this, they will seize you and persecute you. They will hand you over to synagogues and put you in prison, and you will be brought before kings and governors, and all on account of my name" (Luke 21:12). Like Peter, we must be prepared for opposition as we live our lives for Christ.

LEADERSHIP LESSON #74
BE MISTAKEN FOR CHRIST

The members of the council were amazed when they saw the
boldness of Peter and John, for they could see that they were
ordinary men with no special training in the Scriptures.
They also recognized them as men who had been with Jesus.
ACTS 4:13 NLT

When religious leaders questioned Peter and John, they quickly realized two things: they were both common men who claimed no special education or talents, and their spiritual testimony bore a striking resemblance to Jesus'. The crowd that gathered to hear Peter and John speak also recognized the teaching and preaching of Jesus in them. They had healed a man and were speaking the truth just as Jesus had done. These men didn't look like Jesus Christ physically, but they bore a resemblance to Him in their hearts. Those who listened saw Christ in their actions and words.

Have you ever been mistaken for Christ? We are called to imitate Him, to bear His image in our lives and become a reflection of Him to others.

LEADERSHIP LESSON #75
KINDLE YOUR PASSION

"Simon, stay on your toes. Satan has tried his best to separate all of you from me, like chaff from wheat. Simon, I've prayed for you in particular that you not give in or give out. When you have come through the time of testing, turn to your companions and give them a fresh start."
Peter said, "Master, I'm ready for anything with you. I'd go to jail for you. I'd die for you!" Jesus said, "I'm sorry to have to tell you this, Peter, but before the rooster crows you will have three times denied that you know me."
LUKE 22:31–34 MSG

Peter's passion was loud and boisterous and sometimes not quite in line with the message Jesus was trying to communicate. As he served the Lord, he periodically wavered from one extreme to the other. Although Jesus repeatedly tried to prepare Peter and the other disciples for what was about to happen, they could not seem to comprehend it. And Jesus' words to Peter, that he would deny Him three times, must have cut Peter to the core.

But Jesus was right. The fire-filled optimist denied he knew Jesus—three times. Yet his passion fueled his ministry to bring many to Christ after Jesus' death, burial, and resurrection. Peter's outspokenness and transparency of heart drove him to serve God all of his days with a "hair on fire" kind of faith. Peter's life reminds us that we need passion that is constantly kindled by a deep relationship with Jesus Christ.

LEADERSHIP LESSON #76
DEMONSTRATE TRUE LOVE

Now Peter and John went up together to the temple at the hour of prayer, the ninth hour. And a certain man lame from his mother's womb was carried, whom they laid daily at the gate of the temple which is called Beautiful, to ask alms from those who entered the temple; who, seeing Peter and John about to go into the temple, asked for alms. And fixing his eyes on him, with John, Peter said, "Look at us." So he gave them his attention, expecting to receive something from them.
ACTS 3:1–5 NKJV

Have you ever looked past someone? Perhaps it was the harried cashier at the check-out line or the homeless person outside the grocery store. Our brain visually acknowledges that there are people around us, but how often do we really *see* them? Peter and John had probably passed the man at the gate several times before on their way to the temple, but this time they saw him differently—as someone who needed to know Christ. Peter and John gave him their attention. They looked into his eyes and allowed him to see the love of Christ in them. It wasn't pity—but a powerful compassion that changed his life. Peter demonstrated true love and healed the man.

True love requires time to slow down and recognize the needs of those around us. Peter allowed the Christ in him to touch the life of someone else. Ask God to work through you with the power of His true love.

LEADERSHIP LESSON #77
BELIEVE, THEN REST

*So Peter was kept in the prison, but prayer for him was being
made fervently by the church to God. On the very night when
Herod was about to bring him forward, Peter was sleeping
between two soldiers, bound with two chains, and guards in
front of the door were watching over the prison. And behold,
an angel of the Lord suddenly appeared and a light shone in
the cell; and he struck Peter's side and woke him up, saying,
"Get up quickly." And his chains fell off his hands.*

ACTS 12:5–7 NASB

In Peter's day, King Herod ruled what is now modern-day
Palestine and persecuted the Christians there. He killed
James, one of the twelve disciples, and put Peter in prison.
The church was praying for Peter. When God made a way
to supernaturally release Peter from his chains, he was sleeping soundly. He trusted God in the midst of persecution
to take care of him. He believed God was working things
out—and with that reassurance in mind, he rested.

When you trust God to work out the challenges
you're facing, and you've done all you can do by your own
will, you can rest in faith. Peter was certain that his God
who had rescued him before could rescue him again. Faith
allows you to stand firm in your beliefs and rest in the
knowledge that God is able to provide for you in every
circumstance.

LEADERSHIP LESSON #78
KEEP JESUS IN SIGHT

*Shortly before dawn Jesus went out to them, walking on the
lake. When the disciples saw him walking on the lake,
they were terrified. "It's a ghost," they said, and cried out in
fear. But Jesus immediately said to them: "Take courage!
It is I. Don't be afraid." "Lord, if it's you," Peter replied,
"tell me to come to you on the water." "Come," he said.
Then Peter got down out of the boat, walked on the water
and came toward Jesus. But when he saw the wind,
he was afraid and, beginning to sink, cried out, "Lord,
save me!" Immediately Jesus reached out his hand
and caught him. "You of little faith," he said,
"why did you doubt?"*
MATTHEW 14:25–31

If Jesus was walking on water, then Peter believed he
could do the same. He took a leap of faith and stepped
out of the boat. It must have been amazing to do something so gravity-defying. Perhaps Peter even thought,
Wow! Look what I'm doing! But the instant he turned his
focus from Jesus to himself, he began to sink. Our ability
to do the miraculous is not in our own power—but in the
same Spirit that raised Christ from the dead and allowed
Him to walk on the water.

When Peter began to sink, he looked back to Jesus,
who raised him up, and they returned to the boat together.
You have the same power to rise above your difficulties in
life and walk above them when you keep Jesus in sight.

DISCUSSION QUESTIONS

1. Peter dared to be different. How comfortable are you to step outside of your comfort zone and do something out of the ordinary for God?

2. Is the passion of your faith evident in your life to others?

3. Peter was mistaken for Christ—do you live your life in such a way that others see Christ in you—in all you do?

Shadrach, Meshach, and Abednego

FIREPROOF FAITH

STRENGTH IN NUMBERS

Determined to subvert the prophecy that a child of King David would rule over all of Israel, King Nebuchadnezzar killed, castrated, or made servants of as many of Israel's nobility as possible. Only the best and the brightest were spared, stripped of their Hebrew names, and educated for three years in the ways of the Babylonians before entering the king's service. This was the fate of Hananiah, Mishael, and Azariah (renamed Shadrach, Meshach, and Abednego) and their friend Belteshazzer (renamed Daniel).

The foursome quickly rose among the ranks of Nebuchadnezzar's most trusted advisers (much to his other advisers' chagrin). However, while Nebuchadnezzar may have been able to change their identities on paper, Shadrach, Meshach, and Abednego remained loyal to the one true God of Israel, politely declining Nebuchadnezzar's command to worship the huge golden idol he had erected in his own honor. Mortified by their very public refusal to obey, the king devised a cruel punishment of trial by fire. . .which, of course, infamously went up in flames—proving that often the strongest leaders are those who trust God to rule their lives.

DID YOU KNOW?

The kiln Shadrach, Meshach, and Abednego were placed in was normally heated to around 2300°F. That means when Nebuchadnezzar heated the kiln seven times hotter than usual, the temperature was over 15000°F! Third-degree burns occur within five seconds of encountering a flame that's only 140°F.

LEADERSHIP LESSON #79
KNOW WHEN TO FOLLOW THE LEADER

*But Daniel resolved not to defile himself with the royal food
and wine. . . . Daniel then said to the guard whom the chief
official had appointed over Daniel, Hananiah, Mishael
and Azariah, "Please test your servants for ten days:
Give us nothing but vegetables to eat and water to drink.
Then compare our appearance with that of the young men
who eat the royal food. . . ." So he. . .tested them for ten days.
At the end of the ten days they looked healthier and better
nourished than any of the young men who ate the royal food.*

DANIEL 1:8, 11–15

In a world where less than 10 percent of the population
is strictly vegetarian, it's probably hard for most to appreciate Daniel's obsession with eating peas and carrots.
After all, why would anyone pass up food fit for a king?
Free food, no less!

In fact, the thing that's truly courageous about Daniel's veggie crusade is that he was trying to remain faithful to the Jewish dietary restrictions of the Old Testament
while essentially participating in a male beauty pageant.
The consequences of losing were potentially deadly, but
Daniel was confident that remaining true to his faith was
his best chance of survival—and Shadrach, Meshach, and
Abednego recognized that they'd be wise to follow his
lead.

Have you ever been in a situation when following a
friend's unconventional advice saved you from a heap of
trouble? Thank God today for wise friends, and ask Him
to continue intervening on your behalf through them.

LEADERSHIP LESSON #80
UTILIZE GOD'S GIFTS

At the end of the time set by the king to bring them into his
service, the chief official presented them to Nebuchadnezzar.
The king talked with them, and he found none equal
to Daniel, Hananiah, Mishael and Azariah;
so they entered the king's service. In every matter of wisdom
and understanding about which the king questioned them,
he found them ten times better than all the magicians
and enchanters in his whole kingdom.

DANIEL 1:18–20

It was no accident that Nebuchadnezzar favored Shadrach, Meshach, Abednego, and Daniel above all the other young Jewish nobles. "To these four young men God gave knowledge and understanding of all kinds of literature and learning" (Daniel 1:17). However, God's gifts don't come with instruction manuals—it was up to Shadrach, Meshach, and Abednego to determine when and how to utilize their God-given talents according to His plan. Did they want to be so far from their homeland, forced into the service of a megalomaniac? Of course not! But they stayed positive, recognized that God had a purpose for their lives, and relied on the resources He empowered them with.

God has never stopped providing His people with everything we need to achieve great things, but it's always our responsibility to utilize His gifts as He desires. When times are tough, dare to dig deep and uncover the emergency resources God has stored up in you.

LEADERSHIP LESSON #81
CHOOSE WISE FRIENDS

Then King Nebuchadnezzar fell prostrate before Daniel and paid him honor and ordered that an offering and incense be presented to him. The king said to Daniel, "Surely your God is the God of gods and the Lord of kings and a revealer of mysteries, for you were able to reveal this mystery."
Then the king placed Daniel in a high position and lavished many gifts on him. He made him ruler over the entire province of Babylon and placed him in charge of all its wise men. Moreover, at Daniel's request the king appointed Shadrach, Meshach and Abednego administrators over the province of Babylon, while Daniel himself remained at the royal court.
DANIEL 2:46–49

The friendships in your life are vital to your success. You become like those you surround yourself with. Together Daniel, Shadrach, Meshach, and Abednego determined they would keep the laws of their God and not defile themselves. When King Nebuchadnezzer decreed that all wise men be killed, Daniel asked for time to interpret his dream. He went to his friends and asked them to pray and fast. All their lives depended on God's intervention.

When your life is on the line, you want someone supporting you whom you trust—someone you can give your heart and life to for safekeeping. Strong leaders are wise to invest their lives in the right friendships. Pray and ask the Lord about the friendships you should have. He will help you make wise choices.

LEADERSHIP LESSON #82
FIND STRENGTH IN NUMBERS

"Is it true, Shadrach, Meshach and Abednego, that you do not serve my gods or worship the image of gold I have set up? . . . If you do not worship it, you will be thrown immediately into a blazing furnace. Then what god will be able to rescue you from my hand?" Shadrach, Meshach and Abednego replied to him, "King Nebuchadnezzar, we do not need to defend ourselves before you in this matter. If we are thrown into the blazing furnace, the God we serve is able to deliver us from it, and he will deliver us from Your Majesty's hand. But even if he does not, we want you to know, Your Majesty, that we will not serve your gods or worship the image of gold you have set up."

DANIEL 3:14–18

Unwilling to compromise their faith and break the commands of God by bowing to another idol, these three young men stood shoulder to shoulder in faith, believing God would rescue them from the flames of the fiery furnace. Imagine how they must have taken courage and strength from one another as they prayed together for divine deliverance in such a dreadful situation.

It can be difficult to stand strong against society for what you truly believe, but it makes it a little easier when you don't have to go it alone. These three men walked through the flames together, and though they had each other, they also had another with them—He looked to the king like the Son of God. You don't ever have to walk through flames alone. That same Son of God who stood with them will stand with you.

LEADERSHIP LESSON #83
Have Unwavering Faith

*Then Nebuchadnezzar was furious with Shadrach,
Meshach and Abednego, and his attitude toward them
changed. He ordered the furnace heated seven times hotter
than usual and commanded some of the strongest soldiers in
his army to tie up Shadrach, Meshach and Abednego and
throw them into the blazing furnace. So these men, wearing
their robes, trousers, turbans and other clothes, were bound
and thrown into the blazing furnace. The king's command
was so urgent and the furnace so hot that the flames of
the fire killed the soldiers who took up Shadrach,
Meshach and Abednego, and these three men,
firmly tied, fell into the blazing furnace.*
Daniel 3:19–23

Has there ever been a time when you believed in something so strongly that you just knew it had to be true? These three men had unwavering faith. Even the king's men died as they followed orders to throw Shadrach, Meshach, and Abednego into the flames. That might have been a little unsettling for the three friends to see them die—but then again, maybe it encouraged them. Perhaps it reinforced for them that God was on their side.

Whatever you are facing, it's time to go to God and encourage yourself in His presence and through His Word. Settle the matter in your heart and mind and know that you know God's perspective on the situation. Then you can come through the fire with unwavering faith.

LEADERSHIP LESSON #84
SET AN EXAMPLE

Then Nebuchadnezzar said, "Praise be to the God of
Shadrach, Meshach and Abednego, who has sent his angel
and rescued his servants! They trusted in him and defied
the king's command and were willing to give up their lives
rather than serve or worship any god except their own God.
Therefore I decree that the people of any nation or language
who say anything against the God of Shadrach, Meshach
and Abednego be cut into pieces and their houses be turned
into piles of rubble, for no other god can save in this way."
Then the king promoted Shadrach, Meshach and
Abednego in the province of Babylon.
DANIEL 3:28–30

The king was going to make an example out of Shadrach, Meshach, and Abednego, but their trust in God turned the tables and *they* become the ones setting the example instead. Their unwavering faith coupled with God's intervention on their behalf changed the law of the land. King Nebuchadnezzar praised God and decreed their freedom to serve God. Their deliverance was a great victory to all the Jews in captivity.

Leading requires taking the initiative to do what's right because it's right. It may anger some kings, shake up the rules, and turn up the heat in your life. If you're willing to set the example, you may allow God the opportunity to influence the hearts and minds of others around you.

DISCUSSION QUESTIONS

1. Shadrach, Meshach, and Abednego were positively influenced by their friendship with Daniel, but how can friendships have a negative impact on a person's ability to lead?

2. Tempering is the process of strengthening steel through intense heat and gradual cooling. Think of a time when you stood up to spiritual adversity. How did that experience make you stronger? How can you impart that strength to others?

3. Shadrach, Meshach, and Abednego didn't have to stick together, but they chose to stand united rather than go it alone. Where do your loyalties lie? How far would you go to defend what's most important to you?

4. Leading by example is often touted as an admirable trait, but how can we embody it? Make a list of ten simple ways you can actively live for Christ that will lead others to Him.

Solomon

A WISE BUILDER

LEARNING THE HARD WAY

Solomon, the third king of Israel, was the wisest man who ever lived. He spoke three thousand proverbs and wrote 105 songs (1 Kings 4:32). A diplomat, trader, collector, and patron of the arts, he succeeded his father, David, as king. Men of all nations came to listen to Solomon's wisdom, and he fulfilled his father's dream by building God's temple. As a young man, he asked for wisdom to lead God's people, but his personal life demonstrated that even the wisest man in the world can make mistakes.

Throughout most of his reign, he applied his God-given wisdom and enjoyed the fruits of prosperity, security, and peace for the nation of Israel. Yet his choice to marry pagan women who served other gods to seal political agreements eventually robbed him of his relationship with God. He failed to obey God in this regard, and unlike his father, David, who was quick to repent, he did not learn the lesson of repentance until near the end of his life.

Fast Facts about Solomon

- Second son of King David and Bathsheba
  (2 Samuel 12:24)
- Instructed in the ways of the Lord by King David
  (1 Kings 2:1–3)
- Became king of Israel after his father (1 Kings 1:28–30)
- God offered him anything, and he asked for wisdom and
  knowledge (2 Chronicles 1:7–10)
- Spent seven years building God's temple (1 Kings 6:1, 38)
- Had more riches and wisdom than any other kings of the
  earth (1 Kings 10:23)
- Chose to follow other gods (1 Kings 11:11–13)
- Served as king of Israel for forty years (1 Kings 11:42)

LEADERSHIP LESSON #85
MAKE WISDOM A PRIORITY

*"Give me an understanding heart so that I can govern
your people well and know the difference between right
and wrong. For who by himself is able to govern this great
people of yours?" The Lord was pleased that Solomon had
asked for wisdom. So God replied, "Because you have asked
for wisdom in governing my people with justice and have
not asked for a long life or wealth or the death of your
enemies—I will give you what you asked for!
I will give you a wise and understanding heart
such as no one else has had or ever will have!"*
1 KINGS 3:9–12 NLT

When presented with the guarantee of anything his
heart desired, a young king of Israel could have
asked for riches, the destruction of all his enemies, or a
long life—but instead of all that, Solomon asked for wisdom. He asked God to give him a heart of understanding so he could effectively lead his people—God's people.
Wisdom isn't just knowledge, but the aptitude to incorporate that knowledge into making choices that have far-reaching benefits.

Solomon asked for the right thing, and God, pleased
with his request, made him the wisest man to ever live.
He also blessed Solomon with the things he didn't ask
for—wealth, honor, and a long life. Throughout the Bible
we are encouraged to make wisdom a high priority. Solomon's desire for wisdom and guidance remains a shining
example of what all leaders should strive for.

LEADERSHIP LESSON #86
NEVER SUBSTITUTE WEALTH FOR WISDOM

*Solomon built up a huge force of chariots and horses.
He had 1,400 chariots and 12,000 horses. He stationed
some of them in the chariot cities and some near him in
Jerusalem. The king made silver as plentiful in Jerusalem
as stone. And valuable cedar timber was as common as the
sycamore-fig trees that grows in the foothills of Judah. . . .
The LORD had clearly instructed the people of Israel,
'You must not marry them, because they will turn your
hearts to their gods'. Yet Solomon insisted on loving them
anyway. . . . In Solomon's old age, they turned his heart to
worship other gods instead of being completely faithful
to the LORD his God, as his father, David, had been.*
1 KINGS 10:26–27; 11:2, 4 NLT

Even though Solomon was the wisest man to ever live,
he still chose to go against his own good judgment
from time to time. God commanded that His people not
marry foreigners. He warned them many times that foreigners would lead them into worship of other gods. Solomon's disobedience to marry and love these women was a
sin, and it did separate him from God. As he accumulated
wealth—the very wealth God had granted him—he lost
sight of his need for God in his life.

Perhaps Solomon forgot that it was God's wisdom
that provided the wealth he enjoyed and the ability to
provide for so many wives. Successful leaders realize they
must never allow wealth and success to be a substitute for
God. We must keep our eyes on Him instead of ourselves
and remember that He has given us all that we have. He is
the source of all good things.

LEADERSHIP LESSON #87
NEVER ABANDON GOD

I, the Preacher, was king over Israel in Jerusalem.
And I set my heart to seek and search out by wisdom
concerning all that is done under heaven; this burdensome
task God has given to the sons of man, by which they may be
exercised. I have seen all the works that are done under the
sun; and indeed, all is vanity and grasping for the wind.
ECCLESIASTES 1:12–14 NKJV

In writing the book of Ecclesiastes, Solomon gives the reader a look back on his life, especially the period of time he lived distanced from God. Solomon wrote stern warnings to those who may be tempted to take the lonely path he chose. He demonstrates that life without God leads to pain and emptiness.

Solomon's firsthand narratives show us that even if you have knowledge, possessions, pleasure, or money, those things are worthless if you have no relationship with God. The greatest lesson we could learn from Solomon's life is found in the truth that wisdom comes only from God, and real happiness is the result of living your life to please Him.

LEADERSHIP LESSON #88
LIVE WITHOUT SPIRITUAL COMPROMISE

Did not Solomon king of Israel sin by these things?
Yet among many nations there was no king like him,
who was beloved of his God; and God made him king over
all Israel. Nevertheless pagan women caused even him to sin.
NEHEMIAH 13:26 NKJV

If one thing is evident from Solomon's legacy, it's that you can't compartmentalize your life. You can't disobey God in one area of your life without it affecting the other areas of your life. As a young man, Solomon recognized his need for wisdom, but he went against his father's last words and the commands of God by marrying pagan women for political reasons. He made a pact with an Egyptian Pharaoh and took his daughter as his wife. She was the first of many wives he married to seal political agreements.

Wisdom is only effective when it is put into action. Solomon's disobedience separated him from God. Even as the wisest man in the world, his reasoning slipped. We must do what is right in every area of our lives in order to live without compromising our spiritual integrity.

LEADERSHIP LESSON #89
ACCEPT THE HARD TRUTH

Wisdom is in the presence of the one who has
understanding, But the eyes of a fool
are on the ends of the earth.
PROVERBS 17:24 NASB

Solomon's wisdom was world-renowned. The Queen of Sheba heard of King Solomon and journeyed to see if the rumors about him were true. Once he answered all of her questions, she declared, "The report I heard in my own country about your achievements and your wisdom is true. But I did not believe these things until I came and saw with my own eyes. Indeed, not even half was told me; in wisdom and wealth you have far exceeded the report I heard" (1 Kings 10:6–7). Leaders from all over the world sent their men to sit at Solomon's feet and learn from his counsel.

Wisdom is the outcome of wise counsel. Sometimes the hard truth can prove extremely difficult to hear. The average person wants to stay where it's comfortable, but true leaders will step outside their comfort zone and pursue the truth.

DISCUSSION QUESTIONS

1. Solomon's compromise cost
    him much. Is your life free from
    compromise? If not, what is it costing
    you?

2. As you pursue God and grow in
    relationship with Him, you can also
    grow in wisdom. How are you seeking
    God and seeking wisdom?

3. Do you value wise counsel? Whom do
    you go to for counsel in your life?

SCRIPTURE INDEX

"A THIEF LIVES I̶ ̶ ̶D̶O̶W̶S, J'ROLE."

"Most people want the light of the sun to warm their bodies. A thief may want it, but he may not have it. A thief is silent. While others can speak their ideas and thoughts and feelings, a thief must keep all that to himself; he seeks solitude and secrecy while others seek companionship.

"Most important, a thief steals. You do not take from the world, you take from others. Yours is a life without remorse. That is the key. The magic will leave you if you feel shame for what you have done. Others can afford shame. We cannot.

"Close your eyes."

J'role did. A wind seemed to crawl over him, cold and wet. Magic? Was this it?

"The darkness you see is your own darkness. Cherish it. It is yours, neither to share nor to give. Within your darkness you are safe. . . ."

EARTH DAWN

THE
LONGING RING

Christopher Kubasik

A ROC BOOK

ROC
Published by the Penguin Group
Penguin Books USA Inc., 375 Hudson Street,
New York, New York 10014, U.S.A.
Penguin Books Ltd. 27 Wrights Lane,
London W8 5TZ, England
Penguin Books Australia Ltd, Ringwood,
Victoria, Australia
Penguin Books Canada Ltd, 10 Alcorn Avenue,
Toronto, Ontario, Canada M4V 3B2
Penguin Books (N.Z.) Ltd, 182–190 Wairau Road,
Auckland 10, New Zealand

Penguin Books Ltd, Registered Offices:
Harmondsworth, Middlesex, England

First published by Roc, an imprint of Dutton Signet, a division
of Penguin Books USA Inc.

First Printing, November, 1993
10 9 8 7 6 5 4 3 2 1

Series Editor: Donna Ippolito
Cover: Romas
Interior Illustrations: Robert Nelson

 REGISTERED TRADEMARK—MARCA REGISTRADA

Printed in the United States of America

I once had to go to the Hollywood unemployment office for cash so I could eat. The woman behind the desk asked me if I was seeking employment. I sheepishly replied, "I'm writing. I hope to sell what I write." I was certain she'd bounce me out of the office. Writing wasn't something I *sought* each day. I just did it. She said, "Perfect. Writing is work, you know. You're just not employed yet."

This book is for her.

BOOK ONE

Torran & Samael,

I am Mountainshadow. Alone among dragons I have taken interest in mortal races. And now I have taken interest in you two.

Bother yourselves not with wonder at a letter from a dragon. My ways are my affair, and no concern of yours. Perhaps if you agree to see your father, he will tell you of me. As it is, I have written to tell you of him.

Yes, your father. You have not seen nor heard from him for some thirty years now. How you mortals squander your few precious years on this earth. Your lives are slow mornings against my centuries; yet you let fear and pain swallow your hope and joy . . .

Enough. My studies are my business.

Having had occasion to spend time in your father's thoughts, I can say that he longs to meet with you again. Yet he is afraid of you. Afraid? Yes. I know you two fear him; or rather, I suspect as much. Most likely you fear each other, though none of you wishes it to be so. That is why I offered to act as intermediary, and now write you on his behalf. He agreed.

He is old; his flesh soft and dry, his bones brittle. Fear of life can make your kind commit acts of terror, and fear of death sometimes produces acts of contrition. It is such that your father wishes to conduct with you.

As for the two of you, why would you care to hear from the man who terrorized you and left you? I cannot say, but I have seen such desires in mortals before.

Do you wonder at my mention of spending some time in your father's thoughts? I am not the first creature to have shared his mind. Once, in J'role's youth, a Horror lived inside him. You are surprised? You did not know this? No, nor did anyone else. So now I offer the story of his first adventure. If you read it, you will

*better understand the man who is an empty space in
your hearts.*

*Indeed, the tale is more complete than even he could
have remembered. Having lived in his thoughts I know
of many memories and sensations that have dimmed
in his own consciousness. It was an odd experience.
I have never ... I ...*

*Enough. Expect no more of me. Send me no reply. I
am done.*

*He believes he loves the two of you, and from what I
know of the mortal heart, that is so. If this tale touches
you, tell him.*

*I am,
Mountainshadow*

1

Your father, as a boy, had horrible memories; they lay buried in his mind, too terrible to confront by daylight, yet too powerful to be ignored. So the memories emerged while he slept, winding their way through his dreams. The dreams tried desperately to remind him of things past, things he had to know if he was to live his life, but the mortal mind's defenses against horrible truths are strong, and J'role did not heed the memories.

So he slept, and in his sleep he cried out for help and sweated and rocked back and forth like a small babe. And when he awoke, he remembered nothing.

This was the way of things in your father's youth.

J'role, seventeen years old, long-limbed and silent, stood in the shade of a tree. The ritual scars along his cheek bones formed thin lines, like stitching in leather. His face revealed nothing, his body still as the tree beside him. Around him his fellow villagers busied themselves with their daily tasks: farming, pounding bronze into plows and shields, milking goats and cows. J'role owned nothing, and had nothing to do. He had long since given up trying to work for anyone else in the village. His fellow villagers would have nothing to do with him. Cursed and mute, the son of a mother who went mad during the Scourge, he might taint them. No one took chances back then, so soon after the invasion.

The creature in his head said, "Let's go talk to someone."

"No," J'role thought, his face betraying nothing. No one suspected that a Horror lived within his thoughts, and no one could know if J'role wanted to stay alive.

"Come, just a few words. You've been silent for so long. How many years now?"

"Nine," J'role thought.

"Nine years! No one should remain so silent."

"I must." His face was grim with miserable purpose.

"Still upset about your mother?"

"Quiet!"

"Oh, you are."

J'role turned his thoughts from the creature, gazing out toward the craggy mountains that ringed the valley of his village. Whenever he looked at them, he thought about the dragons his father had spoke of over the years. Could any living thing be as big as a mountain? He did not think so, but then, J'role thought very little that his father told him to be true.

Down the dirt lane was Ishan, the bronzesmith, casting a spell on the plow he was crafting. A sprinkle of blue glittered down from his fingers and into the metal, then he raised his hammer and continued pounding the plow.

"Magic," J'role thought.

"What about it?" asked the creature.

"If I could learn it, I'd get rid of you."

"Unlikely."

"I'd try."

"Well, one way or the other, someone must first teach you magic, and there's little chance of that, is there?"

J'role glanced up and down the dirt lane that led in and out of the village. At either end the long brown road tapered off and out of sight, vanishing into the twisted hills. The sky above shone brilliant blue—a blue so bright it hurt.

On the road to the south J'role spotted something—*someone*—approaching.

He moved, turning to get a better view, so slightly and so carefully that few would have noticed the movement even if looking directly at him.

It was not a villager approaching. No one had left the village for weeks. A traveler? An adventurer? Someone to beg coins from? J'role hoped so. Having used up the good will of Brandson the tavern keeper, the only way he would get food for his father and himself would be to buy it.

With the startling grace of a cat, J'role shed his stillness and started toward the edge of the village. It was not a run, exactly, being both lighter and fiercer. A dragon's flaming breath rushing through the air. A slight expression appeared on his face, nothing anyone could name precisely as happiness, but something nonetheless. And inside, safe from the world, J'role was happy. He loved nothing so much as motion, to feel his muscles working throughout his body. As he strained to overcome the earth's pull he felt joy.

Somehow, despite everything, he could move.

Few eyes fell upon J'role as he darted through the huts and trees of the village proper, in part because J'role's motion called so little attention to itself. But even those who did catch his body flashing past paid little heed. It was only J'role. The mute, cursed boy. Running again.

As long as it's away from me, J'role imagined them thinking.

He reached a tree at the edge of the village, ducked behind it, then peered out from behind. He drew in a breath. What was it that approached?

Not a man certainly. Too large and stocky for a man, with long arms and shoulders too wide. A troll? His father had told him about trolls. But J'role imagined them to be even bigger than the stranger walking down the road.

What was it?

Ever since his people had left the stone corridors of the kaer seven years ago, he'd seen the tall, thin elves with their olive or pale skin and tight-lipped smiles. He'd also seen some lizard-folk, the thick-skinned humanoids with powerful tails and bountiful good nature.

But whatever approached now, J'role had never seen before.

An ork, he realized finally. The teeth, the grayish hue of the flesh. An ork. His father had told him stories about orks. Stories his father had heard from his father, who had heard them from J'role's great-grandfather before that. Stories passed down for four hundred years as the world hid from the onslaught of Horrors roaming the world.

As the ork got closer, J'role saw that the hair on his head was thick and stiff, and that he wore a patch of black cloth over his right eye, tied in place with a strip of leather. The ork's other eye was large and yellow, his ears pointed. Jutting up from his mouth and over his upper lip were two large teeth. He wore thick boots, and his clothing was made of rough leather. From the ork's shoulders hung a tattered blue cloak—the blue of the sky just after sunset when the stars first appear. Hanging from a thick belt around his waist was a sword without a scabbard; sunlight gleamed on the metal, running up and down the naked blade. The metal looked smoother than any J'role had ever seen, better even than Ishan's work. And Ishan was good.

Seeing the blade, seeing the extraordinary sight of an ork, J'role began to wonder if maybe there *were* dragons the size of mountains.

When the ork was some twenty feet away, J'role stepped out from his shelter, right out onto the road. He walked up to the stranger as if he'd been expecting him, stopping to bow low at a distance of some six feet. Was this the way to greet an ork? He could only try and find out.

The ork laughed out loud, a sound rough and rich as rocks crashing down a mountainside. "I've had many abrupt greetings upon entering a new place, but none so welcoming! It seems my tired feet have brought me to the right place after all." And he laughed again.

Looking up, J'role saw the ork smiling down at him. The stranger's open, happy face caught him off guard, and for a moment he wanted to embrace him. In fact, he almost spoke. He caught himself just as the muscles of this throat tightened.

The creature in J'role's head sighed. "Say hello to the ork," it said, coiling about J'role's thoughts like a dragon's tail around its treasure. "You want to, don't you? You like him. Something about this freak . . ."

"Be quiet!" J'role thought harshly, a look of anger—or perhaps desperation—passing over his face. But he'd learned not to show anger around people. It raised too many suspicions.

If the ork saw the look, he did not let on. Regaining control, J'role quickly put on a smile—a smile just *so*—with an even mix of supplication and eagerness to please. He'd used the same smile on previous travelers who'd passed through the village, and over the years he'd polished and rubbed it well, like a magic ring: shiny, bright, potent.

"Ah," said the Garlthik, his good-natured smile melting into something sly. "You want something." He spoke the dwarven tongue, as did everyone in J'role's village. It had become the language of trade in the time before the Scourge, and then the standard language throughout the land. But the ork's vowels were short and sharp, and sounded strange to J'role's ears.

A crowd had gathered by now, and J'role knew he had to

act quickly if he wanted to milk the ork. He touched his fingers to his throat, then held his hands wide.

"Mute? That's a shame. A lad your age should be shouting at the stars. You want money, I suppose."

J'role nodded, hopeful and pathetic, but still smiling. Always smiling at anyone he approached.

The ork reached his thick fingers into a leather sack attached to his belt. "I'm tired, I need a place to stay." He leaned close to J'role, drawing him into a cozy conspiracy. "A safe place." He drew a coin that glinted of silver out of the bag. "Do you know of such a place?"

J'role nodded.

"Will they let me stay there?"

He nodded again. The ork handed him the silver, and when the ork's large, rough fingertips touched J'role's palm, the boy became lightheaded. It was as if he'd finally found magic. He could not name it exactly, but there was something so *alien* about the touch. Different. He found it amazing to be meeting such a strange man straight out of one of his father's stories!

"It's a shame you can't tell me your name," said the ork, "But I am Garlthik One-Eye. Come," he said, clasping J'role's shoulder with one heavy hand, "take me to my place of rest."

"His name is J'role," Charneale said from the gathered crowd.

"Oh, no," thought J'role, while the creature in his head said, "Don't you want to harm *this* man? Couldn't we talk to *him*?"

Charneale, the village magician, stepped forward, flanked by his three apprentices, two girls and a boy, all J'role's age. "His parents named him J'role," Charneale added. His face was thin and gray and wrinkled. "I am Charneale, magician of Thyson. These are my pupils." All four wore colorful robes sewn with elaborate patterns to keep the Horrors away when they cast their magic.

J'role hated Charneale, though the beautiful robes drew his eyes and made him long to wear something so wonderful. Charneale's robe had a lightning blue background. Against the blue were red swans, yellow stars, gray and white mountains. On special nights, when the great magics were cast, the swans flapped their wings and flew along the surface of the robe.

"I am Garlthik One-Eye," said the ork, and he thrust out his hand to Charneale, but the magician ignored the gesture. J'role, observant and still, saw anger flash across Garlthik's face, but it passed quickly—so quickly that no one else noticed it.

Speaking as if J'role were not there, Charneale said, "The boy has been an idiot since his seventh birthday."

Garlthik peered down at J'role with his one good eye. "He seems sharp enough to me. He just can't talk. Or won't."

J'role swallowed. Did Garlthik see? Could Orks see a Horror in a person's head?

Charneale said, "His family is cursed. His mother was possessed by a Horror, his father is a drunkard, and the boy is an idiot."

"What happened to the mother?" Garlthik asked softly, strangely intent. "Did you get the creature out?"

Charneale raised his chin, piqued. "We had little time. We were still living in our kaer, and we believed our defenses had been breached. . . ."

"You stoned her," Garlthik said in a quiet, accusing voice.

"We performed what rituals were required—"

Garlthik snorted.

"The taint was deep in her," said one of the girls, obviously reciting a well-known phrase.

"I'm sure," answered Garlthik. "Nonetheless, the boy seems fine to me. Thank you for your time. The sun is setting, and I'd like some sleep."

With his hand on J'role's shoulder, the ork turned toward the village proper. But Charneale had not done. "What, may I ask, is your purpose here?"

"Well, sir, the world is a dangerous place, filled with creatures and evil thoughts. I sought a quiet village like yours for some comfort."

"You may have it, but I suggest you stay away from the boy and his father."

"Garlthik One-Eye has wandered one too many mountains to be afraid of a mute boy and his diseased father, magician."

"You are an adept, aren't you?"

J'role looked up at the ork. He could work magic! What other surprises did Garlthik One-Eye possess?

"In my own fashion."

"Take nothing while in this village."

"I take only from those who have something worth stealing. And as far as I can tell, this village has little to offer a traveler with taste."

Charneale gasped, J'role smiled, and Garlthik directed J'role forward down the lane. Again, the odd sensation from the ork's touch. The ork lived adventure. The ork lived hope and expectation. Combat. Impossible deeds. His heavy touch transmitted all these experiences and more. J'role struggled to find the words in his thoughts.

"He has lived as you have not lived," said the creature.

"Yes," thought J'role. "Lived. He has lived."

"Lived as you have not, lived as you never will. You will never know hope and expectation. You will never know impossible deeds. You are nothing and you will never have anything you want."

Normally the creature's words would have plunged J'role into depression, a despair as deep and empty and dark as a chasm from one of his father's stories. But not today. Instead, J'role trembled inwardly with both fear and excitement. He knew his association with Garlthik One-Eye might bring down on him further misery from his own people, for the ork had been rude, and that was bad. But he was also excited; as long as Garlthik remained in the village J'role had an ally against those who had for so long shut him out of their lives.

He had a friend.

As they walked toward Brandson's Tavern, Garlthik twice looked over his shoulder. J'role saw this, and perceptive though he was, could not be certain if the ork was looking back at Charneale and the villagers who stared after them, or something else, something far away along the southern road. Something distant and following Garlthik.

Garlthik caught J'role watching him. He smiled a broad, toothy smile. "Your people, are you from a nearby kaer?"

J'role nodded and pointed off to the Red Hills, where the shelter still stood, dark and deserted.

"Well, you're doing well for yourselves," the ork said, looking round at the rice paddies and tall trees. "The effects of the Scourge will not last long in this area of the world, I'm certain."

J'role smiled back politely, but in his heart he was troubled. The Scourge was ending everywhere but in his own head.

* * *

Even as J'role stepped into the large common room filled with tables and the central fire pit, a dozen of the patrons of Brandson's Tavern gasped and stared openly at the ork behind him. Their collective gasp of surprise and shock was like the sound of wind rustling branches just before a rain. J'role was pleased; for once they could not simply ignore him. His companion was an ork.

J'role saw them struggling with their own thoughts— Should they let the ork in? Why shouldn't they? Why should they? Their indecision cost them the chance to protest, for before anyone could speak, Garlthik had closed the door behind him.

J'role pointed Brandson out to Garlthik, and the ork walked up to the weary-looking man who wore a smock stained with beer and the juices of roasted meats. As with Charneale, Garlthik extended his hand and introduced himself. Unlike Charneale, Brandson returned the handshake, but without the well-known smile he usually bestowed on neighbors and guests.

The two discussed the price of a room: Garlthik would stay at least three days, though he might leave at a moment's notice. This disturbed Brandson, making him wonder if he was inviting trouble into his establishment. But Garlthik produced silver coins to pay in advance for all three days. Whether he left early or not, Brandson could keep the money. Brandson accepted the coins, and the two shook hands again. This time Brandson smiled his famous smile.

Garlthik turned to J'role. "I've got to get some sleep, lad. "Here's your pay so far." He dug his thick fingers into a leather sack strung onto his belt and produced another silver. Brandson's eyes widened. "Come back later, and I'll tell you some tales of my adventures. How's that, eh?"

J'role nodded enthusiastically. He loved stories, but wanted the *real* stories, not his father's lies

Garlthik picked up his sack and turned to climb the stairs. For the first time J'role realized how weary the ork was, who leaned heavily on the railing as he walked slowly up the steps. The blue cloak, the blue of the sky just after sunset when the stars first appear, had a big gash running down its length. Under the cloak, J'role spotted a rip in the ork's shirt, and beneath that, the flash of a wide purple scar.

Halfway up the stairs Garlthik stopped, drew something

from a small sack attached to his belt. The object was too small for J'role to make out, but Garlthik stared at it a long time. Then he clenched his fist around it and laughed softly. He raised his foot halfway to the next step, then stopped, turning his head unexpectedly, looking directly at J'role, catching the boy staring at him.

The good humor in the ork's face suddenly left. In a gruff tone he said, "You shouldn't look where you're not invited."

J'role desired to run away as quickly as possible. But he stayed rooted to the spot, unable to move, afraid that motion would betray a weakness that Garlthik would use to harm him.

Without a change in his grim expression, Garlthik turned back up the stairs and on to the second floor.

When Garlthik had gone from sight, J'role turned to Brandson. Over the years the two had worked out a rudimentary sign system, which J'role now used to buy some bread and cheese with one of the silver pieces Garlthik had given him. Brandson gave him change and wrapped the food in a large piece of cloth, which J'role put under his arm as he left the tavern to find his father. He decided not to show his father the change he'd received, nor the second silver Garlthik had given him, fearing that his father might take the money to spend on drink. All he would show his father was the food.

"Time to feed Dad?" the creature in his thoughts asked.

J'role ignored it.

2

He dreamed of many things, not all bad. But all forgotten.

When J'role was only six months old, he began to speak. The words "Mama" and "Papa" were quickly followed by full sentences, and by the second year of his life he began to have full conversations—still limited by the viewpoint of a child, but much more complex in structure than the talk of other children his age.

His parents took pride in his speaking, his mother especially. Red-haired and large, she carried him around the moss-lit corridors of the kaer, introducing him to the other inhabitants of the shelter. Other adults, massive like his mother, leaned down and cooed over him, delighted to engage him in conversation. His mother beamed. She held him tight.

By the time J'role reached the kaer, the stars had spun around the earth, and the stars looked down on him, bright and clear. He had not meant to wander the dry land between his village and the kaer at this late hour, but he had searched everywhere for his father, checking all the usual hiding places. Behind Brandson's barn. In a shallow ditch near Ishan's warm furnace. In the copse of trees near the north end of the village, where Jaspree's influence ended and the land became dry and lifeless, ruined by the work of the Horrors over four centuries.

All the while the creature in his head said, "You know where he is. Why do you delay?"

The creature was right. J'role did know where his father would be—back in the kaer. He invariably went there these days, safe from prying eyes and the company of others. Only children daring each other's courage ever returned to the kaer, and even those excursions stopped once the children realized J'role's father had adopted the dark caves as his home.

So now J'role walked across the flat, dry distance between the farmlands and the kaer, carrying the bundle of food for his father. The moonlight, soft and gentle-blue, illuminated the barren landscape the Horrors had left behind. Stones. Chalky dirt. As J'role walked, the desolation around him seeped into his spirit, as though he were walking through a giant reflection of what he carried within himself.

"You could kill yourself."

"Don't,' J'role begged, half-stumbling as the creature's words drove into his thoughts.

"Wouldn't it be easier?"

"Why don't you leave me alone? I don't—"

"Don't what? Want to give up. Give up what? Hurt anyone? Who would you hurt? Only your father. Maybe. And he probably wouldn't notice that you were gone."

The truth of the statement stopped J'role in his tracks. He dropped the bundle of food to the ground. For a moment his hands and arms felt stiff and detached from his control, then he slammed his fists into his forehead, wanting to knock the thing out of his mind. He slammed his head again and again, beating his fists wildly about his face until he became dizzy and dropped to his knees. Still he punched himself, flailing until he could no longer feel his hands or the flesh on his forehead and face.

He dropped forward, leaning on his forearms, breathing heavily, tears in his eyes from the pain.

"I like it when you do that."

J'role sometimes thought that if he hurt himself enough, the thing would get full of pain and finally leave. It never worked.

J'role's ancestors had helped build the kaer generations ago, carved it out of the soft rock of the Red Hills the way people all over the world had built shelters to protect themselves from the Horrors. An old empire of strong magic had given warning to the world of the coming Scourge, and had counseled everyone how to protect themselves. Staring at the Red Hills J'role wondered what had happened to the old empire.

Before him, lit by the blue moonlight, the Red Hills looked like a giant shadow rising from the ground.

Why did his father have to come *here*?

Setting the bundle into the crook of his left arm, he began climbing up the hill to a ledge some thirty feet up. The rough rock dug into the fingers of his right hand and the soles of his feet, but, as with running, J'role found the exertion exhilarating. His breathing increased, and several times he almost fell back down the hill. But he caught himself each time—with only one hand free—and continued. He took pleasure in that. A smooth climb would not have been as much fun. He liked near misses and last-minute saves.

Reaching the ledge J'role sat down to rest, staring at the round entrance to the kaer. Symbols used to ward off the Horrors ringed the large opening, symbols just like those on the magician's robes. A long dragon wound its way around the entrance, and all around the dragon were drawings of trees, suns, plants, water. Animals of all sorts: jaguar, boar, hypogriff. The dots and dashes around the pictures broke the sounds of the objects' names into bits, those bits which the scribe wanted to use to form a new word. J'role knew this because his mother had once explained it to him. She had not understood what the words meant, how to read or write them, but she understood enough about how the words were formed, and J'role remembered what she'd told him about reading and writing.

If only he could read. If only he could write. But who would take a cursed, mute boy on as an apprentice?

He got up and approached the entrance, wanting to find his father and then leave as quickly as possible. Shattered rocks lay strewn about the circular opening, the remains of the day Charneale had decided it was safe to smash open the sealed entrance so that the people could re-emerge into the world. J'role's father had been so happy that day—too happy—laughing, singing, talking so quickly that J'role could only just make out his father's rushing conversation: *Everything will be all right now, we'll start again. Spirits, how lucky we are to be given this second chance!*

The moonlight illuminated only the first few feet of the tunnel, after which all became black. The darkness, J'role knew, extended deep into the hill. He'd forgotten to bring a brand, or rather, he'd been hoping to meet his father returning to the village somewhere across the desolate landscape.

J'role's thinking became unbalanced when he thought of the kaer.

Luckily, someone, most likely his father, had left three brands on the ground near the tunnel entrance. With the flint he pulled from his pouch, J'role used one of the shattered portal stones to spark a flame to life on the tip of the brand. The fire grew quickly, greedily gulping the air. The red light lapped at the corridor's red stone, turning the walls black.

J'role picked up the bundle of food and moved forward. He picked his way carefully, very quietly now, because some *thing* might have moved into the dark corridors of the kaer. He also moved carefully because the entrance tunnel had once been full of triggers for traps to keep the Horrors out—pits, poison arrows, and other more arcane, magical means of destruction. Although the devices had all been disengaged when Charneale opened the kaer, the floor was littered with trip wires and spear tips that could drag an unwary visitor to the floor.

Soon he reached the central Atrium, a large, circular chamber with a great fountain in the center. During the Scourge, magicians had cast magic to draw water from the very stone of the fountain. A pillar rose from the center of the fountain's bowl, and atop the pillar stood a statue of Garlen, the spirit of healing and home. The statue was not carved from the stone of the Red Hills, but of white marble. The flickering red flames bathed her form, turning it rose-colored, giving the illusion of movement to her intricately sculpted gown, color to her cheeks. Her arms were raised, welcoming; her hips wide, her breasts large. She would take care of everyone. Or so Helvar, one of the Garlen's questors in the kaer, had said.

J'role turned from the statue, saw the many corridors leading out of the Atrium and into the hive-like maze of the kaer. Which way did he go? Where was his father nursing his drink?

J'role stood still, quiet, as still and quiet as the statue of Garlen behind him. Sometimes . . .

He heard it. The singing. Low and sad. Though he could not make out the words, he knew it was a happy song, something about love, or adventure. Or a farmer's song, one they sung to keep spirits high while toiling under the sun. His father only sang happy songs, but he sang them all sad.

J'role moved toward the singing, crossing the Atrium and

listening at the entrances of several tunnels. Finally he found the right one and proceeded.

He walked for what seemed a long time, though it was only the darkness and memories stretching out his thoughts that made the short walk seem long. Once, when he had lived in the kaer, floating lanterns had provided constant, safe illumination, following alongside anyone moving through the corridors. Now, as J'role crisscrossed the tunnels—picking up the trail of his father's singing, losing it, finding it again—only the red light of his brand flickered along the red walls. Cracks and crags in the walls vanished and appeared as the firelight danced. The scuttle of strange creatures moving swiftly through the darkness echoed softly.

He had never heard such things in his youth.

And the smell. Things moved in and out of the tunnels now, strange things even his father's tales did not describe. Or so J'role imagined.

He passed the large hall where all his people ate, the rooms where Charneale taught his pupils. Down to his right the corridor led to the chambers where his family had slept. He was glad his father wasn't down there. The memories clawed at J'role as he passed those rooms, though he could remember no specific incident.

He just didn't like the place.

When the singing was clear and loud enough for J'role to make out the words to his father's favorite love song, a song he used to sing to J'role's mother, he realized where his father was. It was a place where he did remember what happened.

Did his father have to be there?

Maybe he could set the bundle down here, leave it for his father? When his father got hungry, he'd stagger down the corridor, find it. Eat.

Wouldn't that be enough?

No, what if his father passed out from drink and hunger, passed out and never found the food, starved to death with his meal only fifty feet away?

Would that be so bad?

J'role's muscles tightened in horror at his thought.

"J'role," said the creature, its tone full of mock concern, "did you just realize something about yourself you don't like?"

J'role's hands trembled, and to shake off the terror of his

thoughts he moved forward, concentrating on how much his father had done for him.

"Like what?" asked the creature.

J'role had no answer.

He turned a corner and saw a brand jammed into a crack in the wall, the tip ablaze with yellow-red light. Bevarden, his father, sat on the ground, back to the corridor's wall, his head tilted back, singing his song. "And never will I—" He stopped singing and turned abruptly toward J'role. "Who is it? Who's there?"

The sight of his father's face in the red light shocked J'role. Skin taut, eyes deep; a death mask. Dirty, ragged cloth for clothes. Arms and legs thin, belly bloated. Was this how his father really looked? Then Bevarden's face softened, a smile appeared. "J'role," he said happily, dreamily. The terrible sight blurred into something much more comprehensible and familiar. Bevarden raised an arm, gesturing for J'role to approach. "My boy, my precious boy," his father said as J'role came closer. J'role smiled in return.

His father kept his arm extended, so he could take J'role's hand. But J'role stopped a few feet away. Just beyond was the pit, fifteen feet wide, and very, very deep. Eight feet down from the pit's brim glowed the surface of the pale blue liquid. It was thick, and bubbles appeared every so often.

The home of the dead.

When they'd put his mother in the pit, after stoning her to death in the fountain of the Atrium, with everyone in the kaer participating, the water no longer flowing so they could collect the blood, the statue of Garlen looking on ... After they'd stoned her, according to the ritual to drive the Horror out of her body and out of the kaer, they brought her body to the pit and threw it into the viscous blue liquid. She followed many other corpses who had died much, much more peaceful deaths.

For weeks afterward J'role had returned to the pit when no one else was around, waiting for her to come back. It seemed to him, eight years old at the time, that she should. She had been punished, and wrongly so, because it was he who had the Horror in his head and not her, and it was his fault they thought she was possessed, and now it was time for her to come back.

Every time he stood at the edge of the pit he tried to say how sorry he was. He would open his mouth, forming his lips into the shape to make the sound *I,* rolling the tip of his tongue to the edge of his teeth, desperately wanting to say, "I'm sorry." But as soon as he began to make a sound, he felt his jaw turn prickly, lost the sensation of his tongue, and knew that the creature was still in him, ready to take control of his mouth should he try to speak. So he said nothing.

Nothing, even after all these years.

"What is it, lad?" asked his father. "Oh, the pool. Yes." He turned and looked into it. "Lost in there among all the other dead." He picked up his flask from the floor, placed the spout to his mouth, and took a long swallow. Then he leaned his head back slowly, until it came to rest against the stone wall, eyes closed, happy. Happier than when he smiled at J'role, and J'role knew it. Truly happy. He remained motionless for a moment, still savoring the drink, then slowly turned his head toward his son.

J'role, confused, eager either to leave his father quickly or to please him, knelt down on the stone floor and set the bundle before him. He unwrapped it and the food spilled out.

Bevarden smiled at him. "Ah, J'role, my fine boy. How good of you." He rolled over and picked at the bread with his fingertips. "Can't say I'm hungry right now, though."

J'role tore off a bit of bread from the loaf and raised it to his father's mouth, as he'd done so many time in the past.

"No, no. Not hungry now." His father closed his eyes. His face suddenly contorted with deep pain. "Why?" he whispered to no one, as if J'role had suddenly gone and he was free to voice all his confusions aloud. He then placed his hand on J'role's knee. Unlike Garlthik's hand, which was rough and alien and full of something strong, the touch of J'role's father was familiar—horribly familiar and weak and tied to misery. "Thank you for the food. You're a good son. Did you beg some money?"

J'role nodded.

"From some adventurers?"

He raised one finger.

"Ah. A man with a sword?"

J'role nodded, but barely. He knew what was coming, and did not welcome it.

"What I could tell you about adventurers! Your great-great-great . . ." He stumbled, having lost track of the count long ago. "Grandfather, who traveled far and wide, even once visiting the island of Thera far to the southwest, the very man who entered this kaer four hundred years ago, he told many stories of his adventures. He encountered a great many creatures across the land. He even fought Horrors, before they became so great in number and there was naught to be done but seek shelter in the magical kaers." He slumped against the tunnel walls, his eyes closed tight. "Oh, the stories I heard when I was a boy! What I would give to be young again, to know I had the opportunity to go off on the same quests that have traveled the family memory all the years we waited for the Scourge to pass." He looked at J'role, saw the disappointment on his son's face. He faltered.

Immediately J'role felt bad: he hadn't meant to reveal anything. He knew he had to react faster, know when people were going to look at him. Reveal only what people wanted to see, or nothing at all.

His father continued. "Ah, and who's to say I won't go yet. You're right, J'role, you're right. I've got it all planned out in my head. There's a treasure waiting for me. I'm just in the middle of my life. I could make it happen. I need only make the preparations. It'll all be so easy." He stretched himself out on the floor. "Just the preparations, and then it's a sojourn for me. What more need be done? The life of wealth and adventure, eh, my son?"

He reached out to take J'role's hand. J'role clamped down his thoughts, felt nothing, let his father pull him close, cradle him in his arms. "It's ours when we want it, son," he said softly. "Ours when we want it. Ah, life can be so grand. Who knows, I might get enough money, find the magic to grant you your speech again. Eh? Wouldn't that be something? Magic to get your speech back. There are finer magicians than Charneale in the world, mind you, and with enough money—the money from a treasure guarded by a dragon or perhaps from a kaer not as fortunate as ours, empty of life now, but still full of treasure. With preparations one could go out and find these things, claim them, forge a destiny." For a moment Bevarden's thin arms tightened too much, and J'role thought his father might start to hit him as he sometimes did, his thoughts confused by drink. A quick, tearful apology always followed.

But no violence came. His father's voice trailed off as he rocked J'role in his arms.

J'role was stiff as a corpse, eyes wide, uncertain. The silence of the kaer enveloped him like his father's arms, and he felt momentarily transported to the earliest days of his childhood. Born in the underground world of tunnels and magical lights, he had existed without a true conception of the world outside. Until the day Charneale announced that the Horrors had gone from the world and it was safe again to go outside, J'role had believed he would spend his whole life within the corridors of stone. Living in the earth did not seem strange at the time. But now, having lived in sunlight, returning to the kaer invited uncomfortable sensations he could not identify. It seemed a strange thing to do, to return to the dark recesses of one's childhood.

Then he heard the faint echo of shouts through the corridors, all edged with anger. To J'role's well-developed perceptions, the shouts carried one clear message. Somewhere within the kaer's corridors, danger had gathered.

3

J'role is seven and something has happened. A day ago. A week ago. Months ago. The dream is a buried mystery, and within the dream the memory of another mystery.

His mother is close to him, her face a breath away from his. "Speak to no one. Speak to no one. No one but me, do you understand?"

She touched his face, her hand so warm and wonderful, but he flinches at the touch. Something is wrong.

His mother turns away, upset. She bites her lip. Walks a few steps away, then turns suddenly and comes back. Kneeling next to where he sits, she hugs him tight. She begins to cry and then say she is sorry.

He does not know why.

He cannot remember why.

But he has made his mother unhappy, and he decides to keep the promise she asks of him. He will speak to no one but her.

J'role got up quickly, disengaging himself from his father's arms. Drifting down the dark corridors of the kaer came the sound of shouted orders. He turned and placed a hand on his father's shoulder, tried to wake him up, but his father pushed him away.

And what if I wake him up? J'role thought. What if he shouts at me for waking me? If we stay here, we might be safe.

He stood and walked with his wary grace back up the tunnel, toward the sound of the voices, hoping to get close enough to hear what was happening. He left his torch behind, not wanting to call attention to himself. Turning a bend he suddenly entered total darkness. He walked carefully now, one hand brushing the rough stone wall. The barking orders continued, but now the words sounded harsher, as if the people shouting had moved farther away from one another.

Suddenly a voice rushed down upon him from out of the darkness. It was a man's voice, the syllables crashing off the corridor walls, coming closer and closer. "Verin, stay by the entrance! Don't let him get back out!"

Now a light spilled down the corridor, faint at first, turning the corridor walls the color of dried blood. Gripped by fear J'role turned and rushed back the way he had come. The darkness seemed to swallow him, and because he ran with fear, it dug its way into his eyes, removing all sense of direction and balance.

Without warning J'role slammed into a wall. With a cry he fell to the ground.

"Wait! I heard something! It must be him!"

J'role scrambled up, pressing his hand to the wall, firmly now, to steady himself. He touched his other hand to his forehead and felt warm, sticky blood. A desire to be a child crawled over him. The man would be on him in a moment, and all J'role could think was how he wanted his father to come and save him. Couldn't he do that? Just this one time, just once, come and do that for him?

Seeing the dim red light appear around a corner snapped J'role back into action. He continued through the darkness, moving quickly, but this time with one hand pressed firmly against the stone. Virtually blinded by the dark, he kept thinking he would trip over something—a stone, a body— something. The rough wall scraped at his palm, but it gave him comfort rather than pain. Compared to the impenetrable, insubstantial darkness through which he ran, it was solid and real.

Then his groping hand found only thin air and he fell into a side tunnel. The fall terrified him, but this time he stifled any sound. He rolled quickly against the base of the tunnel wall, tucking himself tightly into the shadows. The firelight became brighter and brighter out in the main corridor, the sound of footsteps coming closer. Then the light of a flame washed over him, and J'role was sure the man running down the corridor would see him.

But the footsteps only hesitated at the junction. For the

merest instant J'role glimpsed a man dressed in black leather, illuminated by torch light. Then the darkness descended again, comforting J'role as he lay breathing quietly. He started tucking his body deeper into the shallow hole he'd found when he remembered his father.

The man in the leather armor was heading straight toward his father.

J'role got up, dizzy from the wound on his forehead, and once more began to move down the corridor, putting first one hand then the other against the left wall for balance. After walking no more than twenty yards he heard his father cry out. That made J'role move faster, but not so fast as to run the same risks as before. He used the wall for balance and guidance until the light from flames ahead lit the corridor for him.

Three torches lit the scene: his father's torch jammed into the wall, J'role's own torch on the ground, and the torch carried by the man in leather. The man stood between J'role and the brilliant collection of flames, his features hidden from J'role, his body a red-tinged shadow.

The stranger leaned over Bevarden, his free hand around the man's neck, pressing his head against the wall. "You must have seen him! Why else are you here? You're working with the ork, aren't you?"

His father, wide-eyed, gasping as if staring straight into a nightmare come true, sputtered, "No. No. No ork." Then he shut his eyes, as if trying to deny his assailant any reality.

"Listen!" shouted the stranger, jabbing his torch into Bevarden's rough shirt. Smoke rose from the coarse cloth, and Bevarden screamed. The man laughed, and Bevarden tried to shrink himself into a small ball.

Shame burned at J'role's cheeks, and then it was anger driving him—anger at his father—as he charged the stranger. He screamed, and as he opened his lips he felt himself lose control of his mouth. His tongue writhed of its own volition and seemed thick and strange in his mouth. A prickly sensation ran over the flesh around J'role's mouth and he heard the words stream out.

Words . . . things like words.

A conflagration of syllables and sounds, some recognizably human, others not. They tore at his mind even as he raced down the tunnel, screaming them at the top of his lungs. He felt his muscles, his tongue, forming the noises, but he had no idea what he was saying.

As the tall thin man whirled toward J'role, he dropped the torch and clutched his hands to his face. J'role's father screamed in agony—a moaning so deep and mournful that it matched the wail he had uttered while watching the villagers stone his wife to death nine years before.

Without thinking J'role shoved his thin arms into the chest of the stranger. The man fell back, J'role's momentum carrying them both just over the edge of the pit. The man cried out, and J'role, realizing what was happening, twisted and desperately caught hold of the edge with one arm. He quickly swung one leg up onto the edge, then felt a hand grab his back. It was the stranger, who also had one hand on the edge of the pit, and another one on J'role's shoulder as he tried to climb up.

Their faces were inches apart, J'role still babbling uncontrollably. The sensation of his mouth moving without his will terrified him, and he tried to scream, "Help me!" but the sounds and screams and cries and noises only continued louder and faster, broken now by harsh laughs.

Frozen in terror, the man stared wildly for a moment at J'role. Then he began to claw his way frantically over him, the movement nearly sending the boy down into the pool.

As the man climbed over him, J'role tried to roll further away from the pit, all the while still babbling and crying and shrieking.

J'role and the tall thin man cleared the edge of the pit. J'role struggled to get away, but the man flipped him over and pinned J'role's chest down with his knees. Behind them, J'role heard his father sobbing. Grabbing J'role's head between his hands, the man began to slam it against the stone floor.

Slam.

Slam.

Slam.

Slam.

"Stop it! Stop it! Please! Stop it!" the man screamed at J'role.

J'role felt himself losing his sense of place; the up and down motion, the rhythmic pain, suddenly felt normal. A blackness seeped into his vision. But still the noise from his

mouth continued. He tasted the salty tears of the man as they
fell into his open, ranting mouth.

Through all the screaming and pain and motion, a single
thought burned straight to the center of J'role's thoughts.
"I'm going to die." He welcomed the idea. The creature in
his head purred.

Everything outside this white-hot thought suddenly faded
to the background, though he was still aware of the crying
and the screaming and the sharp crack of his skull against
the floor. Terror filled him.

What would happen if he died with the thing in his
thoughts? Would he just keep ranting, never truly dead, alive
just enough to support the Horror?

With a sudden, desperate burst of strength he grabbed the
man's wrists and tore his hands away from his head. Without
pause he rolled the man to the right. The man scrambled
wildly to keep his balance, arms waving in the air, but J'role
sent him tumbling into the pit, giving him a final nudge with
his last bit of strength. The man shouted—a short, abruptly
cut-off cry for help.

J'role's mouth continued to babble as he stared up at the
torch-lit ceiling, but the sounds came softer and softer.

Then a blessed silence fell. His mouth was sore, but still.
He crawled to the edge of the pit and looked down. He saw
nothing but the blue, bubble-pocked liquid.

Behind him his father sobbed.

"I'm sorry," Bevarden said amid his tears. "I'm sorry."

J'role crawled toward his father. His words—the noises
from his mouth—had caused his father the pain that now
wracked him. He wanted to hold his father, to somehow
make everything all better.

But before he could reach his father, more light entered
the corridor. J'role looked up.

Fifteen feet away stood a tall man wearing magician's
robes—red like the blazing heart of a dragon; against the red
were intricate silhouettes of trees, their branches beautiful.
The magician's eyes were blind white orbs. His right hand
was raised, and in the palm was an eye with a deep-green
pupil. It stared down at J'role.

Behind the magician was a woman. She was as tall as the
magician, but with wider shoulders. At her side was a long
sword, but the weapon in her hands was a short sword.

"Well, this is a strange night," said the magician. "Do you know where I can find my friend Garlthik One-Eye? And if so, would you please tell me where?" The words were calm and friendly; the sound of them heavy with menace. The eye in the palm blinked.

A strange sensation passed through J'role, a combination of dread—for he had never seen anyone like the magician before him—and a sense of thrill. He'd just vanquished the stranger who had assaulted his father. His voice, which had always seemed a curse, had helped him. Could he use it again?

Keeping his face still, ignoring the sobs of his father, J'role opened his mouth to speak to the magician. If the voice confused the magician and the warrior, he might be able to grab his father and run. Perhaps not. Perhaps only he would run. Who knew? But the sensation of fight was strong in him now, and he knew the desire to try rather than surrender.

His mouth dropped open and he felt the rush of the creature's control rush up like a thick snake in his throat. The snake squeezed its way into his tongue and J'role felt it begin to move without his willing it.

The first sounds—low cries, unintelligible syllables, some panting, a giggle—came out. The warrior dropped her sword. The magician took a step back, placing his eyeless hand against his chest. His father screamed. "Please," he shouted, high-pitched, "I'm sorry. I'm sorry."

The thrill grew greater in J'role. A pride began to grow in him. He could harm so many people. He had denied it for so many years, but no more ...

The magician, his eye-hand still raised high, spoke a word that J'role could not make out over the cacophony of his own speech. A blue flame jumped out from the hand, and in terror J'role watched as a webbing of blue light warped itself in the air around the hand. The webbing, like a cloud of soft blue cotton, flew through the air, slamming into J'role's mouth and wrapping tightly around his head. He tried to continue speaking, but the gauze grew tighter and tighter, choking his tongue back into his mouth, cutting deep into the corners of his mouth, until he could do no more than moan.

The warrior quickly seized her sword from off the floor. The magician took a few curious steps forward. His father now had his hands held high in front of his face, with the rest of his body curled tightly into a ball.

J'role raised his hands to try to pry away the webbing, but his hands became stuck to the material and he could not tear them free. Feeling helpless, J'role decided to stay on his knees rather than risk the magician's further wrath. His head throbbed, and in his ridiculous position the desire for conflict quickly dissipated.

"What is it?" asked the warrior of the magician. J'role could see now that her eyes were red-rimmed, as if she'd been crying. "Is he a magician? A nethermancer adept?"

"I'm not sure," the magician said, a strong note of curiosity in his voice. He seemed the least affected. With his eye-hand held high, he approached J'role. The eye looked down and peered at him. It blinked. "Hmmm," said the magician.

"A Horror?" asked the warrior. She took a step back at the word she spoke.

"I don't . . .," the magician began uncertainly. "Perhaps. But the boy himself is not." He spoke a few more words J'role had never heard before. A pale green light radiated from the eye, washing over J'role's flesh and forcing him to close his eyes. "No, there's . . . something inside him."

"Inside him?" She hefted her blade, as if ready to split J'role open and kill the creature.

"Not the body, Phlaren," the magician said wearily. "The creature's spirit. It's in his . . . thoughts, if you will. I don't know where the thing's body is."

J'role felt nervous. He'd thought he'd found a way to use the Horror to his own advantage, but by revealing his voice, he had revealed all. A sweat began to trickle down his forehead as he remembered his mother's fate.

"He's good," said the creature.

"Please . . .," thought J'role.

"No. He really is. Most humans wouldn't be able to see as much as he's seen. Do you think they'll drop you into the pit? Pelt you with stones? Slice off your head?"

"Kill him?" asked the warrior, taking a step forward.

"Not just yet. Garlthik ran in here. He may have been coming to meet them. They may be of use."

The magician walked up to Bevarden and kicked him in the side. "You!" he shouted.

Bevarden came out of his tears, surprised, and looked up. He saw J'role on his knees with a glowing blue gauze

wrapped around his face, then glanced at the magician, then the warrior. His mouth opened and closed slightly, over and over again like a fish desperate for water.

"Where is Garlthik?" the magician asked.

"I . . . I don't know . . . I'm just . . . I'm nobody."

"Have you seen a tall man? In leather armor?" asked the woman.

J'role remained completely still. Bevarden looked to J'role, then mimicked his lack of response.

"This is a waste of time," the warrior said, hefting her sword.

"So impatient, Phlaren. Obviously they've seen him, or they would have answered. By not answering they show they're hiding something, which means they know something about Yarith that they'd rather not say. Most likely that they've killed him."

The warrior's face changed, softened a bit, then became hard and cold. "Oh."

"Am I right?" the magician asked J'role. He slammed his foot into J'role's stomach so quickly it caught J'role completely by surprise. J'role fell onto his back, aware he was now dangerously close to the edge of the pit. He stared up as the magician spoke to him. "Listen, boy, if I didn't kill you before, I won't now. Phlaren might, but she'll listen to me. Now just tell me, so we can move along, did you kill a man in leather armor."

J'role glanced at the woman, whose face muscles were held tightly. A thought occurred to him: As long as the other man's death remained a mystery, she would keep her hatred of him alive, ready to snap at any moment. But if he were to admit the deed, she might still hate him, but the event would no longer have a place at the front of her thoughts. It would slowly slip away.

He nodded.

"Where is the body?"

He nodded toward the pit. The magician craned his neck and said, "Oh. Well, so much for him."

"We kill them now," said the woman.

"Not yet. Get the boy. I'll get this misshapen lump moving along."

The magician and the warrior escorted them to the Atrium, where they sat J'role and his father against the fountain. Torches ringed the area, casting huge shadows along the walls. The magician had removed the spell, and the warrior had bound J'role and his father with ropes. A strip of cloth gagged J'role.

The magician had half a dozen allies who entered and left the Atrium in the search for Garlthik. It seemed from the shouts that echoed through the corridors and the constant regrouping that took place in the Atrium that the magician's companions were constantly finding Garlthik's trail, only to lose it again. The magician, the woman warrior, and two other men armed with swords remained in the Atrium, determined to prevent Garlthik from leaving the kaer.

While the other men and women hunted the tunnels, the woman warrior roughly searched J'role and his father. She found the coins from Garlthik—J'role thought she would certainly take them—but only tossed them aside, and they clattered against the stone floor. J'role glanced at the money. Had it been only a few hours ago that he'd met the ork, received the money from him?

Whatever she was looking for, the warrior did not find it, and when she was done, she stood and turned away.

The magician remained seated on the edge of the fountain. "Who is this?" he asked Bevarden, gesturing to the statue.

The reply came dry and tired. "Garlen. Our protector."

"Ah. Interesting. I'd heard that people had made statues of the spirits during the Scourge." He looked at the statue for a few moments. "And how did your people fare? The village nearby—I assume the people came from here."

"Yes."

"And did Garlen keep your people safe?"

Bevarden's voice cracked. "Some."

"You lost someone?"

"Yes."

"Spirits are for the weak. Why depend on the force of another? I'd rather depend on my own wiles. If I fail, I cannot sit and blame another and be bitter."

"Some of us," said Bevarden, his voice suddenly sober, "are very weak."

"Yes," answered the magician. "I depend on that."

The sound of shouting echoed through the corridor, then a scream, and cries for help. "Ushel! Chie! Go, go!" said the magician harshly. The two armed men rushed down the tunnel from where the cries sounded. J'role could just make out the sound of metal striking metal. Another scream. And then another. The woman warrior started for the corridor. "No," said the magician. "Not yet."

Silence fell. The warrior's body tensed. The magician turned and faced the corridor, his hand raised, a blue crackle around it. The tension swept J'role up: What would emerge?

Footsteps approached, slow and staggering. Then Garlthik stumbled out of a tunnel and collapsed to the floor. A short man with a stocky build and curly black hair followed. Blood dripped down his temple.

"Where are the others?" asked the magician.

"Dead."

"All?"

"All."

"Garlthik," the magician said softly, his voice icy with anger, "you have cost me much time."

Garlthik raised his head from the ground. "You should have let me be. Easier for all of us."

"And leave the lovely ring with the likes of you? I think not."

The ork tried to rise up to his hands and knees, but the small man rushed up and threw himself onto Garlthik's back. The ork collapsed to the stone floor with a great sigh. "I'm not going anywhere, Slinsk," he gasped.

"That's what you said outside of Harash."

Garlthik smiled, his huge teeth arching up from his lower jaw. "Yes. I did. Very well." He paused, then said, "I don't have it, you know."

The magician said, "Did you search him?"

"Not yet," answered Slinsk.

"I lost it during the chase. Don't really know where it went. Somewhere in the tunnels." He coughed and blood came up over his lips.

The magician turned to Phlaren. "Help Slinsk search him." She walked over to Garlthik and hoisted him by the neck. As soon as his body was erect she slammed her fist into his stomach, doubling him over. Then she jerked him back up.

Garlthik remained still whole Phlaren held his neck and Slinsk approached to begin his search. Suddenly Garlthik moved quickly, his right arm seeming to vanish as it moved behind him, grabbing something from his cloak. A dagger appeared in his hand. Just as Garlthik was swinging the dagger toward Phlaren, the woman brought her hand down on his arm. His arm's bone snapped sharply as she broke it.

J'role saw a glint of silver—small as a firefly—rush toward him. Distracted by the appearance of the weapon and the pursuant struggle, no one else saw the silver ring fly across the room from Garlthik's free hand toward the fountain.

It fell to the ground with a light *tink* and rolled to a stop a few inches from J'role's outstretched legs. J'role glanced toward the ork. Though Garlthik grimaced in terrible pain as Phlaren and Slinsk drove him back down to the ground, his one eye met J'role's gaze and he nodded slightly.

4

Some memories did come clearly to him while his slept, but these memories were the pleasant dreams. He remembered how his father would make him laugh when he was a little boy. His father had the improbable ability to juggle colored stones, up to six at a time. He could also do cartwheels and handstands and backward flips and could fall on purpose but make it look like an accident.

J'role was the envy of all the children his age, for his father was a clown—and who would not envy having a clown for a father?

J'role's father was the kaer's clown. When he worked he wore a costume of black and white, with bells on the tips of his boots. They jingled softly through the rooms of their home when he was getting ready for work.

Everyone in the kaer knew Bevarden. At that time only a few hundred people lived in the kaer, families who had lived together for generations, so this was not strange. But of all the people in the kaer, J'role's father was the most beloved. "Jolly Bevarden," the adults called him, as did the children who were old enough. The youngest children of the kaer simply called him the Clown.

In later years J'role dreamed of following his father out to the Atrium, where his father would tell stories and juggle and fall. Against the bleak non-memories of so much of his youth, such thoughts gave him comfort.

But they confused him as well. How was it possible to remember the past so fondly, yet feel so bad when thinking about childhood?

Garlthik met J'role's gaze for just a moment, then Slinsk, the nimble man, and Phlaren, the strong warrior, slammed the ork's head into the smooth stone floor of the Atrium. Phlaren and Slinsk beat Garlthik's head repeatedly—Slinsk with a particular joy, J'role thought.

The attack riveted his attention—it seemed more real than real—an intensity of violence J'role had not seen since his mother's stoning nine years earlier.

But the sounds of flesh punching flesh and Garlthik's cries finally forced his eyes away. He could not tolerate watching the pain. Turning his head, J'role saw the ring Garlthik had thrown to him. Silver and smooth, it rested only inches away from his feet. He knew immediately that when Garlthik had stopped on the stairs and stared secretively at the object in his hand, it was the ring he'd been looking at.

And undoubtedly it was the thing Mordom and his companions sought.

He looked to his father, uncertain how to proceed, desperate for counsel. Should he hide the ring, and thus help the generous ork? Or perhaps try to escape with it and sell it? He knew it must be valuable. Or perhaps he could claim it, cover it with his foot, and then use it to barter for his and his father's life?

Or maybe he should simply ignore it.

Looking at his father J'role realized that the tired man would, as usual, be no help. Bevarden sat with his gaze turned away from Garlthik's beating, eyes closed tight. In that moment J'role hated his father. The man could do nothing—not even look! His father mumbled something through tightly clenched teeth. Listening carefully, J'role heard him saying "preparations" over and over again. Bevarden winced each time Garlthik cried out in pain, but his brief prayer continued.

In that moment J'role loathed his father with a clarity that rivaled the ring's pure silver gleam. The man would never do anything! The thought of being like his father in any way repulsed him, and in his father's inaction came J'role's decision for action.

The beating had stopped. Garlthik lay completely still. Slinsk turned Garlthik's body over as if it were a corpse. While Phlaren stood guard over the ork, sword drawn, Slinsk rifled through Garlthik's clothes, searching for secret pockets and ripping the lining out of the wonderful blue cape.

J'role moved his foot slowly, carefully extending it toward

the ring on the floor. The movement was awkward, but he could do nothing about that. If someone spotted him, he would deal with it then. His bare toes just reached the ring, but he could not actually snare it and bring it closer. He lowered himself even more, sliding down along the wall of the fountain, gaining the precious inches he needed, when his father suddenly spoke.

"J'role," Bevarden said softly, eyes still closed. J'role drew in a sharp breath and froze. He glanced at Mordom, who stood facing Garlthik's body, and Phlaren and Slinsk, now searching through Garlthik's pockets. No one glanced back; the ork had their complete attention.

"Did you mean what you said?" his father continued. His mouth hung open slightly, the bones stretching the flesh thin. Bevarden's eyes were wide and wet.

J'role had no idea what his father was talking about, unless it was something from some other time. If so, he certainly did not remember. Then J'role thought for a moment that his father might be referring to the sounds that had come out of his mouth earlier. But that was gibberish, and he dismissed the thought.

"I'm sorry," his father said again.

J'role nodded, hoping to keep his father quiet. The nod worked, and his father turned his head and closed his eyes once more.

J'role continued to slide his body down against the fountain, finally managing to get the ring under his toes, and began slowly to drag it back.

"What are you doing?" asked Mordom. J'role looked up, surprised to see the wizard's head still facing away. Only the palm of his hand with the eye was facing him.

J'role froze, uncertain what to do. His foot hid the ring, so he wasn't worried about that. But his body was stretched out as if he was doing *something*—maybe trying to escape.

The wizard turned his body toward J'role and walked toward him. The scarlet robe fluttered, and the bare tree branches painted on the robe seemed to sway back and forth as if in a mild wind. He walked up to J'role and with his eyeless hand slapped him across the face.

J'role's sight went red, then black, then came back.

The wizard grabbed J'role by the neck and started to drag him up against the fountain's wall. Struggling to keep his face from revealing the effort of his work, J'role tried to curl his toes around the ring. Let me get it, he thought over and over. Let me get it.

As J'role caught the ring under his foot, an extraordinary sensation rushed over him as he touched it. The metal was as cold as the ice a wizard could make with his magic. Yet a heat emanated from it, a warmth of memories—

—of something—

—something J'role could not remember, but thought he should.

"Now stay," said the wizard, his voice low. J'role realized he had closed his eyes when the strange sensation filled him. Mordom had apparently read his expression as one of fear. "I am in no mood for childish attempts at escape," he said. J'role nodded, and the wizard turned with his strange hand toward Garlthik.

The sensation turned into a low buzzing in his mind as he kept his foot pressed tightly against the ring. All that remained after the initial shock was an emptiness in his chest; a tunnel to his heart filled with a cool wind.

"Does he have it or not?" Mordom asked his companions.

"It isn't on him," said Slinsk.

"He could have put it anywhere," said Phlaren throwing her arms wide. "Anywhere in the kaer."

"He ran everywhere," said Slinsk.

"But I don't think he would have simply tossed it away in the tunnels," said Mordom. "He would have hidden it carefully . . . or maybe left it back at the tavern where we found him. Perhaps he hid it in his room. Is he conscious?"

Slinsk smiled an odd smile. "Not at all."

"Very well. Phlaren, bind him. We'll torture him if we have to when he wakes up. Slinsk, go back to the tavern and search his room."

Phlaren said, "They'll be wary now. We killed at least five of their people in the attack."

"Exactly," said Slinsk with a laugh. "They won't be expecting anybody to come back."

"Whatever you think best," said Mordom. "Just search his room carefully."

Phlaren tied Garlthik tightly. It seemed to J'role she went to absurd lengths to secure him. Yards of rope were used to bind the ork's ankles and wrists, his arms and legs bent behind his back. Phlaren used complicated and strange knots.

When it was all done, very little of Garlthik remained visible; he was a bundle of hemp. She dropped him down onto the floor near J'role and Bevarden, and went off to confer quietly with the wizard. Mordom kept the eye of his palm toward them.

Garlthik still breathed; the bundle of hemp pulsed slightly. This gave J'role great comfort, for he didn't know what to do next and certainly could not count on his father for help. Bevarden was still praying, mumbling soft supplications to Garlen.

Minutes passed, and then, through a slight slit in the rope, J'role saw Garlthik's eye open. "Do you have it?" Garlthik said softly. He spoke with such pain J'role wanted to reach out and comfort him.

J'role nodded slightly, casually, as if dropping off to sleep.

Garlthik nodded back. "Distract them. Somehow. With only two of them here, we might get out."

"J'role?" said his father as if coming out of a dream. "Who is this?"

The green eye shifted slightly. "Your father?" Garlthik asked.

J'role nodded.

"Listen, old man," whispered Garlthik, and J'role found himself embarrassed, for he realized his father looked much older than he really was. "We might be able to leave here alive. But I need those two over there distracted. I can get free if . . ." He gasped for air and winced.

"Do you know him?" Bevarden asked J'role.

J'role nodded, this time with his eyes wide, hoping his father would cooperate. He desperately wanted to be able to talk—not make the abominable sounds he had made earlier—but to speak with words, so he could explain everything to his father so he'd be quiet.

But, of course, that was not possible.

"I want a drink, J'role. I want a drink so bad."

J'role turned to his father. The man's head rested against the fountain; his tongue flicked over his lips, desperate for beer.

How J'role hated him! He was so weak!

J'role would never be so weak. He would die first.

He rocked his body forward—once, twice—then rolled up onto his knees.

Mordom turned his body, raised his hand. "What are you doing?"

With a deft maneuver J'role dropped his hands low and grabbed the ring off the floor. Even as he stood up he saw an odd green glow, like blades of grass on a warm morning, emanate from within the knots binding Garlthik's hands. J'role rushed a few feet to the left, neither toward Mordom and Phlaren, but simply away from Garlthik. Phlaren drew her sword.

"J'role!" Bevarden cried. "What are you . . ." He rolled forward and tried to get up. But with his hands bound behind his back he lost his balance and tumbled to the floor. His chin slammed into the stone, but he continued the struggle to get up. A red smear dripped from a cut just under his lip.

A panic seized J'role. He had meant to put his own life in danger, not his father's. Looking after his father was too much work.

"Both of you, sit down!" shouted Mordom.

J'role turned and saw Phlaren, her long sword drawn, walking toward him and Bevarden. Then Mordom gave a cry of warning to Phlaren. Garlthik suddenly loomed behind Phlaren, leaped onto her back and grabbed her neck with his good arm. The two of them collapsed toward J'role, who jumped quickly out of the way. Phlaren and Garlthik crashed down to the floor, Phlaren with a cry of pain.

Garlthik jumped up, a bloodied dagger in his hand—where had he gotten that? J'role wondered—and slipped the blade through the knots that held J'role tight. His hands free, J'role scrambled up, realizing that he still held the ring in his hand.

He knew that nothing would make him let it go.

Mordom turned toward him, his ruined white eyes ghastly in the firelight. He raised the eye-hand and a red bolt arced through the air.

J'role stood paralyzed with fear, thinking now he would die, when suddenly his father crashed into him, knocking J'role out of the way. The wizard's bolt caught Bevarden full, drawing a horrible scream from him.

"Run, boy! Run!" shouted Garlthik.

But J'role found it impossible to move. He stared down at his father, who rocked back and forth on the floor, the flesh burned off his right shoulder, exposing red muscle and yellow fat. He whimpered, then said, "Just something to drink, son. A little drink. I promise, then I'll get everything together. Preparations. We'll make. Preparations. With preparation we can make anything happen."

Garlthik's rough hand grabbed J'role by the back of his shirt and knocked him toward the entrance tunnel. He heard Mordom speak the strange language again, and this time intense fear made him rush for the kaer's entrance. He heard the clatter of metal, a shout, and then plunged into the darkness of the tunnel. He ran and ran, finally arriving on the ledge outside the kaer's entrance.

The night air, cold and damp, crashed into his flesh, and for a moment he felt safe, as if by being under the stars he had somehow left all the troubles behind. He grabbed the rope in his mouth, and pulled it down around his neck. Then he heard Garlthik shouting for him to keep running, the voice getting closer and closer.

J'role rushed for the edge of the ledge and jumped off, balancing himself on two legs for the first few yards of the steep incline. Then he hit a series of rough patches and began to tumble wildly down the hill, totally losing his balance. He rolled into the base of the hill and collapsed among another group of stones. He heard the sound of more stones coming down from above him, and he moved quickly out of the way as Garlthik joined him at the base of the hill.

Without a backward glance the ork grabbed J'role by the shirt and half-carried him to some boulders fifty yards away. J'role bounced along, and the ork breathed heavily with the effort. When they'd slipped into the shadows of the rocks, Garlthik slammed J'role against a tall boulder with his good arm. J'role realized that he should have felt pain, but his body was now too beaten and torn to register new shocks.

"Do you have it?" Garlthik demanded with a sharp whisper, his one eye glaring down fiercely. A stench of beer roiled out of his mouth. "Come on. I didn't have time to finish them. They'll be after us in a moment."

J'role realized that the only reason the ork had helped him escape was to secure the ring—there wasn't a bit of real concern in his face.

J'role had left his father behind to die.

He nodded softly. He let all the rigidity of his body seep away into the night air. As J'role hoped, Garlthik loosened his grip in response. J'role hesitated an instant, then broke free of the ork, rushing under his right arm and back toward the kaer.

He'd only gone a short way when Garlthik tackled him, knocking him to the ground. The ring flew out of J'role's hand and skittered a few feet away.

A horrible emptiness crashed into J'role's chest. The tunnel to his heart created by the ring had sealed shut, and he missed the chill wind terribly. All thoughts of his father forgotten, he fought Garlthik desperately to regain the ring. They crawled over each other, kicking and crawling, arms outstretched to reach the moonlit glint of silver. J'role remembered Garlthik's broken arm and slammed his hands into it. Garlthik cried out in agony, and J'role almost got by him. But the thick fingers of the ork's good hand wrapped themselves around J'role's ankle and pulled him back away from the ring. A horrible, deep fury roared out of Garlthik's mouth, and J'role thought the ork might bite him with his massive teeth.

"Speak!" the creature in his thoughts demanded. "Speak! Let me help!"

In his fury to reach the ring, J'role did not hesitate. As he began to breathe the strange sounds into Garlthik's ear, the ork clutched his head and rolled away.

Now freed from the ork's grasp, J'role rushed for the ring, grabbed it, and began running toward the kaer. His mouth kept moving, his voice still screeching and uttering sounds. He ran on another thirty feet. Then, afraid he might drop the ring, he slipped it onto his finger.

And collapsed to his knees.

The moment the ring was on his finger a terrible longing washed over him. The sensation ripped through his chest; it tore at every dream he ever had, knocking them from his heart, replacing them with nothing but a desire for something he could not identify. It felt like the longing for his mother. Or his desire for a sober and strong father. He thought of his desire to be held. He remembered his friends from when he was much, much younger, none of whom spoke to him any longer. He thought of his desire to live a life of adventure. He thought of so many things, but knew that not one of them was exactly the thing he longed for. The ring suggested something else, something better than anything he had ever dreamed of. In his heart he knew that if he could just find what it was he longed for, he would never, never need or want anything again.

The sensation was so strong in him that he did not immediately realize he was speaking words.

Words!

When he noticed it, he touched his hands to his lips, for he could not at first believe it. His lips moved without his volition, as when he made the creature's noises. But he was speaking words now. Whole words. He listened to himself.

". . . white pillars, as pure as clouds, rising up, supporting arches carved with reliefs showing the splendors of the world . . ."

He listened to himself, stunned. At first he did not know what he was saying. But then realized he was describing the details of a city—a city of such wonder that it matched the tales his father used to tell J'role as a boy. He remained on his knees, listening to himself speak of gold-plated streets and chariots that flew through the sky, of great temples, each supported by a single pillar of emerald-inlaid marble. His words enthralled him, for he could almost see images of the city in the corner of his mind. He sought out the images, desperate for a glimpse of its beauty.

Only because the night air was cool did he realize he was crying.

A shadow fell over him, the light of the moon suddenly gone. He looked up and saw Garlthik staring down at him. The ork looked totally baffled as he stared at J'role with his one eye, head cocked to the side. He looked at the ring on J'role's finger and then asked quietly, "What are you talking about, boy?"

J'role spread his arms wide as his mouth continued to move without his will.

"Come," he said, leaning down and gently helping J'role up. He glanced back toward the kaer, and J'role did too. They could see no one. "If they haven't come after us yet, it means they'll be after us any minute. Come."

J'role pointed toward the kaer several times.

"He's dead, boy," Garlthik said quietly. "He died from the wizard's spell."

With the ork's big arm draped carefully around J'role's

back, the two walked off into the night, J'role's voice a whisper, telling of fountains that poured water filled with small stars and of statues that danced and flew through the air.

5

After Bevarden had done his pratfalls and juggled and made jokes and made everybody laugh, he settled down and told stories.

Each day the people in the kaer survived another twenty-four hours in the stone corridors, prisoners in their shelter of safety. But they knew that generations ago their ancestors had walked the world—a world alive with magic and adventure and a brilliant sun and a blue sky and things called jungles so thick with trees and plants you could not see through it from one side to another. Bevarden reminded everyone of these things.

He acted out stories of adventurers seeking magical elements in craggy mountain peaks, encountering primitive troll tribes. Of ancient warriors defeating the first Horrors that came to the world hundreds of years ago when the invasion was just beginning. Of sailors who traveled huge, rolling, uncovered roads of water called rivers. He spoke of the elves of the Wyrm Wood, with their delicate and perfect faces, their love of the jungles, and their powerful magic with all things living. He reminded people of the dwarven kingdom of Throal, whose language they all spoke. And the powerful Theran Empire that had provided the means to fend off the Horrors.

J'role watched his father and ached to leave the confines of the kaer. And he loved his father, for the man was full of life and energy and spoke of passions and valor and the challenge of being alive. He looked around at the audience assembled in the Atrium and watched everyone enjoying his father playing the part of heroes and trolls and dwarfs and elves. And even though they knew all the stories, they lis-

*tened, for Bevarden kept fresh in their minds the memories
of the life waiting for them at the end of the Scourge.*

Garlthik and J'role walked for a long time that night. The
stars and moon cast a pale light down to the earth, creating
soft shadows of a few scraggly trees along the barren
ground. Garlthik picked the path, and J'role, who continued
to speak of the beautiful city, knew only that he was getting
farther away from his village and the kaer.

As they walked Garlthik took a small vial out of the
pouch tied to his belt. He removed the stopper, and drank
down the contents of the vial. Hours later, long into their
walk, J'role made a connection between the vial's contents
and the fact that Garlthik's groans of pain had ceased and he
no longer held his left arm in agony. A magical potion.

Normally J'role would have been astounded to see such
powerful magic, but not this night. The small tunnel to his
heart created when he had first touched the ring had become
so achingly beautiful and overpowering he cared for nothing
but the words that came without thought from his lips. The
small tunnel had opened into a vast cavern of cold desire.
All he wanted was the promise of happiness that the ring
and the images of the city carried. To know that there actually existed a place where he could finally feel whole . . .
J'role had always believed that such a place or a person or
an object—something—could exist. But he had never been
able to guess what it might actually be.

Now he know. The magic city he now spoke of.

Spoke of!

It astounded him further that he was still speaking. It was
true he did not have control of his tongue, his jaw, his lips.
As ever he found himself disconnected from his own body
in the matter of making sounds with his mouth. The words
came to him out of the world's magic. He looked around at
the barren hills and the scraggly trees and the piles of boulders and stones that dotted the pale blue night. From somewhere in this emptiness came the words. He had no idea
why he said what he said. He had no actual picture of the
city in his thoughts. He responded to the images formed by
the words, moved to tears on occasion, from weariness, yes,
but also from a longing for what he spoke of. The more the
city's details grew in his mind, the more he longed for the
city.

* * *

Garlthik eyed him curiously as they walked. J'role, who listened to himself with the same interest as Garlthik, sometimes met Garlthik's eye. The ork raised the brow over his good eye, stared down at J'role as they walked on the quiet, cool night. These shared looks made them companions sharing a mystery: the mystery of why their third companion—the strange words—carried on so.

Finally, after many hours, J'role's throat began to hurt from the talking. The distanced sensations of his lips moving by their own had been replaced by a numbing pain. His mouth was dry. It occurred to him that it might never stop. He stumbled and fell to his knees.

"What is it?" Garlthik asked.

J'role put his hands to his face, touched his lips. They writhed under his fingertips like snakes. A panic came over him. He put his hands together to remove the cold ring. But even as he did so, a horrible feeling overwhelmed him: give up the longing? Despite the agony of his muscles, he wanted to continue to hear about the lovely city. For the first time in nearly a decade he knew hope, and giving that up seemed too terrible.

"You want to stop talking?" Garlthik asked.

J'role nodded.

"Take off the ring."

J'role drew his hands close to his chest, hid the ring under his free hand.

"You can put it on again later," the ork said, and touched his heavy fingers lightly against J'role's shoulder. "I'm not going to take it from you."

The boy eyed the ork curiously.

"No, really, I'm not. I don't think so. You've got something about you—you were mute—correct? And now you start describing a city when you put on the ring. Something about you . . . You're connected to where this ring leads." Garlthik turned his face away and put a weary hand to his forehead. "Please, take it off. I've seen some stranger things, but this image of your mouth flapping away, with you not paying any attention. It's too disturbing."

A strange happiness filled J'role. He realized that Garlthik and Mordom and the others wanted the ring because it led to something valuable, not because it was valuable in itself. Garlthik was surprised by J'role's words, which meant that he hadn't known what the goal was, only that it was something wonderful. And now J'role knew the goal was the city he spoke of. And if Garlthik was going to the city, and wanted to bring J'role along, then he would reach the city as well. Everything would be all right.

J'role decided to remove the ring, if only to rest, and as soon as the ring left his finger a horrible pain crashed into his jaw, as if metal hooks had dug into his teeth. He dropped to the ground, groaning. But more than the physical pain was the terror of losing the sweet longing. He still held the ring in his hand, and from the ring there came the thin tunnel of desire to his heart. But nothing could compare with the full longing for the city. It had been so clear, so specific. If he could just find the city everything would be complete. Finished. And now there was nothing. Just a memory that he once had something, now gone.

"Come on, boy. Let's find a place to sleep for the night. If they're after us, we'd best hide."

Garlthik leaned down to help J'role up, but at the ork's touch J'role's mind filled with an image of his father lying on the ground, his shoulder torn open by the blast of the magician's spell. The ring and its magical city had kept J'role's head crammed with a longing for the city. But now released, J'role could think of nothing else. He shook his shoulder away from Garlthik's touch, stood, and started back the way they had come.

"Where are you going?" the ork barked, exasperated.

J'role looked out over the still landscape. He had never been so far from home, a six hours' walk. He'd never needed to navigate back to his village from such a distance, and the landmarks he'd used all his life were useless now. Worse, he'd paid no attention to the way they had traveled.

He thought he saw the tip of the Red Hills, low and dark, but he couldn't be certain. Then he thought he spotted a large rock formation that was just east of his village, but realized it was too round at the top, too wide at the base.

J'role felt as if he were floating in a great void, lost forever to everything he'd known.

No. He could get back. He'd find it.

With his legs aching, the dried blood cool and itchy on his forehead, he started back in what he thought was the right direction. He clutched the ring tight in his hand, not only to hold on to the slight feeling of longing, but because it was all he now owned, his only connection to his home. To his father.

"Where are you going, boy?"

He heard Garlthik take a few heavy strides toward him and then a big hand was on him, spinning him around.

The ork leaned his huge face in toward J'role's. "I said, where are you going?"

J'role stared at the ork for a moment, afraid. Garlthik had attacked him earlier. He might do it again. He pointed back in the general direction they'd come.

"What do you want to go back there for, lad? That magician is certain to crisp your flesh if you should ever meet him." The ork smiled like a friend giving advice, but J'role could not believe him.

J'role shook his head, then clenched his fists as he tried to figure out how to communicate his concern for his father. Finally he tapped his chest with one hand, then raised the hand above his head. Garlthik peered at him, uncertain. "I could just speak at him. And then run," J'role thought.

"Don't," said the creature, suddenly harsh in J'role's thoughts after so many hours of silence. "He may have magic you don't understand. He might kill you."

It seemed odd for the creature to be giving him advice—and helpful advice, at that—something the thing in his head had never done before. But remembering the magician's spells and his father's ruined shoulder, J'role decided not to use his voice. But he wanted to go back.

"He's dead," Garlthik said simply.

J'role remembered now. Garlthik had told him, but he'd lost the meaning of the words under the power of the ring. Why had he put it on? He'd forgotten everything when he put the ring on. He should have gone back! He could have done something.

He flung the ring down on the ground, whirled away from Garlthik, started walking. Letting go of the ring—a quick flash of cold in his hand, suddenly gone—he wanted it back. Part of him wanted to scoop the ring back up, put it back on. Feel the desire, the aching, delirious desire of longing to see the city. But he kept moving. Maybe Garlthik was wrong. Maybe his father hadn't died. J'role couldn't know for sure. So much happened so fast.

"BOY!" Garlthik shouted after him. Again the heavy steps followed. Rough hands grabbed him, whirled him around once more. The broad face that peered down at him showed no pretense of kindness now. The large teeth that protruded over Garlthik's lips heaved up and down. "You will not go, do you understand? Your father is dead, and there is nothing you can do to bring him back. And I want you. Do you understand? There's something about you. Don't know what it is yet. But you have something . . . That city you described. I'm looking for that—I think. You can help me. I'm certain of it. Everybody who's put that ring on is looking for *something*. But I've got you. I'm going to find it—we're going to find it. And when we do, we'll be rich. Do you understand? Rich! Only the potential for wealth could make my heart hunger so!"

My father, J'role thought.

"Dead," said the creature. "You let him die when you deserted him. There's no need—"

"I didn't mean to!"

"But you did. You did mean to."

A wet chill touched the flesh of his back.

"Do you remember what he asked you? 'Did you mean what you said?' he asked. When you were shouting in the corridor by the pit. Do you remember?"

"Yes, he asked me that. But it was you who spoke. I didn't say anything."

"Oh, yes you did, J'role, young J'role, J'role the bringer of madness. You did. I let you speak clearly. I let you speak directly. That's why it's so dangerous. Most people can only use words—poor tools, words. But I speak with a clarity—I speak hate clearly. Purified. Absolute."

"But how . . ."

"It's my talent. Alas, my only talent." With a laugh it said, "We're all limited in our own way. I found all the hate he held in himself and twisted it back on him."

"And my mother?"

"The same. And the fool in the tunnels, now locked in eternal embrace with your mother at the bottom of the corpse pit."

J'role sank to the ground. An emptiness filled his chest as he thought of the ring. The ring clarified emptiness, made such an aching longing comprehensible. It also gave him a hope: to find the city meant being free of the emptiness.

He wanted that very much.

He looked up and saw the ork looking down at him, confused. "Listen to me," he said carefully. "We need each other now. They're after both of us. And we have the power, together, to find the greatest treasure of all the treasures. Let's you and me work together. An alliance." He extended his large hand.

J'role nodded and slowly stood. He took the ork's hand and shook it.

He walked back to the ring, picked it up, immediately feeling better. The longing caused by the ring's touch pained him, but it was purified, absolute. He did not place the ring on his finger, however. That would be too much right now.

They found an outcropping of large boulders among some hills, and here they sought out a shelter. Soon they found a small cave-like hole formed by three tall boulders leaning against one another. As they settled down J'role began to shiver. Garlthik was cold, too, and set up a small pile of dry sticks he had found while searching for the cave. He reached into the pouch on his belt, and J'role thought he might be looking for another magical item for use in starting the fire. Instead the ork pulled out a piece of flint, which he sparked against the stone floor of their shelter. Soon he had a fire going.

Without another word Garlthik lay down and slept. For a few moment J'role watched the flames grow and wither frantically in their brief lives. The orange and yellow light played over Garlthik's rough, wrinkled face, which looked so peaceful now. Again he wondered at the fact that he had only met Garlthik One-Eye that very day.

J'role stretched out on the ground, the heat of the fire comforting him as his father's body had so often given comfort when J'role was younger. He thought of his father, now dead—simply gone—and then of Garlthik. They were so very different, yet J'role was strangely linked to each one, a horrible imbalance based on awkward dependency.

He tried to imagine what it would be like to have the most important person in his life be someone with whom he was on equal footing. But he couldn't think of how it might happen.

When they set out in the late morning of the next day, Garlthik was in the same jaunty mood as when J'role had first met him. He hummed a song, smiled his broad, toothy smile. His tattered cloak, still as blue as night when the sun had just set and the stars first came out, billowed around him, and his sword swung at his side. The sky stretched overhead, a pale blue streaked with long, wispy clouds. They walked east, rising higher and higher into a long mountain range.

Every so often Garlthik would stop humming and ask J'role questions.

"Did you actually see the city in your head? I mean, pictures of it?"

J'role indicated no.

"Just words, eh?"

Then the ork would continue to hum, a bit of a skip in his walk.

"Did you see any people? Or landmarks of any kind?"

Again J'role indicated no. And as the day wore on and he continued to answer the ork's questions in the negative, he wondered what worth he really possessed for Garlthik, and what the ork might eventually do with him if he proved himself worthless.

The walk itself exhilarated J'role. Where the previous night he had been terrified to realize how far he was from home, now the distance he put between his village and himself sent a strange, unknown excitement coursing through his muscles. He could feel his former life fading from his body, like an old splinter sliding out of flesh. His past would be meaningless to the new people he met. No one would know that his mother had gone mad, that his father was a drunkard. They would know only that J'role was a mute, and no more than that. No one would know he was cursed.

"We'll keep walking until I think of something," said Garlthik. "I want to put distance between Mordom and us."

And so they walked.

As J'role saw mountain ranges he'd never seen before, saw rivers running crooked and blue-green that he'd never known existed, he was overwhelmed by the realization of how *much* there was in the world. By walking forward into it, new possibilities opened for him. The promise of . . .

Something else.

6

When he was seven, before everything went wrong, something lived in their home with them.

Their home consisted of three rooms—a sleeping room for J'role's parents, one room for J'role, and a central room between the two where they gathered and played. It was a luxurious place to live within the tunneled corridors of the kaer, but J'role's father was an important man.

The thing—a shadow of a thing—a wavering white shadow—sat in the corner of the central room for days. J'role never looked straight at it, for it frightened him. His parents never said anything about it, so he thought it was his own problem. He never said anything.

He spent more and more of his time in his bedroom, trying to avoid the gaze of the strange thing. When he had to leave his home, he rushed through the room, desperate to avoid its gaze. His mother asked him why he was so nervous. Once he pointed at the thing. It laughed a raspy laugh. His mother saw nothing.

At noon they ate berries and roots that both J'role and Garlthik knew how to find and knew were safe. It was not easy work, finding the food, for though the sky was clear and beautiful, the land around them was desolate. It spread out like death, a wasteland testament to the thoroughness of the Horrors, who had in one way or another consumed everything they encountered. Strange furrows twisted their way through the rocky brown dirt of the hills, and the ground showed odd-shaped bulges. Sometimes the weird patterns of the land grabbed J'role's attention, distracting him so that he could no longer walk, nor think on anything but the sight before him. The chaotic pattern of the land spoke to him in a way he could not understand, as if it reflected the worn and ragged mind inside his skull.

After eating, they continued on their way. Garlthik had stopped asking questions and contented himself with humming. However, J'role's own curiosity had taken root. He tugged on Garlthik's arm and held the ring up in his palm, for Garlthik had permitted him to carry it. Still walking, Garlthik asked, "Yes?"

J'role pointed to the ring, and then shrugged his shoulders.

"Ah," said Garlthik. "Not sure, actually. Magic of some kind. But I'm just an adept, not a magician, and there's much of magic I don't understand. I only know how to think about magic in a specific way—as a means of procurement—if you will. But as to its—" he spread his arms wide, searching for the words—"as to its *fundamental* nature, I am blind. Magicians know. Mordom, that crafty dragon's breath ..." Garlthik's green eye gleamed bright. "He knew more than he was saying, of that I'm sure." With that the ork fell silent and resumed his humming as if the matter were closed.

But what J'role wanted to know was about the ring itself. After carrying it for half the day, he had time to think about its strange effect on him. He wondered why someone had taken the time to make such a ring. As he continued to walk he slipped the ring on his finger ... and instantly began to speak, unable to resist the sweet images his mouth held. Again, he did not know what he would say before the words came out, but as the sounds waited, touching his tongue like delicious dates and nuts, all he had to do was unleash them and listen. He stopped, unable to move on, and Garlthik turned to stare at him. J'role spoke of vaults filled with piles of artifacts and magical treasures, of pictures painted on huge marble walls that moved when anybody looked at them, of towers where ships of stone docked after traveling through the air from distant lands.

J'role pointed at his mouth, then summoned the will to remove the ring. He took it off his finger and stared up at Garlthik. The ork seemed disappointed, like a child who has just been told he must wait until the next night to hear the rest of his favorite bed-time story. The mention of treasures had surely caught his interest.

Once more J'role pointed to the ring.

"All right," said the ork, turning and talking over his shoulder as he continued. "But let's keep moving."

J'role hurried a few steps to catch up, and when he had, Garlthik continued.

"The ring is from a city, I think—and I am close to convinced after seeing the odd effect it had on you. From the wonders you describe, it must be an ancient city of the Theran Empire. Perhaps it's somewhere nearby. But I don't know much about the world. Nobody does anymore. I've got to find out if anyone knows of such a city. I don't suppose you do?" He waited for a response, and J'role shook his head. "Anyway, that's why I want you by my side, young J'role. I believe you can help me to solve the mystery, though I don't know in what way yet."

J'role remembered his father telling him about the Theran Empire many years ago, but his father had obviously not known much about it either because he had said very little. What he did know was that the empire once ruled the province of Barsaive, which included J'role's village as well as lands in all directions, and had created the knowledge to build the kaers.

"Yes, you see. A mystery. What happened to the city—if there was a Theran city here in Barsaive?" Garlthik asked. "Did they survive the Scourge? If so, do they need help now? If they do, a reward must await whoever comes to their aid. And if they did not survive, well, all the better, for then the city itself is the reward for whoever finds it. Mordom I think, knew more of the ring than he ever let on—and probably more of the city." Garlthik touched his thick fingertips against his eye-patch. "The man possesses magic the likes of which I have never seen."

But J'role's thoughts had wandered far from the ork's words. A city filled with magicians! A city filled with people who could make statues dance and chariots fly through the air! What wonders might they perform on J'role himself? Could they remove the creature from his thoughts? Might he once again have his voice? Certainly if the people of the city were in trouble, and J'role helped save them, such a reward would be little enough to ask. J'role added a skip to his walk as he continued along.

Garlthik saw this and smiled. "So, now the quest intrigues you, does it, lad?"

J'role looked back and nodded.

"I thought so. I thought I saw something of it in your eyes when first we met."

J'role stopped now, looked carefully into Garlthik's face for an understanding of his words.

"You've got the spirit, boy. That's all I meant. You are an adventurer, aren't you?" He smiled a gigantic smile, his mouth forming into a cave, his huge teeth lining the edges like stalagmites and stalactites. "You long for it, don't you? And I'll bet you don't even see it for what it is, you're so hungry for it. You're a starving man let loose upon a feast— eating everything up so quickly you can't even taste it."

J'role shrugged, uncertain.

"No! Look about you." Garlthik stepped up to J'role and turned him around, placing a strong hand on J'role's shoulder. Standing behind the boy he gestured out to the hills and rivers and mountains that rested on the lowlands below them. "I'll bet you're thinking, 'Got to get to some treasure. Got to reach some monsters. Have an adventure.' But this is it, J'role. Simply being out—wandering, traveling. You've left what you knew behind, and now you're wandering into the unknown. This walk, this walk we've taken just today, how many people from your village have ever traveled so far? Right now they're toiling away in their fields, trying to prove that they're worth something in the eyes of their neighbors, struggling to get enough to eat, to feed their families. The children grow up just like their parents. They're all going to sit around on the patch of ground where they were born. They won't learn anything about the world. They won't live through anything they haven't been taught how to live through."

Garlthik stared down into J'role's face, looking for a sign of comprehension. Finding none, he drew in a breath and started to speaking again.

"That's what an adventure is, my boy. Doing what you don't know how to do. I've never traveled to a lost city before. I've never walked over this spot before. What's over that hill? What might try to kill us next? I've no idea." He spread his arms wide and tilted his head back and smiled at the bright sun. "This is it."

Then he leaned down toward J'role and lowered his voice. "You see, it may seem quiet now, but that's just a trick. In an adventure, the adventure is always present, even if it doesn't look like it. You're an adventurer because you're alert to that. I can tell. Saw it back at the cave when I threw you the ring. You're ready to seize the moment when it presents itself. Most folks, they could even *be* on an adventure, and when it got quiet, they'd think the adventure had stopped. They'd let their guard down. Then, next thing they knew, something would come flying in and kill them. Or a treasure would present itself and they'd miss it. Just like that. That's why they have to stay home. At home you know everything." Now his gaze floated away from J'role and out along the tops of the hills. "You know everything oh so well at home," he added quietly.

Garlthik stared silently out at the hills for a good, long while, and J'role joined him in contemplating the land below. At first he could make no sense of Garlthik's words. Yes, it was true he had never seen this land—the winding river, the barren dirt, the scraggly trees, the hills and mountain tops. But similar sights existed a day's walk from his village. What difference did it make?

He glanced up at Garlthik, who was staring out as if hungry, feasting on the sight before him. J'role tried to imagine what Garlthik saw, and looked back out at the landscape. He tried to suck the sight in through his eyes, as Garlthik seemed to be doing.

And slowly, something began to happen.

He noticed a bird, or at least he thought it was a bird, hopping around on the ground far, far away by a lone tree. It was only a dot, but it moved and bounced around, as if struggling with something.

Then he saw how the water in the river folded over just slightly as it passed a bend in the river. And he saw how the trees, what few there were, each bent in the wind, creating an odd pattern of motion when viewed all together from this distance.

He began to understand. Though he'd noticed many of the same things in his own village, he'd never seen this particular group of objects and motion before. This combination was unique. In fact, when night fell, the shadows would change, the bird would leave. Not only had he never seen it before, it existed only in this moment.

It all seemed terribly fragile.

Thoughts of his father came to him. His father was very fragile. Now gone.

Without thinking about it, J'role began to walk, continuing along the route he and Garlthik had been traveling all day. He watched his feet take steps over the ground before him, and then vanish from sight as his body fell forward again and again.

"Wait up, boy," Garlthik called. J'role did not slow his pace, but the ork quickly caught up. They walked on in silence.

A question occurred to J'role: Did Garlthik have a father he loved? What had happened to his father? Did he ever see him anymore?

That night they made camp on top of a ridge that offered them a view of anyone approaching from the south and the west. "And if they're after us," Garlthik said, "that's how they'll come."

They built a small fire in an alcove formed by rocks they piled high to keep the light from giving away their location. Then they settled down to the food they'd gathered that day. Purple berries with a somewhat bitter taste and half-ripe fruit from a tree that J'role had never seen before, but which Garlthik assured him was safe to eat.

Despite the meal, J'role was still hungry. He caught Garlthik's attention and pointed to his stomach. "Aye, me too, lad," the ork said. "But if there's a drawback to being an adventurer, it's this: you can't always have what you want when you want it. In four days' time we might be as wealthy as kings. Then again, we might just starve to death before four days are out."

J'role thought about the words. He thought of how much time the farmers of his village spent tending their crops, how much toil was involved, and how often they still ended up with very little harvest to show for it. Garlthik might be wise in many ways of the world, but not in all. Everyone risked not having what he wanted when he wanted it, just by being alive, adventurer or not.

As night came on, he stood gazing out over the land below. The cool air washed gently over his face, and the fire buried between the stones kept his legs warm. The mixed sensations delighted him. Extremes, he thought. I like them more and more.

Then J'role spotted two orbs of light bobbing their way

across the land, still distant, but getting closer. Crouching down, he poked at Garlthik's chest. The ork, who had just closed his eyes and begun to drift off, at first pushed J'role's hands away. But then he opened his eyes, saw the look on the boy's face. J'role pointed over the rocks.

Garlthik quickly scrambled up and looked in the direction J'role pointed. J'role thought that Garlthik looked horribly frightened as the ork removed his torn cloak and used it to smother the fire. When the flames had become no more than embers, Garlthik stood up and stared back out over the rocks. J'role joined him.

The orbs had gotten closer, and J'role saw now that they were lanterns. He had only seen such devices once before, many years ago when a group of humans and a troll had traveled through his village. Each lantern hung from poles atop wagons that were making their way across the land. Drawn by horses, the wagons rocked side to side over the sloped and rocky ground. J'role could not make out who rode in the carts, but there seemed to be about three people in each one. He also thought he saw shadows, tall, like large men, moving alongside the carts, but he could not be sure.

Next to him, Garlthik relaxed. "Not them. Just travelers. Wonder what they've got?" He lowered himself back behind their shelter of boulders. "We'll light the fire again when they've passed on a bit."

J'role knew what they might have—and he wanted it. He tugged on Garlthik's arm, then pointed at his stomach and then over the boulders at the merchants.

Garlthik laughed and brought his hand up to his mouth and smothered it. When he'd gained control of himself he said, "And what will we do, young J'role? Go up to them and beg for alms? Those travelers are escorted by obsidimen. Not the type of folk who are usually too generous. I doubt we'd get within fifty feet of them, even with peaceful intentions, before those brutes slammed into our meager bodies with their stone hands. Wouldn't even see them coming if they're worth their pay."

J'role wanted to know what obsidimen were, but knew that getting out of the question would be too much work; he didn't even know how to begin. Instead he kept his mind fixed on the issue of food. He gestured back over the rock again, and then he mimed walking along silently, his knees bent, creeping along.

Garlthik smiled. "Steal it?"

J'role nodded vigorously.

"Lad, maybe another time. Certainly, I've stolen from more difficult marks—but I always had help."

Indignantly J'role pounded his chest with his fist.

"Yes, yes. You're here to help. But you're not especially well trained."

J'role pointed to himself again, then mimed sneaking through a door, opening a barrel, pulling out apples. Garlthik cocked his head to one side. J'role gestured back over the boulder, several times in a row, trying to build the impression of distance.

"Oh. You've stolen . . . You stole when you lived in your village?" Garlthik first looked astonished, then smiled again. "Well, that is a surprise. Wouldn't have . . . All right. Do you know the talents?"

J'role furrowed his brow, at first not understanding what Garlthik meant. Then he realized that he meant magical talents. He had never thought that there would be magical talents for thieves, just as there were magical talents for Ishar, the village metalsmith, but it made sense. He remembered the green glow that poured out of the knots that had been holding Garlthik. That was probably one of them. He shook his head.

"That's it then. We'll be building our appetites tonight." He rolled over to go back to sleep.

J'role knelt down beside Garlthik, grabbed the ork's arm and shook it.

"No, no. I can't do it alone, and boy, you're just not ready."

An idea came to J'role. He pointed first to Garlthik and then to himself, over and over again. Then he took the ork's heavy hand in his and clasped it.

"What do you want, boy?"

He continued to point to Garlthik, and then himself.

"You want to—be me . . . ? To learn from me? You want me to teach you the talents?"

J'role nodded.

The ork laughed quietly. "We won't be done in time to get that caravan . . ." Garlthik shook his head and waved his hand, a sober look coming over his face. "You probably don't know this, but when you pick a discipline, it shapes how you see the world. Everything feeds into this sight. That's why the magic works. Once a thief, you'll always be a thief. You'll always think like a thief."

J'role patted his belly. The ork laughed, then looked somberly at J'role, as if weighing something out. "All right then. In the morning." He started the fire again, and rolled over once more.

For a long time J'role stared up at the stars. The tiny points of light seemed to form countless patterns, just like the picture language common to the name-giver races. Though J'role could not read, he'd seen words carved in stone, words formed from a picture of a dragon's head combined with a few dots and circles. Next to that would be a cat, and next to that an image of a jaguar, each altered slightly to produce different syllables.

As J'role looked at the sky he wondered if the stars too formed patterns—words written across the night.

He could not sleep, and after an hour or so he took out the ring. The silver cold against the flesh of his palm and reminded him of the wonderful, overwhelming desire he'd felt earlier. He craved to feel that longing once more, but it the thought also made him afraid. It took complete possession of his thoughts. Two days ago, putting on the ring had made him forget even about his father dying on the floor of the kaer.

The memory of his father sent a shiver through J'role. What a horrible son he was! How often had he wished the man dead! How could he have wanted that for a man who had tried so hard? So, so hard. An empty ache took hold of J'role's heart; he felt incomplete, as if he still needed something from his father that would now never be provided.

Without even thinking about it, he slipped the ring onto his finger to escape the sadness. He felt his tongue come alive without his will, and the tingling spread across his jaw. He rolled away so as to not disturb Garlthik, then stood up and walked over to a rock and stared out over the barren, windblown landscape, listening to himself speak.

He said, "Fine stones, each as pure white as sun-bleached bones, led to the city from all quarters of Barsaive." An astounding sight greeted him as he stared out over the barren, dark landscape. Several miles away a thin line glowed as pure as the stars above, reaching off in either direction as far as he could see.

A road.

7

The memory of the nightmare is slight. Not as horrible as what is to come, but all connected somehow, a thread in the web of despair. A little matter, really. Probably not worthy of being relegated to the realm of nightmares. But there it is. He is four. The thing in the corner has not yet arrived. His mother is alive. His father happy.

His mother speaks to him one day when his father is gone. He is her pride, yes. She can show him off to the neighbors, yes. He is facile with language. "Just like his father," everyone says, smiling. So happy.

"Be careful," his mother warns. Her face is serious. "Don't be like your father. People will expect too much. Don't speak so much. Don't show them how clever you are."

Yet she continues to show him off, and he is expected to perform. When speaking to others, if he says the wrong thing—and he never knows what that might be—she looks down. Frowns. He is always disappointing her. He doesn't know why. Everyone else thinks him so clever.

When they are alone, she looks at him and sighs. He turns away. He wants to do the right thing, but does not know what that is.

One day she stares at him for a long time. "You're just like your father," she says quietly, hopeless.

He stared at the remarkable sight before him, not listening to a single word he was babbling. The road had not been there before. He would have seen it. It *glowed*. Tears formed in his eyes, and he did not know why. Was it the magic of the ring? The longing was strong within him now, stronger than it had been at any time since he'd worn the ring. The road was of course tied to the city, and the city was the source of the longing.

But no. The tears were for something else. For his father. Here, right before him, something so strange and marvelous. He wished his father could be beside him to see it. Though Bevarden had spoken of many miraculous things, he'd spoke of them only through the memories of others. But he too had known a longing—to actually see the magic of the world—the extraordinary. Everything had gone wrong, though, back at the kaer. First with his mother, and now . . .

J'role wished his father could see it.

A road of starlight. It was the kind of thing Bevarden always suggested they would find together.

He turned toward Garlthik, wanting to wake the ork up and show him.

Then he turned back toward the road. Could he show the ork the road? He fought down the ring's power to make him keep longing for the city, and pulled the ring off.

The road vanished. The barren lowlands again became mundane and stark.

J'role nearly cried out with excitement. But years of training had taught him not to speak out spontaneously, and the creature's warmth in his thoughts always kept the need for silence immediate.

He rushed over to Garlthik to shake the ork awake. When J'role was within five feet of the fire Garlthik suddenly rolled over and sprang up, sword drawn, eye alert and startled. J'role stopped dead.

"Spirits, boy! Don't ever do that. Not unless you want to be able to carry your head in your hands." The ork looked around, seeking possible enemies, then relaxed. "What is it now? Don't you need sleep like the rest of us?"

J'role pointed toward where he had seen the road, then held out the ring in his other hand. The ork lost his indignant manner and eyed J'role carefully. "Something about the ring? The city?"

J'role nodded excitedly, then started walking toward the rocks where he'd seen the road. Garlthik followed.

When they reached the rocks where J'role had seen the road, J'role swept his hand through the air, gesturing to something out in the darkness.

"Is the city out there?" the ork asked.

J'role shook his head, and handed Garlthik the ring. The

ork took it and said, "You want me to put it on?" J'role nodded. "Ah, don't know about that. It hurts to wear the ring. A sweet hurt, but a hurt nonetheless."

J'role simply stared at Garlthik.

"All right."

The ork slipped the ring onto one of his large fingers. Immediately a strange expression shrouded his face; his body shook slightly and the shoulders slumped forward, as if an old wound had suddenly opened. J'role became apprehensive, wondering if the ork was in pain. Then Garlthik gave a strange smile—almost like a frown, but happy enough to be different. He sighed, his eye closed tight.

J'role tugged on Garlthik's arm. The ork opened his eye, and looked toward where J'role pointed.

A pause, and then Garlthik asked with a breathy voice, "Should I see something?"

A panic seized J'role. Had he imagined the road? He looked out across the starlit land. Of course, he saw nothing. With a sudden lurch he fumbled at Garlthik's hand for the ring. He had to put it back on, to be sure. The ork immediately pulled his hand away. "No, no. Just ... Let ... Feel it ..."

Knowing he could not force Garlthik to give him the ring, J'role simply waited as the ork stared up at the sky. He thought he saw a single tear appear under the ork's good eye, a soft and small object that seemed incongruous with the ork's rough, bulky body.

After many minutes Garlthik's body twisted harshly and he began to gasp for air. He put his hands together and wrenched the ring from his finger, throwing it to the ground. J'role grabbed it and held it tight in his hands as the ork doubled over, breathing heavily. "Oh, please, oh, please," Garlthik said over and over.

As he held the ring in his hand, J'role was amazed to realize how small it was. It fit him perfectly, and yet it had also fit Garlthik's finger, easily twice as big as any of J'role's. Could the ring change size? Starlight glinted off the silver as the ring rested in J'role's palm, and he saw clearly that the ring could not possibly have fit any of Garlthik's massive fingers at its current size.

The ring wanted people to be able to wear it. It wanted everyone to be able to wear it.

He turned back to where he'd seen the road earlier and slipped the ring on his finger.

The road appeared, glowing like a river burning with white fire.

Knowing he would never be able to make Garlthik understand what he saw, J'role leaped onto the rocks and then over them, running down the long hillside toward the road.

"Wait, boy!" Garlthik cried with a gasp. J'role could hear a strain in the ork's voice. "Wait!"

J'role did not. Either the ork would follow him or he would not.

Garlthik did follow. But J'role had enough of a head start that the ork never caught up. J'role ran and ran, continuing for fifteen minutes, and then another thirty. The cool night air washed over his skin, the shining road stretching out ahead like the finish line of a race. His heart pounded with effort and exuberance. He spoke all the while, describing carpets that floated through the air and beautiful gowns and robes worn by all the citizens of the strange and miraculous city.

Finally, with his lungs raw from the effort of running and talking, he reached the road. Its brilliance against the darkness of night blinded him at first, and it took several moments for him to look directly at it. Made of thick slabs of stone, it stretched off to the east and west. J'role walked up to the edge of the road and touched his fingertips to one of the stones.

The stone felt only slightly cooler than the air, and then J'role realized that his fingers had actually passed through the surface of the stone, vanishing slightly into the white glow. He pulled his hand out quickly.

Behind him came Garlthik, gasping for breath. "What are you . . . ?" he began. "What's gotten into you, lad?" He staggered up to where J'role knelt and walked right through the stones of the road.

J'role looked up at the ork, startled. Could the road still be invisible this close? He removed the ring from his finger, and immediately pain cut through his mouth from the incessant talking he'd done while running.

The road vanished.

He rubbed his jaw with one hand, holding the ring out to Garlthik with the other. He didn't think Garlthik would see anything—the ork had already suggested that there was a special connection between J'role and city. Maybe he could see things Garlthik could not when he wore the ring.

Garlthik took the ring. "What is it? What *is* it?"

J'role gestured up and down the road.

The ork looked in either direction. "I don't see . . ."

J'role jumped up and jabbed his finger at the ring in Garlthik's hand. "I don't know," Garlthik said. "Not again, not now."

J'role slammed his open hands against Garlthik's chest.

The ork half-smiled, half-staggered back. "All right, all right." He slipped the ring on his finger, sighed as before, then gave a harsh gasp. Though J'role could not see the road any longer, he knew Garlthik was looking in the direction it lay. "A road," Garlthik said, "a ruined road."

The momentary joy slid to confusion. *Ruined* road?

"How did you see this from back there?" Garlthik asked. "The stones are barely visible in the dirt." Then he saw J'role's confusion, struggled with his desires for a moment, then pulled the ring off. He looked at the empty ground. "You did see it, didn't you? A road?"

J'role nodded, but his face betrayed frustration. The two of them began an awkward exchange of words and gestures, each one trying to explain to the other what he had seen. J'role quickly grasped that Garlthik had seen only the ruins of a great road. But he could not communicate to Garlthik that he had seen *more* than that. A road, yes. But whole and magical. They eventually gave up, not a little annoyed with each other.

"Well, a road, at least," said Garlthik. "At least we agree on that."

J'role nodded.

They continued on their way for three more days, taking turns wearing the ring and following the road, both ruined and whole. They came near several small villages, much like J'role's, but they stayed clear of them. Garlthik had lost all his money when Slinsk searched his pockets, and so they had no means to purchase food. "People won't trust us unless we show money," Garlthik said. "If we had some, we'd be as good as family."

Their hunger increased daily, for the brown landscape yielded little sustenance. Although J'role had been hungry in the past, he'd always known that if things got too bad, someone—if only Brandson—would notice and give him some food. And if that failed, he could sneak into someone else's food stock to steal some rice and corn and berries.

Still, despite the lack of food, J'role's spirits remained high. As he continued to walk, the hunger transformed from a sensation of lack to a sensation of cleansing, as if the emptiness let him carry only himself and nothing more.

And he wrestled with the mystery of the road; why did each of them see something else? Were they seeing the road at different times—J'role's view from the past, Garlthik's from the present? But the present view was that there was no road at all. Could it be that each saw what he wanted to find? Garlthik would be pleased to find a ruined city, empty, with treasure waiting. J'role wanted a living city, filled with wizards who could remove the thing from his thoughts.

He did not know. It all made no sense.

As he had promised, Garlthik began J'role's apprenticeship as a thief adept. At first the ork's words confused J'role, for he expected Garlthik to speak of weaving magic spells or the careful ways one could sneak about, and instead the lessons consisted only of the ork rattling on about what an adept's talents were *not*. J'role thought that Garlthik was simply stalling, not wanting to teach him true magic at all. But he had no means to protest, and did not know what he would say if he could, so he listened. And slowly, because he could not express his impatience, he began to learn.

"A magician weaves spells. An adept does not," said Garlthik, his attention caught for a moment by a flock of birds, no more than dots, cutting across the blue sky. J'role thought he could hear their contented cries as they moved together in elegant flight. "Magicians write down their intricate, arcane works in grimoires. We do not. Magicians are trapped by their pasts as they create elaborate preparations for the future. We are not. We," he said as the flesh of his cheeks rolled back, revealing his astounding smile, "*find* the magic, right where it is, at that moment, and letting ourselves go in that moment, float upon the magic."

J'role looked up at Garlthik, startled. He lifted his hand, palm down and fingers spread, and let it move up and down, like a bird floating on the wind.

"Yes. Strange, isn't it? Or so it seemed to me too, when

I was a lad your age." Garlthik paused, just a half-beat, looking down at J'role with a sudden, tiny flash of sadness. Then he smiled. "But it's true. The magic is all around us. But most folks don't think in terms of the *moment*. They don't know how to let themselves respond to what's happening to them—right then and right there. And that's the adept's secret. Not much of a secret, actually. Most of them will flap their lips about it to anyone who will listen—a bad idea, I think. But there it is."

They walked on in silence for a few minutes as Garlthik searched for the right words. "Now don't get me wrong. Magic doesn't just happen. Paying attention to the world is work, and every so often it makes sense to study something in detail. Like the rope Slinsk and Phlaren tied me up with. That was a mistake on their part. I knew that rope well—I studied all the rope we had when we were working together, just in case something like that should come up. I knew my hands, I knew the rope, so in that moment, even though I couldn't see my hands, could feel barely anything but pain from the broken arm tied around my back, I was able to know exactly what to do to free myself. I knew how the rope met my hands, knew just how to tug it, knew just how much pressure was needed at each moment, all because I knew *that* rope so well.

"Anyway, that's why a metalsmith is so good. He gets to know the metal before he works it. Or the archer who floats on the magic. He knows his bow inside and out. Knows every nick and exactly how it's balanced. When he draws an arrow into it, he's got something a regular archer doesn't have: the feel of the world binding his hands to the wood of the bow, the bow against the air, and the air against his hands. It's all connected. There are good archers, but none are so good as those who know the magical side of whatever they're in contact with. That is, archer adepts. And we, lad, will be a pair of thief adepts."

And so it went. At first Garlthik spoke little of thieving itself. He tossed out ideas about the world and magic over and over again, all strange at first, but easier to understand upon each hearing.

One morning J'role woke before Garlthik. Rather than wake the ork, he stood and turned slowly around. A breeze touched him. He looked down and saw how many shapes and sizes of grains of dirt made up the ground on which he stood. All rested against each other, an impossibly enormous number of them, on and on, forming the land that stretched out forever and ever, wrapping itself around the world, all flowing beyond his vision, but all connected, oddly, to the very spot where he stood. "So," he thought to himself, "this is magic."

Toward evening they saw a village ahead. Like J'role's village, it was surrounded by farmland—patches of green that radiated out in wider and wider arcs, forcing their way into the brown and dry lands beyond. A small river ran beside the village, and a large mill rested on it, its water wheel turning steadily and slowly.

"We'll be staying there tonight."

J'role held up a palm, empty.

"Not to worry, lad. I've still got this." The ork leaned down and slid a wad of thick black clay off the edge of his boot sole, revealing a small compartment. J'role caught a glimpse of silver. Then Garlthik sent one of his fingers into the hole and fished out a small stone, no bigger than a fingertip. It was cut with several facets that caught the sunlight and turned the light silver and blue. The sight transfixed J'role; never had he seen anything so beautiful.

"My first haul," said Garlthik wistfully. "A diamond ... You've never seen one before, have you? Beautiful stones. Stole it from a merchant in a citadel far south of here. The old man who taught me to steal, he told me to get it. It marked me. We'll use it to get lodging and food tonight."

He started down the slope leading to the village, but J'role caught the ork's arm and stopped him. The boy shook his head. He didn't want Garlthik selling his beautiful stone for the comfort of lodging and food. He patted his stomach and shook his head again, then pointed further along the route they had been traveling.

Garlthik laughed. "Don't worry about it, lad. It's something I want to do." He looked down at the stone. "It was ridiculous for me to keep it all these years. Not like me at all. An adept's got to be true to himself, J'role. If you don't behave as you truly are, the magic will know. It'll turn you out. This ... This has been a bit of vanity. I'd never hold on to something like this. It's as if I was waiting for something to go wrong, keeping a little extra hidden away just in case. Well, my boy, I'm not a 'just in case' ork. I either make it or I don't. So let's go spend it now and get it over with. We'll have a roof over our heads, some good food in our bellies, and supplies for the rest of the trip. If they've any pack animals to spare, they'll be ours as well."

They went down to the village, meeting a few stares from farmers along the way, and even more when they reached the village proper. It occurred to J'role that almost everyone they'd seen in the villages they passed had been human. Remembering how strange Garlthik's appearance had seemed to him at first, J'role wondered what it was like to be Garlthik, alone in a world of staring eyes. And then he realized with a start that outcast and alone was exactly the way he'd lived his own life. Until now.

8

In one of his nightmares, J'role wakes from his sleep.

He is six or so. From the central room his mother has just let out a cry so loud it woke him. He is startled for a moment, but then hears a soothing whisper. He thinks at first it is father. But the voice is too deep. It is strange. Not the voice of anyone in the kaer.

Then J'role realizes that it is the voice of the thing in the corner.

In the center of the village they found the local tavern, a big inn very much like Brandson's, the tavern in J'role's village. When Garlthik first presented the diamond to the tavern keeper, a thick-bodied woman with red cheeks and clever eyes, she looked slightly left and right, knowing instinctively that the ork had gained the treasure in some underhanded manner.

But when Garlthik began to speak with her, it was in a voice J'role had never heard from him before. The ork's tone was at once soothing and cunning. He never stated that the stone was stolen, yet with sly glances he clearly implied it was. J'role watched the woman, and realized that part of her wanted nothing to do with the stolen diamond, yet another part was drawn to the idea of buying such merchandise. Not only would she get it at a bargain price, but it would be *stolen treasure*. He saw the eagerness building in her eyes. A story to tell her select friends, J'role guessed: "Well, in walked this ork, hungry as could be, tattered cloak and such, and he comes straight up to the bar, making sure no one else could overhear, of course, and in his hand he's holding . . ."

She didn't seem the sort to have trafficked much in stolen

goods, but from the strange look in her eyes, J'role saw that she wanted to give it a try, if only once.

J'role wondered if he was any different. He had left his village, a place where most people stayed forever, to take up traveling with a creature who had one green eye and thick yellow teeth so big they poked up over his lips. Watching Garlthik bargain, J'role realized how thankful he was to the ork for getting him away from his village.

"I can't give you coins," the woman said, staring at the diamond, the negotiations finished, "but I'll give you the food and lodging you asked for, and I'll make arrangements with Hyruss the miller's son about that horse. She won't be fast, but she'll carry the food you've bought."

"And the sword and the dagger?"

"Yes, yes," the woman said with distaste. "The weapons as well." J'role did not think she minded the sword by itself; it was arming an ork with a sword that was giving her trouble.

"You've been most kind," said Garlthik. "Now if you could let us have two legs of lamb, stew, and ale, we'll fill our bellies well and then we'll retire upstairs."

"I can't give you anything until I've been paid," the woman said, hand outstretched.

"Good tavernkeep, we have nothing to pay you with but this stone, and certainly its value exceeds the meal and one night's lodging—as we have already discussed. When you have arranged the food and the horse, I'll gladly give you the stone. I assure you, the investment will be well worth your time." The word sounded awkward coming from Garlthik's mouth, as if they were too large to fit comfortably. Too formal and friendly. Yet he got them out, and the woman agreed. She turned to shout at a boy—her son?—to bring some lamb and stew.

J'role and Garlthik took a table near a window looking out in the direction they had just traveled. Garlthik stared from the window with the same haunted look he had worn when first they'd met and the ork had turned around to see if anyone—Mordom, J'role knew now—followed.

The ring now hung under J'role's shirt, tied around his neck by a thong. Thinking about the past brought thoughts of his father, which suddenly made him acutely aware of the ring. The cold metal against his chest tempted him to put it

back on his finger. He suddenly felt incomplete again, and
wanted the thing that would finally make him whole.

Despite the desire, J'role did not put on the ring. He
didn't want to begin babbling uncontrollably about a lost
city while surrounded by strangers; he and Garlthik had already attracted enough attention. Instead he joined Garlthik
in looking silently out the window.

It seemed strange now to see the world outside enclosed
in a frame. J'role longed to step outside the tavern and be
lost once more in the boundless world, feeling his connection with everything continuing on forever—a sensation
nearly impossible to experience while looking through the
square edges of a window. Yet he also felt a strong desire to
stay right where he was. Though the world lost its indefin-
able, lovely quality when framed, he found it easier to relax.

The boy soon brought the food. The lamb was so tender
it seemed to melt in J'role's mouth; and the stew, warm and
full of carrots and corn and beef, made his cheeks tingle and
filled his belly so deeply that he thought he might never
want to eat again.

J'role and Garlthik swayed as they stood, their full meals
mixing with their exhaustion. The boy who had served them
led them upstairs to a room with two mats on the floor and
a window covered with a coarse, ragged cloth. The sun still
shone, and small circles of light formed by holes in the cloth
dotted the floor. Without any thought of either future or past,
J'role dropped to his knees and spread himself out on one of
the mats.

Just as he closed his eyes the creature in his thoughts said,
"So, you'll find the city?"

It had been so long since the creature had spoken that it
took J'role by surprise. "Yes," he thought, his mind slipping
into a pleasant darkness.

The creature slid back into his thoughts, curling up as
comfortably as a cat before a fire, and said no more.

The slow, precise sound of hoof beats, the snort of horses,
words whispered, a clatter of metal all floated into J'role's
awareness. He awoke with a start.

Darkness. Outside the window he heard the sounds continue. Through the holes in the cloth he saw the stars.
Garlthik still slept.

J'role rose quietly to his feet. In three steps he was across the bare floorboards and looking out the window through a tear in the cloth.

Below he saw a man handing his horse's reins over to the tavernkeep's son. The man was round in the middle, and wore a thick scarlet jacket with matching pants, all trimmed with gold. A large man—no, not a man—one of the lizard-folk his father had talked about. Green-skinned, tall, with a long, thick tail. He held a large sword and stood warily, obviously guarding the man, keeping an eye out for anyone who might approach out of the darkness. J'role wondered what it was like to be so big. Big as Garlthik, and then bigger. With a huge tail that could be used to trip enemies. The guard's long, snouted head turned right and then left, as if sniffing for possible danger.

Suddenly J'role felt something beside him. He gave out a gasp, and felt a rough hand cover his mouth. "Shhh," said Garlthik, releasing J'role immediately. "If we travel together, you must always wake me when there's news. Understand?"

J'role nodded, and stepped aside to give Garlthik a clear view of the scene outside. "Ah. Good. He's the one." With that cryptic statement Garlthik turned from the window and returned to his mat. "Might as well turn in. Unless I miss my guess, there won't be anything more to do with them tonight. We'll let them get comfortable."

J'role had no idea what Garlthik was talking about, but he had no wish to try and sort it out now. He was too tired.

The fat man and his guard entered the tavern. J'role heard their voices, but could not make out the words. Unable to gain any more information—and with not the slightest idea what he might have been trying to find out anyway—he too returned to his mat and the sweetness of sleep.

The next day J'role and Garlthik went down to the common area to enjoy a breakfast of warm bread, cheese, and milk. They had just sat down when the lizard-folk guard came down and took a seat across the room. Though armed with a sword and possessing a fine row of razor-sharp teeth, the lizard-folk seemed oddly shy and small. He curled his clawed hands around his broth and glanced about furtively as if afraid someone would see him looking.

One time J'role's eyes met the guard's, and instead of turning away, as J'role would have expected, the lizard-folk smiled, the tip of his tail thumping up and down against the floor.

"What are you doing?" Garlthik muttered, his voice not much louder than a whisper, but strong and serious.

J'role saw that the ork kept his head down, as if concerned only with swirling the mead in his mug. He didn't know what Garlthik was talking about.

"What are you doing looking about like that, making eye contact? You only do that if you need a mark to take a liking to you. We don't need that. Now he's paid attention to you. Now he'll remember you. You are a thief. You don't befriend anybody, understand? There are the people you steal from, and that's it. The only people you don't steal from are the people who don't own anything worth stealing. And you don't befriend them because they're not worth befriending. If they ever end up owning something, then you can steal it. But they're not your friends. Understand?"

J'role did—just barely—and he nodded his head.

Soon the portly, finely dressed man also came down to the common area. J'role eyed him carefully, keeping Garlthik's warning in his thoughts. He noticed that the rich man wore a ring with a bright stone that shone blue with the light it caught from the windows. It was bigger, much bigger, than the one Garlthik had bartered to the tavernkeep. The rich man took a table separate from the one where the guard sat.

"Tonight, when the reptile is on watch," said Garlthik, "you'll go in and steal that diamond—the one on the trader's finger. They're going to stay at least another night. He's well-fed and well-dressed. Once his kind stop moving, they stay put for a while."

J'role looked up at Garlthik's face and then down at his food, afraid of showing undue attention to the conversation.

"It's your test, boy. Your initiation. And your payment. I paid my mentor with coins I begged in the citadel. You haven't paid me yet. And you owe me for my diamond. That ring on his finger. You owe me. We'll do it tonight. Best be back on the road by then. I do believe Mordom has lost our trail, but better to be on the safe side."

A tight tension crawled over J'role's chest. The lizard-folk looked very strong. To steal something from him would be a difficult task. Dangerous.

"You'll do just fine," said the creature, even as J'role's thoughts slipped into fear. He had the strange desire to be sitting alongside his drunken father back at the kaer. "You'll do just fine."

"What?" thought J'role. It was the first time the thing in his thoughts had ever tried to offer comfort, and the words startled him.

"I like you, boy. Didn't you know that?"

"No."

"Well, I do."

"Will you let me talk now?"

"Talk? I'll always let you talk." The creature laughed; something oily passed through J'role's thoughts.

"I mean . . . like other people."

"Why would you want to talk like other people? I've given you an amazing gift."

"I don't want it."

"Well, no matter. No. I told you years ago, we'll be together until you die. I don't suppose you want to kill yourself?"

"No."

"Well, then there's nothing to be done, is there?"

"Why don't you leave?"

"Not until you're dead. Not until you're dead."

The cold ring hanging against J'role's chest seemed to dig into his flesh. If he could only find the city. They would be able to help him.

"I'm going to go speak with the weaponsmith," said Garlthik, standing up. "Do what you will, but be back here tonight. Get some rest, as a matter of fact. It's going to be a busy night."

That night, long after the sky had turned black and the stars blanketed the world and the people in the village and all throughout the land were asleep, Garlthik woke J'role. J'role's mind stirred itself from a deep dream: his mother, holding him in her arms when he was a child. Her flesh was a light gray, strong as stone, but soft and comfortable.

"Wake up. It's time."

The moon had passed toward her monthly death, and only dim light from the stars passed through the holes in the curtain. J'role made out Garlthik's big body, no more than a thick shadow, moving on all fours on the floor. The old, worn floorboards creaked under him. But softly. Softer than they should have.

A scrape of stone against metal, once, twice, a spark, a sudden flame. An oil-soaked rag wrapped around a short stick set on a metal plate bursting with white illumination. It lit Garlthik's face now, the shadows carving up through the heavy fat and muscles, and fear came to J'role. A monster, he thought, just as his father had told him about monsters when he was a little boy.

A little boy? When had he become a big boy? Why did he no longer feel like a boy at all?

The light cast Garlthik's shadow huge against the wall as he hunched over the flame. "Come here."

Garlthik did not look at J'role as he spoke, but continued staring at the flame, as if it were a memory of years gone by, burning away. His voice was gruff and serious, not at all the way J'role was used to hearing the ork talk. The voice commanded him; drew him to something he did not understand. He moved closer, crawling on his hands and knees.

"Here," Garlthik said, almost angry, but J'role could not be sure. The ork extended his long arms and grabbed J'role by each wrist, tugging him closer to the flame until the two of them faced each other, the heat of the fire between them, the oily smoke rising up into their faces.

The heat turned J'role's flesh warm, making him think of when he was five and had the fever, and how Xiasass, the priestess of Garlen, old then, dead now, came to his room in the kaer and prayed for his health. Her hands were thin and wrinkled, but her touch was gentle, like smooth stone. Marble. The marble of Garlen's statue itself, which J'role had once touched out of curiosity when no one was looking.

Xiasass soothed him as he looked into her face. She smiled at him as she prayed. People get so old, he had thought, looking up into her face. I might live after all.

Garlthik's hands were thick and coarse, not comforting at all. He gripped J'role's wrists tightly, his face set and staring at J'role's, as if daring J'role to look back at him. But J'role could not bring himself to stare into the ork's face. It overpowered him, forcing his courage back.

He took a quick glance at Garlthik, saw the eye patch, thought of Mordom for some reason he did not understand, and then realized that Garlthik's green eye matched the green eye on Mordom's palm!

What enemies the ork had! Did he really want to be with Garlthik? What was he doing? He could die—or worse. Why did he want to be an adventurer, as Garlthik described? Because of his father's stories? His father was a liar who had fed off the tales of his ancestors but never done anything to actually *live* what he spoke of. To get away from his village? As J'role thought of his home, it suddenly seemed more pleasant than he realized. Why not go back? He could get by; some stolen fruit here, an egg there, a crust, some scraps. Watching the villagers live their lives, raising their families. A comfortable observer. Why not just go back?

But Garlthik's thick, strong grip against the muscles of J'role's wrists held him against the desire. The hands were not thin and old and caring like those of Xiasass. They were huge, hard, rough. They did not comfort. But they did hold. They possessed a different kind of strength. The hands of Xiasass had cared for him when he was weak. Garlthik's hands asked him to be stronger.

Did J'role want to be stronger?

He looked at Garlthik's broad face, toothy and maimed. The ork merely continued staring back at him, expressionless, waiting. J'role held his gaze. For a long time they gazed at each other. The heat of the flame made the air between them waver; the coiling, black smoke rose into J'role's nostrils, making him dizzy. But he held Garlthik's stare until he thought he saw the tug of a smile at the edge of the ork's mouth.

Garlthik did not smile, though. "J'role," he said finally, "do you want to be a thief?"

Not just steal, J'role thought. *Be a thief.* Not to be me stealing, but be someone who steals. To be someone new.

J'role wanted very much to be someone new.

Yes, he nodded. Yes.

9

J'role listened as carefully as he could to his mother talking to the thing in the corner of the other room, but he could not make out the words. He heard only tones. Soft and somewhat menacing from the thing in the corner, fearful from his mother.

He climbed out of bed, carefully and quietly, making no sound, his feet light against the warm stone floor. A heavy curtain hung between his room and the central room, and a bit of light from one of the floating, magical spheres in the other room made its way through it. The light was greenish, for that was the color his mother liked at the hour just before bedtime.

Taking small steps with his small feet, J'role moved toward the curtained doorway. One step after another, drawing in long, silent breaths after each successfully accomplished step.

After a long while he stood only two feet from the curtain. All he could hear now were whispers, but his mother still sounded frightened.

J'role wanted to move forward, wanted to do something. He imagined rushing forward, pushing the curtains aside, saving his mother from the thing in the corner of the other room. Yet something held him back. He realized that she was talking to it. She had not shouted for help. She had not raised her voice and demanded that it leave the way she had done when J'role's friend Weshthrall broke one of her glowpots.

Maybe she wanted to talk to the thing in the corner. He listened again.

The conversation continued.

He would ask her in the morning.

He turned silently and crept back to bed. It was many hours before he could sleep, for the whispers in the other room lasted a long time.

When J'role answered Garlthik's question with a nod, the ork smiled and squeezed the boy's wrists. It didn't hurt, and J'role realized the ork was simply happy that J'role wanted to be a thief. But the ork quickly became serious again, the fire between them illuminating his face.

"A thief lives in the shadows, J'role," he said. "Most people want the light of the sun to warm their bodies. A thief may want it, but he may not have it. A thief is silent. While others can speak their ideas and thoughts and feelings, a thief must keep all that to himself; he seeks solitude and secrecy while others seek companionship.

"Most important, a thief steals. You do not take from the world, you take from others. You do not exchange goods or coin to support your life, you simply take. Yours is a life without remorse. That is key. The magic will leave you if you feel shame for what you have done. Others can afford shame. We cannot. Do you understand?"

J'role nodded. He didn't know if he could keep from feeling shame, but it seemed a lovely ambition. How nice never to feel bad again.

"Close your eyes."

J'role did. A wind seemed to crawl over him, cold and wet. Magic? Was this it?

"The darkness that you see is your own darkness. Cherish it. It is yours, neither to share nor to give. Within your darkness you are safe." Garlthik tightened his grip on J'role's wrist. "Open your eyes." Again J'role obeyed. "Remain still. Move nothing, do nothing, but listen for the sound of your own heart." J'role concentrated on listening to his heartbeat. Instead he heard many, many other sounds—his breathing, the wind lightly touching the window curtains, the hiss of the fire before him. Insects outside. But as the moments wore on, the sounds gradually faded away, one after another, each vanishing into the dull roar that became a great silence. Soon only the beating of his heart remained. J'role nodded his head slightly.

"This is your silence," Garlthik continued. "Where you live now, there is no other sound that matters but your own heartbeat. The cry of an infant, the sigh of a young woman, the pleadings of an old man, they are all overwhelmed in the silence that is yours, the silence of your life."

Garlthik paused, and in his face J'role saw a touch of concern—out of place with the serious tone the ork had been using. "Make no sound," he whispered. Then, without warning, he dragged J'role's left hand forward, lowering the boy's forearm into the flame.

Pain tore through J'role's arm. He tried to jerk his arm away, but Garlthik held it tight. He wanted to cry out, but was afraid to. Afraid of what he might say, might do.

"This pain is yours and no one else may know of it. The pain you have felt all of your life, all of it now comes to this point. This moment is yours and in your heart it separates you from every other person in the world. In your isolation you may take what you want, do what you wish. Now you are adrift from all, and none may know you. You owe nothing to anyone, but everything is yours for the taking."

Garlthik released J'role's hand and the boy fell back, rolling to the floor. He clutched at the burned flesh with his right hand, but immediately pulled his hand back, for his touch only increased the pain. The smell of burned meat filled the room. Tears formed in J'role's eyes. It felt as if someone were removing the flesh of his forearm with a sharp blade, over and over again, taking only a little layer of flesh each time. The creature in his head turned this way and that, writhing with pleasure.

Why did Garlthik do this? As J'role rocked back and forth, cradling his maimed arm, he saw Garlthik stand, the flame casting his shadow onto the ceiling.

"Get up," he said, bending down to brush his heavy hand against J'role's cheek.

J'role remembered the potion Garlthik had used to heal his broken arm after the fight at the kaer. Was he going to cure him now? The boy looked up at the ork with pleading eyes, but Garlthik only said, "Get up now, or I'll leave you here and go after the city myself."

J'role stood. Every bit of motion ripped pain through his arm.

"This is your first talent. My teacher taught it to me as my first talent, and you'll need it to steal the trader's ring." He gestured to the area immediately in front of J'role. "Now walk, but don't make a sound."

Yes, thought J'role, as he clumsily staggered forward, the

pain darkening his vision, making even the bright flame vanish in and out of his sight. He just wanted to do what Garlthik said to do, to please him, so he'd cure the burned arm.

Garlthik's rough hand grabbed him from the back. "That wasn't silent, you little fool." The ork pulled J'role back to where he'd been. "Do it again. Haven't you listened to a word I've said? What did I say on the road?"

J'role tried to think back to what Garlthik had said on the road, but the pain lanced his thoughts, turning any idea he had into a hot red flash. He raised his arm toward the ork, tears streaming down his face, his mouth firmly shut.

"What? Is that an excuse? I had my arm *broken,* boy, and I made my way out of a series of good knots. Do you think pain is an excuse? Pain is what feeds you. Without pain, there is no *thief* magic." He relaxed his grip on J'role's neck. "Now, think of the pain, think of what I said on the road. The magic will support you."

J'role started to focus on the pain, desperate to please the ork—desperate so he could finish the ritual and run away and never see Garlthik One-Eye again.

"No, you're just panicking now. Feel it? You're tightening up against it. You're thinking about the future, thinking about when the pain will be gone and you'll be safe. That time may never come. What's that doing for you right now? Forget anything but now. What do you want to be right now?"

Gone, J'role thought fiercely. I want to be gone and invisible and safe. He hated Garlthik for tormenting him. Then an idea came to him, floating just above the pain, skimming across the surface of his thoughts from a place J'role could not fathom. He realized that was it. The desire to be safe, to hide from the pain.

He focused on the pain and felt how miserable he was. He no longer wanted to get away from Garlthik but to get away from everything. He didn't want to exist in the world anymore. He felt his desire to vanish wrap around him. There was nowhere to run, nowhere to be safe. The pain he felt now would haunt him forever, as his mother's death haunted him, as his loneliness haunted him, as his father's death and his father's weakness haunted him. As his betrayal of his father haunted him.

There was nowhere to escape but into himself, into the pain, into the magic.

A lightness curved around him, then threaded through his body.

Magic?

"I am only pain."

"Yes," said the creature.

"No," J'role thought fiercely. "This is mine. You can't take this from me."

"I won't. And the pain has always been yours. But I can enjoy it. I will. You've picked a perfect discipline."

J'role forced his mind closed against the thing. It spoke no more. He stepped forward. He did not want to be noticed by anyone, and when he stepped forward he felt the pain in him arc around under his feet. The magic wrapped around in a way he could not see, only feel, tingling his flesh, connecting it somehow to the wood—the very grain of the wood—and somehow, he stepped just the right way, or the wood responded to his step in just the right way, he could not be certain because it all—everything—blended together at that moment, and he did not make a sound. He continued to walk forward, amazed at the silence of his steps, the sound of his heartbeat the only sound he knew.

The pain in his arm still burned, but it fed him now, a terrible anger at everything. He turned to Garlthik. The ork stood with his arms crossed, smiling.

"Welcome, thief. And now J'role, your first test as an adept. You must steal the rich man's ring."

J'role knew it was true. Stealing the ring was what he had to do. It would be good to steal the ring. His arm hurt, but knowing the rich man owned that lovely ring hurt even more. It should be his. He felt the magical ring against his chest, the longing strong. Stealing the ring would not stop the longing, but it would hold it off for a bit. Yes. Steal the rich man's ring.

J'role stood on the windowsill and reached his right hand out along the exterior wall of the tavern, looking for a finger hold. His left arm hung limply at his side, the pain harsh and hot, but also a wellspring of determination.

His fingers explored the wood of the wall, searching for loose joints and—there—he found a small hole. Before this night J'role might never have thought it possible to use the small gap between two boards as a finger hold; in fact, it would never have occurred to him to climb across the exterior of a building two stories up. But that was the way Garlthik had insisted he reach the rich man's room.

"The door will be guarded," he said, "perhaps with a trap, perhaps even with magic. Better to take the window. They won't be paying as much attention to it."

Now J'role stretched out his toes, again looking for a support hold. Under his bare toes, each grain of the rough wood seemed to reach up and grab his flesh. Finally he found a toehold, and although he could barely press his big toe into it, he knew it would support him. His body, it seemed, was lighter. He felt as if he could let go of the wall and float into the sky. But even as the idea occurred to him, he knew that, no, he could not do that. It was the act of climbing the wall, sneaking about to steal the ring, that the magic rewarded. Flying would be too ... direct. Climbing, finding the small crevices and hanging on by the edge of the body—that was a thief's work.

Putting his weight on his single toe and placing his finger between the boards, he stepped off the windowsill and onto the wall of the tavern. There, suspended above the ground by no more than a few bones and muscle, tenuously connected to the wood of the wall in a fashion he could barely begin to understand, J'role hung for a moment. His heart beat faster in excitement. He wished the people of his village could see him now!

Then he remembered his task, and reached his free arm, his burned arm, out in search of another gap in the boards. In this way he made his way slowly across the wall toward a window at the other side of the building.

The pain tore so viciously through his arm by the time he reached the window that he almost wished he could chop the limb from his body if only to be free of the pain. Yet, he also accepted the pain. Anything he wanted was his by the right of pain. The more pain, the more he deserved to take what he wanted.

And now he wanted the fat man's precious ring.

The window curtain hung loose, moving back and forth in the cool night breeze. Perched on the ledge, J'role touched the edge of the curtain—not a sound!—and peered into the dark room.

The rich man and the lizard-folk slept on their cots.

On the wall J'role saw his shadow—dim, but definitely present in the fuzzy frame of light formed by the window. The sight startled him, as though somehow he should have been safe from such concerns. His shadow should meld with the other shadows of the room, he thought. That would make sense.

Could Garlthik do that? Perhaps. And perhaps J'role would also be able to with practice.

Quietly, ever so quietly, he lowered his left foot into the room. When it touched the floor he deftly brought the rest of his body in. Soundlessly. Perfect.

He looked across the room and saw the fat rich man asleep. The man looked so peaceful. No pain at all. On his finger, the ring.

J'role could just go get it, creep up silently, take it and be gone. But the lizard-folk might turn and see him, catch him from behind. The risk was too great. Could he sneak up to the guard, slit his throat quietly? Maybe. It seemed a good idea. Garlthik had given him a dagger, tucked now into the top of his pants. He drew the blade out. The handle seemed warm and comforting in his palm.

Pain, pain, pain. And now he would give some.

J'role began to move across the floor. Eight feet, then six. Four.

A scream cut through the tavern. "Mother!" a boy wailed.

J'role froze in place, uncertain what to do. The guard stirred, but did not wake. Footsteps raced up the stairs, came closer down the hall.

His grip on the knife tightened. He had to kill him now, get the ring, get out . . .

The door crashed in.

In the door frame, a flash of a face entering from darkness. Slinsk. "Mordom, he's here!" the dark-haired man shouted. "The boy's here!"

J'role turned and ran for the window, had just reached it when a hand grabbed at the back of his shirt and pushed him down. He fell, slamming his chin into the window frame as he went.

Noises filled the air. From down the hall he heard Garlthik shout and then the sound of metal upon metal. Behind him came a cry of alarm from the tall lizard-folk, followed by two more screams.

J'role turned himself around, and the pain in his arm blossomed. The magic's strength had left him. Where was Garlthik? What should he do?

He looked around the room. On one cot rested the corpse of the rich man and on the other the guard, their throats slit into jagged crimson gullies. Slinsk kept his back to the wall, his eyes on J'role. In one hand he held a blood-drenched short sword. How had he killed them so quickly?

"I've got the boy!" Slinsk shouted. From the next room the sounds of combat continued. "New friends, lad? They didn't last you very long, did they? Didn't Garlthik tell you? Everyone he associates with dies an early death."

J'role began to get up.

"NO!" screamed Slinsk.

J'role froze in place. Slinsk seemed horribly on edge, but less sure of himself than back in the kaer.

From next door Garlthik screamed again. Slinsk smiled, seemed to relax. "Mordom, he made up something special for our ork friend. Something left over from the Scourge."

A chill passed along J'role's spine.

"Please," J'role heard Garlthik gasp. "Please stop . . . Mordom . . . I'll give you . . . Please stop."

The sound of Mordom's muffled voice came through the wall.

"Wait! The boy!" Garlthik gasped. "He's got it."

The ring felt like ice against J'role's chest. How could Garlthik betray him and their quest so easily?

"If that's all you've got to offer, then you'll die," Mordom's dry, precise voice declared. "I'll need more if you want to live. Bargain with me, Garlthik. Like the time we first met. You know more than you ever let on."

"So . . . do . . . you," Garlthik said, his defiant spirit returning. For a moment J'role thought that the ork had found a means of escape. Maybe he'd only told them about the ring to stall for time. But then Garlthik screamed again. Outside, J'role could hear the sounds of villagers shouting to one another.

"Don't waste my time. I'll find it with or without your help," Mordom said with great impatience.

More shouts from outside. Slinsk carefully maneuvered himself toward the window, keeping his blade toward J'role. Reaching the window, he pulled the curtain back slightly and looked out. He sighed.

Once more Garlthik screamed. "He can speak of the city.

Ha! You knew, didn't you? When he puts on the ring, he talks . . . please, ahhhh . . . He talks of it. The city. He's connected to it somehow . . . Mordom, my good friend, I only tricked the boy. Gained his trust. An elaborate lie. I would never—" Outside, the cries of the villagers had become louder. Garlthik gasped for air, an infant too tired to sleep, but Mordom said nothing.

An image came to J'role's mind—Mordom cracking his skull open, searching for the creature in his thoughts, searching for his connection with the city. He would be no more than a small spider for Mordom's inspection, an object of curiosity—the way the boys in his village used to pull the legs off insects just to see what they would do.

Footsteps approached from the hall. "I think we're surrounded," said Slinsk even before Mordom appeared in the doorway.

"No matter. I can handle them," said Mordom as he came through the door. J'role had forgotten how disturbing was Mordom's face—narrow and strong, with the pure, white eyes. The wizard raised his hand and the eye—Garlthik's eye—stared at J'role. "I have something to show you," he said slyly.

Then Mordom turned slightly, tugging at someone standing behind him. Over the magician's shoulder J'role saw a long, pale face. Almost disembodied, it was like the face of a ghost as it came floating out of the darkness.

10

The next day, his mother looked at him strangely. Not at him, really. At everything. She seemed very frightened, but also as though she wanted to keep the fear tight to herself. His father noticed it too, but when she asked, she said only that she was tired.

J'role's body tensed as his father stepped into the room, assisted by a push from Mordom. He felt embarrassed, acutely aware of the corpses on the cots as if they somehow incriminated him instead of Slinsk. He didn't want his father to know what he had become.

He need not have worried. Bevarden kept his eyes on the ground, as if ashamed. When he finally raised his head to meet J'role's eyes, a giggle escaped his lips before he quickly dropped his gaze once more. Then he covered his face with his hands, and J'role thought he heard his father weeping softly, but he could not be sure.

The eyes Bevarden had just shown J'role were unlike the ones he had seen all his life, even these last years. Empty, lacking any vitality, they seemed to be the eyes of an infant.

No, something else. All the babies J'role had ever seen searched the details of life with intense fascination. His father's eyes were the eyes of a *dead* infant, the muscles relaxed, the sight useless.

J'role moved toward his father.

"Ah, ah," said Mordom and raised his other hand. "You can't have him just yet. First, you have something I want. Boy, listen to me. I have a certain ability with . . . the Horrors. Specifically those that assault the mind. I can help your father. I can help *you*. But I will need your cooperation."

From the next room Garlthik's whimpering continued.

J'role shook his head.

"You're making things difficult," said Mordom, sounding sincerely disappointed. "We can end this all quickly. Please."

What to do? J'role felt his thoughts tugged in too many directions. He wanted to rush to Garlthik's side—at once wanting to help him and to flail at him with his fists. How dare the ork betray the secret of his speaking? Now that Mordom knew, he would undoubtedly kill him. J'role also wanted to rush to his father's side, to get his father away from the vile magician, even though it was obvious he'd never make it past Slinsk and Mordom. And finally, he wanted simply to run, to make a mad leap out the window and leave everyone behind.

He felt the thief magic tugging at him, whispering to his bones and muscles to flee and forget about the wounded ork in the other room and the broken man on the floor. This last choice, he realized, was a thief's choice. The magic coiled around him, encouraging him to flee.

But, he thought, my father.

"You can't save him," the creature said, unfolding its words like a dark flower in his mind.

"What?"

"You can't save him. And you don't want to save him. He is broken and useless. Flee. Find the city. Get your glory. Do something for yourself."

The creature's voice carried a new quality, something akin to duplicity. Perhaps it was because the thing had so seldom lied to J'role that he immediately discerned the lie. Why the creature in his thoughts kept encouraging him to find the city, J'role did not know, but why should it be at the expense of abandoning his father? He had already left the man to die once. The instant he began the first step toward Slinsk and Mordom, J'role realized he expected to die, and he found comfort in the thought, cold and moist, like the ground after rain. If he were dead, no more creature. No more father to worry about. But until that moment. . .

By the time his left foot and then his right had touched the ground in his graceful walk across the room he felt the magic gone, like the sun's light slipping out of a room with the closing of the shutters. The thief magic had deserted him when he decided to fight for his father rather than retreat for his own safety. Alone now, with no one. Mordom smiled at him as a crackle of blue light formed around his hands. J'role returned the smile.

A cry of pain cut through the wall to the other room. Phlaren, J'role realized, as everyone in the room turned to look at the wall. A heavy thud slammed against it, and then another. Suddenly the wall cracked open and Garlthik One-Eye crashed through it, sending shards of wood scattering about.

Bevarden gasped and cowered, scrambling across the floor in search of safety, finally resting in a pool of the fat trader's blood. Slinsk raced toward J'role from the right, his blade rushing at J'role's chest, while Garlthik charged from the left, leaving Mordom to finish his spell.

J'role kept his attention focused on Mordom. Slinsk brought his blade down swift and hard, but Garlthik swung up and parried with his sword. Out the corner of his eye J'role saw a grimace on Garlthik's face and a stream of syrupy black liquid dripping from a fissure in the side of his head. The image grasped at J'role attention, but he tore his gaze away and focused on Mordom.

The magician watched J'role approach with the green eye in his palm. The eye blinked once as Mordom spoke some strange words. Then the wizard touched his face with his other hand, the flesh suddenly transformed, torn open to reveal muscle and bone, but more disturbingly, becoming the image of Bevarden.

The ruined visage grinned at J'role, confusing him about where his father was. It overwhelmed J'role with a cold fear, and his only thought now was of running away; not running to escape, but to hide.

Fighting off the fear, he focused on his father so he could help him. He charged forward, crashing into Mordom and knocking him out into the hall. With a loud gasp Mordom fell to the floor as J'role slammed the door shut.

Whirling back toward the room he found his father whimpering and beginning to back away. J'role grabbed him by the shirt and dragged him toward the window. Behind him he heard the sound of blades beating against one another.

His father began to cry, softly, his head hanging down. J'role wanted to say, "Please don't," but held his tongue and raised his hand to his father's face. His father pulled back at first, but then leaned in, seeking comfort from J'role's touch, pressing his tears against J'role's palms.

From the hall Mordom called for Phlaren. J'role looked through the hole that Garlthik had created in the wall, and saw the big woman warrior struggling to her feet, blood trickling down her temple. She hefted her sword and staggered toward the hole. Spotting J'role, she smiled and increased her pace.

Slinsk screamed as Garlthik disarmed him and slashed with his sword, cutting a gash all the way from the man's collarbone through the leather armor down his chest. Streaming blood, Slinsk collapsed to the floor, staring up in surprise at Garlthik. The ork laughed and said, "I'm better than you!"

J'role waved his arms and tried to get Garlthik's attention as Phlaren rushed in from behind, slamming her sword against his back. The ork's thick skin absorbed some of the blow, but he still cried out in pain as he whirled around to fend off the attack.

J'role looked out the window and saw many villagers milling about outside the tavern, as if they wanted to get in but could not. Some people spotted him and cried out for others to come and help. When the villagers had gathered below, holding their arms up, J'role seized his father by the shoulders and forced him out the window. Caught off guard, his father could do little more than give a short cry, and then he was out the window.

"Go!" shouted Garlthik, now backing slowly toward the window as Phlaren closed in on him and J'role.

Then the door flung open and Mordom entered.

Without pause J'role flung himself out the window, in the moment of free fall wondering once more what it was like to be dead. Then he felt hands slap against his shoulders and legs, breaking his fall. Slamming into the ground, he thought he'd broken a leg, for the intense pain rivaled the pain in his arm.

Strange hands seized and jerked him away. Then Garlthik landed beside him, cursing in pain, clawing at himself, his thick arms and legs contorting in odd ways.

Then he heard a roar from the villagers, and saw Mordom looking out the window, his hand pointing down. The villages sent a hail of stones and sticks up at the window, forcing the magician to retreat inside.

As the villagers helped J'role to his feet, he looked to his right and saw two figures at the door of the tavern. Skeletons, he realized, armed with swords, waiting patiently for anyone to try to enter the building. None of the villagers had made the attempt, though several men and women were trying to distract the skeletons so others could get by. But the skeletons did not move away from the door, and a stalemate had been reached.

The siege started at night, with Mordom and the others trapped inside the tavern. The villagers carried J'role, his father, and Garlthik a short distance away from the tavern and set them down on the ground. Water was brought, and a questor of Garlen arrived. The questor was a woman in her twenties, older than J'role, but he still thought her very beautiful. When she smiled down at him, he realized that everything would be all right.

Praying to Garlen, she tended to each one of them, touching the tips of her fingers to their wounded bodies. As J'role awaited his turn, he overheard some of the villagers talking.

"Burn them out, I say," said one man, whose friends identified him as Hobris.

"Aye," said another. "She's as good as dead. Everyone in there is."

J'role remembered the screams they'd heard just before Slinsk entered the room. There was little chance that the villains had left anyone alive as they searched the tavern for the ring. J'role turned his head and saw the villagers—now at least four hundred strong—ringing the tavern, brandishing torches and rocks and sticks.

Hobris leaned down to J'role. "Who are they, boy? Do you know?"

J'role shook his head and touched his throat.

"Did they do that to you?"

J'role nodded. He didn't want them wondering about it.

The questor, Valris, said, "This man is . . ." She stopped, searching for the words, staring down at Bevarden. "I've taken care of most of his injuries. He will need time to rest. But his thoughts . . ." She turned to J'role. "Did the wizard do this to him?"

Again, J'role nodded. This time he told the truth.

"We've got to kill them. Worse than Horrors," said a woman.

Hobris said to the questor, "The wizard ruined his voice.

See to that as well as the arm." He then walked off, presumably to deal with Mordom and the others.

The questor touched J'role's throat. She spoke a prayer to Garlen, and a wave of memories washed over J'role. Images of his mother and Xiassis came to him, and for the first time in many years he felt himself relax into peace.

"Can you talk now?" she asked.

Could she actually have healed him? He paused, but felt the creature in his thoughts, though it tried in its crafty way to be still, and shook his head.

She frowned, somewhat troubled, and turned her attention to his arm.

A cheer had begun to rise up from the crowd now, and J'role saw them waving torches and beginning to pile wood around the base of the building. He was stunned by their festive atmosphere. Did they know something he didn't? Would it all be over so easily?

A window at one corner of the upper floor opened and Mordom appeared, waving his hands in a simple pattern. A group of people screamed, falling to the ground, dropping their torches.

The crowd fell silent for a moment, drawing back. In that silence Mordom said, "I want only . . ." His voice was rich with power and rage. But the mob swelled forward once more, throwing more rocks as well as their torches up at the window. Under different circumstances, J'role thought, with fewer people, Mordom's commanding voice and the use of the horrible spell might have been enough to send everyone fleeing. But not now.

Mordom retreated from the window. A young girl threw off her long dark cloak, revealing a bright orange robe with patterns of leaves and flames upon it. She waved her arms and a stream of fire rushed from her fingers to ignite the base of the building and the wood piled around it. The villagers threw their torches into the kindling, and a thick, billowing smoke began to rise up around the building.

Beside him, J'role heard the questor gasp. Turning, he realized that she had finished her work on him while he'd been watching the fire, and his arm and leg were both now whole and well. An unfamiliar sensation of well-being coursed through him—a gift from the passion of Garlen.

The sensation quickly evaporated, however, when he looked at what had stunned the questor. She was staring at

Garlthik, where a black shadow writhed in the crack in his head. The ork was whimpering, and without a moment's hesitation the questor reached in and tried to pull the shadow out. Garlthik screamed with pain and clawed at the questor's hands.

She called for help, and a few villagers came and forced Garlthik's hands to the ground. She drew a deep breath, pressing her hands against her face for a few moments, smearing her cheeks with Garlthik's blood. Then, from a bag tied to her belt, she withdrew a pair of small metal tongs.

The shadow writhed beneath the tip of the tongs as she brought them up. With a deft motion she snared a tentacle, and began to drag the thing out. Again Garlthik screamed, and again he struggled to stop the questor. But the villagers rested on him and kept his arms pinned down.

After a long time the questor finally succeeded in pulling the shadow thing out of the wound in Garlthik's head. It clung tenaciously, but was finally plucked out of the ork's skull with a final, sickly sound. The questor grabbed a bottle from her pouch and stuffed the thing inside it. The shadow squirmed about for a moment, then the glass shattered, sending shards deep into the questor's flesh. After a moment of surprise, the shadow was nowhere to be seen.

For a moment J'role thought about asking the questor if she could help him with the creature in his head. But then he remembered what Mordom had said, that the thing's body was somewhere else, only its spirit resided in his thoughts. As Mordom seemed to know a great deal about the Horrors, J'role decided he was right.

Garlthik relaxed now, and the questor began soothing him, beginning the process of healing.

"I need a drink," Bevarden pleaded softly just to J'role, so no one else could hear. "Please, I need a drink."

A crackle of flames cut through the night air, and J'role turned and saw huge flames claw their way up the sides of the tavern; the smoke rose up so thick that it blurred the stars above the fire.

Garlthik was just getting up, the questor done with him, and he turned with amazement toward the fire. He was wobbly, but the crack in his skull was gone. "What are they doing?" he asked with rapidly growing enthusiasm. "Are they burning them out?"

At that instant a terrible crash erupted from the tavern.

J'role thought a wall had fallen, but instead saw a golden light emanating from the roof. A chariot, with three sides and two wheels, erupted from the roof. It was made of something that reminded J'role of smoke, for he could see the stars through it. Standing on the chariot were Mordom and Phlaren. Resting against one side of the vehicle was Slinsk.

Nothing pulled the chariot, though Mordom held two reins that extended several feet before vanishing into thin air. A gasp rose up from the mob as the chariot rose and swung around in a wide arc, flying back toward them.

"Where is the boy!" Mordom cried.

Garlthik hustled J'role into the shadow of a tree, then quickly ran back to drag Bevarden into the shadows as well.

The shadows wrapped around J'role, comforting him. Dark and protecting, they touched his flesh and worked their way into him, and he felt the thief magic grow strong within him. The magic touched his muscles and told him to run, passing from the shadows of one tree to another, leaving his father behind. He was better off on his own.

The chariot rushed low to the ground, tearing through the startled crowd, knocking the slow and surprised out of the way. J'role's father, apparently amused by the sight, began walking out of the shelter of the shadows, a smile of wonder on his face. J'role swallowed. His father's actions would betray him . . .

. . . and more than that . . .

. . . what? . . .

. . . his father would be in danger.

A cloud passed from J'role's thoughts. Yes. His *father.*

He stepped quickly forward and wrapped his young hand around his father's wrist, pulling Bevarden back as one would a child who has stepped too close to a fire. In doing so he felt his chest tremble in a kind of fever. When the sensation passed, J'role realized that the thief magic had left him. It wanted only that he rush away from anyone he might care about.

Mordom was still screaming at the villagers below, demanding that they surrender the boy. He cut around the area in a wide arc, peering into the shadows as his magical chariot sped by. The villagers had re-grouped now, picking up sticks and rocks and throwing them at the chariot as it passed. As the chariot rushed toward the tree sheltering

J'role, several rocks slammed into the chariot's passengers. Mordom raised his hands to cover his face, and in that moment, J'role dragged his father down, with Garlthik following. The chariot whooshed by, then shot up into the air. Growing smaller and smaller, it crossed the night stars swiftly, then vanished from sight over the top of the distant mountains.

J'role stood quickly, dragging his father to his feet. He felt immensely relieved.

Garlthik saw J'role's face and said in a tone of warning, "He'll be back for us. He's just gone until he thinks it's safe to come back. Come, we'd best be going. He knows we know about the city now. His determination will increase."

J'role nodded and gestured in the direction of the magical road.

"Let's go then," said Garlthik, starting to walk. J'role, holding his father's hand, followed. "What are you doing with *him*?" Garlthik asked.

The question surprised J'role. He hadn't really considered it. He was just bringing his father with him. It seemed to be the thing to do.

"Do realize what a burden he'll be?" Garlthik said in reply to J'role's silence.

Pointing first to himself and then to his father, J'role tried to remind Garlthik that this man was his father.

"Yes, yes, your father," said Garlthik. "I don't care."

Angry that Garlthik was dismissing him so—even though he thought Garlthik might be right—J'role began to walk toward the magical road with his father in tow. The only other possibility was to leave his father in the care of strangers. And that he did not want to do.

Garlthik angrily walked up beside him. "All right, lad. All right. But know this, the thief magic will leave you, and leave you at the worst time, if you keep betraying it like this. You didn't do what you went in there to do, did you?"

J'role thought for a moment. The ring! He'd forgotten all about it during the carnage. He shook his head. No, he didn't get the ring. How could he have?

Garlthik brought up his hand. In the center of it rested the fat man's ring. Though stained with blood, the large diamond was bright against the night's darkness. "A thief," he said, "never forgets his work."

11

*Later, when everything had happened, J'role's mother said
to him, "Don't speak. Never speak. Speak to no one but me."
His father was at the Atrium, entertaining everyone. He and
his mother were alone at home.*

*He started to ask her a question. "Not even Father?" But
he felt the prickly sensation in his mouth, and he lost control
of his tongue, and began to babble the high-pitched squeaks
and cries and gasps and strange sounds. His mother
wrapped her arms around him and drew him close, trying to
smother the sound of his voice. For a moment he felt safe,
and then he discovered he could not breathe.*

*"Oh, my baby. Oh, my baby," she cried. "No one but me.
No one but me."*

As J'role, Bevarden, and Garlthik started to walk away,
the villagers circled them, openly curious, their torches
forming a ring of fire and smoke. J'role knew they would
have too many questions if he simply tried to leave, questions he had no way of answering. His fists tightened in
frustration. Why couldn't he talk? Why was the thing in
his head? Everyone stared at him, slightly afraid, as the
fury built on his face. The creature in his thoughts only
chuckled.

"Good people," said Garlthik. "Thank you so much for
your help in saving us from that villain. . . ."

"Merith said you gave her a diamond!" shouted one villager.

"Did she die because of your hand?" shouted someone
else.

"Did the magician attack to get the diamond back?"

Other cries sprang up, and then a general commotion of

noise. The threat of Mordom gone, the villagers were free to vent their suspicions on the strangers in their midst. The ring of people tightened.

"Why don't you tell them you're innocent," the creature in J'role's thoughts laughed.

"Be quiet," he told it, his lips tightening as he argued in his mind. And then he had an idea. Yes, he thought. Maybe I will. He removed the cord from his neck, slipping the ring off and putting it on his finger.

He began to speak of the city. Unexpected words came out of his mouth, telling of towering spires whose walls were carved with scenes in miniature, images of everything from raging battles to lovers exchanging flowers alongside a stream. All the scenes moved and shifted, like massive plays staged by hundreds of actors. His voice continued without his prompting, telling of the white walls that bounded the city. Pure white, as white as the clouds on a spring day, majestic. He described how the city's roads were carved from marble whose beautiful veins of pink ran the length of the streets.

At first J'role only listened to his own voice, his eyes shut as he imagined the city of his words. But as he continued, he began to look around at the crowd. They stared at him with wide eyes, their lips parted slightly, as if thirsty for his words. Soon many began to smile, and J'role realized that the description invoked in them a wonder—the same wonder that drove him forward toward the city. The same wonder his own father had inspired in the people of his kaer. He was telling them of their world's past and of the future that might await them.

The villagers stood around him, enraptured. He was giving them dreams. They wanted to hear his words.

As his mouth and tongue worked themselves into words and sentences, tears began to form and roll down his cheeks. He didn't notice them at first. When he did, they confused him.

Why? Why am I crying? he thought. The creature made no comment, but J'role knew the words he spoke were not those of the thing in his mind. He had the attention of the crowd, and his words gave them pleasure. But the ideas he spoke came from somewhere else, a place he could not understand. Whatever pleasure he took from these people was a lie.

He pulled the ring off his finger, the metal burning icy

cold against his flesh as he gripped it in his palm. The crowd parted for him. He grabbed his father's hand, then walked on past them, followed by Garlthik. The crowd remained silent.

He had to keep moving. He had to hide from Mordom. He had to reach the city first. In that moment J'role had no idea why. It was just something to focus on. Something to do, to keep busy, so the hurting didn't eat out his heart with its intensity.

J'role hated his father. It was early afternoon, and the two of them were seated in the shade of a tall rock. Garlthik rested on another rock nearby, letting the warmth of the sun wash over him.

As J'role stared, his father picked at the grains of dirt scattered along the ground, holding them up before his face, grinning in wonderment like a child. Twice he tried to show the sand to J'role, and the second time J'role knocked his father's hand away sharply. Cradling his hand against his chest, protecting the sand, his father looked hurt for a moment, as if about to cry. Then he apparently lost interest in trying to please J'role, and fell to staring at the sand once more.

"Drink?" his father said to no one in particular.

J'role stood, the rest over. His father, confused, looked up. J'role leaned down and extended his hand, taking his father's wrist, helping him up. He'd learned to keep hold of his father at all times. If not carefully tended to, Bevarden would go wandering off somewhere.

The creature said, "I don't know how you go on."

"Quiet." The creature had offered neither support nor suggestions of suicide of late, only odd sarcastic comments. Ever since J'role had found the ring, the thing in his head had become different from all the other years it had shared his thoughts. It seemed, in fact, somewhat confused.

"Drink?" his father asked. He shivered slightly, though the air was warm, and wrapped his arms around himself.

For two more days they walked, traveling as quickly as they could to stay ahead of Mordom. Garlthik eased J'role's concerns about Mordom's chariot—a rare magical device that could only be used once, he said. Apparently Mordom thought being trapped in the tavern was an emergency worthy of its use. Still, the magician was powerful and wily, and they did not want to give him the chance to find them.

They ate what food they could find. Hunger came often, and when they passed near a village, J'role was tempted to enter it and steal some food. Garlthik was wary of approaching a village, however, for Mordom always seemed to find him whenever he did so. He preferred to stay in the middle of nowhere, following the magical road.

On the second day after leaving the village, J'role spotted a group of travelers to the south. He thought he made out Mordom's bright robes, but could not be sure. Traveling with the man in the robes were two others: one small and wiry, the other one tall. Slinsk and Phlaren? Again, the group was too far away to be sure.

Following the general direction of the road, J'role and Garlthik dragged Bevarden to the other side of the hill to avoid detection. Later that night J'role slipped the ring on and found they were still on their way along the road, which appeared just as new and glowing to J'role. When Garlthik put the ring on, the road was old and ruined.

Mordom's group, if that was who it was, seemed to be heading in the same direction. J'role wondered if Mordom knew something about the city's general location. Maybe he knew much more. J'role wished desperately he could discuss these matters with Garlthik, but he could not. And since the fight with Mordom, Garlthik had become strangely sullen and rarely spoke. He often walked at a distance from J'role and Bevarden.

J'role wondered at first if it might have to with the thing that Mordom had placed in Garlthik's head. But then he decided that no, it was not that. But he was not sure what the reason was.

It was strange traveling with his father and Garlthik. Bevarden alternated between simple-minded smiles and open tears. Garlthik brooded. Neither offered conversation, and J'role was silent too. The three of us might as well each be traveling alone, J'role thought.

"Don't forget about me," the creature said.

J'role did not respond.

* * *

"The ring," said the creature. A red haze bled over the western horizon and the eastern sky was turning dark purple.

"What?" thought J'role, tired and wishing only to rest.

"Try the ring."

"What?" he thought again. Why did the creature taunt him so?"

"Do it! If you want to find the city, do it!"

The creature's tone so startled J'role that he stopped in his tracks and began to fumble about for the ring on the leather cord.

"Why are you . . . ?" he began to think, but he'd already slipped the ring on.

The sky flashed bright and he stumbled back.

"Father!" he cried. His father did not respond. Garlthik ran up to him.

"What is it? Are you all right?" Garlthik asked.

J'role opened his eyes. Even in the light of the setting sun the brilliant glow of the city on the hill ahead blinded him.

The spires, the towers, the magnificent walls—everything was as J'role had described it. It shone as brilliantly as if the sun itself had settled on the earth.

"What is it, lad? What do you see?"

J'role responded with his babbling words describing the city. He pointed in the direction of the city.

"Go!" said the creature.

"The city?" Garlthik asked. "Is the city there?" He grabbed at J'role's hands and fumbled to get the ring off. He grabbed so roughly that J'role thought the ork would shatter his bones.

J'role pulled his hands away, then removed the ring before Garlthik could attack again. He threw the ring to the dirt and fell back.

The city had vanished from J'role's sight.

"Passions," Garlthik said softly. "We've found it." He hesitated only a moment, then charged toward the hill where J'role had seen the city. Forgetting about his father, J'role followed.

Garlthik outdistanced him, and by the time J'role caught up, the ork stood at the top of the hill trying again and again to move forward. Each time, at the same place, he came to a dead stop as if running into a wall, then took a few awkward steps back.

"What is this?" Garlthik cried. "We *FOUND* it!" He turned toward J'role, gesticulating wildly. "There's a huge *fissure* in the city wall, but I can't get through!"

J'role started at this announcement. He had not seen a fissure. The city had been intact.

Garlthik dropped to his knees and began weeping. He begged to the sky to be allowed in. "It's empty," Garlthik cried. "Just bones and ruins. Ours for the taking."

Lightly, J'role placed his hand on the ork's shoulder. Garlthik looked up sharply, but his expression softened when he saw J'role. J'role held out his hand, and with slumped shoulders, Garlthik handed over the ring.

J'role placed it on his finger.

Towering white walls stood before him, blazing with the light of a thousand stars. Nearby were the gates of the city—also made of the white stone and held in place with massive gold bolts and silver hinges. His mouth began babbling again, the uncontrollable descriptions pouring out. He walked up to the gate, desperate to get inside, and put his hand against the stone to test how heavy it was. Drawing closer he heard the racket of countless voices from the other side of the wall.

His fingertips touched the edge of the massive gate—and then passed through. His hand, and then his arm up to his elbow disappeared into the stone. Beyond the gate he felt a kind of *nothing*. Not the cool air of night. Not the cool air of anything.

He turned toward Garlthik, who only stared at him in confusion. "What do you see?" he asked. "The city? Are you seeing something?"

J'role nodded. He turned back to the gate. Could he get in? He stepped closer, pressing his other hand through it, then a leg. His chest. The creature in his thoughts began to breathe faster, hungry. Anticipation. Then J'role pressed his face toward the gate . . .

And stopped.

He could get no further. It was not like encountering a solid wall. It was more that his muscles seemed to freeze up and refused to move any further. He drew up all the strength he could muster and tried to make himself move forward. His arms began to shake, and he felt his neck muscles tighten and tighten. He gasped even as descriptions of the city continued to flow from his mouth. He heard himself speak of fountains made of flowers that produced wine as pure as the sky, and of wizards that floated about on magic carpets while traveling within the city walls. All he had to do was get inside. They'd be able to cure him! They could cure his father! He knew it had to be true. They were miracle workers. They could do anything!

He felt himself crash to the ground. Immediately he opened his eyes, expecting to see the wonders of the city surrounding him. But all he saw was Garlthik, staring down at him, framed by the night sky. "Sorry. It looked . . . as if you had stopped breathing. I was frightened."

J'role jumped back up and charged the gate, then felt himself slammed out just as his body began to enter. Over and over again he tried to enter the city, and soon the creature in his head was screaming and wailing in his thoughts, screeching for J'role to do something until J'role stopped speaking of the city and began screaming and wailing as well.

He lost all sense of time and place and was startled to find Garlthik shaking him. "We have to go. You've made so much noise, and Mordom might be near. We have go to *now*."

"No," said the creature in his thoughts. J'role felt it sliding quickly in his mind, fidgety and desperate. "Don't go. Wait for the wizard. If he comes he'll show you how to get in. He'll know how."

"No. He'll kill me."

"No, he won't. Just wait."

"We have to go now," Garlthik said again.

The longing consumed J'role now, and he wanted only to get into the city. Everything—*everything*—he'd ever wanted waited within its walls. His voice. His mother's love. A father he could count on. If only he could get in.

He shook of Garlthik's hand and began to walk the length of the wall running east from the gate.

"What are you doing?" asked the ork.

Looking for some kind of entrance, J'role made his way along the wall, pressing his hands into the permeable stone, so cold to the touch.

Something! He glanced up every few feet, scanning the towering walls for a window or a mark. Seeing nothing, he continued on. At certain spots he placed his hand through the surface of the wall, but as before, he could feel nothing beyond the wall.

He thought suddenly of his father. But the creature in his thoughts said, "If you're going to search, *search*. Keep moving!"

"Yes," he thought and turned his attention back to the wall. Large stone blocks, about one yard by one yard, their joints nearly imperceptible, formed the wall. He knew little of stonework, yet the perfect cuts and joints of the stones could not be ignored; whomever had built the city must have used magic in cutting the stone and building the wall.

Admiration for the monumental achievement spurred him on, for again he appreciated the power of the people living inside the walls of the city. But how to get in? Why didn't they come out?

His mouth was going numb, and despair drifted into his soul. He slipped the ring off his finger. The city, the road . . . everything vanished from sight. He stood near the top of a wide, flat hilltop, Garlthik dozens of yards away.

He ran past where the road would be if he could have seen it, and then put the ring back on.

Now he saw nothing but what he had seen before. He ran forward, toward Garlthik. When he had gone far enough to be outside the walls of the city, the city's brilliant light glowed from behind him. He collapsed to the ground in frustration.

"Someone is coming," said Garlthik, walking up to him. "We can't get in. I don't think Mordom can either. But we have to go." In the distance J'role saw a group of people approaching, one of them carrying the torch. At some point it had become night.

He scrambled up and ran down the hill to find his father, which took much longer than he would have liked. The man sat silently on the ground staring at the stars, tears in his eyes. All the while J'role was searching, the creature insisted that he wait for Mordom to arrive.

"No," he shouted back in his thoughts. Then he and Bevarden met up with Garlthik and they stole off into the night.

They had gotten only a quarter of a mile away when Garlthik whispered harshly, "Down. Get down." J'role dropped to the ground, dragging his father behind him. Bevarden, who had been shaking for some time, gave out a startled gasp. The three of them rolled into the base of a shallow ditch. J'role looked over the lip of the ditch, staring back toward the hill where they had seen the city.

The orange flame of torches bobbed in the distance. "It's them," Garlthik said softly. "I know it's them. I knew I should never have trusted that wizard. Something about him. Never stops. I hate people like that."

J'role looked up at Garlthik in surprise.

"Except myself, of course," he said with a smile. "Come. We'd best get a move on. It's dark. They won't spot us as long as we stay in these gullies. We should be able to stay ahead of them."

The boy touched the ork's shoulder, then shrugged, then pointed.

"Ah, where are we going?" Garlthik asked, voicing J'role's silent question. "Well, I think I know where we might get some help finding out about the mysterious city. I don't know for sure, but it's worth a try. Down south of here."

He got up, but J'role caught his arm, and shrugged once more. "Who are we going to see?" the ork asked. "Let's just leave that as a surprise for you, lad."

J'role shook his head. He'd had enough mystery since meeting Garlthik.

"No offense, lad, but I'll just keep it my secret."

Leaping up, J'role faced the city's hill, and began waving his arms. Garlthik grabbed him roughly and slammed him down to the ground. Bevarden merely stood watching the whole incident without moving.

"I should just kill you now, boy," Garlthik whispered. "I should just twist your neck."

J'role stared up into the ork's furious face, trying to hide his fear. He didn't think the ork would hurt him, but he could not be certain.

They rested on the ground for a few moments, Garlthik leaning over J'role, his hot breath streaming down into J'role's face. Seeing a strange series of expressions pass over the ork's face, the boy realized that Garlthik was trying to decide whether or not to trust J'role. Finally Garlthik glanced over at Bevarden—a long, wistful glance—and then looked back down at J'role.

"Throal," he said. "We're going to see if we can talk to the dwarfs. The stonework of the city was good. Good enough to be from the Kingdom of Throal. They might know something about it we don't." Then he rolled over and sat up, staring off into the distance.

It made sense to J'role. His own father had told of the kingdom's legendary facility with architecture and engineering. J'role might even have thought of it himself, given time. So why did Garlthik hesitate to tell him?

Then J'role realized it didn't have so much to do with Garlthik telling or not telling him about the dwarfs. The ork's reluctance had more to do with telling J'role anything. He's a thief, J'role thought. He depends on thief magic. He never gives anything away.

And then J'role thought, "But he did. To me."

12

One day, his mother began screaming during one of Bevarden's performances. She did not scream anything in particular. Just words. Just screams.

She tore at her hair and scratched her face with her fingernails until she drew blood. Several people grabbed her and tried to stop her. But she was enraged and very strong.

J'role, who was now mute, ordered by his mother to remain silent in the presence of anyone but her, rushed to his mother's side. He wanted to hold her as she had held him.

When she saw him come near, she pushed him away and screamed and screamed and screamed.

They walked through the night, the air humid and warm, the starlight turning the rock-strewn terrain pale blue. The ring was around J'role's neck, hanging from its leather cord and resting against his chest. The cold longing tapped against his chest, making it very difficult for him to walk away from the city. Beside him, Bevarden coughed softly.

The chirping of insects surrounded them, echoing the buzz that raced through J'role's thoughts. The creature gave him no peace, but J'role tried to sort out the mystery of the city, his father and Garlthik followed behind.

"Where are you going?" the creature demanded.

"To Throal." J'role was weary of the thing's badgering. It had railed at him for hours.

"But you saw the city!"

"I couldn't get in!"

"You didn't try! You're useless!"

J'role focused his attention on the city. "It was there. And it still seems to be there. But I can't get in. . . ."

"So you should go back and try again!"

J'role ignored the creature, puzzling instead over the mystery of the city. "Why can't I get in?"

"Because you are a miserable thing not worthy to be alive! Oh, just put a blade through your veins and let us end all of this . . ."

"Unless they don't want anyone to get in. They have so much magic . . ." He thought of his own kaer, buried deep in a hillside, protected with runes and heavy enchanted stones. "What if they built their city so it would be gone during the Scourge? What if it's partially here, on earth, but partially somewhere else, so it would be harder for the Horrors to find it?" The idea drifted, a leaf in the wind, unsettled.

A pause, and then he heard the creature hum, and then it said, "Yes."

"Yes?"

"Yes, I think you are right."

J'role continued to walk, but slowly, his body matching the wariness he now used in thinking his thoughts with the creature. "You do?"

"I am what your people call a 'Horror,' you know. I have a bit of insight into the methods of the people of the city. It was well protected." He paused, and then added dismally, "I myself could not get in. I don't know if any of those from my home ever did."

"Why should I believe what you're—"

The creature screamed, sending such a sharp pain through J'role's temples that the boy had to clutch at his head. "I'm helping because I choose to!"

"Please stop," J'role thought quietly as the terrible rending of his thoughts continued. "Please stop."

Garlthik put his hands on J'role's shoulders. "Are you all right?" J'role nodded. He noticed that this father had wandered far ahead. His coughing was louder now. Garlthik released J'role, and walked on.

The creature's tirade subsided. "I hope I won't have to do that anymore. Now, will you listen to me?"

"Yes."

"Fine. So. The city is there but not there. How did they do that?"

"How do I know? I thought you were going to tell me!"

The creature remained silent for a moment, then said tersely, "I don't know enough. It's your foolish world; you know more about it than I."

"I could get as far as the walls," J'role thought, dismissing the creature. "Maybe the walls are the key. Like our kaer's doorway, they are the source of the magical defense." Even as the idea came, J'role began to doubt himself. How could he even make guesses at how magic worked?

But the creature said, "Yes. That might be it. Who made the walls? The dwarfs Garlthik spoke of?"

Bevarden began to cough so wrackingly that J'role thought it might tear the man's throat apart. He raced over and helped his father sit down. The night was warm, yet Bevarden shivered as if trapped in a spell of ice. "Please, I'm sorry," he repeated over and again.

"We've got to leave him, J'role," Garlthik said. J'role looked up at the ork in surprise. "Truly, we do. He's becoming ill. He'll slow us down. Give us away to Mordom."

Bevarden suddenly pulled J'role close and embraced him. Despite his weakness, the embrace held J'role tight. As their cheeks met, J'role felt a tear falling between their flesh, and he did not know whether it was him or his father crying. They stood for a long while like that, holding each other, feeling their chests move against each other as they drew in and exhaled breath.

Finally Bevarden pulled away and stared at his son. He took J'role's face in his hands and tried to speak. "I . . . ," he managed to squeak out, the sound twisted and distorted. His mouth contorted and he closed his eyes against the struggle. "Sorry . . . ," he said finally. Then he lowered his head, and began to weep, coughing all the while.

The eastern sky was turning golden red. They had walked all night. Weariness massaged its way into J'role's body. He needed rest. Bevarden needed rest. Probably even Garlthik needed rest.

He spotted a small copse of trees in the distance, the large, leafy branches just barely illuminated by the lightening sky. That would do for now. Mordom might or might not have followed, but it was too tiring to juggle every possible doom in his thoughts. He stood, holding his father's hand, and began walking toward the trees with Bevarden in tow.

"J'role, if you don't want to kill him, I will."

The words so startled J'role he stumbled slightly. When he turned back to look at Garlthik, the ork stood without a bit of hesitancy in his posture. J'role simply shook his head, revealing neither his fear nor his anger. Then he turned back toward the trees and walked on.

Garlthik followed.

Sleep did not come easily to J'role. First his father's coughing kept him awake, and when Bevarden finally fell asleep, J'role couldn't sleep for wondering if Garlthik was waiting for the chance to slit his father's throat. Exhaustion finally took its toll, and with the coming of dawn, J'role at last dropped off to sleep.

When he woke later that day, the sun was high above, brilliant as a dream. Garlthik sat against a tree, cleaning his sword. His father, still alive, slept.

"Good day," Garlthik said without looking at J'role.

J'role glanced about, taking in his surroundings. Earlier he'd been too tired to really look around. Now he saw that they were in the midst of about twenty trees, all three times his height and with thick branches spreading out overhead. From the rough branches grew long, large leaves that offered shade against the noon sun. J'role had never seen so many trees growing in one place. He wondered if magic was at work, for his village had needed magic to grow crops in the fields. To grow trees like these seemed just as difficult a task. He also wondered who could afford to use magic for something as frivolous as making trees when growing crops was so much more valuable.

On the ground under the trees grew grass, green and several inches high. J'role had never seen the stuff before, but he had heard it said that grass was one of the things the Horrors had ruined.

He touched the grass, so smooth and giving so easily under his fingers. He plucked a blade and examined it. So small, thin. What did it do?

As he looked around for any other strange sights, J'role suddenly let out a gasp.

Immediately beyond the copse of trees, the ground was as barren and brown as most of the other places they had traveled. But ahead, across a space of perhaps a mile, he saw a brilliant island of green: a forest. Catching the leaves, the sunlight shimmered emerald as the leaves fluttered slightly back and forth.

"J'role? What is it?" asked Garlthik as he stepped up

alongside him. Then the ork too began to stare at the forest, drawing in a long, deep breath. "Last night I thought that was a hill."

J'role nodded slowly. When he looked around he saw that the copse to which they had retired was only one of several groups of trees circling the massive forest. It seemed to J'role that the copses were distant parts of the forest, and that some day they would all be linked together, forming a monstrous wilderness of trees.

The thought terrified him.

"Look," said Garlthik, pointing to the north. Perhaps some three miles back was a trio of travelers descending a hill. Though none seemed to wear scarlet robes, J'role knew magicians sometimes covered their bright and colorful garments to disguise themselves. "If they've followed us this far, they might be able to walk right up to us." For a moment Garlthik pursed his lips together, then finally said under his breath, "He must have something. Something."

Garlthik was already gathering his things and stuffing them into the sack he carried. "We'll have to move quickly."

J'role walked over to his father. The man's flesh was gray and his breathing very shallow. He shook his father awake, and as soon as Bevarden opened his eyes, the coughing started again. He reached up and grabbed J'role's arm. He looked J'role straight in the eye, but the boy thought his father did not recognize him.

"Drink?" he begged. "I need something to drink."

J'role shook his head and dragged his father up to his feet. He realized suddenly that he was as tall as his father, probably had been for some time. Exactly when, J'role wondered, had he gotten bigger? Or his father smaller?

Garlthik had already left the shelter of the trees and J'role ran quickly, dragging his father along, to keep up. The ork maneuvered their path so that the trees they had just left behind would hide them from the magician's sight for as long as possible. Bevarden smiled an idiot grin at the forest, and actually increased his pace.

J'role looked back and saw that Phlaren—he could see her long hair clearly now—had traveled away from Mordom, and was now signaling to Mordom and Slinsk, who remained hidden from view behind the copse. She was starting to get closer, slowly at first, but then at a run.

"Come!" said Garlthik, running quickly toward the forest.

J'role, still holding his father's hand, stood in place watching Garlthik dash away. He could not move forward, even with his father struggling against his grip to get to the forest. The forest was too *big*. It seemed to J'role that the overabundance of life would wrap itself around him and choke him. The thought of approaching the forest made him tremble.

His father turned to him, leaning forward like a child held back from a treat by a parent. "A forest," he said plainly, a bit of a smile in his eyes. "Elves."

"Come ON!" shouted Garlthik, with a wave of his arm. Phlaren would reach J'role any second now if he did not move.

The wash of green filled his vision and rooted him to the spot.

Garlthik took a few steps toward J'role, then threw his arms out wide in frustration and started rushing toward the wood. In an instant he vanished, swallowed up by the thick green.

I don't stand a chance now, J'role thought weakly. His father stared at the trees and licked his lips. We don't have to go deep into the forest, J'role decided. We don't have to go deep at all. With a sudden lurch he started to run toward the forest. For the first time in the whole journey, his father kept pace.

They raced toward the tree line, and as they got closer it seemed to sweep around J'role, arms coming to smother him. The brilliant green beauty of the leaves became dark and menacing, and the thick maze of branches and trunks became a single, powerful creature that would eat him as soon as he got near. It was too much *life*. J'role thought of the clean, straight corridors of his kaer, or the open plains of the rest of the world. But this *forest* . . . a jumble of angles and lines and *life*.

Closer and closer. His breathing became heavy and labored. Bevarden began to stumble and then finally lost his balance completely. He and J'role tumbled to the ground, a tangle of limbs. J'role glanced back. He could see their faces now. Slinsk, dark-skinned, a hungry smile on his lips. Phlaren, closer, determined and impatient. Far beyond them walked Mordom, willing to let his two assistants handle the first melee. J'role scrambled back up and dragged his father with him.

They ran, and now it was upon them, thick, shading leaves rushing over them like the maws of a dragon. Coarse vines crisscrossed between the trees and hung down to the jungle floor. Bushes caught their legs and scratched them. Birds sitting in trees suddenly took flight, the flapping of their wings like water flowing swiftly over rocks.

J'role did not want to go in any deeper, but he heard the crash of footsteps behind them. "Danger," Bevarden said, and giggled in glee as if the thought of impending danger was the best thing in the world. J'role ran on, holding his father's hand.

They continued to speed through the trees, the sounds of their pursuers close behind at first, then growing more and more faint. Shafts of shadows cut across their route, and after fifteen minutes J'role realized that he had no idea which way they had traveled.

He tried to listen for Slinsk and Phlaren, but could hear nothing over the sound of his own heavy breathing. He noticed that the tree trunk against his hand felt exceptionally warm. He attributed it to his own heated state and did not think about it until he pulled his hand away.

It was wet and sticky, the palm covered with blood.

J'role stared at his hand and then at the tree bark, which oozed with blood where he had touched it.

Then the tree moved.

It uprooted itself and backed away from J'role. A face, formed from the knots in the tree, stared down at him in horror. It bellowed something at him in a language J'role could not understand. He only had time to catch the slightest motion out the corner of his eye before he realized that a flurry of activity was rushing toward him from all directions.

He turned his head and found himself staring at a spear tip only inches from his face.

The spear was made of wood, the tip of smooth stone, the point so sharp and perfect it had undoubtedly been created with magic. J'role slowly lowered his gaze down the length of the pole until he saw the hands that held it—gnarled branches lined with thorns. The hands belonged to a long and thin creature. It had legs and arms, a head and chest, but its entire body was made of branches covered with thorns and leaves. Though the creature had the shape of a person, its interior was hollow, like the cages containing beautiful

colored birds that J'role had seen travelers carrying through his village. Like cages, the thorn men carried animals inside their bodies, but these animals—small birds, squirrels, rabbits—were all dead, the bodies in various states of decay. Even in the heads of the thorn men, where one expected to find a face, J'role saw only the rotted flesh of a ferret, now hairless and gray-pink, or the small, frail bones of a sparrow.

Dozens of the creatures stood around them. His father smiled at them. "Hello," he said, and then asked, "Am I dreaming?" He asked the question intently, obviously expecting an answer.

Something fluttered down before J'role; a leaf, he thought at first. But as it hovered before him, he saw that it was actually a tiny human, floating on wings formed from two coarse brown leaves. The tiny woman's face was framed by straight white hair and thorns grew from her skin.

No, he realized. They grew out *through* her skin. He saw a drop of clear liquid ooze out one of the tears in her flesh. It rolled down the short thorn, hung suspended from her body for a moment, and then fell to the ground. She stared at him, cocking her head from one side to the other, then fluttered off to look at Bevarden. Although she had tried to hide it, J'role had clearly seen pain on her face.

No one said anything. More of the small winged people flew around the nearby trees; they stared, but none came closer. When J'role looked directly at them, they flew around a tree and out of sight. The tree he had touched spoke again, this time as if asking a question, and J'role heard some of the small people answer, their responses a jumble of chirping noises.

The little white-haired woman came back and floated before J'role's face, her wings beating the air to hold herself in place. She said something to him, but he could not understand the words. A thorn man attempted to encourage an answer with the stone tip of his spear.

"I . . . ," said Bevarden, and all the thorn men and winged people moved back.

The woman flew over to him. This time J'role could hear words he understood formed in the small sounds of her tiny voice. With faulty accent and many mistaken words she used the common dwarven language. "Why . . . ? Tribute . . . ? Queen."

Bevarden gestured toward J'role, tried to form a word,

and failed. Then he fell into a coughing fit and collapsed to the ground. Thick droplets of blood came up from his throat and spattered the ground. J'role was astonished to see the ground quickly soak up the blood, like parched earth drinking rain water.

Oblivious to Bevarden's pain, the little woman repeated, "Tribute! Queen!"

"I think we need a present," said the creature in his thoughts.

J'role knew he had nothing to offer. He spread his arms wide.

"Good, good," the creature said sarcastically. "Confound them with your simple-minded honesty." Then it shouted in J'role's thoughts, "Give them the ring. Maybe they'll know what to do with it!"

He had forgotten about the ring. Its magical touch had become a permanent hum against his perceptions. As soon as he thought about surrendering the ring, he felt like crying. He forced the idea from his head.

The patience of the creatures had run out, and they began to chatter wildly. The thorn man in front of J'role tapped the tip of his spear against J'role, and though it did not pierce his flesh, a hot pain lanced through his chest.

The winged woman circled about them and said, "Come!" The thorn men arranged themselves to escort Bevarden and J'role. J'role helped his father up, and soon they were on their way into the heart of the forest.

13

When J'role had first stopped speaking, his parents said it was only a strange whim and he would grow out of it. The other children of the kaer could not understand such a concept. At first his friends were worried for him, but as the days, and then the weeks, passed, the other boys and girls began to sense that something was strange about J'role now. They avoided him, for his haunted eyes carried a weight of misery that even the high spirits of children could not shuck off. It was simply not fun to be with him.

After concern turned to avoidance, abuse set in. The children—even his best friend, Samael—began to taunt him, daring him to speak. But J'role never did, remembering his mother's instructions that he must not.

But how he wanted to! He knew something crawled in his thoughts, something so vile and corrupt that even his mother's mind had begun to splinter against the strange sounds he made when she asked him to speak to her. When the children pointed and laughed he wanted to open his mouth and let loose the horror in his thoughts; he wanted the perverse screeches and babblings to fly through the air and crash into their ears and replace their smug mockery with the misery that filled his mind each day.

He never did. His mother had warned him never to speak, and he did not.

So he listened to the laughter of the children echo down the corridors of the kaer, and imagined himself playing with them, which only made the creature in his mind taunt him all the more.

Surrounded by the thorn men, J'role and his father walked through the strange forest. A chatter of talk came from the small winged people who swarmed among the trees. The trees were also filled with more faces, staring down at J'role as he passed, their eyes and mouths formed by blood-soaked knots. The leaves and branches of bushes and other, lower trees seemed to reach out for him, brushing against his flesh, examining him. After J'role and the others had walked for a while, he realized that the ground was more than soft—it was damp. With a shock he saw that the dark moisture oozing up around his bare feet was blood.

At another point J'role was startled by the grotesque sight of a man, at least eight feet tall, staring at them through the trees from a hill thirty feet away. The man's flesh seemed torn in places, flapping like clothes hung out to dry, with wide stains lining the wounds. But the man was far away, and J'role wondered if perhaps his eyes had tricked him.

The more he walked, the more he felt overwhelmed by the forest. The very ground seemed to shiver, as if something moved underfoot. And everywhere—*everywhere*—there was life. Moss grew on the rocks. Leaves formed a nearly impenetrable canopy overhead. Tiny plants grew in the absurdly fertile ground. Insects buzzed up close to his eyes and then flew away again. The never-ending trees crowded around, reducing J'role's range of vision to only a fraction of what he was used to. It was as though the forest were crawling over him, trying to smother him and absorb him into its overabundant life. His gaze kept shifting from one place— one living thing—to the next.

Too much. Too much.

They walked for an hour or more, and J'role wondered if the forest had somehow grown to cover the world the moment they had entered it. Then up ahead, just beyond the thick labyrinth of trees, he saw flashes of a gathering of people. They had been sitting on the ground, but were now standing and staring at the approaching entourage. J'role could just make out that the people were tall and thin, with high foreheads. Some seemed to have green complexions, while others were as white as the full moon. When Bevarden also caught sight of the strange people ahead, he covered his mouth with both hands, eyes opening wide. Then he looked down at the ground, his mouth still covered, like a child trying to pretend he hadn't caught on to a surprise.

As they continued on J'role saw more and more of the people, all clustered in groups, all staring. Some were following the entourage now, but from a distance. Straining to get a better look at them, his eyes darting from side to side trying to catch glimpses of the thin strangers, he did not notice the clearing until they were almost upon it.

Sunlight poured into the clearing like a heavy rainfall, washing it with golden clarity. At the center towered a circle of eight giant trees, trees bigger than anything J'role had ever seen, their trunks as thick as taverns. The branches of the trees wound around each other in intricate patterns, as if they had been grown to become ordered and through the order, beautiful.

Flowering vines grew between the trees, beginning on the ground and climbing high overhead. The vines grew thick enough to create walls—walls covered with huge green leaves and white and violet flowers at least two hand-widths in size.

Throughout the wall of vines were openings, like windows, each covered in elaborate spider webs. The webs caught the gold of the sunlight and broke it into a rainbow of colors.

The whole structure, J'role suddenly realized, was a castle. Though he had never seen one before, his father had often spoken about them. The castles in his father's stories were made of stone, however. Not a single one supported this structure. It was all grown and made from the living earth. Its beauty caught at his throat.

Next to him, Bevarden spoke a single word, his voice that of someone who feels finally justified in some secret argument with himself. "Elves," he said, and dropped to his knees. His eyes were wide, as though trying to suck as much of the sight into memory as possible before the image suddenly vanished. Seeing his father's face, J'role realized how much Bevarden's tales had meant to him. His father hadn't considered them mere stories at all; he must have needed to tell them as much as the villagers needed to hear them. The need for hope had prompted him to give hope.

And so another legend that J'role had dismissed as pure fancy was proven true. Would the elves be as beautiful and kind as his father had described?

Opening outward at the base of the castle were two tremendous doors made from rose bushes grown so thick they blocked all light. A flight of broad white steps led down from the doorway to the clearing. Staring at them, J'role re-

alized the stairway was made of bones—bones of so many
shapes and sizes he could not imagine what kinds of creatures they were from. These strange, rare bones had been fitted and formed with careful craftsmanship to create flat tops
and sides.

At least sixty of the people—elves—who had followed
them through the woods entered the clearing. They wore
gowns and cloaks made of vines and flowers; and their skin
was studded with sharp points, which J'role assumed to be
some kind of armor. Some of the elves were quite human in
appearance, with hair and stern faces. But others had leaves
for hair, or arms formed like branches, or were not very human at all, seeming closer to being trees, walking on roots,
with faces only visible when they blinked, revealing their
knots to be eyes.

As they arrived in the clearing they knelt, facing the opening doors.

The thorn man next to J'role gestured down with his
spear, and J'role thought it best to join his father and the
others. The creature in his thoughts snickered at the display
of respect. "Strange what you all think is important," it
sighed.

From the castle door stepped eight more of the thorn men.
They flanked either side of the stairway, one guard to the
side of each step. Then several elves walked out, each more
elegantly adorned than the last, their elaborate garments created from roses and purple-flowered vines and wearing
capes of lilacs that trailed to the ground.

Following these came four elves with human shapes, but
whose bodies seemed to be both flesh and tree bark. As the
efour moved stiffly down the stairs, they grimaced in pain as
the tree bark shifted against their normal flesh. Their mouths
and eyes were severely distorted, as if their bodies had not
grown quite correctly. Each one wore the brightly colored
robe of a magician. The robes were scarlet, and shone as if
moist with blood.

The magicians and the other elves took up positions on
the stairs. Then all turned toward the door. From the pitch
dark of the doorway emerged a phantasm of white and red;
a woman so *beyond* life that for a moment J'role stopped
breathing. Her flesh reminded him of the white walls of the
mysterious city; her red hair flowed down around her shoulders like watery fire. The wide white skirt of her dress was

sewn from countless petals, and like the clothing of the other elves, it covered her, but left just enough bare to make her flesh enticing. Her long limbs aroused J'role, and rendered the ring that rested against his chest nearly impotent in its ability to focus his desires.

He looked to the elves gathered in the courtyard, all kneeling. Their faces were upturned, staring at the woman. They did not smile exactly, but each wore an expression of profound comfort as if by her presence the woman bathed them with grace. From the way their bodies arched toward her, leaning forward slightly, straining, J'role knew each one longed for her approval, and that any one would, if need be, leap up and die for her at a moment's notice. Without thought.

The woman stood on the white steps, slowly sweeping her gaze across the clearing, bestowing smiles on her subjects. They accepted the smiles like a lover's kisses. Finally her gaze came to rest on Bevarden, an old, tired man who stared at her with a plea in his eyes, and J'role, a young boy so afraid of showing his desire that he had made his face into a mask. She then walked down the last of the steps and crossed the clearing.

As she drew closer, the rustle of her dress flowed into J'role's senses, and he felt himself swept away by the possibility of being near her. . . .

The small, winged woman flew to the beautiful, red-haired woman, and they spoke softly as the woman in white continued to approach.

And then she stood before him.

"And so you have come to my forest," she said. Her words were in the dwarven tongue, but from her mouth the rough language seemed as beautiful as light rainfall.

J'role looked away, afraid of revealing too much, as if she could read his thoughts if their eyes met. But the temptation was too great . . .

He gasped when he looked up at her. Beautiful she was, yes. But, like the small woman with dead leaves for wings, thorns also grew from her flesh. Long, thin thorns. Each one pure white, and each splitting her beautiful flesh from the inside out. He realized that what he had thought to be armor from a distance was actually these thorns that grew from within the bodies of the elves. Droplets of ruby blood rolled down from the thorns of the majestic elf before him. The droplets remained suspended for an instant on the tips of their thorns, then fell off, dripping down the woman's skin and clothing, but leaving no mark or streak of their passing. Only the woman's face betrayed the truth: a slight twinge of pain, almost completely masked as if by years of practice. She smiled like a gracious hostess.

"Do I startle you?" she asked. Coyly. Mock surprise. Perhaps hurt. It was impossible to tell.

J'role could only nod. He sensed her mood shift from generosity to sharp anger to soft playfulness. Like a wind in spring, he thought. She frightened him, and he wanted suddenly to be out of the forest.

Then she lowered her hand to his cheek; her delicate white hand, the thorns small but razor-sharp. Just the tips of her fingers touched his flesh, the thorns so close, but not quite touching . . .

Warm. A tingle passed through his skin. What did she look like under the gown?

"Ah, I frighten you, do I? Or"—and here she chuckled—"do you frighten yourself? You have desires that you believe to be dangerous."

She slid her fingertips under his chin and up to his other cheek. So wonderful. And yet the thorns . . .

"And my touch frightens you. The thorns. I see that your kind did not need to resort to such tactics during the Scourge. The Horrors seemed to find my people a particular delicacy. To protect ourselves we were forced to adopt desperate measures." She raised her hand before her, turning it, admiring it. "I used to wonder how we would get rid of them when the time came. The thorns, I mean. Now, they seem so much a part of us." She looked down at J'role once more. "And I'll wager you sealed yourself up—well, not you, you being just a boy. But your people. Common enough, from what I remember. And you're still sealed up, aren't you? Like us, your defenses feel quiet natural."

She waited for J'role to respond, and when he did not, she turned her head and stepped over to Bevarden. J'role's shoulders slumped in tremendous relief. How he wanted to touch her, and how glad he was that she was no longer close enough.

"And who is this?" she said to Bevarden. His father tried to mouth a response, but only a small noise and a bit of spittle came forth. A look of distaste passed across the woman's face. J'role saw terror form in his father's eyes; his chance had come and gone. He realized that all his father had ever wanted stood before him, but he was incapable of even speaking.

Then, with frightening speed, the distaste left her expression, and she stepped back and smiled.

"I am the Queen Alachia. And you are my guests. And now, what have you brought me?"

J'role lowered his head, not sure what would happen next, but guessing that it would be awkward. Perhaps even dangerous. They had nothing to give.

"You entered my forest. Surely you have brought a gift." When no response came, she laughed delicately and said, "Oh, I think I see the confusion. You think I am asking whether you have brought something expressly for me. That's not at all what I mean. I mean, what are you going to give me?"

J'role spread his arms and shook his head.

"Nonsense. Everyone has something to give." She stepped up to J'role, touched her hand to his face once more. Her touch burned desire deep into his body and all he wanted was to bury his face against the palm of her hand, against her abdomen, against . . .

Without warning she dragged a thorn in one of her fingers across his skin. It dug just slightly into his flesh, but he felt blood swell up and run down his face. He tried to back away from her, but the hands of two thorn men held him in place, their thorns digging into his shoulders, increasing his pain. "You see," said Queen Alachia, "there is always something to give. There is always blood." She removed her hand and the thorn men released him.

The cut on his cheek felt like nothing he had ever experienced before. It hurt, yet he longed for more.

A memory flashed in his thoughts, something hidden, as if in a nightmare: a flash of metal in someone's hand. "Come here," the person said. He could not remember who. The memory ate at his thoughts, and he suddenly forgot all the strange sights around him.

"Very good," said the creature. "I thought I'd have to tell you everything myself."

Then he was back in the clearing, the sun bright, the elf queen before him.

"I don't want to kill you," she said softly. "I want you to

decide what you will give me." She stopped suddenly. "What is this?"

Gently she lowered her hand toward J'role's neck until her fingers plucked at the cord that held the magic ring.

"Ah," she said with genuine delight as she lifted the thong and removed it from around J'role's neck. "Have you forgotten this?" She smiled at J'role. "I will take nothing unless it is offered. If you have nothing else, will you give me this?"

She leaned down toward J'role, her breath warm—as intoxicating as flowers in bloom—caressing his face. He felt dizzy, and the desire for her seized him again. "You want me, don't you, boy?" she said softly. "I assure you, everything you feel is coming from within you. I have cast no magic upon you." She smiled. "Now, what will you give me? This ring?"

The ring dangled before him, the sun's light glinting on it as it swung slightly on the cord. J'role could no longer feel the longing the ring had given him. He was unmoored now. Whatever he needed—and he still needed so much—he no longer knew where to go to get it. But he remembered the sensation—now no more than an echo of longing. The city promised so much, and he wanted so much to have the ring back, to taste the longing again. Even if the promises never came true, the belief that something could finally make him happy was so sweet.

Yet the queen promised even more. Perhaps she would give him all he craved. Why go on the quest when all he desired, so beautiful, stood right before him?

"Don't you do it, brat," the creature in his thoughts said suddenly.

He looked up at the queen, pleased to distress the creature.

"NO!" the creature screamed. "Don't give it up!"

J'role nodded to the queen.

"What a lovely boy you are." She coiled the cord around her hand until the ring reached her palm. She grasped it and a passionate sigh escaped her lips. She smiled down at J'role, her eyes alive with mischievousness.

The creature raged and ranted in his thoughts, but J'role lost himself in the smile the queen bestowed upon him. "This ring," she said, her breathing increasing in pace. "I know this ring." Her eyes looked off into the distance, as if past the trees that circled the clearing, as if seeing something long ago that she could no longer place. "Where did you get this?" she asked. The commanding tone had left now; she wanted very much to know the answer to her question.

J'role's jaw moved a bit. He so wanted to answer her, to give her anything she asked. But he could not speak. He could never do that to her.

"What does it matter now?" the creature screamed. "You've ruined the only chance for happiness you've ever had!"

"No. Not the only," he told it, still looking at the queen. Yes, he knew now. His mother and the priestess of Garlen who had tended him as a child. Both had given warmth. Love. But this woman who stood before him could give him things he never dreamed of. If only she would hold him in her arms . . .

She touched his face with her fingers, the flesh warm, the thorns kept from his skin. "I know you are not mindless. You are a bright lad. I can see it in your eyes. A clever, strong, handsome boy."

His chin trembled. More, please, more. He was embarrassed at his love of her flattery. A trick, no doubt, but what a lovely trick. He let his thoughts slip away, allowing her words to have their way with him. Her lips moved only inches from him as she spoke. Their motion hypnotized him; the full red lips now, in his thoughts, separated from the rest of her.

"I see you considering whether to speak. Yes? Yes. You choose not to talk. Won't you talk for me?"

He had almost spoken! J'role pulled his face away from her hand. Clamping his jaw tight, he forced himself to think of his mother and his father and what had happened to them when they had heard him speak.

She touched him again. "What is it? Don't you want to make me happy?"

He turned his head toward her, again almost speaking. "Yes," he wanted to say. He nodded.

She stood and extended her hand to him. "Come. I will show you my home." He took her hand, only their fingertips meeting, the flesh of his hand brushing against her thorns, but not cutting. She turned to the thorn men. "The other one will remain here until I return."

J'role looked at his father. Bevarden was staring at the ground, but his shoulders shook slightly, and J'role knew he was crying for all the dreams lost, now passed on to his son.

14

The flash of the blade caught the green light of the glow sphere. His mother, insane, held the blade. "Come here, dear. Come here."

His father was out telling stories at the Atrium. One thought crashed through all others: Home was supposed to be safe.

The elf queen led J'role up the broad steps of the castle, each one formed from intricately placed, polished white bones. Some of the bones were large, some small, but all seemed strange in a way he could not identify. Thinking they might be the bones of Horrors the elves had killed during the Scourge made him wonder what the Horror in his head actually looked like.

As they walked up the stairs they passed the courtiers and elven magicians who were still positioned at either end of each step. All had thorns growing from their bodies. The magicians stared at J'role with disdain, though their faces bled from the thorns and from the scraping of their flesh against the bark and small branches that grew from their bodies.

When they came to the top of the stairs the elf queen gestured for him to pass through the great doorway. Plunging beyond the thick vine walls of the castle was a great hall under a spell of green twilight. J'role entered, followed by the queen, who touched his shoulder lightly, steering him through the corridors. Vines and trees made up the castle's inner walls, a wild profusion of flowers growing from them. Sometimes the flowers formed flowing patterns; other times they showed scenes of battle or portraits of elves. J'role saw that most of the elves portrayed in the flower scenes had no thorns in their flesh.

At one point a shrubbery walked past them, carrying a tray made of dry leaves. Sitting on the tray were cups, each formed from a thick layer of petals. The shrubbery bowed low to the queen, then continued on its way.

J'role and Queen Alachia then ascended a series of staircases that spiraled around tree trunks. The steps were branches carpeted with vines, and all the windows they passed were adorned with beautiful spider webs. The elves on the ground looked smaller and smaller as J'role and the queen ascended the spiraling stairs. Once he caught a glimpse of his father kneeling on the ground, surrounded by the thorn men. The other elves had moved closer, pointing at Bevarden and laughing. He almost felt a desire to be with him. But the queen's fingertips rubbed slowly against his shoulder.

He let the impulse die quickly.

Finally, after climbing many flights of stairs and traveling down many corridors, they reached the top floor of the castle. A long hall extended before them, the walls lined with tree branches that served as shelves. The shelves contained amulets and rings and gowns and silver cloth and countless other items that J'role suspected had served as gifts to the queen, and perhaps the rulers who had come before her.

At the end of the corridor were double doors made from white rose bushes. The queen pushed the door open and J'role entered a magnificent bed chamber. The room had only three walls. Opposite the door, in the place where the fourth wall would have been, was nothing but a wide, empty space. J'role crossed the floor, a springy surface made of tightly woven vines, and then stood staring out into the open space.

Below him the top of the elven forest stretched on and on, forming a vast landscaping of shifting leaves. Beyond the forest lay all the brown of the world, the lands left dead by the Scourge. The stark contrast of the dead world against the forest made J'role reconsider his original fear of the forest. The abundance of life still disturbed him, but he wondered what a world covered in trees would be like, and then he thought it might be wonderful.

"A beautiful view," the elf queen said, suddenly behind him. He felt her breath on his neck, and then her lips touching his flesh, rubbing slightly, dry and arousing. The thorns along her body pricked lightly against his back as she pressed closer and ran her hands down his arms.

Though he knew what would happen, he leaned back into her, desperate for her warmth to envelop him. The thorns on her body bit into his back, sending a delicious pain through his body. Yes, delicious, and so intense that he arched his back and uttered a low moan. The creature in his thoughts purred like a cat, bathing luxuriously in the agony.

This was it, then, the touch and the pleasure and the pain, and J'role thought he could die at that moment; impale himself on the queen's beautiful body and know the pleasure he had always wanted while gaining a final rest so he would never feel longing again. Could anyone want more?

She gently raked her hand along his chest, tearing his shirt open, drawing thin lines of red along his dark flesh. Though the temptation was great, J'role said nothing, only hummed through tightly clenched lips.

She leaned in next to his ear, the thorns on her throat pressing into the skin at the back of his neck. "No words of encouragement?"

He sighed.

"I know you can talk," she said, and the tip of her tongue pressed lightly against the inside of his ear. Her warm breath made him jerk, her thorns tearing his flesh. "What are you afraid of? What is it that you wish to keep me from knowing?" She removed her hands from his chest and he saw they were now smeared with streaks of blood. The leather thong was still looped about her hand, and she loosened it and slipped the ring onto her finger. She sighed and drew him tightly to her. He let out a soft gasp, but pressed himself even closer. Tears of pain formed and rolled down his face. He bit his lip to prevent himself from screaming, yet the pleasure was perfect.

"This ring . . . ," she said, raking his flesh with the thorns in her hands. "I remember this ring . . . from so long ago . . . I was only a small child—four hundred, five hundred years ago—we made this for a city. Yes, Parlainth. I haven't thought about it in so long." As she suddenly pulled back, J'role felt the sticky blood pulling between their bodies. "Why?" she asked, her voice distant and distracted. "Why haven't I thought of it for so long?"

Then, abruptly she turned him around, stared into his

eyes—Ah, to be looked at with such desire! How wonderful!—and pulled him close. They kissed. The thorns drove deep into him now, but he did not dare stop for fear she would not kiss him a second time.

But even as they kissed, he realized she was not responding to her desire for him. Instead, she was using him to fulfill the desire created by the ring on her finger.

It did not matter. J'role would take her love in any form.

She pulled away, blood on her face. She swayed as she tried to stay in control, gasping for air. "Where did you get this? What do you know of Parlainth?"

He leaned forward to kiss her again, but she backed away, smiling. "You want me?" Her white gown, now smeared with his blood, parted easily as her hand pulled at the collar.

He stepped toward her, and she retreated once more. "Tell me where you got the ring. I haven't thought about Parlainth for so long. Not since . . ." She paused, lost in memories, and J'role nearly reached her. But she left her reverie just in time to leap up onto the bed—a rectangular hammock made of vines and matted with a thick layer of broad green leaves. "Not since we helped them . . ." A memory seemed to come to her, and she smiled. Her face immediately contorted from the pain of the thorns.

"We built the ring," she said, ignoring him completely now. "And the dwarfs cut the stones for the walls. The walls held the magic to hide the city, and the ring . . ." She stared down at it, and then looked up at him. "You may go now."

He swallowed. He spread his arms wide, asking for an explanation. Warm blood turned cold and wet as it dripped down his body. The pain began in earnest without the intensity of the moment to sustain him. He stepped toward the bed.

"You can take the stairs if you wish. Or you may simply go out that way," she said, pointing to the opening that looked out over the forest. "Many of my lovers simply prefer just to die. I really can't tell about you."

A fury built up inside him, a self-righteous anger similar to the one that had helped him steal while still living in his village. The fury mixed with his lust and he lunged for the bed. He would die, but against her, her thorns tearing him apart.

From the floor, from the walls, sprang half a dozen thorn men, spears in hand. They blocked his way, dragged him to the ground, their thorny arms ripping wildly across his body. J'role gave a shout of pain, and as he opened his mouth he felt the creature take control. He decided not to fight it.

But the queen sensed the danger even as the noise began. She brought her hands reflexively to her ears and commanded, "Silence him!"

Two of the thorn men grappled his face and squeezed his jaw shut. Their thorns raked across his lips and over his eyes, and he tried to scream again, but could not. His tongue, controlled by the creature, moved wildly in his sealed mouth, but no words escaped. His sense of smell was assaulted by the decayed forest life trapped in the bodies of the thorn men.

"Take him to the pit," the queen said. "I will deal with him later."

Blood now rushed over his eyes and he could see nothing. He only felt himself lifted and carried off by the flesh-shredding hands of the queen's guards.

Down the corridors and down the stairs they carried him. Then sunlight filtered through the blood that washed over his tightly shut eyes. He heard the laughter of elves and the chattering of the small, winged creatures, then felt himself tossed into the air. He fell, much longer than he expected, and braced himself for terrible pain. Darkness embraced him as he suddenly slammed into the ground. Though the ground was not hard, the impact still hurt horribly. Adding that to the pain of the queen's thorns and those of her guards, he was left with neither the energy to move nor the desire to do more than keep his eyes shut and fall asleep. And this he did.

J'role woke to the sound of small movements, with little awareness of where he was or how he had gotten there. A slow groan rolled from his throat, and he carefully stretched out his legs and arms. Then he stopped quickly, for even these small motions sent pain cutting through his flesh. He paused to rest, eyes still closed, feeling damp, cool dirt against his cheek.

"Hello?" someone said softly, and he realized it was his own voice, and all the events with the elves came back to him.

J'role opened his eyes, carefully raising his hand before his face for fear of being stunned by bright light. Blood, dried and still sticky, held his eyelids shut for a moment, and a panic seized him: would he never see again? But the blood cracked and his eyes opened.

Darkness.

He pulled his hand away from his eyes and discovered that he could just discern his father kneeling over him. Beyond that, nothing. He heard a soft voice, his father's, mumbling over and over, "I'm sorry, I'm so sorry. Your Highness. Please. I'm sorry." From the acoustics J'role guessed they were in a small room; a cave, perhaps a tunnel.

He closed his eyes, and felt a deep, numbing darkness slide along his body. At the edge of his thoughts he remembered fully what had happened in the queen's bedchamber. His body ached and pain spread over him in odd waves, but he felt a warmth from the memory. He had finally gotten what he wanted. He had hated the queen for sending him away, but he was happy with the gifts she had given—the touch of her skin, cuts from her thorns. All his life he had waited for something like this.

"All your life?" the creature asked coyly.

"No," he said. "Ever since you arrived."

"Yes. And if you liked it, it's because I'm here. I'm glad you appreciated it. I had a delightful time."

But even as J'role drifted off to sleep, he knew the creature was wrong. It had begun when the creature entered his head, but there was something else. The drowsy darkness consumed him, and he fell into a deep sleep before he could remember what that thing was.

Sunlight streamed down a vertical shaft about twenty feet away, creating a circle of gold. J'role propped himself up and saw that he was resting on the floor of a tunnel that extended out of sight behind him and beyond the circle of light ahead. The shaft was probably where he'd entered the tunnel. He didn't know how he had moved down the corridor away from the shaft. Then he noticed the shallow depression leading up to his own body, and realized someone must have dragged him.

His father sat against the wall of the tunnel, fast asleep. For the first time since they'd left their village, Bevarden seemed peaceful. The tunnels undoubtedly reminded him of the kaer, the place where he had always gone to retreat.

Carefully J'role stretched his limbs. They were still stiff and sore, but did not hurt as much as they had hours earlier. He got up, dizzy, and walked with weak legs to the base of the shaft.

Above him rose a pit about twelve feet across; about twenty feet up, the lip of the pit opened into sunlight and trees. The dirt wall of the pit was lined with tree roots that poked toward the center of the pit. There seemed to be no guards at the top of the pit. Or at least no one staring back down at J'role.

He looked at the tree trunks and realized that even without the thief magic that Garlthik had passed on to him, it would be easy enough to climb out of the pit using the roots as handholds. But with the magic, it would be no problem at all. He smiled inwardly; the elves were in for a surprise if they thought they could keep him in prison!

Hunger chewed at his stomach, but the thought of escaping excited him, and he wanted to get to it as quickly as possible. Finally, he need not depend on anyone but himself. He was the hero of his story.

He moved quickly back to where his father slept, fearful that thinking about the thief magic would make him want to leave Bevarden behind. J'role didn't know what else to do but try to escape and then struggle against the thief magic when he got out.

He decided to wait until nightfall before attempting the escape. Shadows, Garlthik had taught him, are a thief's friend, and J'role wanted as much comfort as possible while trying to climb the pit. Wondering how long the queen had planned to leave them down in the tunnels, it suddenly occurred to him that she might never have thought of letting them out. She had probably forgotten about them already.

When the sun set, the tunnels became solidly black. Not even starlight reached the tunnel, blocked by the large, dark leaves in the tree tops high above. His father sat in the darkness, giggling, sometimes coughing, and other times sobbing. "The elves!" he said, and gasped for air. "Where is the beauty now?" J'role listened to his father, his heart filling with pity and hatred. He knew Mordom had done something to his father, probably probed his father's mind for clues—

and when he had discovered that Bevarden knew nothing, was, in fact, only a hopeless drunk—must have kept him around as a pet.

J'role wished his father were stronger. He'd wished that all his life. Why couldn't his father have done . . . ?

What? What hadn't his father done?

The idea slipped just out of range of J'role's thoughts. It was something he couldn't remember, yet he knew it colored everything about his life.

"I wouldn't work so hard at remembering," said the creature in his thoughts. "You aren't ready yet."

"You know something . . ."

"About you? I know everything."

"Tell me."

"No. Not yet."

J'role waited in the darkness, thinking the creature would taunt him, make him beg to hear what it had to say. But the thing said no more.

J'role stood at the foot of the pit, blocking his father from his thoughts, thinking back to the initiation that had taken place at the tavern. The darkness of the night drew around him like a cloak, and he felt his concerns becoming smaller and smaller, until his cares extended no further than himself.

It felt good. Comfortable.

The roots above him were long shadows melded into the larger shadow of the pit's wall.

Now.

He crouched low, then jumped up, catching the end of one of the roots with his fingers. He swayed in the air, then reached out with his free hand to grab another root. Without effort he felt the rough grooves of the roots, knew their shape, gripped them just the right way so he could cling easily to them.

He felt lightheaded. It was so easy being a thief. One had only to be alone . . .

He moved up the roots, hand over hand, using them to support his feet as he moved up the pit.

No noise from above.

He continued. He climbed two feet, five feet, ten feet.

And then, out of the corner of his eye, he saw a shadow move slightly. He did not think much of it at first, for his concern was on climbing. But then, as he reached his hand up above his head to grab the next branch, the root directly in front of his face uncoiled from the wall like a snake and wrapped around his neck.

15

He is mute, sworn to silence by his mother. His mother holds a knife in her hand. He is allowed to speak to her, but there is little point. He does not speak words; he cannot formulate his fear and confusion into sentences. There is nothing to do but slowly back away in terror.

All the while his mother speaks with a calm, loving voice. It is the same tone she has used all her life. Suddenly he wonders if any of her professions of love were real.

The root quickly tightened its grip around J'role's neck. Startled by its animation, he let go his hold on the other roots in the pit and dropped away from the wall. Now only the writhing root that choked him like a hangman's noose held him in place while his arms and legs scrambled uselessly for purchase in the air. He gave a hoarse gasp for air, and then, arms flailing wildly, tried to grab hold of other roots to prop himself up and keep himself from strangling.

His fingers came within inches of the roots, then he watched, eyes wide in terror, as each flitted just out of his grasp. No matter what he did, J'role could not gain a grip against the surface of the pit; meanwhile the first root bit deeper into his neck. Twisting wildly in the effort to grab another root for support, he felt all the cuts made by the elven thorns rip open. Warm blood spilled over his skin once more.

J'role grabbed the root and propped his feet against the wall of the pit. With the wall as leverage he tried to rip the root out of the wall, deciding it was better to fall back into the pit than be strangled. More roots came at him, encircling his wrists and ankles, arms and legs, crawling over his body.

He was becoming lightheaded as he tried to pry himself free of the root. With what little strength was left he grabbed the root's tip and wrestled to unwind it from around his neck.

Finally he gained the advantage over the root, uncoiling two of the loops from his neck. The root fought back, and J'role thought he felt muscles snaking about under the surface of cold, wet bark. Using two hands now he managed to completely uncoil it, holding the root up like a snake as the tip slashed at his face.

Then all the roots let go at once, plunging J'role back down into the pit. His body tensed for the impact, and an instant later he hit the soft dirt.

He lay there, groaning as his father crawled up next to him. "Don't try anything you aren't sure you can do," Bevarden said, his tone suddenly sober. Then he stretched out beside J'role and fell asleep, curled up next to his son.

For a long time J'role stared up at the pit opening, despair weighing on his body. He'd never get out.

That night he got no sleep. The cuts and bruises all over his body seemed like insects crawling up and down his flesh. What would it be like to die in the pit? No food was available, not even the berries and roots they'd dug up and eaten on the road. That meant he would probably starve to death. How long did it take? Maybe two weeks? In the kaer and in the village, J'role's people had used magic to keep food supplies available. There had been shortages, but no one had ever starved.

Did the pit tunnels exit back somewhere out into the world? Probably not. It would be a very poor prison if they did. As poor a prison as J'role had originally thought when he'd decided to simply climb up the pit and escape.

What was that? A sound?

All his senses alert, J'role shifted, just slightly, so as not to give himself away.

He saw the shadow of something, a faint shape, crawling along the darkness of the corridor. Whatever it was, it was only a few steps away. He slowed his breathing, trying to make no sound. Could he slip into the shadows now? Probably not. Not if it had seen him.

Odd that he should know that, he realized. The magic, when he thought of it, just came to him. He was a part of it now, and as long as he lived by the rules of a thief, it would support him.

The shadow came closer and closer, approaching with great caution. Then it stopped about a few feet from him. Sat up on its haunches. J'role thought it stared at him, but he couldn't be sure. It was small, only about four feet from the ground, perhaps taller when it stood.

Then, as carefully and quietly as it had approached, it turned around and began moving back down the tunnel.

A near panic came over J'role. Should he let the thing wander off? Or should he stop it now? It could be going off to get more of its kind—whatever that was. Or it might have decided it wanted nothing to do with him. Attacking it might only create new problems.

And yet . . .

It crept away, and when J'role thought that its guard was down, he quietly rolled onto his knees. The magic made his motion nearly soundless. On his feet now, walking close to the wall of the tunnel, he began to follow his visitor back the way it had come. It might know of an exit. It might have a master—someone who had been thrown into the tunnel some time ago. Perhaps working together they could escape.

J'role thought briefly of his father. Should he leave him? Would Bevarden panic if he woke and found J'role gone? J'role had difficulty focusing his thoughts on his father; concern for anyone but himself had all but evaporated from his mind. Instead he put all his attention on the placement of his next step. It thrilled him to make no sound as he walked.

He followed the creeping shadow another twenty feet. Nothing was visible. But he heard the thing shift and sigh—perhaps it was standing now—and then continue on. It certainly sounded as if its movement had changed, and perhaps it now walked on two feet.

As he followed, J'role ran his fingers along the wall to keep his sense of balance. They came to turns in the corridor, and finally intersections. Several times he had to stop and listen to determine which way his prey had gone. He made a mental list of the turns he had made, so he could find his way back if necessary.

Finally, when he had gone a long way from the pit, J'role heard a few strange words spoken. The voice belonged to a girl. Then a bright blue light suddenly flared ahead of him.

The light hurt his eyes, and J'role raised his arms before his face.

"Oh," the voice said, definitely a girl's. "I thought so."

Lowering his arms, he saw a short girl, about his age, with a round face and long dark hair, staring at him. A blue fire burned from her hand. It took him a moment to adjust to the fact that she was not a monster. Nor was she—with mud streaking her face and hair matted with grime—like the elf queen at all. Pudgy, he thought.

"Who are you?" she asked firmly.

J'role spread his arms wide, and then pointed to his throat. He shrugged.

"Did the queen send you here?"

He nodded.

She paused, looking at him carefully. Then said, "Me too. I've been here for months. I think. I don't really know. Didn't start keeping track until I'd been down here a while. She said she was going to take care of me later. I guess she forgot. Or maybe later for an elf is different than later for me. For her, later might mean next time the seasons turn. For me it might mean by the time I get bit by a poison spider and die down here. Was that a friend of yours back there?"

Her rush of words startled him, and it seemed she was hungry for conversation. He nodded.

"What do you want? Why are you following me?"

He shrugged, unable to answer.

"How long have you been here?"

He raised his hand, held up two fingers.

"Hours?" He shook his head. "Days?" He nodded.

"You're good at this. You've been mute a while, I take it. You don't have to stand there and think about how to communicate. You just do it. Impressive. Well, I'm going home. Maybe I'll see you tomorrow." She turned to leave. J'role realized she wasn't hungry for conversation. She just could talk a lot.

He ran up to her. She was a magician and might well have the power to get them out. She whirled to face him, the flames glowing around her hands appearing to be very hot, but apparently not affecting her. "I didn't bother you. I don't want you to bother me."

He pointed to himself, then her, then clasped his hands together, and then pointed up.

"If I knew how to get out, I wouldn't still be here. I

tried . . . What can you do?" She stopped suddenly, looking him up and down. "You must have put up some fight."

Her remark confused him for a moment, and then he remembered his cuts, many of them still bleeding. He was embarrassed. A fight? Most of them, the most horrible ones, were from the elf queen herself, from touching her lovely flesh. He tried to brush the matter aside. He once again pointed at her, and then himself. Then up.

She smiled. Her cheeks puffed up, lines formed around her eyes. She suddenly became pretty, despite the mud and grime. "You're persistent. Nice. But you can't climb up the pit. The roots come to life. . . ."

He pointed to the thick bruise around his neck.

"Ah, you found that out," she said, examining his neck. "I don't suppose any of your group are adepts in the discipline of thieving?"

He smiled, poked his finger at his chest.

She looked disappointed. "Well, maybe we'll talk later."

She turned again, and J'role touched her shoulder. She quickly whirled around once more. "Don't do that," she said flatly.

J'role nodded and then pointed at himself.

"Yes. You're a thief. I thought you'd be able to climb up the wall of the pit—or at least I thought a thief would. But you couldn't. Either it's too hard, or you're not very good. Either way, it's no help."

She started down the tunnel. J'role stared after her, trying to figure out what to do. Darkness crept around him as she walked off with the blue fire that blazed around her hand. Frozen with uncertainty, he watched her turn a corner and vanish from sight.

"Not very good," he repeated in his thoughts. He might not have thought much of her, at least compared to the elf queen. But she thought even less of him. He turned and retraced his steps, one hand running along the walls, finding his way back to where his father slept.

The next morning he felt ashamed. The girl had sent him off as a useless boy. And hadn't the elf queen done the same thing? Yet there seemed to be a great difference between the two of them. The elf queen had asked that he give himself up to her. The girl—what was her name? he suddenly wondered—had asked nothing.

J'role knew now it was possible to survive in the tunnels for a long time, even if it was difficult to get out. What did she eat? Had they thrown food down with her? No, she'd been down in the tunnels too long. And he doubted they would have bothered to send food. This was the place for people the queen had forgotten.

A dizziness passed over him, and J'role thought he might fall asleep again. He wanted so desperately to eat. It frustrated him to know that above him was the most enormous expression of life he had ever seen, and only a few feet below ground he had nothing.

Fearful of falling unconscious and never waking up again, he crawled around on hands and knees, looking for something he might have missed. Small plants. Deeper roots that he could eat. Something. He began to dig through the dirt floor, the ground wet and cool as he scooped it up in thick clumps.

"Why don't you just let yourself die?" the creature asked. "If we're trapped down here with these two, what fun in that? There's no sport in talking to your father. Why don't you just scamper up the pit and let those fascinating roots rip the life out of you? *Give up your life, J'role.* Surrender to the misery of your life and stop feeling so bad. This hope you have is making you more miserable than you can imagine."

The creature's words surprised him, for J'role had never considered himself hopeful. Still digging through the dirt, he asked, "Why do you want me to die?"

"Wait. Let me be clear. I don't want you to die. I want you to kill yourself. And to answer your question, I really don't think you're very happy being alive."

J'role stopped scooping dirt. "Then why did you encourage me to go on a few days ago?"

The creature said nothing. J'role waited a moment more, and when he realized the creature was not going to answer, he went back to digging.

The hole was a foot deep now, and as wide. J'role sent his hands down once more and as they bit into the dirt he felt water rush up around them. Pulling away some more dirt, he peered into the hole. At its base was a small pool of water. Seeing a flash of motion he instantly jabbed his right hand down into the pool, trying to catch whatever had moved in the water.

He pulled his hand up, then clamped his other hand over it, forming a small container. He felt something crawling around on his palms as he walked under the opening of the pit to get more light. Above him the sky and leaves caught the sun's light and turned it a soft green.

Carefully he parted his hands to get a peek at whatever he was holding . . .

It was bigger than he expected, black and brown, with shiny, thick skin, and numerous legs. J'role sealed his hands tight before it could get out.

He'd never eaten a bug before, but he'd known other boys who'd done it on a dare. He wondered if he should crush it first or eat it alive. Alive seemed too disturbing a thought, so he squeezed his hands together. When he thought he'd killed it, he brought it up quickly to his mouth so as not to look at it, and shoved it into his mouth. He chewed quickly, surprised to find it did not actually taste bad, and swallowed it.

He got to work, digging for more food. Though it took hours, he found enough to feed himself and his father.

"Does your father appreciate what you do for him?" the creature asked.

J'role did not reply. His father's eyes were empty.

As J'role sat contentedly on the ground, hardly full, but satisfied enough, he realized he'd made far too many assumptions about the nature of the tunnels, and promised himself never to assume a place was barren simply because it looked that way at a casual glance. He would have to examine the tunnels carefully, seek out what could help him, and perhaps learn of the dangers they possessed.

He suddenly had the feeling someone was watching, and quickly turned his head. The girl stood maybe ten feet away, hands on hips, looking at them. "Do you usually just lie around?"

J'role, to his own surprise, smiled.

She laughed, then walked up to him. "My name is Releana. I see you're not always as grim as you seemed last night."

J'role stood and shook her hand.

"And this is . . . ?" she said, turning to Bevarden.

J'role's father simply stared at her, then whispered the word, "Despair." The word sent a chill through the corridor, and the three of them remained completely still and silent for a moment.

"Is he all right?" Releana asked J'role.

He shook his head.

She weighed a thought, then said, "I really didn't know if I was going to come here. I've been alone down here for some time, and maybe I've started to like it. I'd given up hope of getting out, actually. And you know what they say about magicians: 'Where they are is where they stay.' But ... but if you have a plan to get out, and I can help, I certainly will. I don't know if you do, but maybe we could come up with something together. I don't know." When she had finished, Releana took in a big gulp of air, and J'role realized that she had raced through her words, almost without breathing, as if afraid he would interrupt her. He almost laughed.

J'role pointed to her, then shrugged his shoulders.

Her lips pressed tightly as she tried to puzzle out what he meant. "I don't ...," she began to say.

J'role then raised his hands and waved them about in a broad imitation of casting a spell. Then he pointed at her again.

"Oh. Right. What can I do? You have thief talents. I have magic. We have to take stock of our resources. Yes. Well, I'm an elementalist."

They began to communicate. Faltering at first. But Releana was the most patient person J'role had ever met. She did not become frustrated with the gestures he used to communicate. If anything, she seemed completely captivated by the complexity of the problem of "talking" with someone who did not speak.

Her enthusiasm was infectious, and many more times that day the beautiful smile he had seen the night before revealed itself. J'role suddenly thought that being trapped wasn't so bad as long as you rose to the challenge of getting free.

Together they built a plan.

16

He is silent. His mother extends one arm, the glint of the blade hidden behind her back in her other hand. Months have gone by since the thing entered his head. His mother asked him to speak to her. He thought it was dangerous, but she asked him to do it, and he did.

Over the many weeks a strange look entered her eyes. She became nervous. Often she stared at the walls, her attention frozen by the sight of something only she could see. Nothing could bring her out of these spells. His father sometimes asked J'role if he knew what was bothering his mother, but he only shrugged. He knew it was his voice that had altered her mind; he felt miserable about it. He was driving her mad.

Night.

Above, the shadows of leaves. The last songs of birds. Thousands of insects chirping as one. The Blood Wood a single, giant animal breathing in and out.

The shadows of night and loneliness passed over him, seeping into his flesh. J'role felt the magic that bound the world arcing through his body and out into the dirt of the pit. The magic spun outward, into the dirt beneath the whole of Blood Wood, and beyond that, in all directions, out into the world. Where he stood at that moment connected to the kaer where he had grown up, to the room where he had slept as a boy, to the burial pit that held his mother. The world itself formed a tapestry showing his life frozen at that moment.

Releana stepped up to him. She had a spell, she said, that would help him climb better. Though he was only a beginning thief, such a spell would augment his thief adept talents and perhaps give him the skill he needed to get out of the pit.

She took his hands in hers and very softly spoke the words of a spell. The words were in a language J'role did not understand, but in their sounds he heard deep age. She was tapping into the magic of the world, but in a different way than he could. He could only use magic to be a thief, and use it in a way the world allowed. Releana could take the magic and shape it to her own desires. As she spoke, her face became intent and thoughtful.

A tingle passed up through his fingertips, along his wrists, and through his arms. The strange sensation—like being air, J'role thought—spread through his body, leaving him giddy. He smiled. Releana saw this and smiled back. Her pudgy hands felt warm and reassuring in his. His chest suddenly felt empty, as if ready to be filled with a new life. He swallowed. Releana wasn't at all the kind of girl he'd ever thought attractive. She had neither the slender beauty of the elf queen nor the thorns that had somehow drawn him to the elf's touch.

Releana was plain by comparison. But good.

Was that enough? To be drawn to someone who was good?

She let go of his hands.

He looked up at the pit opening, sensed all the parts that made it; the connections between the grains of the dirt, the grains that made up the clumps of dirt, the clumps that made up sections of the wall, the sections that made up the pit. All pulsed in its walls like veins filled with blood.

He pressed his hand to the wall. The thief magic helped him know exactly where to put his fingers now; he sensed which part of the wall would give way and which would not. Releana's magic made him more nimble and light; he could feel it in his muscles and bones.

He poked the toes of his right foot into the dirt, then reached high above his head with his left hand, finding a spot to brace the weight of his body. A gasp came from Releana as he hoisted himself up and began to climb the wall. He moved like a light breeze.

His long limbs, once so ugly to him, thin, like a spider's, he now saw as good. The muscles strong, thanks to Releana's magic. His flesh taut, thanks to his hunger, with no excess weight to hinder his progress up the wall. A new way of seeing himself, a climber of walls. Successful. His body helped him.

Good.

He glanced up. A few feet above were roots growing from the wall of the pit. Already he saw them shift slightly; snakes ready to strike, awaiting their prey. Their slight shifts of preparation sank through the dirt of the pit walls and up through J'role's fingertips. Their tiny tremors pierced his sense of touch as sharply as shimmering starlight reflected off the stones of a stream. He stopped for a moment, taking it all in—it being the world, the sensations, his own body. The world of his youth now seemed so far away. Once, a long time ago, so much longer than the few days that had actually passed, he had been alone, trapped forever, in the village outside his kaer. Now . . .

Now what?

He wasn't.

Now he was a thief using magic to escape the elf queen's pit in Blood Wood.

He looked up, mapped out a path along the pit wall. He could see it all so clearly now. It would be hard. But now he could see the best path—how to avoid most of the roots, which portions of the wall would hold strongest. He might not make it. But then again he might.

A slightly longer intake of breath, just before he began. He'd have to move fast . . .

In some far corner of his thoughts he barely remembered his father. And the girl—what was her name? What could either one give J'role that he wanted?

Up.

His fingers dug deep into the dirt, so cold and damp. The dirt began to give way, his hand slipping out of the wall. But it was all right. He threw his other hand up and then dug his feet into the wall. Even as his new position began to crumble, his hands and feet scrambled for new holds in the wall.

The roots came at him, sending tremors up his muscles like an earthquake. Thwap! The tip of a root slammed at the side of his head. Bits of dirt smacked his face. More roots came for him. The cacophony of sounds and the tumble of motion from the roots—all augmented by the magic—confused him, nearly sending him falling away from the wall and back down into the pit.

But the thief magic came to him, a friend, draping its

shadow arm over his shoulder and pointing to the wall. Focus, it seemed to say, but speaking through his muscles and not through his thoughts.

He scrambled.

Roots nipped at his heels. Bits of bark cut across his face. Before he even knew what was happening, a sharp sting passed over the back of his hand, and J'role knew that a root had drawn blood.

But none had caught him. He moved too fast for that. He dodged one way, then another. Rarely did he move horizontally in trying to evade the roots. Always up. He knew the way to go, and the girl's magic helped keep him moving quickly. Each inspiration for movement came to him as needed, quickly replaced by the next.

It all ended much more quickly than he would have thought.

His hands clutching at the lip of the pit, J'role hauled himself up, staying flat against the ground. The darkness of night covered him like a thick blanket.

His breathing came quickly, less from strain than excitement. He tried to remember what had just happened, and the memories seemed distant, as if they'd happened years ago. He'd been so *alive* as he'd climbed up the pit wall that memories hadn't time to form.

He looked about and saw a few shadows of people walking about. Elves, he thought at first, but he wasn't sure; perhaps they were the thorn men. Trees towered overhead, and he could make out their leaves shifting in the wind, blocking his view of the stars. Several hundred yards away, at the center of the clearing, he saw the Queen Alachia's castle, gray now in the starlit night, gray like the flesh of a rotting corpse.

He heard nothing from the pit below, but knew that the girl—Releana—was waiting for him to do something. To rescue her and the old man. His father.

He looked about. It seemed safe enough.

But should he? He felt something new twisting inside of him now. Not the creature, which he heard breathing lightly in his thoughts, apparently content that J'role had escaped the pit. Not the thief magic, which of course was telling him to leave the dead weight behind. Releana could come, perhaps, for she had something to offer. But his father? His father, the thief magic insisted, was only a burden.

But even beyond the force of the thief magic came a desire to leave his father behind. He did not recognize its source at first, because he'd buried it so long ago. But it came to him as he lay at the edge of the pit, his cheek pressed against the cool dirt. The new thing inside him was, oddly, himself. Smart, strong. Growing. He didn't have to wait on his father. He wanted to test himself against the world without the burden of his father's despair and misery.

He could steal the ring back, travel on his own. Find Throal, somehow. Get the information he needed from the dwarfs. He could save the city. Get his voice back. He didn't need anyone else. The magic would support him. See him through the adventure.

From below came Releana's voice, softly calling for him. "Are you all right?"

Fury cut through J'role. How dare she take the chance of alarming the elves to his escape? What did she think he was doing?

J'role waved his hand over the top of the pit, signaling her to be quiet. Silence followed.

Now what? Leave them or help them?

"Go," said the creature in his thoughts.

The magic tugged at his muscles. Leave now, it said, before he began to feel sorry for his father.

His own instincts tumbled. He wanted to be free . . .

Suddenly an image came to him. It was the two of them: Releana and he walking across a field of grass, the world now regrown and green. They were older. Friends. They'd adventured for many years. Trusted each other. They now wore fine arms and armor.

They topped a ridge. Below them, a valley, stretching wide. A river wound through it, trees growing as thick as the elven wood. Within the sheltering darkness of the trees might be anything. Monsters, wild tribes of humans and trolls. Ancient ruins. Wealth and treasure and magic waiting to be discovered. Work to be done. And they would do it together. This valley would be their home, theirs to take and conquer. A base from which they would build their stories. Maybe J'role could speak; maybe he couldn't. It didn't matter. Releana didn't care. What mattered was that they had known each other for many years. A friendship forged in the midst of Blood Wood, many years before, when they had first started adventuring. . . .

He pressed his cheek close to the dirt, afraid to think any further. Such a thing . . . Could he actually have it? He felt tears build lightly in his eyes. He wanted it so much.

His father's stories . . .

"No," said the creature. "It is not for you, J'role." Something strange had entered the creature's voice. A touch of sincerity. Accidentally, J'role was sure. It knew something, had secret knowledge; knowledge of J'role's future.

No. Not his future. His heart.

"I want it," he begged the creature.

"Want all you want," the creature said lightly. The mirth came back into its voice, a humor poisoned like standing water. "I do not care, nor does the world. You shall not have what you want. Some people don't get to be happy, J'role. Didn't anybody tell you? Your father wanted to see the elves. But I don't think these were the circumstances he had in mind."

Fighting for comfort J'role said, "But he did see them . . ."

"Very well. And you'll find your valley. But don't be surprised if it's littered with the corpses of those you love."

J'role dug his fingers into the dirt. "Stop. Please, stop."

"Go. Leave your father and Releana. They *can't* mean anything to you. If they mean something, you'll only lose them. Why risk that pain?"

"I can have them now," J'role thought, and he brought himself up to a crouch, a new resolve entering his spirit, "They can make me happy now." He looked around. He would use a vine to bring them up, but he must keep them safe from the branches. He had to find a way to do that.

"What are you doing?" the creature asked with genuine surprise. "Your father's nothing but dead weight."

J'role's vision flooded red, and he froze. "He is my father!" he thought fiercely. "I want to bring him."

"Where was your father in your fantasy, boy? He didn't have a place in your little adventurers' group. He doesn't have a place in your life."

"Quiet . . ."

"That's right. No place in yours. But you have one in his, don't you? Servant. Wine-bearer. You clean him up when he vomits. You take the blows when he can't abuse himself anymore . . ."

J'role formed fists and punched himself in the face, over

and over. Appease the thing. Beat himself. It loved that. Make it stop talking. Choking back the gasps of pain, he slammed his knuckles again and again into his forehead and cheeks. He felt his face turning red, the dizziness coming over him as he held back his breath and accelerated the pace of the beating. Numb himself. Take all the pain away by rubbing the flesh raw. If there's nothing left that can feel . . .

The creature purred.

Enough? What would be enough?

He stopped, fell forward onto the ground, supporting himself on his hands and knees. The ground beneath him rocked like mead in a drunken man's goblet.

No more.

Please.

The creature said nothing. Content. Slumbering, as if sated with a full meal.

J'role raised his head. He heard nothing from the pit bottom, but he knew Releana waited. He would help, if only not to be alone with the creature.

Finding two long, thick branches, J'role carried them back to the pit, then placed one on top of the other over the pit's mouth. Next he found a sturdy vine long enough to stretch from a nearby tree all the way to the pit bottom. He tied one end of the vine around the tree, and then flung the rest over the crossing point of the two branches. Thus, the vine hung directly down the center of the pit, supported by the branches.

It had taken Releana and J'role hours to work out all the details, J'role using only hand signals and drawing pictures in the dirt, but they had come up with a plan. All he could do now was try.

In the darkness at the base of the pit he saw Releana tying the end of the rope around his father's waist. At her signal, J'role raised his father a few feet. He weighed little and came easily. Below, his father dangled right and then left, hanging from the rope at his waist.

Releana lay down on her back beneath Bevarden. Spreading her arms wide and exhaling forcefully she let out a powerful rush of air. The vine in J'role's hand went suddenly slack as his father rose upward, propelled swiftly by the column of air from Releana's spell. J'role quickly pulled the vine up, hand over hand, racing to jerk back on the slack.

The next thing J'role knew Bevarden had slammed into the branches that covered the pit, shooting right past the roots before they had time to grab him. It had worked!

Now all J'role had to do was get his father out of the pit.

The vine was taut, with Bevarden's weight supported by J'role's stiff grip. Soft moans of fear escaped his father's lips as he twirled right and then left, suspended over the dark chasm. The long roots snaked and reached for his father from the wall, but they could not reach him.

J'role let his fingers slide over the vine as he moved back to a tree a few feet behind him. There he tied the vine so that it held his father in place above the pit. Returning to the pit he clapped his hands softly to get his father's attention. In response Bevarden only whimpered.

Realizing he would get no help from his father, J'role set his mind to coming up with a new plan. A desire to simply run off and leave the useless man hanging began to bubble up in his thoughts, but he forced it away.

He realized he could control his father's position by carefully maneuvering the ends of each of the branches supporting him. By sliding two ends toward each other, J'role could move the point where the branches met toward the edge of the pit. As the intersection moved toward the edge, so would the vine, and so would his father.

He set to work, moving each branch closer to the other an inch at a time, fearful that if he moved them too quickly one might roll out of place and send his father plunging back into the pit. Slowly but surely the intersection of the branches came toward him, and his father's body approached.

Soon Bevarden hung only a foot away, the branches bending low under the uneven distribution of weight. J'role reached out and touched his father's head. Bevarden looked up, saw J'role, and smiled a child's grin. "Son," he said, surprising J'role. He'd thought his father couldn't recognize him anymore.

The thin, worn man reached out toward J'role, and his hands felt like well-worn leather. Too soft. They had the touch of death about them.

J'role helped Bevarden up, led him to a spot a few feet away and sat him down. Bevarden stared at his son, perhaps with pride, but J'role could not be sure. He was no longer able to read his father's face.

Returning to the pit, he lowered the vine to Releana, who waited with arms upraised. She tied the vine to her waist, and then J'role gave it a pull, lifting her a few feet off the ground. Facing down toward the dirt, she spread her arms wide as she had done before, and again exhaled forcefully. Once more, a terrible rush of air expelled from her mouth. The air crashed into the ground beneath her, spraying wet dirt upward. Then the massive blast of air rebounded straight into Releana, sending her up the pit.

Her ascent was not as vertically straight as Bevarden's had been, and she careened into the pit's wall. Roots lashed out at her and J'role heard her choke back a scream as the vine tugged wildly in his hand. No matter. The force of the air blast kept her moving up the pit, and he continuously hauled in the vine's slack, tossing it behind him as Releana's body raced toward him.

Suddenly the motion stopped and he heard her cry out in pain. Peering over the edge he saw her only a few yards down, hands clinging tightly to the vine. Several roots had wrapped themselves around her legs and waist. On her face was a mixture of pain and fear.

J'role swung around the edge of the pit to get better leverage from the branches. He could no longer see Releana, but he heard her soft whimpers of agony. He pulled as hard as he could but the roots would not give her up.

Again the thoughts came to him. Leave her. What did she mean to him? He had already saved his father. Wasn't that enough?

He almost gave in to the impulse to drop the vine and run off as quickly as possible, when he felt someone come up and grab him from behind. In his surprise J'role jumped and nearly let go of the vine. But then he recognized his father's hands. The hands wrapped themselves around the vine, and close to his ear his father whispered, "I'll . . ."

The voice trailed off, the thought incomplete. Then Bevarden began to pull, arms wrapped tightly around his son. Together they tugged as hard as they could.

A shriek came from the pit as the vine suddenly slackened, and J'role realized they had freed Releana from the roots. J'role and Bevarden hauled up on the vine as quickly as they could until Releana's hands came up over the edge of the pit. She climbed up over the edge, her legs bleeding with raw wounds.

J'role breathed a sigh of relief.

And then he heard the barking of the dogs.

17

His mother stepped toward him, dagger in hand. "No, no. Nothing to fear," she said. "It's all going to be all right now. Everything will be all right."

He turned to get away, to hide in his room, but she grabbed his wrist fiercely and snapped him back toward her. "I'm sorry," she said. "I'm so frightened." She held him close for a moment, then pulled back, the smile leaving her face. "Why did you do these things to me?"

J'role wanted to know why too, desperately wishing he knew how to stop hurting her. But he didn't have the answer.

Turning quickly, J'role saw two pairs of gleaming red eyes rushing toward him, moving low to the ground. One dog barked as it leaped through the air, trailing a mist of glowing red breath. Its night-black fur made it nearly invisible against the shadows; all he could see were the spectral eyes and mist floating from its mouth.

Releana looked up, spread her arms, puffed up her cheeks and exhaled, just as she had done in the pit. A rush of wind poured from her mouth and slammed into the dogs, sending the one in mid-leap back over on itself and then tumbling to the ground. The other dog continued its rush forward, going straight for Bevarden, who screamed like a child waking from a nightmare.

J'role's thief magic said, "Run!" Instead he threw himself at the dog attacking his father, tackling it, throwing his arms around its back. The two of them rolled off Bevarden and into the bushes.

J'role had never felt muscles as strong as those that now rolled and bucked against his arms and chest. The dog turned its head left and right, straining back as far as it could, snapping and growling at J'role. The teeth finally caught his forearm, and the animal bit deep. Though J'role wanted to scream in pain, he clamped down on the urge, afraid of releasing the voice of the creature inside him. The pain made him lose his grip, and the dog scrambled free.

It rose onto its hind legs and whirled around, its breath summer-hot on J'role's face. It barked once, then lunged forward. The moment stretched out; the burning eyes seeming to come at J'role's face forever, then he rolled out of the way and the dog bit down on empty air. Now closer, it reared back its head for another bite, when suddenly the flesh along its neck was pierced by a spray of long needles. Blood spattered J'role, some of it falling into his open mouth. The dog let out a cry and its eyes rolled back into it head.

"Over there!" someone in the distance called.

"They're coming," said Releana.

J'role tried to spit the blood out of his mouth, but the taste clung to his tongue. He looked around quickly. The two dogs lay on the ground, both pierced by dozens of long, thick splinters of dirt formed by Releana's magic. His father also lay on the ground, curled up like a child, whimpering softly.

"Not now," J'role thought.

"Now, and always," the creature said.

J'role rushed to his father's side and helped him up.

"What?" his father screamed, terror blazing in his eyes.

"There!" came another voice from the distance.

J'role clamped his hand over his father's mouth and pulled him up. Releana rushed ahead. At first J'role thought she was going to run off, but she waited for them to catch up. Then he saw that she was scouting their route, making sure they didn't rush into a thick wall of brambles.

Then came more shouts, the sounds of more dogs. The leaves and branches and bushes dragged at J'role, Releana, and Bevarden as they ran, catching their legs and clawing at their eyes and faces.

They ran for a few minutes when a thorn man suddenly sprang up from the ground, cutting them off from Releana. Bevarden said, "No, no, no."

J'role grabbed a thick stick from the ground and raised it in front of him. He swung it wildly, blocking the blows of the thorn man's magical spear. Whenever the tip of the spear hit the stick, the air crackled with blue-white light. The energy shot up J'role's hands, and his flesh became more and more numb after each blow.

Through the thorn man J'role saw Releana. She had her hands cupped, a small flame appearing between them. Then she gestured her fingertips toward J'role. A bolt of flame raced through the air, through the thorn man, and then wrapped itself around his stick. The red flames frightened J'role until he saw them parting around where his hand gripped the stick. He felt no heat from the flames. Releana had augmented the stick with magic.

The thorn man pulled back in fear too, though J'role did not know if it was the fear of a thinking person or of an animal panicked by fire. He swung the stick fiercely, the flames casting shifting red shadows among the branches and leaves of the forest.

The thorn man retreated a few more steps, and J'role pressed the attack. Though he knew little of the art of combat, the magic flames from the big stick seemed to help his blows. Red sparks flared up as he struck the thorn man, illuminating the bones of several birds in its bramble chest. J'role smiled at his success.

Yet even as he forced the thorn man back, a strange discomfort overtook him. Fighting so openly, with a weapon of bright fire, felt—*wrong*. There was no other way to put it. A desire crept through his flesh to retreat to the shadows, to hide from his attackers and strike when they least expected it.

The agitation in his body drove him to a fury. He struck wildly at the thorn man, one blow after another. He knocked the spear out of the creature's hands, and the thing stumbled to the ground. With a final, massive blow he smashed in the thorn man's head, and dozens of sparks floated up like fireflies into the night air.

Dropping the flaming stick, J'role looked around for Releana and his father.

He found Bevarden leaning against a tree a few feet away, weeping silently but apparently unharmed. The next moment he looked around for Releana, and was greeted with the sight of two thorn men springing up out of the ground to attack her. She stood about thirty feet away.

The backs of the thorn men were to J'role, and a surge of excitement coursed through his chest. Exactly, he thought, and picked up the spear dropped by the thorn man he had

fought. The weapon felt oddly balanced in his hands, but he
knew it would be more effective than his stick.

He rushed toward Releana's assailants, passing through
the shadows like air, his footsteps wrapped in silence. The
magic laughed inside him, seeing the perfection of his attack. Yes. J'role was certain he would hit.

Releana dodged the thorn men's blows. Ducking and
shifting left and right, she had not a moment's rest to prepare a spell. One of the thorn men slashed its spear against
her right arm, and a crackle of blue energy burst on her skin,
instantly leaving a black scar.

J'role reached her without having made a sound or leaving a trace of his movement. Even Releana did not spot him
through the gaps in the thorn man's body. He pulled his
spear back and drove its tip into the back of one of the thorn
men, wondering only at the last moment if such a weapon
could harm a creature made of branches and thorns.

But the spear's magical nature prevailed, and blue sparks
flew wildly from the tip as it plunged into the thing's body.
The creature's arms flew wide, its spear flung wildly away
from Releana. The thorn man collapsed to the ground, then
lay motionless. J'role whirled just in time to parry the thrust
of the other thorn man.

He heard Releana's voice, then flames sprouted at the tip
of his spear. J'role felt oddly giddy, and the moment seemed
to freeze in his awareness. Before him stood a creature made
of brambles and magic. He himself held a magic spear, now
made more powerful by the spell of a magician. Despite all
that had happened in his life, and no matter what would
come next, everything he might ever have wanted from the
fantastic had come his way.

His father hadn't lied at all. There was adventure in life.
J'role knew now, however, that one could not define the
terms of the adventure.

The thorn man stabbed his spear at J'role, and caught him
full in the arm. A horrible pain coursed through his flesh,
and he staggered back. Raising the spear just in time, he
blocked another blow, and then shoved the spear forward.
The creature leaped out of the way.

The maneuvers cost J'role his balance, nearly sending him
to the ground. He recovered just in time to dodge another
blow from the thorn man. Jumping away from the attack, he
whirled around and plunged his spear into the creature's

right shoulder. The sparks flew wild, and the creature reeled back.

The two of them stalked each other now, moving in a wide circle around an undefined point of contention. Behind the thorn man, J'role saw Releana grab dirt from the ground, speak a few magic words, and toss the dirt at the thorn man. The dirt transformed into the same kind of darts that had killed the dogs, but the darts passed harmlessly through the thorn man's hollow body.

The creature made a stab, then another. Each time J'role just barely dodged the attack.

Releana looked startled as she stared at some bushes back the way they'd come. J'role saw her wave her hands in the formation of another spell. A moment later an elf, his flesh pocked with thorns that pierced his flesh from the inside out, broke through the bushes, brandishing a sword and shouting, "Here, here!"

As J'role continued parrying with the thorn man, he saw Releana raise her hands again, and release another spell. A spear of ice formed under her fingertips and raced through the air. It slammed into the elf's chest, creating a red blossom on the elf's shirt of white petals.

In that instant the thorn man turned his focus from J'role, turning slightly toward Releana. J'role lunged forward and pierced the thorn man's chest, which began to glow white-hot as fire and sparks from the spear cut through it. The brambles exploded into flames as the thorn man fell apart and dropped to the ground.

"Come. We've got to go! Now!" Releana cried.

J'role hesitated. He wanted to go back and get the ring. He knew where it would be. On the shelves outside the elf queen's chamber with all the other gifts.

How could he leave the ring with the Alachia?

How could he leave her?

Without even thinking about it he began to walk back toward the castle. A hand caught his arm and he turned sharply. It was Releana, looking concerned and confused. "We have to *go!*" she whispered harshly. "The Blood Wood, all of it, belongs to the elves. There's no place to hide. I already made that mistake. We have to get out. Now."

He stared at her as if he'd never seen her before. Her words were full of practical, direct concern. Their abruptness seemed to pull him out of a dream. Yes. He had to go.

They had almost died just trying to escape. What hope did he have of sneaking back to the castle, getting to the Hall of Gifts, and then escaping from the forest? He could not even explain to Releana what he would be doing. He would have to take his father with him . . .

No. No. There was no way.

Releana tugged his arm again.

"What is it?"

Just everything, he thought. Just everything.

"Not everything," the creature in his thoughts said. "The ork told you where to go next. That kingdom. Throal?"

"Yes," thought J'role. "Throal."

"Exactly. He's probably still on his way. You can catch up to him."

"Yes. Yes. I can catch up."

Suddenly inspired, J'role went over to his father and took the man's hand. "The elves," Bevarden kept saying over and over, as if he'd lost a child. "The elves . . ."

The three of them pressed on in the darkness. Neither elves nor dogs nor any other creatures bothered them, but J'role saw the silhouettes of trees moving all during their seemingly endless trek through the night forest. Then Releana spotted spheres of light floating through the air, apparently looking for them. With each step, leaves and branches tugged at their clothes and scratched their flesh.

All J'role's wounds—from the spears, the roots in the pit, and the thorns of the elf queen—began to work deeper into his body. After a few hours he could barely stagger after Releana, who led Bevarden along in the night. He had no idea how long they had been traveling, though it seemed more than likely that they'd been wandering in circles. He had a waking nightmare of stumbling once more into the clearing where stood the great, living elven castle. There the elves surrounded him once more and threw him back into the pit.

J'role's face soon began to feel prickly and he heard things he knew could not be real—random words spoken by his mother, fragments of stories spoken by his father. But the words came so clearly that J'role thought he must be slipping in and out of the past, arriving in Blood Wood as if through some feverish nightmare—instead of the other way around.

"I'm sorry," his mother said to him. *"I'm so frightened."* She held him close . . .

. . . He was confused. The dark trees, the shadows on the ground . . .

A flash of metal . . .

Did Releana know where she was going?

"I want so much to see the elves," his father said.

No. His father *had* said. Right now, in Blood Wood, his father was crying softly.

"They're so beautiful. That's what my father told me, and his father before him. And now I tell you. They live in thick forests, and there is no being fairer or kinder than they. They are strict, but generous." His father looked away and up, as he so often did after J'role's mother had been killed. The elves were a replacement for her, giving him hope in a world without hope. *"I may not live to see them. But perhaps you may, J'role. What a thing, son. What a thing. What a thing to see the world."*

There in the elven Blood Wood, J'role hastened his steps, caught up with his father and Releana. He took his father's hand in his. Squeezed it. His father squeezed back.

They had traveled some short distance away from the forest before J'role realized that they'd left it. The stars, forming an eternal bowl of countless silver flecks, caught his attention first. That was wrong, he thought. He must have dreamed stars.

Then, he told himself, No, that's right. He looked up and around, saw the broad, barren expanse broken only by the mountains and hills in the distance. He could see and see and see. No trees towering overhead, no foliage blocking all sight.

He dropped to the ground and rubbed his hands in the dry, chalky dirt. Lovely. No life, no moisture. It was a land he understood. The forest, he thought, had tried to suck him into it; had tried to make him one more living thing among countless other living things. Here, on the dead soil, there was no confusion. He was himself, no more and no less.

"Grim?" someone said. Who?

He looked up. Yes. Releana. She stared down at him.

"Come. We've got to hide."

Yes. Hide. He had forgotten who he was hiding from, but it was good to hide.

Why did he answer to the name Grim? he thought, rising clumsily to his feet. His name was . . . what? What was his name?

A voice in his head said, "I think she's nicknamed you Grim. You are Grim. It's a good name."

"Yes." J'role thought. "I am Grim."

"Do you want to know what happened, all those years ago? What happened in the kaer? You've remembered more than I thought you ever would. You're so close. . . .Do you want to know?"

A tremor passed through J'role, and he felt his chin shaking in fear. He continued to walk, following his father, who now staggered after Releana's lead. But his thoughts froze. Did he want to know what happened, all those years ago?

A blackness swarmed over him. No. No. No. He did not want to know. He was too close. He'd remembered too much already, and all that he only wanted to forget.

*His mother, holding him, "Shhh. Don't tell anyone. . . .
You'll die if you . . ."*

"No," he said to the voice in his head. "No, don't tell me."

The creature said nothing. Purred.

Soon they reached some rocks piled up on the barren plain. "Here," Releana said, and J'role obeyed by lying down on the ground. Now he could truly rest, for which he was immensely grateful.

He spread out, pressing his face to the cool, dry earth. Home again. Home is lifeless. Home is safe. Home is where the heart is frozen.

18

She pulled him tight once more and he felt her body tense.
There was no doubt in his mind what she was going to do
with him. Do with the knife she held.

He did not struggle, did not pull away. She was his
mother, and he wanted so much to make her happy. To fi-
nally cease causing her so much pain. Whatever he had to
_do._

Why did his voice make her so sad? Why couldn't he
speak to people? Something had happened, but he couldn't
remember what.

Even in his dreams, your father's secrets within secrets re-
mained deeply hidden.

The sky above, now full of rain-bloated clouds, seemed to
swirl slowly. His body shook and ached, and he thought it
would be better to be dead.

"Then kill yourself," the creature in his thoughts said
wearily.

"Quiet," he told it.

Looking around, J'role saw his father staring up at the sky
and saying in a flat, detached voice, "Rain. Rain. Rain."

Beside J'role was the spear he had taken from the thorn
man during the fight in Blood Wood. He didn't remember
keeping it, but apparently he'd never loosened his grip on
the weapon.

Also lying on the ground was Releana, still asleep. It was
the first time J'role had seen her in full light, albeit the light
of a gray day. She wore an emerald green magician's robe,
now smeared and nearly hidden under a layer of mud. The
robe's pattern showed a person—a child, J'role thought—

running. The running child raced for a lone tree standing in leafless silhouette against the green background.

J'role had never seen such a stark magician's robe before. It chilled him, though he did not know why.

Releana's long black hair was loose around her face, her features as plump as the rest of her. Compared to the sharp edges of the elf queen, Releana's soft curves were wonderfully appealing. He wanted to roll over and snuggle up against her.

But even that seemed like too much effort. Skin raw and muscles brittle, J'role could do no more than close his eyes and fall back to sleep.

Releana had built a fire. J'role drew as close as he dared, trying to warm his body, which felt chilled to the bone. Bevarden still stared up at the sky. "Rain," he muttered.

"Feeling any better?" Releana asked, sitting down beside J'role. She, too, was wounded, her legs covered with thick welts, and on her arm the strange black scar from the thorn man's spear.

J'role shook his head.

"Well, you will soon. The wounds are clean now. You just need time." She sounded confident, but J'role knew she was lying. Releana couldn't know for sure. Without a healer he might well die. They both might. Wounds were like that. They started as one obvious point of penetration, and if they didn't kill you immediately, they often festered slowly, draining all the life out of you, corrupting your health until . . .

Until what? How did you actually die? J'role didn't know. Maybe your body just got too tired to go on.

A drop of rain plinked against his temple, startling him. His muscles tightened, but instead of the deluge he expected, the rain began slowly. Big drops that splashed into the fire and fizzled with steam. They landed on his face, cold at first, but soothing somehow. He raised his hand to his forehead and smeared the drops over his cheeks, across his lips, and onto the tip of his tongue.

Bevarden tilted his head back and opened his mouth wide. J'role did the same, rolling onto his back. The drops fell into his mouth at unexpected moments, but they tasted wonderful.

"I've never seen you do that before," Releana said, her voice teasing.

J'role looked at her, puzzled and curious.

"Smile," she said. "It's the first time I've seen you smile. You are often Grim, but I'm glad to see you've got more to you than that."

He looked away, uncertain how to respond. *Unable* to respond. Why was the creature in his head . . . ?

Seeing his deep concentration, she changed the subject with a bright tone, "So? Where are we headed now? Do you have a goal, or were you just wandering like I was? Each has its advantages and disadvantages, and I'm not saying one is better than the other. But if there's some place you're going, and you wouldn't mind, I'd like to come along with you. If that would be all right with you. I mean, I don't have a destination, and I'll tell you," she said smiling, "I'd sure like to have some place to go."

He hadn't thought about that: about her actually coming along. How would he explain it? How *could* he possibly explain it all to her? How could he communicate the enormous complications of a magical ring, a hidden city, the strange, blind wizard with the eye in his hand, the one-eyed ork, and so on . . . Just thinking about it overwhelmed him.

He decided to start with little bits of information. She was a magician. She was smart. J'role figured she'd be able to put some of it together herself.

He propped himself up on one arm and raised his other hand a few feet off the ground.

Releana looked at him quizzically, then her face lit up as she realized he was trying to answer her question.

"A child?" she asked.

He shook his head.

"A short stick? A wand! No? Longer? A staff!"

He shook his head and rolled back onto the ground, already frustrated.

"No, no, no," she said quickly, her voice happy and excited. "We just need to make up more rules. Listen, when I get closer, point your thumb up. When I start guessing worse, point your thumb down. Now. Is a child closer than a wand?"

J'role propped himself back up. She waited for his response, leaning in hungrily, a child waiting for the next round of a game. He found that he liked her immensely.

He held his thumb up.

"A child. It's like a child. A person?"

He mimed stroking a beard, just as he'd seen his father do years ago, in the kaer, when telling a story about dwarfs.

"An old man!"

He raised his hand again, then lowered it closer and closer to the ground.

"A small old man!"

He shook his head.

"A dwarf!"

Her correct guess startled him for a moment, and then he smiled. It had worked. And it hadn't been too difficult.

"You're going to see a dwarf?" she asked.

Not exactly, he thought. How do I communicate Throal?

He did it just as he had communicated dwarf. With patience.

"I've . . . the dwarven kingdom. Actually, I've never seen a dwarf. Only heard about them. Strange, isn't it. I'm speaking to you with their language, but I have no connection with them. Or, I have a strong connection with them, but it's so strong I'm not even aware of it. I'm babbling. Sorry." She stood quiétly for a moment.

J'role realized that she wanted to talk to him. He was supposed to answer. A *conversation*. Not his father's incessant apologies and dreams, but an actual exchange. At the same time, unable to do anything about it, he felt his fever winding its way its way into a headache. The pressure to interact was too much to bear.

"Why do you keep doing that?" she asked, abruptly curious.

He looked at her, exaggerating the confusion on his face so she'd know he had no idea what she was talking about.

"Look like that, I mean. So upset. You're always so serious. Not always. But you seem to retreat to it all the time. Retreat? Is that what I mean?" She thought about her question for the briefest of moments, then answered herself. "Yes. That's what I mean. Retreat. I called you Grim as a joke. But you seem too—serious. I don't know." She drew in a breath and looked at him.

Her words made him feel bad, though he didn't know exactly why. Then he realized that the words struck a chord because they were true. He was often serious. And all he wanted was to be light-spirited.

He could not speak, so he said nothing.

"I'm sorry," she said, realizing she'd depressed him even more.

The words, echoing his father's perpetual refrain, sent a buzz of frustration through his head. The last thing he wanted was to be responsible for making Releana sound like his father. He got up quickly and took her hand in his. Looking into her eyes he shook his head slightly.

As he touched her hand he realized how good it was to have someone near him who actually paid him enough attention to tell him the truth about himself, even if it was truth he didn't particularly like. How else was he going to know how others saw him? How else would he know if his behavior was actually different from what it could be?

Could be?

Yes. Exactly. He was serious all the time because it was his defense against all that had happened to him in his life. He'd assumed it was the only way to survive. Releana questioned his seriousness. Implicit in the question was the notion that he didn't have to be serious.

She assumed he could be happy. She wouldn't have asked the question otherwise.

She met his gaze briefly, then looked down at their hands, then removed her hand from his. J'role sat back down, almost disappointed to lose her touch, but not really. Someone had really paid attention to him. It was so wonderful in itself.

"I ... uh ...," she began, faltering. He smiled at her. In the two days they'd known each other it was the first time he'd seen Releana at a loss for words.

He raised his hands, waving them, signaling that she dismiss her concerns. She stopped trying to talk and he stood up, carefully. When he was up he gestured for her to sit down. She did.

With Releana and his father watching, J'role began to do something he'd never done before. He began to tell a story, just as his father had done in the kaer years earlier. His father had used words, but he had also portrayed all the people and creatures with his body. Drawing on the memory of his father's talents, J'role began to tell Releana of the day he stood in his village seeing Garlthik One-Eye approach. He mimed how they had met and later gone to Brandson's Tavern, and how J'role had seen Garlthik gazing spellbound at the ring on the stairs at Brandson's.

As he introduced new elements of the story, he and Releana played a guessing game of nouns and words until she guessed correctly. It took time, but she was curious and energetic and full of life and loved the challenge of figuring out what J'role was doing.

Hours passed and the rain continued to fall. His father applauded. The day wore on. J'role told his story.

That night the rain stopped and the clouds dispersed, leaving the stars clean and shiny in their wake. Stretched out on the ground, Releana and J'role and Bevarden stared up at the sky, a fire crackling beside them.

Earlier that day Releana had gone off to one of the copses that circled Blood Wood, later returning with enough berries to feed them well.

J'role had not been so happy in a long time. Doing something other than glowering provided its own energy.

Releana said, "My parents were killed by a Horror two years ago. I had already started my apprenticeship as the village wizard. But just a few months ago ... I don't know ... I didn't want to be around the death anymore." She turned to him. "Does that make sense?" She did not wait for a reply. "Death is strange. So I left. I've been wandering, waiting for something to happen. Something exciting, I mean. When I came to Blood Wood, I didn't know what it was. The elf queen asked me for my gift. I didn't have anything. She threw me into the pit. I thought the elves were supposed to be nicer."

"The world," Bevarden intoned to no one in particular, "is dying."

J'role thought that an odd statement. Hadn't the world been growing itself back from near devastation in the past few decades? Or maybe that didn't matter. Maybe deeper down it was dying. Maybe it was already dead and no one knew it yet.

"No," said Releana. "Parts of it are dead. Our parts. But there's life out there."

Bevarden began a coughing fit. Blood came up from his mouth and fell on the ground in thick drops. Releana and J'role both got up and held him. J'role rocked his father.

"We've got to get him to a questor of Garlen," said Releana.

J'role nodded. His father quieted.

"So we're going to Throal?"

J'role nodded again, smiling and relieved. She hadn't yet said she would travel with him. Now he was glad to hear she would.

"Good."

They sat up with Bevarden until he fell asleep. At one point Releana extended her hand and squeezed J'role's. "You're nice," she said. Then, with a laugh, she added, "I'm glad we were miserable together. We might never have met."

They walked south toward Throal. All three were weak, but the need for help and food and healing drove them on.

Releana talked. "The ring makes people care very much about it. And thus keeps people searching for the city."

J'role nodded again, this time listening carefully to Releana. He liked it when she reasoned. He'd never met anyone who did it so intensely.

"So, when you wore this ring, you wanted to find the city?" she said.

J'role nodded, confirming what he had told her the day before.

"It made you long for the city," she said thoughtfully. Then she suddenly added, "A geas!"

J'role touched her arm, then shrugged when she looked at him.

"A geas ... it's a spell. A powerful one. I haven't the faintest idea how to do one, but I've heard about them. But never one like this ..."

She started to drift off into thought, but J'role tugged her arm again.

"Sorry. Thinking. A geas ... It commands a person to go on a quest. If I cast a geas on you, and command you to go find a particular magic sword, you will go off and find that sword. Whether you want to or not. You *do* want to." Her hands were moving quickly in the air now, as if she were casting a series of spells as she spoke. "You want to so much that it's ... it's like being in love. And not fulfilling your quest is like having your love rejected. It hurts terribly. It hurts so much you become ill. But if you fulfill the quest, everything is right in the world."

She fell silent just long enough to draw in air.

"Anyway. I've never heard of a transferable geas before. I mean, the spell is cast upon a person or a group of people. That's it. I give you, Grim, a quest. And you do it. But this ring ... It seems to pass the quest on from one person to the next. Do you still want to find the city now?"

He thought about it. Yes. But not as intensely as when he wore the ring. He didn't know how to express that. But he knew what she was getting at; he definitely felt differently about Parlainth when he'd possessed the ring. He shook his head no.

"But you still want to get the ring?"

He thought about that. Yes. Very much. Why, though? he wondered. Because he wanted the longing for the city to come back. He wanted his soul tied into the quest for the city. He nodded.

"So the ring doesn't pass on the geas. But it leaves a memory with all the wearers. They all want to own the ring. And if you own the ring, you want to find the city."

This revelation troubled J'role. The longing had been so intense he'd thought it was just his and Garlthik's. To discover that everyone had felt it ... Mordom and perhaps countless others ... It made him feel stupid. It cheapened it.

Of course, Releana could be wrong.

"Of course, I could be wrong. As I said, I've never heard of anything like this before. It would take a great deal of magic, a knowledge far beyond that possessed by any other magician I've ever met."

J'role gestured behind them, toward the elven Blood Castle.

"The elves ... ?" Releana asked.

J'role nodded. Queen Alachia had said as much.

A moment passed in the still darkness, and then Releana said with quiet excitement, "The elves made the ring."

He nodded again.

"Well, it would still be hard, even for them. But with enough time. And enough elves working on it ... But what's it for?"

"It's for drinking," said Bevarden, his tone ugly. His mood had begun to shift unpleasantly in the last few hours.

Releana said, "Well, it's to make people find the city. That's it."

J'role tugged on her arm once more, and shrugged again.

"Right," she said. "Why would they create a ring to do that? If they wanted to know where it is, why didn't they just send someone out to find it? Maybe they don't like to leave Blood Wood. But then how did the ring get outside Blood Wood?"

Releana fell silent. J'role thought, If the elves made the ring, how did it get outside Blood Wood? Then he remembered what the elf queen had told him: the elves had made the ring hundreds of years earlier. Before the Scourge. Probably even before the city was lost. But then why did the elves build a ring to find something that wasn't hidden?

19

His father came home just as his mother pulled the blade back to slay J'role. The door opened and his mother froze, a thief caught in the act, not knowing what to do next.

Bevarden stood smiling at them, for a moment not realizing what was happening, seeing only his wife holding his son close.

When he saw the blade in her hand, his face blossomed into horror. Rushing forward, he wrestled her to the ground, knocking the knife from her hand.

She began screaming, crying for J'role's death. She clawed at Bevarden, tears streaming down her face.

Through the open door her shouts and screams carried out into the corridors of the kaer. Within moments other people began to arrive, thinking a Horror might have invaded the kaer. They entered the room and saw the knife on the floor. Saw Bevarden pinning his wife down. Heard J'role's mother screaming for her son's death.

J'role backed into a corner. A woman from the kaer came over and picked him up, held him tight.

Charneale arrived, tall and imposing, and everyone stepped aside to let him pass. He studied J'role's parents as if from a great distance. Then he waved his hands, and in an instant J'role's mother fell unconscious. Startled, Bevarden turned to look at Charneale, fear weaving itself across his face.

"Your wife," the magician said dryly, "is no longer herself, is she?"

Bevarden only stared at J'role.

Subsisting on plants and insects, they traveled a few hours a day, enough to keep increasing the distance between themselves and Blood Wood, but slow enough to give themselves a chance to rest and heal. After five days the wounds had scabbed, the fevers had passed, and it looked as if no elves had followed them. With a clear sky above, they walked a half day south toward Throal, and then traveled another full day after that. Each time they topped a hill all they could see waiting ahead were more dry, rolling hills.

J'role never lost his desire to get the ring, but kept telling himself he no longer needed it. It was the only way to resist the impulse to abandon the others and return to Blood Wood. He also reminded himself that it was the dwarfs who built the stones for the city, and if the stones were the source of the magic, then the dwarfs might have the answer to rescuing the city. And his ultimate goal was, of course, to find the city.

"If they built it four to five hundred years ago, as the elf queen said, it would have been just before the Scourge began," Releana said. She spent more and more time talking about the mystery of the ring, chipping away at the ring's puzzle, trying to find the one crucial crack that would reveal all. She moved her hands the whole time, as if drawing elaborate diagrams in the air for future reference. "Let's go over it again. The ring makes you want to find this city . . ."

J'role nodded.

"Was it ever really there? I mean, were you seeing something from—I don't know, another plane?—or was it a city that used to be there, and you were seeing its ghost?"

J'role thought about it. The words he had spoken did not seem to paint a picture of a city the Horrors might have built, though of course he could not be sure. But he held up two fingers, indicating the latter possibility.

"Second . . . You were seeing a ghost. Then where did it go? Cities don't die. They don't haunt places. Also, you spoke to people, describing this city when you wore the ring?"

J'role nodded.

"But from what you've indicated to me, this city is tremendous. The Therans are the only other people who have achieved that scale of architecture and magic."

"Therans," Bevarden echoed to himself.

"And why has no one heard of the city? You said the ork thought the magician—Mordom—knew something about it. But I've never heard of it. And neither have you."

J'role stopped, furious. He felt her taking away his hope. He grabbed Releana by the shoulder, and pointed at his eyes.

"No, no. You saw it. I believe you. But why does no one remember—"

He made the symbol for the elf queen.

"That's right. You said she remembered."

He nodded vigorously, still angry. Then he recalled that it was in holding the ring that the elf queen's memory of it suddenly returned. And it was only after wearing the ring that she had remembered the name of the city. *Parlainth,* she had said. He raised his hand, indicating a stop in the conversation, then shook his head.

"She didn't?"

He shook his head, then mimed putting the ring on, then nodded.

She said, "The ring made her remember."

He nodded.

"But it doesn't make sense that she wouldn't remember it before. If she helped make the ring . . ."

"Hide what you hold most dear," Bevarden said.

Releana and J'role stopped walking, but Bevarden continued placidly along, looking sometimes at the clouds above and sometimes at the flowers that struggled to crack the surface of the dirt.

Releana raised her hands to her head and rubbed her fingers against her temples. "Oh, my."

"They hid the city," J'role thought.

"From the Horrors," Releana said. "They hid the city from the Horrors."

J'role felt the creature slide across his thoughts, but it said nothing.

"The entire city," Releana whispered. "And then they made everyone forget about it. There may have been records of it. Maybe they used magic to wipe away all records of it."

The implications sent vertigo through J'role's body and mind.

"They removed all traces of themselves, not only moving their home somewhere else, perhaps to another plane, but even taking away all thoughts and memories. Not only would the Horrors be unable to find the city during the Scourge, but neither could they possess some person outside the city and find out that the city was hidden by reading the person's thoughts. Safe. Very safe."

"But what about the ring?" wondered J'role, and he formed his fingers into an *O*, their symbol for the ring.

Releana paced in a tight circle. "That's it!" she said excitedly. "That's the key. Maybe to get the magic to work there was one big, magical cost: they couldn't get back by themselves. They and the city were trapped wherever they are. Only someone on the outside can bring them back. But no one on the outside knows what happened. Doesn't even know about them, for reasons of security. If they told someone four hundred years ago, 'Come get us when the Horrors are gone,' the secret could have been exposed. So they had to come up with a subtler way of getting 'rescued' from their hiding place."

"The ring of longing," J'role thought.

"Whoever touches the ring wants to find the source of the longing. They'll work to solve the mystery, just like you did. And the ork. And the magician. It'll be slow going at first, but they'll work to do it."

J'role smiled. He was going to rescue the city.

Releana saw his smile and smiled back. "Much better," she said.

The happiness left J'role within a few hours. He kept his concerns to himself as they walked, his face a neutral mask. But inside his thoughts he asked the thing in his head, "Am I leading you to the city? Is that why you want to help me find it?" Although the Scourge had ended and most of the Horrors had gone away, many of the creatures, like the one in J'role's thoughts, remained. Would they attempt to attack the city if it returned to the world?

The creature said nothing. J'role knew it did not matter. Would he have believed the thing, no matter what it said?

And did it matter? If Horrors still roaming the world were to locate the city—Parlainth—wouldn't the city have enough power to beat them back? After all, the people of Parlainth had successfully hidden themselves from the all-out assault, not just a few monsters.

J'role comforted himself with that thought. Thinking any other way might make him want to give up searching for the city. And if he did that, the people of Parlainth would not be grateful to him for saving them, and they would not help him remove the creature from his thoughts. Then where would he be? He needed to move forward and hope or else the creature's prompting of suicide would take its toll.

A mist had settled over the land by the time J'role woke. A thin layer of water covered his skin, while an endless barrier of gray spread out in all directions. He got up and woke the others, and soon they were on their way, eager to get moving and warm up their bodies.

The mist dissipated as the sun came up. On they walked, a little further until they realized they were approaching the lip of a valley. Across a broad emptiness they saw land covered with green trees and grass. Bushes and plants dotted the ground where they walked.

When they reached the lip of the valley they were met by an astounding sight. The ground sloped down, rushing toward the base of the valley. Trees and grass covered the sides of the valley, but J'role was delighted to see that the greenery was not as dense and writhing with life as in Blood Wood.

At the center of the valley ran a chalk-blue river at least a mile across. Hovering above it was a thin layer of mist that coiled its way through the air like myriad wary snakes. To the right and to the left the river ran on, winding out of sight as the valley curved tightly in either direction.

"The Serpent," Releana said with awe. "It just keeps going. It goes on forever. That's what my mother told me. It just keeps going."

J'role could not fit such an image into his head. Instead he focused on the section of the river below him, and the sight was no less startling than the idea of an endless river.

Rising out of the river grew spires made of stone, grouped in tight clusters. The river's current crashed against the spires, washing around them in a thick spray on either side. Just below the surface of the water J'role saw the base of the towers spread out, becoming wider, as if they led to underwater fortresses. Docked at one of the spires was a big ship with a huge, broad wheel made up of several dozen paddles at its rear. It seemed to J'role that the wheel must have something to do with how the ship moved, but he could not tell how.

The upper decks of the ship looked more like a large hill carved with dozens and dozens of caves, though the ship was in fact built of wood. No stairs led up to any of the doors, but ropes hung from countless vertical and horizontal poles growing out of the ship; it seemed that these were intended to provide access to the doors for people who felt comfortable climbing and swinging. The ship was painted bright blue and green, giving it a festive air. A word written in glyphs J'role could not understand was painted near the front of the ship.

"Look," said Releana, and J'role turned in the direction she pointed. Another ship, this one red, black, and gold, moved upriver toward the docked ship. The wheel at the ship's rear turned, and J'role realized that the paddles on the wheels pushed the ship forward, using the water as a momentary brace. Thick clouds of smoke poured from chimneys scattered without any apparent pattern or design across the top of the ship.

J'role saw no sign of anyone on board the new ship, but looking back at the first ship, he noticed a sudden flurry of activity. A dozen thin people swarmed out from the spire where the ship was docked. The sun caught their green-scaled skin and bright yellow hats and bright red jerkins. From the water came more of the creatures. They bobbed up to the surface of the water, grabbed the ends of ropes hanging into the river from the ship's poles, and rushed up them like squirrels scaling trees. Thin tails swished behind them. They swung in wide arcs on the ropes, then used their tails to catch other ropes to swing further along the ship.

Now J'role could see reptilian sailors also scampering about on the second ship as well. Large, long black tubes appeared from the windows, all pointed toward the first ship. Sailors were all over the roofs and walls and ropes of both ships now, all jumping up and down and waving swords and shouting at one another.

The sailors of the docked ship pulled in the ropes that tethered their vessel to the spire. The paddle wheel began to turn, and smoke poured out of the ship's randomly placed stacks.

Suddenly the red, black, and gold ship's black tubes began to billow red flames and black smoke. The crack of thunder rolled out across the river and echoed along the valley. Huge balls of fire rushed through the air toward the blue and green ship, but then fell short and crashed into the water. Giant plumes of steam rose into the air like illusory pillars.

A tremendous cry went up from the sailors on the blue

and green ship. Their vessel banked right, revealing an array of black tubes just like the one on the attacking ship. The smoke poured out faster from the ship's chimneys as the vessel picked up speed, traveling a path that kept the fire cannons pointed at the red, black, and gold ship's bow, which was mounted with few fire-cannons. The red, black, and gold ship turned wide, trying to escape the barrage of fireballs that would certainly be coming . . .

But too late. The blue and green ship cut loose a volley of shots that ripped through the air, half finding their target as the distance between the ships continued to close. Six fireballs ripped into the red, black, and gold's upper decks, with two more crashing into the ship just above the water line. Another cry went up from the sailors on the blue and green vessel.

Fires erupted on the struck ship, and J'role saw one of the sailors raise his hands to cast a spell. The incantation brought a huge wave of water rising up from the river and splashing down over some of the flames.

The fires spread as the ship continued its turning. Coming about, it fired three more small volleys, simply trying to keep the blue and green ship at bay. Soon it had turned completely around to beat a retreat downriver, even as its sailors continued to combat the flames.

J'role thought the blue and green ship might pursue, but instead it turned and headed back for the spire where it had been docked.

Releana and J'role looked at each, at first with surprise, and then with broad smiles. "I never heard about anything like this before," said Releana.

J'role had. His father had told the people in the kaer about the t'skrang years and years ago. But J'role knew so little that he didn't bother trying to mime it out for Releana.

"Ah. Some of it is still here. What will become . . . ?" his father said, and then fell into silence.

Releana looked quizzically from Bevarden to J'role, then shrugged. "If we're going to get across the Serpent," she said, "we'd better find out who those sailors are. Because I don't see how we're going to do it without their help."

J'role tugged on her sleeve. When he had her attention, he pointed at each of them and then across the river.

"Yes. We have to . . . Look." She pointed downriver. It took J'role a moment, but then he saw. Shrouded behind a white mist in the distance was a huge range of mountains. "That must be where the kingdom of Throal is. I can't imagine there being a bigger mountain range in the world." Her voice became excited as she spoke of the mountains. And looking at them, J'role could understand why. They *were* huge, and the way they were wrapped in mist seemed to promise something magical. All that was visible of the mountains were vague, hazy blue shapes. The peaks rose into the clouds and out of sight, seeming to ascend all the way up to wherever the sky ended—perhaps touching the stars themselves.

The dwarven Kingdom of Throal.

J'role did not know any longer which mattered more. Rescuing Parlainth or reaching the mountain kingdom across the Serpent.

I could do both, he thought, and smiled.

Laughing, Releana said, "Grim is happy again. I'm going to have to get him another name."

J'role grinned back. Another day, a day only two weeks ago, he would have become angry. Her teasing would have made him afraid, and his fear would have aroused the need to stay separate and become indignant. But not now.

"Son," his father said abruptly, "where is your mother?" Bevarden looked around as if she might just have wandered off for a moment.

An echo of loneliness passed through J'role's heart, and he saw the smile quickly leave the face of his companion. Releana had asked about his mother the other day, and he had communicated that she was dead.

He took his father's hand in his, and felt it shaking. A tremor of fear crawled up his own flesh, and he wondered how much of his life would be taken up sharing the loss of his mother with his father. Grim his name would remain for some time.

The valley's side was steep in spots, but many trees grew from the sloped ground. They traveled with relative ease by sliding down from one tree to the next. Bevarden was often afraid to rush down to the next tree, but Releana gently coaxed him down the slope.

J'role knew he could have used the magic to move with greater ease. It would surely be easier to climb down a slope than to climb up a vertical pit with writhing roots. But he knew the magic would draw him away from the others. And even in his silence, he enjoyed being with them.

Soon the work of getting down the hill had him sweating and breathing faster. Focusing his mind on getting from tree to tree, he turned the work into a game. With the thorn man's magic spear held at his side, J'role raced down to the next tree with Releana to prepare to catch Bevarden. Soon they were nearly slamming into the trees in their efforts. Releana laughed out loud; J'role, for fear of releasing the creature, did not, but smiled broadly. Once more his despairing thoughts left him, shunted out by physical concerns, and he remembered that back in his village he used to run to feel better.

Motion was his ever-present friend.

After half an hour the slope of the valley became gentle. Slowing their pace, both J'role and Releana began to limp, the effects of their wounds taking a toll after their spirited exertions.

From beyond the trees they heard the continuous running of the river. They walked on for another twenty minutes, the water getting louder, becoming something just under a roar.

Then J'role heard voices in the distance. He raised his hand for the group to stop. Releana did so, taking Bevarden's hand to keep him calm in the face of whatever would happen next.

20

---

*His mother cried softly. Charneale closed his eyes and said,
"I've suspected for some time that something had entered
the kaer. You are to be respected, Bevarden Storyteller, for
your attempts to protect the woman you love. But that is not
who she is anymore. Or at least, that is what I suspect. We
will take her and examine her."*

*The woman holding J'role thought he was being very
brave in the face of all the noise and screaming—and the
dagger. It had look as if the mother had actually intended to
actually kill her own son. J'role was stiff and lifeless and
very well-behaved.*

*All the while his impulses were telling him to squirm his
way out of the woman's arm and somehow protest his mother's innocence. It was all his fault, that much he knew.*

But he was so frightened. He really did not want to die.

J'role, spear in hand, moved forward silently toward the
voices. The trees at the base of the river valley provided excellent cover, but he let the magic seep through his muscles
and bone anyway. Within seconds the feeling of closeness he
had shared with Releana dissolved, and he wondered for a
moment why he had indulged in it. The strength that came
from the magic, the knowledge that he would be safe as long
he looked after only himself, far outweighed any benefit he
gained from being with her. Though he might travel with her
as it suited his need, he saw no reason to let her matter to
him beyond that.

He moved forward, his senses once again reaching out
into the world. His feet intuitively stepped over twigs and
around rocks and he made not a sound. Working his way

through the bushes, J'role noiselessly pushed them out of the way.

After traveling a bit he came to a wide brown road. One way led down to the river, for he could clearly see the Serpent framed by the trees, the sunlight shimmering off the swift-running water. The other way led through the trees, and J'role assumed the road worked its way up to the valley's top in an easier fashion than the route he had taken to get down.

Up the road, away from the water, he saw a group of six people walking toward him. The first three wore no more than rags. Around their necks were collars of leather, and their arms were held behind their backs; most likely tied to their collars. They bent their heads low, and their feet barely shuffled over the ground as they walked.

Behind them . . .

Behind them walked Mordom, Phlaren, and Slinsk. Phlaren looked serious as she held the leashes of the three bound prisoners. Mordom's spirits seemed high.

"No, it doesn't matter where they're going," Mordom said, his eyes white and blind, his hand raised high so he could walk safely. "They were heading south. They'll have to get across the Serpent, and so will we."

"How much do you think we'll get for them?" asked Slinsk.

"At least passage across. Maybe some food."

"That would be good," said Phlaren.

They were only a few feet away now, and J'role tucked himself under a bush and stayed out of sight as they passed.

Slinsk asked, "What about Garlthik?"

Mordom answered, "What about him?"

"I want another stab at him."

"He's clever, that ork. Cleverer than I would have guessed. I don't think he's worth my trouble. And I suggest you think the same thing. He's gone now."

Phlaren said, "He keeps turning up."

"No more," Mordom said with certainty. "He's halfway out of Barsaive by now. He didn't speak with the elf queen. Has no idea which way the brat went."

Their voices became softer and softer as they moved on. Slinsk said, "All right. I just want that ring back. Wearing that ring is even better than thinking about shredding Garlthik's flesh with my blade."

"I still think that elf was lying . . . ," began Phlaren.

"The elf *queen* would not lie to me. If she said the boy stole it back, then he stole it back."

Slinsk and Phlaren exchanged looks behind the magician's back. Then Slinsk asked, "What makes you so certain?"

Mordom shrugged. "I have my reasons."

"You have some secret to tell her in that private meeting you had with her," said Slinsk.

J'role could not hear Mordom's reply.

When they had gone too far to hear, he crept back to the others. When Releana asked what he had seen, J'role raised his hand and pointed to the center of his palm. "Oh," she said.

J'role pointed to himself, then indicated the direction in which Mordom and the others had gone. Then he pointed to them, and pointed to himself. Without waiting another moment, he started back for the road, hearing Releana gasp, "What?"

When he reached the road, J'role moved cautiously, but fast enough that he would catch up with Mordom. Glancing over his shoulder he saw Releana and his father following. Releana kept her pace slow, and J'role knew she had figured out what he'd meant—he would follow Mordom, and they would follow him.

Coming to a bend in the road he slowed down, raising his hand for the others to stop. When he had made the turn and saw Mordom and the others still far ahead, he signaled his companions to continue. Then he moved along the roadside, ducking in and out of bushes.

The road ahead dipped down, and Mordom's group vanished from sight as they reached the Serpent's edge. J'role ran quickly. When he reached the top of the dip he saw that the road led down to a wooden dock painted bright green, purple, and red. He wondered if the colors referred to the ships, and if a huge green, purple, and red ship owned the dock.

Mordom's group reached the dock, where many other people waited. Most of them were human except for a few orks. Some had carts loaded with goods, others stood beside large boxes, which J'role assumed had been delivered by carts that had already come and gone.

J'role had enough time to take in this impression of the scene when behind him he heard footsteps. He turned to find

Releana and his father, whom he motioned into the shelter of the trees and bushes to the right of the road. They made Bevarden sit down against a tree a few yards back. The man was pale and almost skeletal, his breathing shallow, his body shaking as if very, very cold. It occurred to J'role that his father was dying. Dying quickly. It wasn't just the wounds and the exertion of running and the lack of food. It was the drinking, and the lack of it. It was his life.

J'role started to feel very bad, and discovered he didn't want to. The thief magic offered him a choice. He took it. He closed off all his feeling for his father. He turned and headed back toward the slope to see what Mordom was up to. Releana followed.

Even hidden behind some bushes they had a clear view of the dock. J'role noticed that the other travelers and merchants had moved away from Mordom and his companions and the three prisoners on Phlaren's leashes.

A single, loud note carried over the waters of the Serpent, and J'role raised his gaze to see the blue and green riverboat approaching. The people on the dock began to bustle about, preparing themselves and their wares. Mordom, however, stood placidly, almost like a ruler of the land, his body straight, but unconcerned.

Within a few minutes the riverboat docked, and a dozen t'skrang men and women dressed in outlandishly gaudy colors swung down to the docks on the ropes that hung about the ship. On their hips they wore scabbards with thin swords. The sailors cheered and cried out in excitement, as if they loved nothing more in life than docking ships. They grabbed lines and tied them to the dock's pylons; they prepared the entrance ramp to the ship's belly; they danced a little.

Seen closer now, the strange bodies of the creatures disturbed J'role. Their long, thin tails twitched back and forth, and he was keenly aware of the long row of bones that must extend from the sailors' spines down to the tips of the tails. Their large eyes moved independently of each other, taking in details from all over the dock. And as they stood stock-still in neat rows, the jerky, segmented movements of their hands, necks, and arms were boldly accentuated.

Mordom stood unimpressed during the whole proceeding. One man, his cart stacked with goods, and two orks, greeted several sailors with handshakes, receiving big smiles in re-

turn. The reptilian features of the t'skrang looked friendly
somehow. They had large eyes, like a child's, and their
snouts were rather cute.

As soon as they had secured the riverboat at the dock, the
sailors suddenly leaped around and did handsprings and
backflips, eventually forming up into two neat rows running
the length of the dock. At one end of the rows stood all the
merchants and traders and potential passengers. The rows
led to a ramp that had extended out from the ship and now
rested on the dock.

Without warning the sailors whipped out their swords and
cried, "Ah-ha!"

Everyone on the dock jumped except the merchant with
the cart, the two orks, and Mordom, presumably because the
first three had seen the display before and because little
could startled Mordom. All the sailors looked up, and everyone followed their gaze.

Standing atop the highest point on the ship—a pole towering above all the others on the uppermost deck—was a
female t'skrang wearing a huge hat with green flowers
attached to one side. She was dressed in garments of bright
purple and green, with big, puffy sleeves and leggings. With
sword upraised in one hand, she took the end of a rope in
her other, and jumped off the pole.

She plummeted down, arcing her back and curving away
from the pole until the rope snapped taut. Then she swung
back up. When the rope was almost horizontal, she let go
and flew through the air, her arms swept back, suddenly as
elegant as a sparrow. Her hat, tied with a string under her
chin, fluttered wildly behind her head. She caught another
rope, and swung around again. Then another and another.
Her motions caught everyone who watched her off guard.
Just when everyone was sure she would continue to swing
left, she would grab hold of a rope and toss herself around
to the right. When they thought she was about to drop fifty
feet to her doom, she startled them by suddenly grabbing a
rope and swinging up higher than she'd been before. J'role
became dizzy watching her, but the sight was also exhilarating. Motion was hers to command.

She caught the end of one rope and suddenly careened toward the dock, swinging in so low that J'role was convinced
she would slam into the dock. But she scrambled up a few
feet along the rope as she swung down, rushing in between

the two rows of sailors, all of whom stood at rigid attention. They did not so much as flinch as her feet ran along the deck and her momentum carried her into two forward flips and finally an astounding double roll, her sword tucked in tight across her stomach. She landed on her feet with perfect balance, raised her sword high, and shouted, "Ah-ha!" with tremendous mirth.

Around her the other sailors echoed her cry.

"Greetings, fellow travelers," she said in dwarven, her accent strange to J'role's ear. "I am Captain Patrochian, and this is my ship, the *Breeton*. With proper passage you will be lucky enough to sail aboard her!"

She greeted the man with the cart warmly, then the two orks the same way. All of them paid her coins, which the captain dropped into a sack held by a sailor to her right. J'role heard snippets of the conversations, in which the captain asked the passengers what they carried and then set a price. One person after another paid the captain, and then walked up between the double rows of sailors, some carrying their cargo by themselves, others getting help from the sailors who dropped down from the ship.

Mordom and his party were last, and J'role saw the captain's body stiffen as Phlaren approached with his prisoners.

"What cargo have you?" asked the captain.

"None but ourselves," said Mordom. "That is, me and my two companions, Phlaren and Slinsk Gorc."

"And these three?" she asked.

"These are our payment. We are currently short on funds . . ."

A tremor ran down the length of the two rows of sailors, like wind traveling through rice stalks.

"They arc slaves?" The question was uttered so softly that J'role barely heard it.

Mordom paused, as if confused by the question. "Yes. Slaves. They are in excellent condition, I assure you."

J'role remembered hearing about slavery from his father and the others while he lived in the kaer. The thought of slavery had always terrified him. Being trapped by another.

"There is no slavery in Barsaive," said Captain Patrochian. "You have made a mistake. Release these people at once." She did not move, and neither did her crew. It was a test, J'role knew immediately. She wanted to see what

Mordom would do. The slaves themselves turned their heads cautiously toward Mordom.

"I . . . ," Mordom began slowly. "It is not my place to correct you. But Theran law is explicit on the issue of slavery. It is allowed. It is common."

Thera! J'role had not given the old empire much thought since the days of his father's stories back in the kaer. The Theran Empire had extended over the entire world. It was the Therans who had encouraged local trade, and thus made the dwarven tongue the common language of the land. But when the Scourge ended and everyone emerged from their shelters, no word came of the Empire. Years passed, and everyone eventually came to assume that the core of the Theran Empire, far to the south, had fallen prey to the Horrors. It was sad, for the Therans had spread the glory of art and architecture throughout the world. But it was also a relief, J'role remembered, for the issue of slavery did not sit well with many of the people of his land. But now Mordom called upon Theran law to justify his actions. Was the Empire really gone?

The captain cocked her head to one side, examining Mordom carefully with her large blue eyes. "Strange that you should cite Theran law. There is no Theran law in Barsaive. The dwarfs rule this land, and they have declared slavery an offense punishable by death. Free these people."

Mordom actually took a step back in surprise. "Captain, I know the Therans have not yet returned, but Barsaive *is* a province of the Theran Empire. Until Thera chooses to release—"

"The decision has already been made, magician. Those who wish to live in the Theran Empire should travel south. As for we natives of Barsaive, King Varulus of Throal has made his intentions quite clear. We are free of Theran rule and laws."

"Free! What—" Mordom caught himself, tripping on his words, and then deftly continued. "We were saved by Thera. They gave us the knowledge to build the kaers and the citadels to protect ourselves from the Horrors. They created the trade ties throughout Barsaive. There would *be* no Kingdom of Throal had it not been for the Therans."

J'role saw the captain nearly lash out, then just as quickly become smiling and cool. "The issue is worthy of a long debate over a good dinner. I suggest we postpone the matter until you are on my ship and we can dine together. But the decision stands. I cannot accept these people as payment . . ."

"Then I'll find another ship that does! And don't bother telling me the other t'skrang captains don't buy slaves. I've traveled up and down the Serpent for some time now."

"I wouldn't, because it doesn't matter. Not only will I not take these people as payment, but you will not be leaving with them." The slaves relaxed a bit, but J'role saw one of them smile. Mordom saw the smile too, and he slapped his eyeless hand against the back of the woman's head.

Two dozen swords suddenly came unsheathed with a sound like wind passing through metal chimes. The captain's blade was out and pointed at Mordom's chest before anyone realized it. "I trust you won't make me kill you. We've only recently painted the dock, and blood stains are so difficult." Her long jaw clacked twice, and a shiver ran over J'role's chest.

Mordom, Phlaren, and Slinsk all tensed. None moved, but in each of their bodies J'role saw readiness for an attack. Both groups stood off like this for a moment, bodies poised, each side ready for a fight, willing even to die to save face. Then Mordom said flatly, "Very well."

He turned and walked away, leaving Phlaren and Slinsk stunned. Then they too walked off, leaving the slaves, who dropped to their knees and began weeping. The captain pulled out a dagger and cut their bonds.

"Where are you from?"

The woman answered. "A village, four miles from here. Up river. We were planting seeds . . ."

"Yes," the captain said. "I can guess the rest. Well, you're too tired and ill-fed to travel back now. If you would honor me by traveling with us a few days, you'll rest and eat well, and then we'll deposit you up river."

"We have nothing to pay you with . . ."

"What? Have you not already given me enough? I was given the chance to do a good deed this day. In the eyes of Lochost I am now blessed. Please. Enough pain is enough. Come aboard." With a flourish she indicated the two rows of sailors, all of their swords now sheathed, marking the entrance way to the ship.

"Thank you," they all said at once.

"And thank you, for accepting my invitation."

The former slaves stood and walked down the dock and entered the riverboat.

"We'll wait another hour," the captain shouted. "Double the lookouts. I don't want any surprises from that magician and his cohorts."

The sailors on the dock and on the riverboat sprang into action. J'role could not tell exactly what they were doing—there seemed to be a great deal of random movement—but they seemed very happy.

Releana said, "I'd rather be on this ship than one that takes slaves as payment."

J'role nodded. He would like to get to know the t'skrang better.

"But we've nothing to pay the captain."

An idea came to J'role. He made the symbol of the city. Releana looked confused. "We give her the city?" she asked.

J'role nodded, then picked up a clump of dirt, held it in his hands before her. He made the symbol of the city once more, then pulled a portion of the clump of dirt away.

"A piece of the city," Releana said, thinking it through. "Oh. A piece of the reward. If we save the city, we will give the *Breeton* a piece of the reward." She paused and looked doubtful. "Captain Patrochian seems the hands-on sort. I don't know if she'll take passage on a promise ... Then again, who knows? We can ask. I think it's a wonderful idea." She smiled at J'role.

J'role felt flattered. The sensation wrapped around him like comforting arms, and for a moment the thief magic retreated.

21

Charneale, the kaer's magician, took his mother away after she tried to kill J'role. No one saw her for many days.

His father remained at home, and no one came to visit. The two of them, Bevarden and J'role, sat in their home, both silent. At first Bevarden simply looked out beyond a place that did not exist. A few days later he began to cry on occasion, and held J'role close.

After that he began to stare at J'role strangely. J'role spent more and more time in his room.

J'role, Releana, and Bevarden waited a few moments on the dock while one of the sailors went to get the captain. Four other sailors remained behind, and J'role thought their clothes even more startling close up. Scarves wrapped around their heads, baggy blouses and loose vests, pants that billowed around their thin legs. The colors were an eyesore of lightning blues, sunrise reds, sea of grass greens, and midday sun yellows. Although they had green scales for skin and long, sharp talons for fingers, their good-natured smiles seemed perfectly at home on their reptilian features.

"You've never heard of the *Breeton*!" exclaimed a sailor named Voponis in response to Releana's question. He wore shiny yellow and scarlet clothes and a rapier at his side. "Why, of all the t'skrang ships that sails the Serpent, there is none finer!"

"Then we'll be fortunate to secure passage on it."

"Him," the sailor corrected.

"Him?"

"Captain Patrochian calls the ship a 'him,' and so will you. Captain's choice, you know."

"No," Releana said with a smile, very interested. "I didn't know that."

"That's one of the rules. The sailing life is full of rules, as I'm sure you understand, you being a magician. When you live by the rules, the river carries you and you float."

"Stories say the Therans had air ships," said another sailor. "But what sport is that? Give me water roiling under me, a river as big as the Serpent. Then I'll show you moving!"

"When we stood at the lip of the river valley," Releana said, "we saw the *Breeton* fighting another ship . . ."

"The *Restorii*," said Voponis. "They don't want us setting up trade ties with the kingdom of Throal. Stupid *fekas*. They're afraid the dwarfs will get too much power now that the Therans are gone. But we need someone powerful if we want to trade. The dwarfs promised to help us."

"The captain knows people in Throal?" asked Releana.

"Indeed. We'll be meeting envoys from Throal a ways down the Serpent in a few days."

Releana turned back and smiled to J'role.

"Have you an interest in Throal?" asked the sailor.

"It is our destination."

"Then you are in luck!" cried Captain Patrochian as she slammed onto the boards of the dock, landing in the center of the group. She flashed her triangular white teeth in a broad grin, whipped off her hat and bowed low. "Captain Patrochian at your service," she exclaimed, then extended her long green hand to each one in turn.

"Releana," said Releana, bowing to match the captain.

As the captain put her hand out to J'role, J'role took it with a bow as well. Releana said, "He cannot speak. I call him Grim."

At that all the sailors pulled back from J'role, and he thought for certain the creature in his head had pushed through the skin and suddenly appeared on his forehead. He touched his temple, but felt nothing.

"What is it?" asked Releana.

"A . . . ," began the captain, scrutinizing J'role's face. Then she smiled, forcing an ill notion from her thoughts. "Just a superstition . . ."

"A silent man brings silence for all," intoned Voponis. The other three sailors seemed to side squarely with him, and remained tense.

"We have customs about many things," said the captain.

She turned slightly to the other sailors. "We shouldn't take them all equally seriously."

Voponis looked as if he wanted to believe her but couldn't quite bring himself to do it. The other sailors didn't seem to change their position, and, if anything, eyed the captain with suspicion.

Releana said brightly, "Then there is no problem, for he is not yet a man."

Silence reigned for a heartbeat, then the captain said, "Ah! There it is." She turned to the other sailors. "He is almost there, but is certainly not a silent man."

The sailors did not seem convinced. But Voponis said, "If you say so, Captain." He sounded relieved. J'role noticed the t'skrang had taken a liking to the strange entourage that wanted passage on the *Breeton.*

"And you would be?" the captain said, turning to Bevarden.

"He's Despair," Releana said without thought, then caught herself and winced. "Grim's father. He's not in very good shape."

The captain put on a strained smile and said, "Well, you wish to go to Throal?"

"Yes," said Releana.

"Four dwarven gold. Pricy, but you must admit, you're a strange lot."

Releana looked to J'role, and then said, "We have no gold to offer. But we have something else. Something that might gain you more than four pieces of gold."

"And what would that be?"

Releana looked at the other sailors. "It's a bit of a secret. . . ."

The captain eyed Releana carefully, then J'role and Bevarden in turn, as if weighing them in some arcane mercantile manner. "What you can say to me, you can say to them." Releana paused, then opened her mouth to speak. Just as she was about to begin, the captain said, "But if we're going to bargain, let's get some food. I'm famished. Please, whether you travel with us or not, be my guest for a meal." She took a long look at Bevarden. "He, in particular, looks as if he could do with one."

An intense rumble emanated from J'role's stomach at the words, and though it had only been two weeks since he'd left his village, his mind strained trying to remember his last real meal.

As he walked up the wide loading plank to the ship, the image of the last fine meal he'd eaten suddenly hit him. It was the lamb Garlthik had bought him the day J'role had been initiated into the way of thief magic. For just a moment he thought wistfully of Garlthik, the man who had dragged his wrist into an open flame. Then the feeling left and J'role thought only of the good, hot meal he was about to eat.

It was wonderful, though strange. Long, succulent fish, dressed with colorful vegetables the like of which J'role had never seen, sat on silver plates on a long wooden table intricately carved with pictures of mountains and dwarfs at work in forges. Wine poured freely from pitchers made of cut glass almost as beautiful as the diamond Garlthik had traded to the tavernkeep. They sat in a wide, low-roofed room with the captain at the head of the table. Another sailor, who the captain introduced as First Mate Nikronallia, sat to her right. Voponis served them food, more of which seemed to appear each time they had cleaned their plates.

J'role started his meal by wolfing it down, but soon the taste so caught his senses that he let the food rest for a moment or so on his tongue, so he might enjoy it more. Releana rushed food into her mouth as well, and no one spoke a single word for some time. Nikronallia glowered at them, seeming impatient at their silent, ravenous behavior. But the captain smiled to see them sate their hunger.

After several minutes J'role realized that his father was not eating, only swallowing down one glass of wine after another, knocking it back in terrible gulps. J'role leaned over and cut up a slice of red fish on his father's plate, trying to encourage him to take some true sustenance. Seeing what J'role was doing, Bevarden knocked his son out of the way, nearly throwing J'role out of his seat and spilling his plate to the floor.

Voponis quickly appeared to clean up the mess and give J'role's father a new plate of food, which the man steadfastly ignored. J'role wanted to apologize to the captain and the others, though he did not exactly know for what. Perhaps, he realized, it was simply to put the matter behind him; a little ritual over an incident that truly needed no comment. Unable to say anything, he simply looked down at his food and con-

tinued to eat. After a moment he glanced up and found
Releana staring at him. He could not guess what she was
thinking.

"She thinks you're a freak," said the creature in his head.
"And she feels even more sorry for you now that your father
has shamed you. Don't think she feels anything for you
other than the lowest form of pity."

"I don't think she feels anything for me . . . ," J'role began
to think angrily, to defend himself. But he let the thought
trail off. What did it matter? The creature was right. He
wanted to look at Releana again, but he blocked the impulse.
Instead he remembered her, thinking that her face was pretty
and her eyes large. And he liked the way she smiled.

The creature laughed at him, dismissing his pleasure.

After the eating had gone on for some time, Captain
Patrochian said, "Well, I think we can let the stuffing slow
down to steady intake now. What say we discuss this proposition of yours?"

Releana and J'role looked up, loath to slow their eating.
But Releana set her fork to the side, and J'role followed suit.
Bevarden continued to drink.

"We are on a quest," said Releana.

Nikronallia snorted, but the captain waved her hand at
him, and leaned in toward Releana. "What do you seek?"
she asked.

"A city. Lost during the Scourge."

The captain crinkled her eyebrows in concentration, which
had the disturbing effect of making her reptilian face look
positively terrifying. "The city's name?"

"We do not know," answered Releana.

Nikronallia snorted again. J'role wished he could say the
name, Parlainth, which the elf queen had spoken to him. But
he could not, nor could he write it.

"We believe that all memories of the city were removed
from the world shortly before the Scourge. Rather than build
the kind of defenses the Therans taught us to use, this city
hid itself . . . somewhere else. In another plane, I suppose."

"If I might be so bold," said Nikronallia, leaning in, a
condescending smile lifting the corners of his mouth, "How
do you know about this city if it is not in this world and everyone has forgotten about it."

"There is a ring that makes the wearer seek out the city."

"Stop annoying our guests, Nikronallia," said Captain

Patrochian. "Your attitude bothers me as much as it does
them." She turned toward Releana. "This ring? You have it?
Is this what you wish to trade?"

"No," she said. "We lost it in Blood Wood. To the elf
queen."

"The elves," Bevarden said suddenly, "have thorns that
grow from within their bodies!" He spoke to the captain, his
tone full of pain. "The flesh is torn, and the blood runs in
smooth droplets down their flesh. They have ruined themselves, you see. They were a dream once." He paused, and
everyone stared silently in amazement. "I had dreams once.
So did my son." He closed his eyes, and J'role realized his
father was going to cry. "I'm sorry. I'm so sorry."

"Voponis," the captain said quietly. Voponis nodded,
stepped up next to Bevarden, then took the man's shoulder
and helped him stand.

"I'm sorry," Bevarden said again.

"You need rest, my friend," said the captain, and Voponis
led him out of the room. J'role stood to go with him, but the
captain motioned for him to sit. "He will be given a cot to
sleep on. He . . . looks as if he could use a rest." The captain
eyed J'role. "It looks as if you could use some, too."

J'role nodded, and sat back down. Unexpectedly he found
himself relieved that his father was gone. One less disaster
waiting to happen. He relaxed into his chair and listened to
the rest of the conversation.

"I take it you no longer need the ring?" asked the captain.

"That's what we think," said Releana. "We need to get to
Throal and do some research. We know where the city
should be. Grim has been there. With the aid of the ring he
saw it. We just have to find out how to bring it back."

"And where is my pay?"

"We think that the people of the city hid themselves before the Scourge to protect themselves from the Horrors. By
hiding all memories of themselves, they were safe, but they
might well need someone to bring them back. If we rescue
them, there will most likely be a reward. We will give you
a share of that."

The captain thought it over, then asked, "Why me? Why
this ship?"

"This ship is safer than other places," said Releana, "safer
even than other ships on the Serpent. We saw you turn away
a magician with one eye on his hand earlier, and that man

and his companions are searching for us and the ring. And
I trust you."

J'role hadn't thought of that, but it made sense. Until they
got off the boat, Mordom would not be able to find them.
J'role then saw Nikronallia staring at him. As soon as their
eyes met, the sailor turned his gaze away. J'role turned away
too, frightened, for he knew something significant had just
occurred, but he did not know what.

"Very well," said the captain. "An enemy of my enemy . . .
And so on. Passage is granted. We will not be going all the
way to Throal, however. We are meeting another ship, the
Chakara, in five days' time. They will have come from
Throal, and will be sailing back there after a trade meeting
between us and the dwarven envoys the *Chakara* is transport-
ing. I will guarantee passage on the *Chakara* for you, and
cover the cost to the *Chakara's* captain. This is my investment in your quest."

"Thank you, Captain Patrochian," Releana said with visible
relief.

The captain raised her glass and said, "May we all find
what we seek most." The others at the table followed suit,
even Nikronallia, who now kept his gaze set on the table.

A dizziness came over J'role, and he realized it was a good
thing the captain had granted them their passage, for he felt as
though he couldn't move another three feet after stuffing himself with food. He stood, then cocked his head to one side and
closed his eyes.

"Ah, yes," said the captain, and J'role opened his eyes.
"Your appetites may have stuffed you all a bit too full."
Voponis returned then, and the Captain said, "All is set. Please
take them to a cabin. And get Ofreaus to visit them and tend
their wounds. Though they were too polite to ask, they're all
in need of some help."

Voponis nodded, and everyone got up to follow him. As the
t'skrang closed the door to the captain's luxurious quarters behind them, he smiled and said, "I've already set up your quarters. I know the captain. She's a fine lady, generous, with a
sense of business. I knew you'd be coming aboard even as I
listened to you begin your tale." Neither of them answered, for
drowsiness had overcome their senses. Voponis said, "Here,
I'll get you to your rooms quick."

He led them through the maze of rooms and corridors that
made up the ship. Every once in a while they caught glimpses

out the windows of the rushing blue river and the green trees along the banks. The sun was bright in the late afternoon, and the world sparkled with light reflecting off water and leaves. The world, J'role realized, was stuffed with beauty. But it was easier to comprehend when viewed from a window frame, rather than when caught up in the middle of it, as in Blood Wood.

They passed other t'skrang, who casually glanced at them. The sailors walked with a swagger down the corridors, or sometimes leaped out the windows, grabbing ropes and swinging out of sight. Luckily, the ship had stairs for the non-sailors aboard, and the group ascended several decks. The sunlight became sparse as they moved away from the edge of the ship, then vanished, replaced by magical, burning stones set into sconces in the wall. The corridors began to remind J'role of the kaer; not as it had been when he was young, but in recent years: his father's refuge lit by torchlight.

Voponis opened a door and J'role saw his father, deep in a drunken sleep. He felt ill for a moment, but forced himself to relax, and the sensation passed.

"Here you are," said Voponis, indicating two empty bunks. Gracefully he extended a hand to Releana, and helped her up to the upper bunk. J'role collapsed into the one underneath. "If you need anything, just come and get us." He then left, closing the door behind him. The light in the room dimmed and J'role closed his eyes. The world rocked under him as he began to drift off, and he thought once more of the priestess who had held him in her arms when he was a boy. Then his thoughts turned to his mother.

"Don't tell anyone," he suddenly remembered her saying. Why had she said that? Not, *Don't talk to anyone,* which was a sound warning, but *don't tell anyone.* What wasn't he supposed to tell?

"Do you really want to know?" the creature asked.

The creature's glee disturbed J'role, and he thought, "No." Better not to know. To leave it all be.

The darkness and the rocking slowly swallowed him, and as J'role fell asleep he felt phantasmal fingers upon his chest, memories of the past come alive. Then came a dream . . .

22

The dreams. Fragments of the past, shaped into a language of sights and sounds only the unconscious could comprehend. The memories came now, but only because his awareness was safely shut off from the truths buried within. His mind coiled around the key question. What had happened between the arrival of the shadow in the corner of his room and the death of his mother? Somewhere between those two events was the moment of true terror.

J'role's thoughts searched and searched, but each time only found the void.

He woke, startled by the dank, wet smell of the ship. The gentle rocking. The darkness. It took him a moment to remember where he was. When he did, he also remembered how tired he'd been, and wanted to roll over and fall back asleep. But his body was alert now, and curious. Despite his wise desire for more rest, part of him wanted to be up and about.

After fruitlessly tossing and turning several times, he sat up, realized he was wide awake, and climbed out of the bunk. He stood a moment, his bare feet touching the wooden floor. Cold. Wet. Comfortable. He listened, hearing the breathing of his father and Releana. Then, echoing up through the wood of the ship, the rhythmic churning of the ship's paddle wheel. Beneath that, the slapping of water against the hull.

He realized his body did not hurt as much as before. A questor of Garlen had obviously arrived and tended their wounds. For that J'role was very grateful.

Standing in the cabin he had the strange sensation that he was watching over his father and Releana. It comforted him.

He indulged in the feeling for a moment, then left the room, closing the door behind him.

J'role wandered down the corridors, looking for Voponis, but found neither him nor any other t'skrang. After turning and twisting through the ship's warren-like structure for a while longer, he suddenly found himself outside. Night had fallen while he slept, and stars dotted the sky.

He stepped out onto a ledge running the length of the ship, a board no more than two feet wide. Below, the dark waters of the Serpent roiled away from the *Breeton* as the ship cut a path toward its meeting with the *Chakara*. The paddle wheel churned through the water with a clean, rhythmic swooshing, sending a spray of water back down into the river.

J'role began to walk carefully along the ledge toward the front of the ship.

A shadow suddenly rushed at him, and he pressed himself tight against the wall. "Good evening," a sailor said in dwarven, swinging by on a rope, his loose clothes flapping as he passed, the rapier at his side momentarily brilliant in the starlight.

J'role waited a moment, letting his breathing calm down, then sighed and continued on. Soon he reached the bow of the *Breeton*, where the wide ship narrowed, though the ship's front was flat. Thick metal spikes and two wooden prongs fifteen feet long adorned the flat edge, and J'role thought they might be for the purpose of ramming other ships.

"Good evening," said Captain Patrochian, and J'role jumped, nearly falling into the river below. "I'm sorry," she said, grabbing him by the shoulder. "Didn't mean to startle you. Out for some air?"

J'role nodded, then turned away slightly, embarrassed that he could not say more.

The river stretched out before them, amazingly wide. The rushing surface of the river caught the reflection of the stars, which seemed to bob and toss in the water. J'role thought of all the times he'd looked to the stars for answers, searching for patterns he could not read. Now the stars floated along the watery path the ship traveled, as if finally leading him to his fate.

"I love this river," the captain said with warm cheer. Her thin tail slowly snaked its way back and forth across the ledge, making J'role wonder briefly whether it had a will of its own. After a moment, she asked, "Are you far from home?"

J'role decided he was and nodded.

"Any rivers like this where you come from?"

J'role shook his head.

"Is the land dry?" She asked the question in a friendly way, not pressing him. Curious.

J'role nodded. He then mimed casting a spell, his hands wide apart and busy. Then he bent down, and slowly raised his fingertips all the way from the floor to his standing height, as if following the growth of a plant. He reached into the air and mimed plucking a fruit, then took a bite.

"Ah. Yes. Magic for the crops. We had to do that at first. Or rather, my parents did. But the Serpent is so fertile ..." Her voice trailed off, obviously full of love for her home. J'role wondered what that would be like, to live in a place that one loved, that one didn't want to escape.

Ahead, on the far right side of the river he saw a riverboat docked among several of the spires rising out of the water. J'role pointed at the tableau.

"I'm sorry ...," the captain said, uncertain.

J'role raised his arm vertically, then pointed again.

"Ah. The spires. Those are the tips of our homes. We t'skrang live in communities under the waters of the Serpent. The spires lead down to our towns. That's where we hid during the Scourge."

How extraordinary! J'role wondered if he might someday visit an underwater town. He would wait until he could ask the captain if he might visit. With words. Until that day, his focus would be on finding the means to remove the creature from his head.

An image flashed through his mind: his body on the ground, bloody gashes across his wrists. The creature in his thoughts laughed.

"You've seen the elves?" the captain asked abruptly. "Your father said ..."

J'role nodded, somewhat surprised by the captain's question. What interest would a citizen of an underwater town have in the elves? Didn't living in such a strange place offer enough delights?

"I've never seen them. My parents heard stories, of course. Passed down through the generations in the kaer. They're supposed to be wonderful."

Yes, wonderful and terrible. And he had seen them and Captain Patrochian had not. She stared over the bow of the *Breeton,* out over the river, eyes full of anticipation of excitement. She had what she wanted, her ship and her travels, yet seemed to long for even more.

Turning back to J'role and meeting his eyes, she gave him one of her frightening smiles, the corners of her mouth pulling down grotesquely. "You are not yet a man, but you have already seen a great deal, haven't you?"

At first J'role thought she was talking about the elves and other extraordinary sights like their thorn men. But a part of him suddenly realized that the captain was referring to the darker, subtler sights that he could not remember, but knew were buried in his memories somewhere. He answered her question with a nod.

"Have you ever swung over the stars at night?"

The question confused him. He shook his head no.

"Come." She addressed him the same way she did her sailors—with the expectation of being obeyed. They walked along the ledge until they came to a hook driven into the wall. Wrapped around it were several ropes. She grabbed the end of one and said, "Watch."

With a mighty push from her legs she swung in a wide arc out over the river. The rope hung from a wooden arm that pivoted on a thick pole, and her momentum carried her toward the rear of the ship. J'role thought she would slam into a wall, but she pulled up her legs and braced them against the impact. At the exact moment the captain made contact with the wall she pushed again with her legs and swung out over the water once more. She swung back toward J'role with a mighty rush, landing on the ledge with perfect balance, wrapping the rope around the hook in the same deft motion.

"You try."

"Me?" J'role almost said. But before another thought could come to him, she'd unhooked one of the ropes and was holding it out. "Just hang on tight. I'll catch you on the way back. Stopping is where the training comes in. And make sure to look down."

She put the rope in his hands. As he thought about giving it back to her, he felt the rough hemp fit comfortably against his palms and fingers. It was just like climbing a wall, he realized. And if he could climb a vertical pit lined with writhing roots, he could certainly cling to a rope.

Without hesitation he turned toward the wall, and with a sharp exhalation of breath he pulled up his legs, braced his feet against the wall of the ship, and pushed . . .

He swung out into the darkness, the red lights of the ship flashing in and out of his sight as he spun wildly around.

"Look down," the captain cried.

He did.

The stars . . . !

The stars bobbed up and down in the wake of the *Breeton's* passage. They whirled around beneath them as if he'd flown up from the earth and now lived among them.

"The wall!" the captain shouted. At her warning he looked up and gained his bearings. As his body rushed toward the wall, J'role used the thief magic to balance himself and pull his legs up toward the wall.

Even sooner than he expected his feet slammed into the wall, buckling his legs. As if he'd been practicing for years, he pushed off the instant his forward momentum stopped, and was out over the water again.

He looked down again. This time he saw his own shadow, his silhouette, rush through the night sky. He gasped as he watched his life finally given a place in the stars.

"Grim!" the captain said, and he looked up to see her only a few feet away, an arm outstretched. He pulled his legs up again, and slammed into the wall feet first. The captain reached out and grabbed the rope, one hand on the hook for balance. J'role nearly swung back out over the water, but Patrochian held him fast and pulled him close to her. Her body shook with laughter.

"Well done, softskin! Well done!"

The motion of her laughter passed from her into his body and he found himself floating in his emotions. The thief magic sulked away like a disappointed child, promising to return when he had room only for it. He wrapped his arms around Captain Patrochian to prevent himself from falling off the ledge, and she held him tight.

"Well done," she said again. "How would you like to put yourself to some use during the rest of the trip? Nothing required, of course. Just something to occupy you so you don't go *restas* while on board. You seem to have the spirit."

J'role looked up at her, uncertain what she wanted from him. In that moment a chill passed through his flesh.

She caught the expression on his face. "No, no. Only if you want to. Maybe you'll like it."

An offer, he realized. Simply an offer. She was giving him something—a chance to work aboard her ship. She loved the *Breeton*, and so it was an offer to share something dear to her. His fear changed to embarrassment. He realized he did not know how to accept a gift that he had not first begged for.

But he wanted to try. He nodded.

The captain kept him busy doing anything that needed doing, and Releana soon joined in. From the storage holds to the engine room, they carried the magic coals that moved the paddles. They cleaned the fire-cannons, the long tubes that fired the magical balls of fire at enemy ships. They helped the crew carry the cargo on and off they ship as they docked at one port after another along the Serpent.

J'role had never had much opportunity to work. He'd coveted the food his fellow villagers grew, but had never seen any appeal in the act of working. His only occupation had been lounging around, carefully observing the moods of his neighbors for the right time to beg for scraps. Though begging was intense work, emotionally draining in its shame, it did not offer the physical release and satisfaction of cleaning the ship and hauling goods aboard.

His muscles strained, his breathing quickened, sweat formed over his skin. The physical thrill was heightened, not by his magic—which separated him from others—but by his *cooperation* with Releana and Voponis and the other t'skrang. Though many of the sailors shunned him out of fear of his silence, J'role quickly became a fiercely active work force on he *Breeton*.

He went to bed tired each day, fell into a deep sleep, and woke up ready for more work. He ate hearty meals on a regular basis, each one as sumptuous as the food Garlthik had bought with his ill-gained diamond.

The days passed, and the Throal Mountains loomed ahead, their tops vanishing into white mist. Like his future, existing, but unseen.

"The dwarfs only control a small portion of the mountains," said Voponis, gesturing at the towering mountain range. "But that small part is still very large. Instead of their homes being laid out flat, like ours in the Serpent, they stretch up and down within the mountains. The surface of the mountains is wild territory, full of strange creatures." He looked embarrassed. "Or so I'm told."

"Grim," Captain Patrochian said, suddenly behind them. Her voice was brisk, as always when J'role was "on duty." "Need more coals for the paddle wheel."

He nodded and rushed off, with barely a glance to Voponis.

The coals were kept in small boxlike containers of a golden metal called orichalcum. The orichalcum could contain magical elements, such as the coals of elemental fire used to power the paddle wheel and fire the ship's guns.

The ship had forty such containers, and Releana told J'role that they were as valuable as the magical fire elements within. She explained that there were magical elements for fire, earth, wood, water, and air. Orichalcum, an enchanted earth alloy, made transportation of the elements safe. She had never seen the boxes before, but had been told about them. All magicians, she said, knew about them, and most sought out containers made from the metal.

The boxes were stored in neat stacks of two layers, four deep and five across. They were cold to the touch, but J'role knew some contained fiery coals that perpetually burned until released from their boxes for use in conjunction with magic.

Boxes that were empty remained on their side, with the small square door on one side left open. Bending down to pick up one of the filled boxes, he suddenly heard voices coming through the wall in a neighboring hold. One he recognized as Nikronallia's. The other was familiar, but he couldn't place it immediately. Curious, J'role leaned closer to the wall, finding a crack that let him peer between two boards.

"Have you spoken to the crew, as I told you?" asked Garlthik One-Eye. He sat on a pile of stained tarps, his thick, gray-green body reclining on the cloth like some decadent king holding court. J'role nearly gasped out loud.

"Those I trust," answered Nikronallia.

"And how many is that?" Garlthik seemed bored with the question, as if Nikronallia was certain to disappoint him.

J'role watched with fascination as Nikronallia twitched with concern and tried to please the one-eyed ork. "Most. All but seven. Most can't stand her flaunting of the customs."

"And the *Breeton* meets with the dwarven envoys tomorrow?"

"Aye. We must—"

"We will. Tonight. We can't risk word of the mutiny traveling downriver ahead of us. But tonight . . . in the darkness. There will be no time for warning to reach the other ship."

"The dwarfs will be the ruin of us all . . .," the t'skrang said bitterly, looking down at the ground.

Garlthik shrugged and stood up. "Not my concern," he said. Nikronallia opened his mouth to speak, and Garlthik raised his hand. "I told you I'd help you," he said. "I needed passage across the river, and this is my fare. But I don't care who rules. I just want their money. Now, of course, I want the boy."

"And you shall have him."

Garlthik blinked at him. "Do you think I need your permission?"

"No."

"Then grant me no favors. And once the dwarfs are dead, you'll sail us to Throal."

"But . . ."

"We'll all go. That's where I'm headed. But kill the father and the other one during the mutiny. I just want them gone."

Nikronallia nodded.

Garlthik paced absently, and then smiled. "To think I should stumble across the boy this way. When you came down to tell me he was on board . . ."

"And you will kill the captain? Tonight?" The fear in the t'skrang's voice revealed why Garlthik was necessary for this mutiny. Apparently no one on the ship felt capable of taking Captain Patrochian's life.

"Tell me when."

Nikronallia hesitated, as if he had one more question to ask but could not bring himself to do it.

"I'm as good as you've heard," Garlthik said impatiently. "Your captain shall sleep in her own blood this night. Have no fear."

"She is . . ."

"She is dead by my hands. Consider it already done."

Nikronallia hesitated again, his departure imminent, but delayed. "How did the boy escape you then?"

A terrible ire crossed Garlthik's face, but then his expression softened to something pitiable. "That magician you told me about. He has an affinity with the Horrors. There are some things even I am afraid of."

Nikronallia's wide eyes widened more, then he nodded and left.

Fearful of being caught, J'role quickly pulled away from the crack, searching for some excuse to look busy.

He remembered the request for the fire coals, and reached down and picked up one of the golden boxes. His breathing felt tight in his chest as he walked toward the door and turned the thick metal ring to open it. Everything done plainly, easily. See. Not doing anything. Just an errand. Captain told me to.

He stepped out into the corridor and closed the door behind him.

He turned. Down the corridor stood Nikronallia, staring at him.

23

One nightmare comes back to him regularly. When he wakes, it is vivid in his memory. Sometimes it is the only thing he can think about for the rest of the day.

In the nightmare Charneale arrives at J'role's home in the kaer. The door slams abruptly open. The magician is laughing maniacally. J'role's mother is at Charneale's feet, weeping and screaming for mercy. But her words are not words. They are the same strange sounds J'role makes when he opens his mouth.

"It is time," the magician intones, and from his chest pours countless rocks. They rush out onto the floor, like water poured into a cup.

Just before he is smothered by the rocks, J'role is suddenly transported to the Atrium. His mother now stands in the fountain. The statue of Garlen hovers behind her, but the statue is covered with a thick tarp. The spirit of Garlen should never witness what is about to happen.

J'role and Nikronallia stood facing each other in the corridor, neither moving, both their faces expressionless. J'role was certain that Nikronallia somehow knew that he had overheard the conversation with Garlthik.

But as the moment stretched on, J'role realized that Nikronallia stared at him not from knowledge, but from uncertainty. He didn't know if *J'role* had overheard *him* plotting with Garlthik. And so the two of them stood, the tall, thin boy and the reptilian sailor, each waiting for the other to make an accusation.

When the suspense became unbearable, they nodded to one another, a terse greeting designed to force the issue. As they mirrored each other, they both relaxed, each believing they were, after all, safe. Each added a stiff smile, and then both turned and walked casually away in different directions.

J'role's hands felt awkward and clumsy holding the golden box. He carried it toward the paddle wheel room, desperately sorting out what should be his next action. He knew he had to warn Captain Patrochian, but Nikronallia had said most of the crew would soon betray her. He couldn't reveal his knowledge of their plan by acting suspiciously. The captain had given him a task, and he had to carry through on it. Then he could return to her, as if for another assignment.

How would he tell her?

He slammed the thought shut. That wasn't the problem now. For now all he had to do was seem calm and unconcerned. Two sailors approached, laughing and chatting in the native t'skrang tongue. Their enjoyment ceased as they stared at him. He'd seen the same looks over the last several days, knew they reacted to him this way because he was mute and because of their superstition. And yet ...

Did they know something? Were these two part of the plot to kill the captain? Releana? His father?

The sailors passed, talking once more, though it sounded to J'role as if they used softer tones now.

Soon he reached the ship's engine room. It was located at the back of the riverboat, a large room with a massive metal container—the engine. The container was as thick and hot as the belly of a dragon. The engine, the t'skrang said, was a gift from Upandal, the passion of construction. No other race had been so blessed.

From either side of the engine extended long, thick wooden poles that disappeared through holes in the back of the ship. J'role knew that the ends of the poles attached to the paddle wheel. Driven by the engine, the poles moved back and forth, sending the paddle wheel round and round, and thus moving the ship through the water.

A t'skrang, dressed in a velvet robe covered with images of water and flames, smiled as J'role approached. Although he was part of the *Breeton*'s crew, this was not a sailor but the ship's magician. "Good," the t'skrang said in dwarven. "Good." He took the box from J'role and carried it to the engine. There he opened the box. Heat bellowed out, the air above the opening shimmering. The magician spoke some words and waved his hand over the elemental fire.

Then he grabbed a thick wooden handle on the engine and yanked it up. A door opened to reveal an interior full of blazing red light and scathing heat. For a moment J'role stood transfixed by the sight; the blaze seemed to beckon with the promise of enclosing safety, but at the same time the overpowering heat within the metal walls made him tremble with fear. To find safety in the engine was to be consumed.

The magician threw the contents of the box into the engine, and the flames roared, a blast of new heat rushing from the interior. J'role watched the magician staring into the flames, apparently very pleased, still holding the box that J'role was to return to the store room. He walked up to the magician and tugged on his elaborate sleeve.

The magician whirled, glowering at J'role, then handed him the box without a word. J'role rushed out of the room and down the corridors toward the storeroom where the orichaleum boxes were stored. He would have preferred to go straight to the captain, but carrying the box around on the upper decks would have raised too many suspicions.

Several sailors eyed him as he ran past, and J'role couldn't be certain if it was from suspicion or curiosity, but he no longer cared. Nightfall was only a few hours away, and that was when Garlthik said the mutiny was to begin.

He returned the box to the storeroom, then ran to find Captain Patrochian.

Passing throughout the twisting corridors and out along the ledges of the ship, J'role encountered many t'skrang sailors. He couldn't help but wonder if they were part of the mutiny. Finally he reached the captain's quarters and knocked on the door, hoping desperately to find her here. "Come in," Captain Patrochian said.

He entered to find her sitting behind her desk, quill pen in hand, ledger set out before her. "Grim," she said, obviously surprised to see him. She studied the concern on his face. "What is it?"

J'role closed the door behind him, wondering how was he going to do this. Some matters were too complicated for gestures . . .

Betrayal . . .

She stood up, anxious now. "What is it?"

He raised his hands, as if an idea would come to him if he started gesturing. But his mind was as blank as before.

She waited. She wanted to understand. He could see that in her eyes so clearly. All he had to do was try, and she would try as well.

He looked around the room, searching for an object he might use to represent Nikronallia. Swords. Maps. The ledger. Her hat. The windows on either side of the ship; wooden frames with small panes of glass. The four-posted bed with the yellow and scarlet sheets.

A panic rose up in him. He saw nothing that might help. He looked back at her.

"Grim," she said, "I have—"

He slammed his hand on the desk, desperate to make her understand that what he had to communicate was exceedingly urgent. She pulled back, startled, then leaned in again. She swallowed. "Do you want me to get one of the others? Will they be able to understand you?"

A knock came at the door. The captain moved toward it quickly, then opened it to reveal Nikronallia framed in the doorway. As the captain stepped aside to let him enter, the t'skrang sailor's eyes locked with J'role's.

"Nikronallia, Grim has something apparently urgent he wants to tell me," Patrochian said crisply. "Do you know of anything wrong on board?"

Nikronallia looked hard at J'role, then said, "No."

"I'm going to get his companions. They might be able to help decipher his concerns. Keep an eye on him, and J'role, keep trying." Without further ado she rushed out of the cabin, shutting the door behind her.

Nikronallia and J'role watched her energetic departure, then turned back to one another.

"So you are concerned about something, are you?"

J'role swallowed. Nodded.

Nikronallia took a step closer, cocking his head to one side, "What is it?"

J'role shrugged, not knowing what else to do.

"Oh, now it seems less important than a moment ago?" Nikronallia leaned his head forward now, intent. "You little curse," he said softly. "Let's see. If you . . . tried to steal the ledgers, I caught you, we fought . . . Yes." Suddenly Nikronallia drew a dagger. "It's a shame your parents didn't drown you at birth and save me the trouble." He lunged toward J'role.

"He's killing me," his mother panted, trying to keep her grip on the knife and scramble back up.

"He's just a boy. Our son."

"A monster. He speaks with the voice of a monster. I can't listen to him anymore. Please. Please, let me kill him . . ."

The images stunned J'role, and he froze in place as Nikronallia's knife plunged deep into his chest, the warm metal splitting his flesh, fat, and muscle. J'role gave out a dry gasp, his arms flailing wide, and he saw blood gush from his body to spray Nikronallia and the objects around the room a deep red. Nikronallia grinned wide, and jerked the dagger out. A new pain, hot and jagged, cut across J'role's chest, spreading over his body like sunlight on a warm day.

He turned and stumbled away. He felt his life leaving him, and was suddenly terrified. An incredible loss came over him, for he had seen the elves and met Captain Patrochian and was on his was to Throal and no longer lived among the villagers who despised him, and had made friends with Releana . . .

For so much of his life he'd wanted to die, but now he wanted to live. He didn't know how things would turn out, if he would ever get his voice back, if he would ever truly be happy . . . But he wanted to find out.

For the first time in his life he wanted to grow older and see what life held.

He stumbled across the room and pulled his hands away from the wound in his chest. Alien and red, his hands caught the sun's light through the nearby window and turned bright and shiny.

He glanced back. Nikronallia approached, stalking carefully, forcing J'role into the corner. "Make it easier for both of us. I can finish you quick."

"He's right, boy," the creature in his thoughts said. "End it now. Surrender. Oh, did I ever tell you what happened when you were seven years old? I can't tell you unless you ask. Part of a bargain."

J'role turned away from Nikronallia and shut his thoughts to the creature. Though it babbled and taunted him, he heard none of the words. The pain helped in this regard.

To his left was a window, its dozens of glass panes sepa-

rated by wooden frames. Outside, hanging from some unknown point, the end of a rope.

He drew in a dry, raspy breath, then charged forward. As
he smashed through the glass, J'role heard Nikronallia gasp
from behind him. The sound of the shattering glass echoed
terribly in his ears, and the shards cut across him like the elf
queen's thorns.

Even as he jumped J'role drew the magic around him, extending his hands, becoming alone once more. He caught the
rope as he flew forward, the momentum carrying him away
from the ship. Below the water roiled wildly, brown and
bubbling. He swung around the rear of the boat, saw the
paddle wheel churning. He wanted to swing just above the
wheel, but felt his grip already slipping. The pain tired his
arms.

"Just let yourself die," the creature said.

Ahead J'role saw another rope. He could reach it. Maybe.
He didn't know.

He tried to regulate his breathing, to calm himself. To focus only on the rope . . . The thief magic spoke to him: Need
no one. Depend on no one. Love no one, and let none love
you.

He drew in a breath, reached out a hand . . .

His rope jerked back, taking him just out of reach.

He stretched as far as he could.

Got it!

He looked up and saw Nikronallia slicing through the
rope with his dagger.

J'role's hopes drained out of him like his blood. The rope
snapped.

He floated for a moment, a thrilling sensation. Then droplets of water splashed over him, and the air turned suddenly
cool.

He slammed into one of the paddles, and for a moment
the world turned black as his knife wound tore open wider.
Moving hurt *so* much; J'role was desperate for a grip on
something.

The paddle was wet and slick; eight feet across, too big to
grip easily. His hands scrambled uselessly for a moment,
then he put his trust in the magic. If he lived alone he could
survive.

He had it. He felt the wood grains under his skin. Even as
the wheel spun, he found a grip on the edge.

Then the river washed over him. His throat filled with water; around him a world of water and swirling bubbles. The pressure of the water pushed him, and he clung to the paddle with all his strength, fearing that if he let go he would be slammed again and again by the other paddles turning.

"You're going to die now. Do you want to know what happened?"

He could not even think to answer.

Crack! The surface of the water. Light! Water splashed all around him as he gasped. The water around him ran red with his blood.

He felt dizzy. Knew he would pass out soon. A shadow far above, Nikronallia watching his demise. J'role pressed his cheek tight against the paddle. Wishing so much that his whole life had been different.

The paddle reached the top, then started back down to the water.

"Tell me," he thought.

The creature sighed. The memories flooded in . . .

The thing in the corner—the creature—said, "Give me the boy, I'll leave you and your husband alone."

"I can't."

"Think about it. . . ."

He crashed into the water, barely aware of his surroundings, the memories so sharp, so real. . . .

Water.

"Will he know? I don't want him to know."

"Tell him you don't want him to talk about it. He'll only remember what he feels comfortable speaking about. . . ."

Air again. He wanted to die now. He could not. . . . How could he live any longer?

A shadow from the sky. Death coming to finish him off, swinging down from the blue sky.

He welcomed death.

"Truly?" the creature asked, pathetic with hope.

Then an arm around his waist lifted him into the sky.

He had no idea what was happening, but surrendered to it.

He turned his head. Captain Patrochian's was looking straight ahead as she hung onto a rope with one hand.

Now they were on the upper deck. She lowered him gently, letting him lie on the ground. She called for help, barking desperate orders.

J'role had to warn her somehow.

He reached up, grabbed her bright yellow sash with his right hand, staining it light pink with his blood. She looked down at him, and he strained his mind. How could he tell her? A bitterness raced in, a fury at his mother . . .

His mother!

He could warn the captain now if not for his mother. He could have spoken all his life. He could have lived his life!

Sailors rushed up around them now. "Relax, rest. Our healer will be here soon," Captain Patrochian said. Then she noticed the stab wound. "What happened?" she asked softly.

Nikronallia arrived on the end of a rope, landing gracefully. Whether the sailor heard the captain's question or not, J'role would never be sure, but without pause Nikronallia said, "He tried to steal your ledgers and escape out the window, Captain. He drew a knife. We fought . . ." He trailed off, shrugging his shoulders as if to suggest the rest was obvious.

The captain looked into J'role's face. He could see her wavering. Releana arrived. She knelt down beside him, touching him gently. Panic overcame J'role, and his breathing quickened. He knew he had to do something—he might die at any moment. If he couldn't warn the captain, perhaps he could force Nikronallia to start the mutiny prematurely—now—before all was in place. This might give them a chance, at least.

With the last of his energy J'role stood and rushed toward Nikronallia. No one expected the sudden movement, and he crashed into the first officer, knocking him to the ground. The exertion almost made J'role black out, but he scrambled over Nikronallia's body and pressed his mouth close against the slit that was the t'skrang's left ear.

The muscles in J'role's mouth and tongue let loose once more, and he babbled the sounds and cries and tortured noises of the creature. He pressed his lips against Nikronallia's scaly skin, straining to keep the sounds as quiet as he could. The creature in his thoughts squirmed with pleasure.

Then hands were upon him and he cried out. Immediately he slapped his own hands against his mouth. His jaw and lips moved wildly against his palms, and he tasted his blood as he tried to force the sounds back down his throat.

Someone threw him to the deck, and he rolled over and saw Nikronallia get up, clutching at his head. The next instant the sailor had drawn his sword, pointing it at J'role.

His eyes revealed fury and hatred and a longing for a taste of vengeance.

"Nikronallia!" the captain cried.

Nikronallia hesitated, wobbling as if drunk, then sliced the air with his rapier and pointed the tip of his blade at the captain.

"Nikronallia," she said again, this time with quiet surprise.

"Your time is through," he answered, his voice raspy, still touching his head with his free hand. With a gesture toward J'role, he said, "You let this thing . . .," then gave a great sob, and lowered his hand from his head. "I want you dead, so very, very badly." He laughed, as if his words both surprised and amused him, and three other sailors drew their blades. The mutineers looked at Nikronallia oddly, as if they knew something had gone wrong. But this was obviously the start of the mutiny.

"What?" asked the captain, thoroughly baffled. "What are you talking about?"

Ignoring her, Nikronallia said to himself, "No, not yet. Not yet." He looked around, confused. "We're supposed to . . . tonight . . ."

The captain looked down at J'role, and he nodded back to her. She understood. He relaxed and rolled onto his back as Captain Patrochian drew her blades. Then he heard the sound of someone screaming a battle cry and the fight began.

24

He did not throw stones at his mother, though in the night-mare he does. In the nightmare the stones are sharp and rough against his hand, and he feels them rub his flesh raw. Blood pours forth. He hurls the stones at his mother, and as the stones float for that singular, frozen, nightmare eternity arc of fall, each one drips his blood.

The stones are still in the air, yet forever moving toward his mother, the strange paradox that only dreams can allow. The stretching of time makes J'role anxious in his sleep, as if he himself is falling forever, toward a pit bottom he cannot see. All he wants is for the stone to reach its destination; his life is stuck as the stone floats along its never-ending path.

"Move him!" Captain Patrochian shouted to Releana, leaping forward to engage the mutineers in swordplay. Her sword clacked sharply against Nikronallia's, then she parried one of the mutineer's blows. Voponis engaged the other two mutineers, and the deck became a flurry of silver swishes of swordplay.

Releana ignored the captain's instructions, preferring to aid her instead. She waved her hands, then cupped them, palms facing forward. Frost formed on her hands, then a spear of ice appeared from out of her cupped hands and flew toward the mutineer who fought alongside Nikronallia. Sparkling in the sun, flakes of ice trailed the spear, then floated down to the deck. J'role, prone and helpless on the deck, looked up at the sight, thinking. "How beautiful," even though he knew the observation made no sense at the moment.

Releana's spear drove deep into the mutineer's chest. His clawed, green hands flew wide as he screamed and fell back on the deck. The spear shattered, sending chunks of ice skittering around his corpse.

Seeing his companion fall, Nikronallia made a panicked stab at the captain.

She parried, smiling, her triangular teeth nearly ghoulish in her love of the fight.

Nikronallia pulled back, then lunged once more, his breath forced from his lungs in an angry hiss.

The captain parried again, then added a riposte that Nikronallia parried just before the captain's blade would have sliced through his shoulder.

Meanwhile Voponis drove the other two mutineers across the deck. The swordplay was fast, and sometimes the three rapiers seemed no more than a momentary sparkle of wind, somehow magically induced to reveal itself for one extraordinary moment.

With a sudden switch in tactics, Voponis laughed with tremendous bravado, brought his rapier up and under the sword of his opponents, swung his weapon in a wide arc, and sent each of the other t'skrang's swords flying off the edge of the ship. The two sailors stood stunned for a moment, then Voponis slashed the air harshly with his blade. Both sailors gasped and jumped back, vanishing from sight over the edge of the ship, splashing into the water below.

Nikronallia saw all this and gave up his fight with Captain Patrochian. Running for a rope attached to a swinging mast, he jumped for it. With one hand on the rope and the other slashing his sword through the air, he swung over the ship shouting, "Now! A call to arms! Follow me! The time to strike is now!"

The captain almost followed, rushing toward another rope, but Voponis caught her arm and spoke quickly in the t'skrang tongue. She looked at J'role, taking in the whole truth of what he'd wanted to warn her about: it was not four sailors who had mutinied, but the entire ship. She would need a plan. She nodded, crossed to J'role, and helped him up.

"We've got to get to the engine room," she said. "If we can take it before the mutineers do, we'll still be in control. Come. We'll use the interior passages. Less obvious that way."

The four of them moved quickly down the steps, across the descending decks, through the winding corridors.

Voponis and Releana helped J'role, and the captain went ahead. Hearing shouts ringing through the ship, they came across two corpses. "They probably refused to join the mutiny," Voponis said sadly.

Minutes later they came across a fight between five sailors; three against two. When the sailors noticed the captain and the others, the group of three turned and ran, pursued momentarily by the other two sailors until the captain called the loyalists back. Their numbers thus strengthened, they continued toward the engine room.

They were almost there when Voponis said, "Despair . . . Grim's father!"

J'role remembered Garlthik's desire to have Bevarden killed.

"We can't split up now," the captain said. "We've got to take the engine room. If we succeed at that, we'll decide what to do next."

Releana looked at J'role as if ready to comfort him, but he killed all his feelings, kept his face stony.

As they continued on, the only other individual they encountered was the ship's questor of Garlen, who also joined the group. "I saw three crew members killed in their sleep," he said. "I awoke just in time, saw the murders, and ran off. The ship is hosting a bloodbath." He glanced at J'role's chest as they walked. "I'll tend to that as soon as we're settled," he said. "You'll be fine."

A terrible feeling came to J'role as they walked down the last corridor. If the engine room was so vital, shouldn't they have encountered trouble by now? But they had not. He suspected that the delayed trouble would be even worse. Though no one spoke of it, the others must have been feeling the same. Their bodies had become more tense, and their rapiers quivered in their hands.

Reaching the door to the engine room, everyone took up a combative stance after they set J'role a few feet back on the floor.

A hesitation. Thoughts evoking the passions of Thystonius and Floranuus. The thrum of the engine grinding the arms that pushed the paddle wheel.

Voponis stepped forward, opened the door.

Through the crowd of legs J'role spotted the engine room's magician. He turned from the engine, slowly, looking surprised. "What? What is it?" he asked.

Everyone relaxed, and in that moment the wizard raised his arms and a ball of fire erupted from his hands.

"Down!" Voponis cried, and even as they all fell back, the fireball rushed across the engine room and caught Voponis full in the chest. He screamed out, and a spray of flames cut down the corridor and splashed over J'role's head.

The captain shouted "NO!" The acrid smell of burnt flesh cut through J'role's senses. Releana, screaming with wordless rage, leaped to her feet and faced the t'skrang magician. She dug her hand into a pouch on her belt and produced a pinch of dirt, which she threw into the air before her. She cast her spell and the dirt seemed momentarily suspended. The magician was in the midst of preparing another spell when he looked up, saw what Releana was doing, and gasped. Even as he was deciding which way to run, the dirt before Releana transformed into crystalline needles that shot through the air and slammed into the magician's face. The needles ripped through his green scales and pocked him with bright red wounds. He stood still for a moment, eyes hidden beneath the blood, then fell forward, dead.

Suddenly the doorway filled with mutinous sailors, their swords drawn. Behind them all stood Nikronallia, smiling. "A little late, Captain!" he shouted.

Captain Patrochian replied tersely. "Really? I think your death will be most timely."

The loyalist sailors jumped up, and the two sides charged each other. Then began a fury of flashing metal and the sharp clanging of swords. Looking back J'role saw that the corridor behind them was empty. He tugged on Releana's leg. She looked where he pointed, then shouted, "Come!" She leaned down to help J'role up, and the two of them began moving away as quickly as possible from the fierce battle.

Four mutineers appeared before them, swords drawn, battle fury on their reptilian faces. Before J'role could even panic, Releana threw more crystalline darts forward in two waves, each wave cutting a mutineer. The other two t'skrang ran off.

J'role glanced back. Nikronallia and his followers drove the captain and her loyal sailors down the corridor.

J'role and Releana made their way down several more corridors, the captain and her men following as they tried to keep the mutineers at bay. When J'role realized that they had entered the ship's supply holds he tugged on Releana's arm, pointing down a corridor to the right.

Releana did not know why J'role wanted to turn, but she followed willingly, as did the others.

J'role knew exactly where they were, however. Ahead, on the right, was the storeroom with the fire-coals. If they couldn't hold the engine room, J'role decided they would at least control the materials needed to make the engine work. He indicated the door, and Releana pushed it open.

Two mutineers, alerted by the sound of the door opening, stood facing the doorway, swords drawn. Both lunged forward as Releana dropped J'role to the ground. She fumbled trying to get more dirt out of her pouch, and the bag fell to the ground. Both mutineers drove their rapiers into Releana's shoulder. She cried out in pain. J'role struggled to get up, though he could feel his chest still wet and sticky from the blood drawn by Nikronallia's dagger. Then a rapier appeared over his head, and someone dragged Releana out of the way. Captain Patrochian had arrived, and she cut down the mutineers with four precise stabs. "Good. Good," she said. "Everyone in."

They got a huge wooden bar braced against the door just as the mutineers began to pound on the door to get in. From his corner spot, J'role took stock of the group: Captain Patrochian, Releana, the questor, and one other sailor. Everyone else had died or fallen in the retreat from the engine room. Including Voponis, most likely killed by the fireball back at the engine room.

"Captain—" the questor began.

Patrochian cut him off. "See to the boy. I need to think."

The pounding of the door continued, and J'role did not see how the captain could contemplate anything, given the racket and the knowledge that her ship had fallen to traitors. She leaned against a wall and closed her large blue eyes.

At least they were alive, he thought, not killed in their sleep. There was that. J'role realized that sometimes sheer survival was the challenge, and success in that the victory.

The questor approached, probed his wound, then began to speak in the t'skrang tongue, with its many long S and T sounds. A sense of well-being drifted through his flesh, and he felt the same sheltering warmth he'd known as a little boy so many, many years ago. Soon he was lulled into a light sleep.

He woke when he heard the captain ask, "Why, though? Why did he do it?" The questor now stood near the door, listening. Everyone else sat on a few scattered boxes.

J'role was instantly alert to the question and caught the attention of Releana. He made the gesture they'd invented for Throal when the had left Blood Wood.

"Throal," Releana said to the captain.

The captain blinked. "The dwarfs . . . ? That idiot is still . . ." She sighed, leaned against the wall. "Getting people to move forward . . . is so difficult."

"What is it?" asked Releana.

"The dwarfs. I've been trying to set up contacts with Throal. I want to use the *Breeton* as one of their agents to reunite Barsaive under their control, instead of waiting for the Therans to return. *If* they return. But some of my kind fear the power of Throal. I had no idea most of my crew belonged to that camp."

A pounding began at the door. Everyone else stood up, alert and tense, but drowsiness had begun to overtake J'role. His consciousness wavered for a few minutes, but finally the pain and loss of blood took its toll. Drifting, sleeping, dreaming, he left the crisis at hand and hid in the safety of his thoughts.

"J'role? J'role?"

He opened his eyes and saw Releana looking down at him. Something bothered him; something was wrong. How did she know his name?

"J'role!" came a cry from outside the door.

Garlthik.

"Is your name, your true name, J'role?" Releana asked.

He nodded, and slowly raised himself. He felt better. The questor sat next to him, touched J'role's forehead, and nodded. J'role looked down at his chest and saw a thick purple scab, six inches long.

"Someone is calling for you," said the captain, "though I don't know who it is."

"J'role," Releana said, taking his hand and shaking it. "It's a pleasure to meet you." Despite the desperateness of the situation, she smiled.

J'role looked to the door. Three large crates had been set against it. From beyond the door Garlthik said, "J'role, listen to me. I know you can't speak, lad. But I've got your fa-

ther. You've got to acknowledge that. I don't want to harm
him, understand. But I can't speak for these cutthroats.
You've got to open the door, boy. That's what they told me
to tell you. Now, you've got to answer me. There's no telling what they might do. J'role!"

J'role looked to the captain, who nodded.

J'role walked over to the door, climbed up on one of the
crates and knocked twice.

"Ah. There's a lad." Garlthik lowered his voice, and J'role
strained to hear. "I don't know if it's really you yet, so I'm
going to have to test you. Knock once for the first answer,
twice for the second. Did I initiate you in a building or a
field?"

J'role remembered the night of the initiation at the inn. He
knocked once.

"Ahhh. And did I initiate you with fire or water?"

J'role remembered Garlthik grabbing his hand and moving his wrist over the open candle. The memory overwhelmed him. He grabbed his wrist with his other hand. It
felt warm to the touch. But he also remembered the terrible
pain with fondness; Garlthik's strong arms holding his wrist
in place . . . He found himself suddenly missing Garlthik. He
thought back to their time together on the road. J'role lowered his forehead against the door. He then knocked once.

Garlthik's voice became something close to a whisper.
"Now, once for no, and twice for yes. Do you know the
ways now, lad? Do you enjoy being a thief?"

J'role hesitated. Yes. And no. The pause lingered. Finally
he knocked once. And then twice.

"Well, then there it is," whispered Garlthik. "For only a
thief knows how confusing his talents are. Boy, listen.
They're going to bash this door down. They would have
blown it open already, but for fear of the fire-coals within.
But they will enter. *Make things easier.* I've spoken for you
and your friends. As a thief, I've got a certain influence with
folks like these. They asked me to help them and in return,
I'm getting to Throal. I want to take you along with me. I've
stopped them from killing your father. But I can't hold them
off for much longer."

J'role was stunned by Garlthik's bold lies. For a moment
he wondered if Garlthik had changed his mind. Maybe he
would come through.

No. He wouldn't come through. He realized now he had

pinned his hopes on Garlthik when they'd left the village, just as he'd once had hopes for his mother. Don't hope, he told himself. People don't come through.

"Now," continued Garlthik, "I know you won't be able to persuade the others to surrender. And not just because you can't speak. They'll hold out until the end because they'll be hoping things will turn their way. This is no time for hope, J'role, except for hope in me. I can save you. I can save your friends. At some moment, soon, you'll have to open the door. There'll be a flash of activity, but I'll get it settled quick. Will you do this? Twice for yes."

J'role hesitated, not sure how to answer, not sure if lying would do much good. But it seemed it would buy them time. He knocked twice.

"Good lad. Good. I'll be waiting."

J'role pulled away from the door, and found the others waiting expectantly. He pointed to himself, then mimed pulling the bar up from the door. They all nodded. "Who is that person?" asked the captain. J'role shrugged, uncertain how to answer, too upset to try.

"What about your father?" Releana asked.

What about his father? His chin began to tremble. He hated this! Why did he always have to look out for his father? His mother had put the thing in him. Where had his father been? Why couldn't his father just be dead and gone?

After a moment the captain gathered everyone to the far side of the room. When they had all formed a tight group, she whispered, "I estimate we'll reach the *Chakara* within a few hours. I imagine that they'll try to attack her and kill the dwarven envoys. Since the *Chakara* won't be expecting the attack, Nikronallia will be able to get close enough to board her, and take her. He can stop the dwarfs, cause enough trouble to slow trade with them, and he gains another ship into the bargain."

Her strong, determined tone pulled J'role up from his misery. She paused, and everyone waited expectantly.

"I can't let this happen. I can't let the *Breeton* be used for this purpose. I'd rather see her sink. And sink she will. We have the means to do it, right here," the captain said, gesturing at the golden boxes containing the fire-coals. "We can burn the ship down."

"Captain," said Releana. "I'm not sure this would help, but I have some elemental air with me." She tapped the small pouch with her magical supplies. "I could combine it with the elemental fire—the fire-coals—to produce an explosion . . ."

The captain smiled. "We can rip a hole in this room, right at the water level, and the ship will flood. There is a chance we can survive the explosion if we're crafty, but no guarantees." She looked at each of them. "I cannot make this decision for any of you. If you would rather surrender . . ." Her voice trailed off.

J'role knew that of anyone in the room, he was the only one who might survive if they surrendered. But he had no desire to surrender. These were the people who had stood by him. He would rather die with them than sacrifice them for his own survival. In his mother's own painful way, she had taught him that much at least.

Each one nodded in turn. They would sink the *Breeton*.

25

The rocks, in his nightmare, fly through the air and strike his mother's forehead. The other inhabitants of the kaer throw stones at her, too. Children, adults. Everyone. Charneale has gathered everyone for this purpose.

She stands in the fountain at the center of the Atrium, covered with her own blood. It runs down her face, soaks her gray robe. She is weeping, screaming for mercy. The blood splashes the cloth covering the statue of Garlen.

She screams for mercy, but none is given. She is possessed by a Horror, so the magician Charneale believes, and the ancient ritual of cleansing the kaer must be performed.

J'role sees his father in the far corner of the Atrium, just behind the ring of people throwing stones. Bevarden leans against the wall, weeping.

In the nightmare J'role is suddenly beside his father, who does not see him. J'role stares up at his father's face. At first he thinks his father is grieving for his mother, on her knees now, barely alive, swaying back and forth in the fountain.

But as J'role looks into his father's eyes, he realizes something else is at stake. There is another pain his father carries.

Captain Patrochian explained where the fire-coals should be placed for best effect. Some on the floor, forming a wide circle that would let the Serpent's waters rush in. Some on the wall that faced out toward the river, to help get water into the hold. Some against the door, so the water would flood the rest of the ship. And some placed on the walls that led to the storerooms on either side.

"Our job," she said, "is to get as much water into the ship as possible. As the water rushes in, the ship will sink a little more, and then more water will come in, and so on, flooding more and more of the ship." She hesitated, her large blue eyes looking down, then, "Until the *Breeton* is dragged to the Serpent's bottom."

Everyone got to work, setting up the boxes where the captain had indicated. They pulled the nails from packing crates and pounded them into the walls and floor to make braces to hold the boxes in place. While hammering at the nails, they could hear the mutineers shouting to know what was going on inside the hold. "Ignore them," the captain said tersely.

Then Garlthik arrived, pleading with J'role through the door, telling him to think of his father. J'role steeled his heart, and set his focus on the task at hand.

Finally the mutineers began to batter the door down. Nikronallia promised they'd bring out a cannon if they had too, despite the threat of the fire-coals. "If you care at all about the *Breeton*, Patrochian, you'll open up now!"

"It's not mine anymore, you idiot," the captain answered under her breath. "I don't care at all." But J'role knew she was lying.

Everyone but Releana began to drag the crates they'd set against the door back to one corner of the hold. The crates would serve as their shelter from the blast.

They hoped.

With the crates gone from the door, only the wooden bar remained in place. As the mutineers continued to beat and pound on the door, the bolts lowly began to give way.

Outside the door J'role heard someone shout, "Captain Nikronallia, we've spotted the *Chakara*! We'll be on her in minutes!"

"Be up in a minute," Nikronallia called. Then, "It's all over, Patrochian. Surrender."

"We're still thinking it over."

"Bah!"

The mutineers continued to pound on the door. It shuddered and creaked and began to crack.

As Releana set to work opening each of the golden boxes, the room's temperature immediately began to rise. From her pouch she withdrew her own golden box, which J'role assumed was also made of orichalcum, though it was smaller than the ship's boxes. She opened it and then seemed to be pulling out a string, though nothing was actually visible. She walked to each of the boxes and appeared to be tying

knots out of something invisible at the edges of the heat that
flowed out of each box's opening. Every so often she reacted with pain, as if she'd burnt her fingers. Watching her
actions J'role imagined Releana tying strands of air and fire
elementals together, as if they were made of long, invisible
tendrils.

All magic passed through the astral plane, the place where
it was most real. Thus, it might be possible that the bits of
elemental air and fire existed in one form in the physical
world and in another form on the astral plane. Watching
Releana work, it occurred to J'role that she, a magician,
could probably see into the astral plane and manipulate those
parts that were the true magic, the parts that existed on the
astral plane, using actions on this plane, the plane of earth.

Hearing a sharp creak coming from the door, J'role turned
to see a huge gash running down its center. Releana also
turned to look, then began working faster. After three more
loud thumps came from the door, the bolt began to bend.
Releana had just finished her work and huffed over to the
crates, ducking behind them with the others. It looked to
J'role as if she were still holding a piece of invisible string.

"Never mix magical elements," she said with a mischie-
vous smile. "Very unstable."

She waved her hands as if about to cast a spell, but Captain Patrochian interrupted, holding up a long green finger.
"I wouldn't want anyone to miss the show," she said with
grim humor.

At that moment the door crashed open. The captain
dropped her hand and Releana let loose her spell. Flames
jumped from her fingertips, each one like a flying mouse
made of fire, all rushing about in the air on their own little
errands as they followed the path of the elemental air
Releana had tied all around the room.

J'role stared at the mutineers, all of whom looked totally
surprised. Then the captain grabbed him by the shoulders
and dragged him down behind the crates.

One explosion after another ripped through the room,
bathing the walls in harsh red light. Screams and the shriek
of wood ripping apart filled the air, following by the sound
of rushing water. J'role unfolded himself and felt water
spray over him.

"Out! Out!" cried the captain. Everyone scrambled up
from behind the crates. Water rushed up like a fountain from

the hole in the center of the hold, and more water poured in from the hole on the side of the ship. Water already covered the floor completely, spilling into the two adjoining rooms through the holes created from the blast. The corpses of the three mutineers who had charged into the room lay on the floor, the blood from their ruined bodies seeping into the flood.

As three more mutineers tried to rush into the room, Captain Patrochian jumped forward, her sword flashing, and drove them back. "GET OUT!" she screamed at J'role and the others.

"A captain abandons last," said the questor quickly. "If we want her to leave, we'll have to get off first."

The water was already ankle-deep, and still rushing in fiercely. J'role had no idea how they would fight their way through the pressure of the water. He felt hands suddenly grab him, and heard the questor shout, "Hold your breath!" J'role had just enough time to grab some air and close his mouth before the t'skrang were stuffing him out through the hole in the side of the ship. The water rushed against face, forcing his eyes closed.

Suddenly the pressure against him changed to become a pull back into the ship. Opening his eyes he saw that he was in the water, the surface only a few feet above him. Shining through it, the bright sun shimmered and wavered in and out of focus. He moved his arms and legs, trying to swim as the captain had instructed when they'd been setting up the fire-coals.

But the water rushing into the *Breeton* pulled him back. He slammed into the hull of the vessel, and then started to crawl along the ship, trying to get away from the breach. His lungs began burning for air. He almost gasped instinctively, but years of resisting the impulse to open his mouth kept him from doing so now.

Hands grabbed him, and then he did gasp, water rushing into his throat and down into his lungs. He tried to scream, afraid death had finally caught up with him. A moment later he broke the surface of the river. He coughed up the water he'd swallowed, and air poured back into his lungs, sweet and wonderful. The sailor from the storeroom floated alongside him. "All right?" he asked awkwardly, as if not familiar with the dwarven tongue.

J'role nodded, looked around. The *Breeton* towered

above, already listing in their direction. Releana, Captain Patrochian, the questor, and the sailor who had helped him all bobbed nearby in the water.

"Yistorl!" cried the captain to the t'skrang sailor. "Take J'role. I'll help Releana." The sailor took J'role under his arms from behind. Then, with J'role resting against his stomach, he started swimming on his back away from the *Breeton.* J'role turned his head and saw another ship, probably the *Chakara,* approaching. With the t'skrang doing most of the work, the group began moving quickly toward the *Chakara.*

Nothing happened for a few minutes, and J'role thought that their greatest worry would be getting to the *Chakara* before the t'skrang tired. But then he saw red flames blossom from the *Breeton* and fireballs cut through the late afternoon sky. Most of them arced overhead, flying toward the *Chakara,* but some fell short, splashing into the water around them. Thick pillars of steam rose up, towering over them, and the water became uncomfortably hot.

Under the captain's encouragement, the t'skrang swam on, slowed by their young companions, but pressing on nonetheless. The *Breeton,* now listing sharply, turned, changing its course to run them down. If anything would save them, it was that the ship would be considerably slowed by the water it was now taking on.

Though the *Breeton* did not rush toward them as fast as Nikronallia surely would have liked, it did gain on them. J'role thought it only a matter of time before the ship overran them, catching them in its wake and then throwing them against the paddle wheels to be battered and crushed to death.

His mind had ample time to turn the image over and over, until, unexpectedly, shadows loomed above and behind him. Startled, J'role jerked his body around and fell off the sailor into the water. When he spun around, he saw a group of t'skrang in a long, low boat. The *Chakara* had sent out a boat to help them!

Some of those aboard shouted words in the t'skrang tongue and began helping the group into the boat. A sailor extended his hand toward J'role, and soon they were all aboard. The *Chakara*'s sailors grabbed oars and began rowing as quickly as they could. Still the *Breeton* followed, bearing down on the small craft as it raced toward the

Chakara. Both ships began shooting balls of flame at one another, and as the long boat neared the *Chakara*, more and more of the *Breeton*'s fireballs splashed nearby.

J'role looked forward and saw the *Chakara* turning about, realizing he'd been wrong about the intent of the *Breeton.* The ship wasn't trying to run him and the others down. It was trying to intercept the *Chakara.* The long, sharp prongs that extended from the bow of the *Breeton* loomed near now.

As the *Chakara* turned, the ship's sailors dropped rope ladders down to the longboat. Shouts of encouragement and cheers of enthusiasm filled the air as the sailors waved the crew of the longboat and J'role's companions up the ladders. They had only begun working their way up the ladders when a fireball crashed into the stern of the longboat, shattering it and igniting the remains. Spurred on by the heat, they all rushed up the ropes, and again Releana and J'role were aided by the t'skrang.

J'role had just put his feet on the deck of the *Chakara* when the ship shook violently. He looked to his right and saw the *Breeton* towering above; its prongs had pierced the hull of the *Chakara.*

Immediately dozens of t'skrang sailors swung overhead, slashing with their swords as they passed one another. With the t'skrang in their bright, gaudy clothes, the scene looked like a produce cart had overturned sending fruits and vegetables flying wildly through the air. Cries and shouts and curses rang out. The sailors landed with elaborate flips and dives and rolls on each other's ships. It was terrifying and glorious; deadly serious and absurd. A gurgle of giddy excitement rushed up J'role's throat, and he thought for a moment he might both cry and laugh.

A mutineer dropped down beside them, and the captain cut him through the abdomen without a thought. "I'll never have enough of this river," she said under her breath. Suddenly the ship lurched again, this time to starboard. "The *Breeton!*" she cried. "It will drag us down as it sinks!"

J'role looked over the side and saw that the *Breeton*'s two prongs deeply embedded in the *Chakara.* When the prongs and the *Chakara*'s breach reached water level, water would pour into the *Chakara*'s lower decks, plunging the ship down to the bottom of the river along with the *Breeton.*

"What can we do?" asked Releana.

The captain looked back at the *Breeton*—wistfully, J'role

thought—and then said, "We've got to back her up. Get to the wheelhouse and turn the paddle the other way." With that she ran for the edge of the riverboat and threw herself over, grabbing a rope at the last moment and flinging herself over to the *Breeton*. J'role could think of nothing he would rather do than try to keep up with the captain's headlong, reckless energy. He rushed forward and imitated her, swinging back over to the *Breeton*. Releana followed immediately behind, shouting, "I just hope I live so I can tell someone about all this!"

When they reached the deck of the *Breeton*, J'role grabbed a sword from off the deck, prying it out of the hands of a dead sailor. He waved it once through the air, the swishing sound making him suddenly giddy. The captain looked down at him, winked, and then the three were on their way, running along the deck to the rear of the riverboat. The wheelhouse was located on the top deck at the stern, and they had a long way to go.

They fought their way through the mutineers, engaging them in groups of up to six at a time. The captain fought with her skillful swordplay. Releana with her magic. And J'role, slipping his thief magic around him, sneaked up around their opponents, striking from behind. Skirmish after skirmish they fought, each of them taking nicks and cuts. By the time they were halfway there, each was trailing drops of blood in his or her wake.

The captain, who had taken the worst of the damage, finally fell to her knees. "Go on, go on," she said. "Pull the lever all the way back . . ."

"But . . . ," Releana said.

"GO!"

They went. They fought on. They made their way along decks and up ropes. They were wary now, avoiding fights when they could, fighting quickly when they couldn't. Around them a choppy sea of conflict—swords, shouts, the clinks of rapier against rapier . . .

They reached the wheelhouse, a square room sitting atop a platform and surrounded by windows on all sides. They came up low, under the windows, intending to catch the mutineers inside off guard. With a signal to Releana to wait a moment, J'role walked up the stairs to the wheelhouse door, and tried it. Locked. Inside he saw two mutineers. They seemed content to wait safely inside as the battle raged around them. Nikronallia was not among them.

It occurred to J'role that, being a thief, he should be able to unlock a door. He didn't know how to do it exactly, but like so many other things about being a thief, he trusted it would come to him if he lost himself in the magic.

He quieted his thoughts. Let the loneliness soak into his muscles and bones . . .

Yes. It came to him now. He placed his fingertips against the lock . . . Yes . . .

No. He felt his magic falter. He was positive he should be able to manipulate the lock by using magic; he sensed the magic within, wanting him to do it. But he knew the task was simply too difficult to accomplish without some practice and thought. That was for a later time.

He signaled Releana to come up the stairs, then stood and smashed the glass of the door with the pommel of his sword. Quickly he reached in and undid the lock. As he pulled his hand out, one of the mutineers jabbed his rapier into J'role's arm. He fell back just as Releana cast a spell. She dropped to the ground and breathed onto the floor. A thick layer of ice rushed across the room, suddenly sliding under the feet of the startled mutineers, who slipped and tumbled to the floor.

J'role jumped into the room, driving his rapier into the chest of one of the t'skrang. Releana killed the other one with an ice spear she produced from her hands.

J'role spotted the lever. Though it was labeled in t'skrang, it was pushed all the way forward, and it seemed obvious that pulling it all the way back would reverse the *Breeton*'s direction. J'role scrambled for the device, slipping on the blood and ice that covered the floor. He reached it, and pulled it all the way, then he and Releana breathed a sigh of relief as they heard the paddle grind to a halt and start up again. He looked out the rear window and saw the wheel in full reverse. Slowly the ship began to back up.

J'role turned toward Releana. His smile quickly vanished, for right behind her stood Nikronallia, blood-stained and grim.

Even as Releana turned in response to J'role's visible fear, Nikronallia was pulling back on his sword, getting ready to run Releana through. Releana just had time to cry out in surprise and terror when a knife flashed in the door frame and caught Nikronallia full in the neck. The mutiny leader gurgled blood for a moment, then fell backward over the stairway railing.

"Lad!" Garlthik One-Eye exclaimed, his bulky ork body filling the doorway. "Are you all right?" He paused for a moment, taking in J'role's reaction. When J'role only stood there impassively, he said, "Thank the gods and goddesses you found help. I've been a prisoner to these—"

J'role rushed forward and slammed into Garlthik, sending the ork over the railing. The ork bounced on the deck below, then plunged into the Serpent.

"We've got to get off!" shouted Releana. As if confirming the urgency of the danger, the ship listed sharply and threw them to the deck.

26

He dreamed of her putting the thing in him. His mother stood beside his bed, her fingertips pressed against his chest, gently massaging his skin. "Like this?" she asked. The white shadow in the corner replied, "Yes."

As the ship rocked and listed sharply, J'role and Releana fell to the deck. Dazed, he lost the impulse to get up and move, but Releana was quickly at his side and tugging on his arm. "The *Chakara* isn't holding the *Breeton* up any more," she said. "We've got to go!"

J'role came out of his strange disorientation, and the two of them fled across the upper deck, trying to get to the *Chakara* before the *Breeton* capsized. Balancing carefully on the deck's steep angle, they worked their way through the corpses and the blood. The fighting had stopped, and both the *Chakara*'s crew and the *Breeton* mutineers who wanted to surrender had begun a retreat. Ahead dozens of t'skrang swung from the sinking ship over to the *Chakara*.

J'role and Releana were halfway down the length of the ship when J'role suddenly thought of his father.

Where was he? Was he still alive?

Releana ran on a few steps more, then turned to look when she realized J'role had fallen behind. He waved her on toward the *Chakara*, then turned toward a passage leading to the lower decks. Releana must have read his mind. Running back toward him, she said, "They might have found him already, Grim . . . J'role. Some of the *Chakara*'s sailors might have gotten him off the ship."

J'role hesitated. She might be right. But he couldn't wait. He started down the stairs.

A moment later he heard Releana following. He felt much better.

With the ship now tilted at a forty-five degree angle, J'role and Releana had to walk with one foot on the floor and one foot at the base of the wall. They ran through the ship, Releana calling, "Hello? Hello?" over and over again. They found corpses, but no Bevarden. Eventually they reached the lower decks, and as they headed toward the starboard side they saw passages filling with water; further on some cabins were completely submerged.

J'role wondered if the ship would soon begin to sink faster, with he and Releana trapped aboard, unable to find an exit before the decks they now wandered flooded with water.

J'role tapped Releana on the arm, then pointed one way for her, and another for himself.

"Good. We'll cover more rooms that way. We'll meet in five minutes. I think that's all we have ... J'role. I'm sorry. But I think we must leave soon."

They broke apart. Alone now, J'role felt the thief magic come warm and strong upon him. It gave him a valuable sense of balance, allowing him to move quickly through the tilted corridors without falling into the water that now lapped at his thighs. The magic focused him, made him need no one and nothing but himself. He would survive. He knew that. He would endure.

"Why don't you let your father die?" the creature asked. "You know that's what you want."

J'role did not answer, because, in some way he could not understand, he knew that the creature was right.

He checked cabin after cabin, pushing aside bits of wood that floated in the flooding, blood-stained waters. Time was running out, but he could not give up.

Passing another corridor that tilted up steeply, he heard the sound of crying. The corridor tilted up, and a voice so like his father's seemed to emanate from somewhere along it. J'role began to climb quickly up the inclined floor. After climbing another fifteen feet of corridor, J'role found that the water had risen enough to cut off the passage he had traveled. The ship was sinking faster.

Finally he came to the room where his father wept. He looked inside and saw Bevarden resting at the bottom of the room, where the floor met the ceiling. A thick cord was tied around his hands and feet, and he stared down. "What is the world? What is the world?" he kept asking over and over through his tears.

J'role slid down the floor, and his father looked up, shocked as J'role appeared beside him. Then the fear turned to joy. "My son. My son." But even this emotion evaporated, replaced by deep-lined sadness across Bevarden's thin, tired face.

His father's sudden shifts of emotion filled J'role with a kind of anguished frustration, but he set about untying his father's bonds. His fingers moved nimbly and quickly. Though the sailors had created an extraordinary puzzle, J'role's thoughts cut quickly through the maze of cord. As soon as Bevarden's hands were freed, he grabbed J'role and held him close.

J'role flailed his arms and forced his father away. The man's touch sickened him. His father looked at him, stunned and hurt. "J'role . . . My J'role . . ." Then, as if perceiving some deep knowledge from the look in J'role's eyes, he said, "I'm sorry." He looked away. "I'm sorry. I didn't . . . Your mother and I . . ." He gasped for air.

J'role stood, grabbed his father, and helped him up. He handed one end of the rope to his father and then climbed with the other end up to the door. After looping the rope around the doorknob, he slammed the door against the wall, trying to get his father's attention. But Bevarden simply stared at the rope, his jaw moving without words.

Down the passageway the water was rising faster and faster. J'role slammed the door against the wall again and again. Finally Bevarden looked up at him. "You . . . ," Bevarden began. "The elves are wrong, J'role. All wrong. When we emerged, the world was supposed to be wonderful. Perfect. I had heard . . . things."

Confusion swirled in J'role's thoughts. He knew now what had happened. His mother had betrayed him to the creature, the white shadow in their home in the kaer. Why had his father always been so upset? It was his mother! Why did his father turn to drinking? Why had his father become so weak?

Energized with furious impatience, he slid back down to the bottom of the room and quickly tied the rope around his father's waist. Then he scrambled back up, and began dragging Bevarden toward the door.

"I loved ... I loved ... your mother very ... You see, J'role. I loved ... And she wanted ... She thought ... She had to ... You see ..."

J'role only half-heard the words, for he was putting all his effort into dragging his father up the tilted floor. The memory the creature in his thoughts had given him came to him now, and he felt his mother's fingertips on his chest, casting the ritual that allowed the Horror into his head.

"I'm sorry ..."

The apology! Always the apology! Over and over again the apology! All these years he'd heard his father apologizing. J'role never really knowing what for.

That, J'role realized as he tugged on the rope, was the true legacy his father had given him. Always apologizing. J'role had spent his whole life up until he met Garlthik thinking he had to apologize to everybody. Only now did he realize he was not whole, but he did not have to spend his life apologizing for it.

"Please ...," his father begged, but for what J'role did not now.

J'role wanted to scream, but held his tongue. Instead the anger inside him seized his muscles, and he slammed his foot into his father's face. Bevarden cried out with terrible pain, the blood smearing his features. The ship creaked and tipped backward.

"Now, didn't that feel good?" asked the creature.

It did not. J'role felt a terrible shame. He wanted to cry. But he choked back the impulse. Why had he hurt his father like that? Bevarden began to cry once more. With two more heaves he had his father up to the door frame. He stared at his father, and saw empty and pathetic eyes.

Why had everything been like this?

Fearful of what he might do next, J'role began to climb up the floor, knowing he would have to keep moving to higher ground until they finally made it out the other side of the ship.

"Let him die," the creature suggested.

"Quiet!" J'role thought fiercely.

The thief magic tugged at his muscles. The ship *was* sinking faster now. With his father slowing him down, he might not make it out. Should he ... ?

He looked down toward the door. His father looked up at him, longing deep in his eyes, longing for love from his son.

"I just . . . So much wanted to make you happy . . ."

Then why weren't you stronger! J'role thought fiercely.

Bevarden reached his hand up toward J'role. "I'm sorry . . ."

J'role ignored his father, tried to beat down his fury. He tied his end of the rope around his waist and began climbing up the passage. Soon the rope went taut, and he looked back and saw his father had not yet begun to climb up after him. He simply sat in the door frame, staring at the opposite wall.

J'role snapped the rope. His father turned languidly and looked at J'role. He smiled. The rising water lapped at Bevarden's feet.

With the fear of drowning growing in him, J'role braced himself in a doorway and began to drag his father up the passage. Bevarden offered no help. When J'role had dragged his father a dozen or so feet, the rope, now wet from the rising water, slid through his hands. The rope burned deep into his palms, and Bevarden splashed into the water below. The pull of the rope tugged at J'role's waist and he slid down into the water after his father.

The two of them splashed wildly in the water for a moment, Bevarden's cries for help filling J'role's ears like a nightmare. Finally he found the floor and began to climb out. But his father grabbed him from behind and the two of them went deep into the water once more.

Again they twisted and turned, splashing with panic in the water, the cord that bound them wrapping so tightly around them that soon both had lost the free motion of their arms and legs. J'role could not keep afloat, and he found himself dragged under the water, his throat choking with water. He came up for air, and his father grabbed him, apologizing and begging for help.

His father's weight carried J'role under the water once more, and this time J'role became dizzy from the lack of air. His feet found the floor of the corridor, and he pushed up, forcing his father back and beaching the surface of the water.

His father grabbed him again. J'role freed his right arm and pushed his father away. Bevarden cried out in despair, and clutched at J'role's face, as if he only wanted to hold his son in a tender embrace for a moment.

Once more J'role was forced down under the water by his father.

When next he came up for air, J'role was screaming.

His mouth moved wildly, his tongue out of control. Screeching and screaming and babbling and cursing, he launched himself toward his father, slamming into him. The two of them splashed through the water and J'role forced his father toward the wall. Bevarden's face contorted in terrible pain, and he tried to grab his ears to protect himself from the sounds. But the tangled rope kept his hands from his head. So he shook his head wildly back and forth.

Without thinking, J'role slammed his father against the wall. He screamed into his father's face. His father shut his eyes, opened his mouth into a wide O, cried out. Tears ran down his face.

So *weak*. So *weak*. And each time J'role thought the words, the creature in his mind whispered, "Yes."

The words built themselves into a steady rhythm, and soon, with a matching rhythm, he slammed his father against the wall. An exciting pleasure ran through him. He did not mean to do it, but it all happened nonetheless. Screaming with the creature's voice, he grabbed his father by the throat and smashed his head against the wall with a sharp crack. He did it again and again until splashes of blood radiated onto the wall, forming a scarlet frame around his father's contorted face. Suddenly his father's eyes opened wide, startled. He tried once more to speak, looking directly into J'role's eyes, but not a word came out. Finally he heaved in a sharp, dry breath.

Then stillness.

Immediately J'role pulled his hands back. He saw his father's blood swirling around him in the water, and he screamed and screamed, clawing at the ropes, desperate to disentangle himself from his father's corpse. The cords grew tighter and tighter until he realized he was strangling himself.

"Yes," the creature said, the words crashing through his thoughts even as he struggled. "Yes. Let yourself die. Kill yourself now. How can you go back? How can you go back to that young girl? Think about what you have just done!"

The creature's words made more and more sense.

How could he have . . . ?

He tightened the rope around his neck, felt the harsh burn against this flesh.

"Yes, yes. Take your life. End it!"

J'role's strength withered away as continued to strangle himself. Dizziness came next, and finally he had trouble seeing. When the darkness closed around him he splashed into the water, aware only of drifting in the water, happy at last that it would finally be over.

Hands grabbed him.

"J'role!" Releana shouted.

The creature whined like an angry cat.

She was in the water with him, uncoiling the rope from his neck, from around his body.

He was confused. Disappointed. Finally he would have been able to let all the pain go. Why was she here?

When she had removed the rope from his body, she looked at Bevarden. J'role thought for sure she would scream or push him away. But she did not know he had killed his own father. She said, "J'role, I'm sorry. But we can't take your father's body with us. We don't have time."

He nodded, too stunned to do anything but listen to her instructions.

Was it obvious? Wasn't it written across his face? How could she not see?

But the two of them climbed out of the water and worked their way up the passage. They reached another one and turned right, running now on the edge where the floor and wall met. On and on they ran, leaving Bevarden's corpse behind, though J'role did not feel any more distance from the body no matter how far they traveled.

They raced through the ship until they found an open window that led out onto the tilted balcony right outside. They were near the bow of the *Breeton* now, and not much of the ship remained above water. Around it a terrible undertow had formed. If they tried to dive in and swim to the *Chakara*, they would most likely be sucked underwater. And now the *Chakara* was beginning to pull away, its crew probably desperate to get their ship away from the undertow.

"J'role! Releana!" he heard Captain Patrochian cry, then saw her on a mid-deck of the *Chakara* waving her arms. J'role and Releana ran down the side of the *Breeton*, leaping over windows and doors. As they reached the bow the captain swung a rope over from the *Chakara*. J'role stretched as far as he could over the edge of the bow and caught it. He had only just fixed his grip when the *Chakara*'s movement pulled him off the *Breeton*. He stretched out his hand and grabbed Releana by the wrist, and the two of them swung out into the space between the ships. They swung swiftly to the *Chakara,* where the sailors grabbed J'role and pulled him and Releana over the railing.

All remained silent a moment, then Releana said, "I'm sorry, J'role."

He said nothing. For once glad he had no choice.

A t'skrang from the *Chakara* approached. "'Scuse me lad, but we fished an ork out of the river. Captain Patrochian said you might know who he is. Now I know you can't talk, but can you signal us what to do with him? We'll be hanging the mutineers, of course, but we really don't know if this one was involved."

J'role looked past the sailor and saw Garlthik, bound just as his father had been. With his one good eye fixed on the J'role, the ork smiled his toothy smile. The look clearly said, "Whatever you decide, lad. It's all been rough, and I'll take whatever you give me." J'role knew that with a nod or two to the right questions he could condemn the ork to death. Hadn't the man plotted the murder of nearly everyone on ship?

Including Bevarden.

J'role glanced at Releana. Better not to form ties, he felt the thief magic tell him. You don't know who you might have to kill next.

Garlthik had warned him of this during the initiation. The lesson was well taken.

He looked once more at Garlthik, knew he had more in common with the ork than anyone else on the ship. He shook his head, and to everyone's surprise, including Garlthik's, he pointed at Garlthik and shook his head. Then he walked off alone, clutching his forehead, looking for someplace safe to fall asleep. Some place where he would be safe from the memories.

27

"Am I doing this the right way?" his mother asked. The creature purred in response. J'role felt something slip into his head, slick and oily, and it slid through his thoughts.

Although only a small child, an astounding insight came to him: he had always had one place of privacy. His thoughts. His mother had bartered that off.

He would never be alone again.

"We owe you our thanks!" said Borthum, leader of the dwarven envoys from Throal. He raised his mug high, and all at the table did the same. The *Chakara*'s captain, a t'skrang with a white stripe running over his head and down his back, was hosting them in his stateroom. The guests included the captain of the *Chakara*, Releana, Captain Patrochian, and seven dwarfs from Throal. The dwarfs wore loose, square-cut clothes covered with spirals that wound around each other in fascinating patterns. On their feet were thick shoes with pointed tips that curved up. Their long beards were braided and flat as boards. On their heads they wore round hats, each inscribed with symbols that J'role, of course, could not understand. Some wore earrings.

They were friendly, and not at all suspicious of J'role, though he sat glum and unresponsive throughout the dinner. He had tried to avoid the meal, but Captain Patrochian insisted he accept his hero's honor. He was afraid that too much protesting would raise suspicions, so he'd agreed to come.

But J'role couldn't think about food. All he could do was keep trying to prevent the memory of his dead—murdered—father from entering his thoughts. He was convinced that someone at the table already knew what he had done or else would figure it out by looking at him and catching a chance gesture that revealed too much.

In the din of the dinner conversation, just at the edge of his thoughts, he heard Releana ask the dwarfs about the stones for a city they might have cut before the Scourge. The dwarfs had cut the stones for many cities and citadels, but knew of none in the vicinity Releana described. She asked for permission for her and J'role to enter Throal and search through the dwarven records for any hints of such construction. The dwarfs laughingly agreed that they could do nothing but accede to the request. "Heroes," one of them said, "are well respected in Throal."

During the meal another one asked, "And what is the matter with your grim friend?"

Some of the guests at the table, those who knew that J'role had lost his father, looked aghast. "His father, sir, died on the *Breeton*," said Releana.

The dwarfs looked appropriately ashen.

"His name, sirs," continued Releana, "was once Grim, but is now J'role."

"He is a thief adept," said Captain Patrochian, "but an honorable one."

The dwarven leader raised his mug. "Here is to fallen fathers, then. And to honorable thieves, rare though they may be!"

All raised their cups, and most drank deeply. All but J'role, he touched the liquid to his lips, and thought he might never drink or eat again.

"There's a branch of the Serpent, the Coil, which flows down from the dwarven mountains," explained Captain Patrochian to J'role and Releana the day the *Chakara* docked at the foot of the mountains. "But it's far too rough for our ships. The rest of your trip will be overland."

"And what will become of you?" asked Releana.

The captain drew in a long breath. "I'll stay on the *Chakara* for a while. Ships are rare to come by, but I might obtain funding from King Varulus for a new one. I've given the envoys my offer. They'll carry it back to Throal for me." She looked away, and then back at them. "But this is not the talk for now. Good luck to you. And to you especially, J'role. For someone who was supposed to bring bad luck, you undoubtedly helped save dozens of lives with your warning. Thank you." She extended her hand, and he took it.

But though their flesh touched, J'role felt nothing in the moment. His body seemed insubstantial, as if nothing about him was real anymore.

The others said their goodbyes, and soon the entourage was on its way to Throal. It consisted of eight dwarfs, Releana, J'role, and Garlthik, still bound. Because J'role would not incriminate the ork for the mutiny attempt, Garlthik's fate fell to dwarven justice. Rumors of the exploits of Garlthik One-Eye were known through the area, and the dwarfs recognized him. "Fame," whispered Garlthik to J'role, "is a loathsome thing to a thief. Quite a paradox for those who are of legendary quality, eh, lad?" He laughed conspiratorially, but J'role shunned him.

They would reach the gates of the kingdom on the next day. The dwarfs had donkeys with saddlebags full of food, and so the group remained well fed. J'role kept to himself, eating alone and keeping slightly away from the rest of the group; he knew they thought it was because he mourned his father's death, and they were partially correct. But in truth he did not know what to think about what he had done. He remained separate because he *felt* so apart from them. He had done a thing that none of them would have done.

And more, a part of him had begun to enjoy the fact that he had killed his father. There seemed a power to it. Finally he was free of that tired old man! Finally the whimpering and begging and apologies had come to end.

Still, even as he tried to find strength in his actions, tears rolled down his face.

It was at twilight, when the stars began to dot the dark violet curtain drawing over the western horizon, that Borthum, leader of the dwarfs, spotted the riders. They approached from the south, creating a billowing wall of dirt behind them. "Arms," Borthum said calmly. The dwarfs drew their weapons wearily as if they had already responded to the same command far too many times.

"Who is it?" asked Releana, scraping up some dirt from the ground and holding it in her hands.

"I don't know," said Borthum. "We never know until it's time to fight." The dwarf, his round face hidden partially behind his heavy beard, seemed impassive. But his head shook slightly.

* * *

Though the daylight was dying, the riders were identified long before blows could be exchanged. All J'role could make out were the animals they rode—large beasts, as tall as men, with a smooth, hairless hide.

"Scorchers," said Garlthik.

"Aye," agreed Borthum. "Ork scorcher." He eyed Garlthik.

A tingle passed along J'role's spine; an anticipation of violence. Death. He had no need to draw the magic close around him; it had seeped deep into his being now, resting comfortably. And he knew that whatever came of the encounter, he would do whatever necessary to survive. He couldn't even try to fight it. He was so alone in the world, the magic would turn him into a puppet and make him live.

"Will there be a fight?" asked Garlthik.

"Most likely. Though I wish it were not so. We have no antipathy toward them. We even have relations with several of the tribes. But who knows? Sometimes they attack. Sometimes they don't." He pointed to a hill with a sharp, flat side. "We'll prepare ourselves there, and make a circle."

"I can speak to them," said Garlthik as they walked toward the hill.

"I'm sure you can."

Garlthik stiffened. "Don't think I'll be spared because of my race. As they are ambivalent toward your people, so are they ambivalent toward all outsiders—even other orks. I don't relish the idea of them finding me bound in these ropes. These raiders have a harsh sense of worth, and anyone weak enough to be captured is usually killed."

Borthum looked carefully at Garlthik, as if weighing out the value of precious stone. "Perhaps ..."

"If they are violent, and they do want a fight, I will be the best one to undertake the negotiations." Garlthik looked toward the orks, and J'role followed his gaze. There were at least thirty of the raiders. The ork looked surprised. "I've never seen them in such strong numbers."

"They've been organizing for some time now," answered the dwarf. "Or what passes for organization among them." He paused for a moment, then said, "Here is what we will do. We will let Garlthik One-Eye speak with the orks if needed."

One of the dwarfs tried to interrupt, but Borthum raised his hand.

"If they decide to attack, we will fight to the end. But know this, the battle will be difficult. Not all shall live. Which is why I will give Garlthik his chance. I would rather let him speak than lead us into such a lopsided battle. If it comes to a fight, a fight it will be, whether Garlthik speaks or not. Untie his ropes."

"What?" asked one of the dwarfs.

"Untie him. He'll hold no authority with them if he's bound."

Two of the dwarfs reluctantly undid the ropes, and Garlthik smiled at J'role. The boy had no idea what the ork was up to, but it being Garlthik, some scheme was surely at work. Garlthik then walked away from the group, and came to a stop at twenty feet. He stood tall and firm.

J'role suspected that Borthum also had a plan in mind. He walked over to the dwarf, who stood shoulder height to J'role, and touched the dwarf's shoulder. He pointed toward Garlthik, and then shrugged.

The dwarf smiled. "I do not think he wants us dead, and I do not think he wants to escape," he said softly. "I have checked his knots every half hour this day, and he has—by my observations—made no attempt to free himself. I had expected to re-tie his knots all during our journey, but there has been no need. This strikes me as odd. Unless he wishes to reach our mountain kingdom and gain access to it."

The approach of the ork riders turned thunderous now. Their beasts were huge: giant, six-legged animals with gray hides and large faces tipped with monstrous horns. The orks on the backs of the beasts were no less terrifying. They wore thick leather armor made from tanned hides. They had adorned their heavy, gray-green faces with dyes of some kind—lines and circles of red, yellow, blue, and green. In their hair they wore bits of bones as additional adornments. On their backs they had slung bows, along with quivers. In their arms they carried large, heavy lances.

They rode in a great spiral around the hill that Borthum had designated as their point of defense. The trotting of the beasts consumed all other sounds, and rumbled in J'role's chest. He watched their speed. Dodging his way out of the circle might be difficult, but he could get through them if he had to. From there, he did not know. There was little shelter in the area. The trick would be to leave the instant the fight broke out. His exit might not be noticed in the initial skirmish, and he could simply run and run.

The spiral tightened, eventually slowing as the raiders came to a stop. Their beasts snorted, and the raiders stared impassively. The three orks in the lead looked down at Garlthik.

Garlthik raised his arms, and J'role faintly heard him speak strange words. Garlthik halted several times, apparently having trouble with some of the sounds. This impression was confirmed when the raider orks laughed and turned to one another, ignoring Garlthik and speaking to each other. Then the lead raider looked down at Garlthik and cut him off, speaking over Garlthik's attempts at the ancient ork tongue.

Around J'role the dwarfs subtly hefted their weapons, waiting for the conversation to suddenly break out into a brawl.

But Garlthik shook his head, and tried again. This time he did better, his words running more smoothly than the first time, though there were still starts and stops. He gestured to the group behind him, and specifically to J'role. This concerned J'role, and his concern only increased when the ork leader turned to look directly at him.

The conversation continued for some time, with Garlthik gesturing in the air with his hands. J'role saw Borthum watching the conversation as if he suspected some kind of trick, but the dwarf held his ground and said nothing.

Then came a long pause, and it seemed as if the raider leader was weighing out much more than whether or not to go into battle. Finally he nodded, and shouted commands in the ork tongue to his followers. The spiral quickly broke up and the group sprinted off into the darkness.

Garlthik stood for a moment, then his shoulders heaved with a heavy sigh. He turned and came back to the group as Borthum crossed toward him.

"You spoke for a long time."

"No thanks? They wanted to kill you."

"Thank you. What did you talk about all that time?"

"My background. They wanted to know who my family was. I lied and connected it to distant relations of theirs. That part was lucky. I might well have connected it to their most hated enemy."

Borthum paused, looked at Garlthik carefully. "Lucky."

"Yes."

Borthum turned from Garlthik and announced that they would make camp for the night.

A sound woke J'role. Without thinking abut it, he rolled from where he lay, then stood straight up. Garlthik knelt beside where J'role had slept, and he looked up at J'role with a grin. His one good eye caught the dying light of the fire's embers and turned it solid red. He raised a finger to his lips, then crooked it, signaling for J'role to approach.

J'role examined Garlthik carefully. The dwarfs had tied him up again, and the ropes still seemed to bind him. Garlthik had crawled or rolled over to where J'role slept. He did not appear to be armed. J'role approached, and knelt down near Garlthik. They faced each other, as they had on the day Garlthik had initiated J'role at the tavern. The red light framed them, flickering, shifting from red to black to red again.

"Are you all right, then?"

J'role shook his head, cutting off the ork's friendly, concerned tone, not wanting to hear any more pleasantries. He pushed at Garlthik, hoping the ork would simply leave him alone.

But Garlthik spoke again, this time with a seriousness in his voice. "I know, I know. You think I turned on you. But I didn't, you know. I'll tell you honestly, I would have killed the others. And though I can see you're upset about your father's death, him too. I would have, and I say it with no shame. I don't feel shame, that's what gives me my strength. But you? No, lad. Not you. You're still weak." He smiled gently once more, his large teeth sticking out over his lips. With a concerned, comforting tone, he went on, "You're my student, you see? We're bound."

J'role turned his face toward the ground. He wanted to take the words into his heart, but they frightened him.

"Think just of this then, lad. Dig deep inside yourself and give my questions some time to take root. Do you think you're incapable of doing what I did? Would you have done anything different?"

J'role knew the questions all too well. They had already taken root and he didn't want to think about them anymore. Hadn't he killed his own father? There was no need to contemplate the matter. He lay back on the mat the dwarfs had given him for sleeping and turned his back toward Garlthik.

"Very well," said the ork quietly. "Yes, I understand. I see. Well, good night."

J'role heard him crawling off. After watching the embers dying for half an hour, he finally fell asleep.

The gloom that weighed on J'role lightened as they traveled around an outcropping of large rocks and then reached the entrance to Throal.

Three giant arches had been carved into the flat face of the mountain; the center arch stupendously large, the ones on either side only astoundingly large. Even the mountain that towered high above the arches could not make them seem small. Massive stones had been fitted around the edges of the archways, and they glittered gold in the sunlight. A long train of pack animals was leaving the kingdom along a road that rolled out from the mountain. Compared to the arch, they looked like no more than insects.

J'role's group approached, and reached the road that led south from the mountains. On the road they met some other travelers, mostly dwarfs, but also elves—without thorns—orks, obsidimen, the strange creatures made of black stone, thick-bodied lizard-folk with powerful tails, and humans. Some carried baskets filled with beautiful statues or cloth. Two or three had wagons, well protected by a complement of guards who looked sternly at J'role when he eyed their goods.

As he approached the gate J'role was certain he would pass out from fear as he walked under the arches. It seemed impossible that such arches would be able to support themselves.

Releana stepped up beside him. "It's beautiful, isn't it?"

J'role almost turned and answered, feeling a warm desire to join her in her amazement. He caught himself, and faced forward, with not even a nod. He was aware of her walking beside him for a moment longer, felt strongly her desire to be with him, just to show she cared. But his coldness won out, and he saw her shadow on the ground fall back in the entourage.

Better, he thought to himself. It's better this way.

They walked up to the arches, and J'role saw that the gold-plated stones that framed them carried inscriptions, just as the entrance to his own kaer had stones with inscriptions. J'role realized that once all these gates had been bricked up, to shut out the Horrors, and only in the last few decades had the dwarfs torn the walls down and opened the kingdom to the world.

He could not understand the glyphs on the stones, of course, but they fascinated him just the same. Pictures of griffins and strange, three-headed men and the sun and the stars and all the things of the world seemed etched out in the gold plating. Though he could not understand them, he knew that the Horrors, in some strange, magical way, could. They read the glyphs and turned back.

The creature in his thoughts snickered and said, "*Most* of us turned back."

The entourage passed under the arches and then into a large cavern beyond them that stretched as high as the arches themselves. The sunlight reached only so far into this massive antechamber, and the air cooled suddenly.

Around the cavern stood dozens of stalls, all displaying wares, yet these took up only a small portion of the massive chamber. The rest of the area was kept clear, as if the space were being reserved for others who might wish to set up shop at the gates of the city.

Travelers from the road haggled with the merchants, trading their wares or trying to purchase goods with coin and jewelry. The merchants were as varied in face as the travelers on the road—elves, t'skrang, dwarfs, stone men, thick-bodied lizard folk. He even saw a few tiny winged people selling delicate silver jewelry. After all the groups he had seen thus far, the elves and the t'skrang and the ork scorchers, all of whom had stayed with their own kind, the racial mix at the kingdom's entrance startled J'role. Everyone seemed pleasant and cooperative. Despite his dour state, the sight had the odd effect of lifting his spirits.

All throughout the bazaar area were many dwarven guards who stood by the archways and walked around the booths. They wore metal armor of polished silver and carried heavy axes and maces. Like the dwarfs J'role's group had traveled with, their beards were neatly trimmed, though their demeanor was grimmer. They eyed everyone carefully. And again, like the floor space for the bazaar, there seemed to be more guards than were needed, all in expectation of more merchants and travelers.

Borthum called three of the guards over, instructing them to take Garlthik to the prison and lock him in a cell with magical locks. The guards looked with some awe and trepidation at Garlthik, who smiled down at them with his toothy grin. Then the dwarfs nodded and led the ork away.

It seemed possible to J'role that he might never see the ork again. But something stirred within his soul, and he felt that his time with Garlthik One-Eye had still not come to an end.

28

He is seven. There is something crawling in his thoughts.
His mother stands beside him, breathing heavily. Weeping.

"Hello, J'role," the creature in his thoughts says. "You're
a good boy, aren't you?"

J'role is afraid. He thinks nothing. He says nothing.

"Yes, yes, you are. And do you now what good boys don't
do? They don't upset their parents. You know that, don't
you? Look what you did to your mother. She's crying. You
should feel terrible."

Several corridors, each forty feet tall, each with an arched
ceiling coming to a point, led out of the huge antechamber.
The dwarfs led J'role and Releana straight ahead, down a
corridor that in turn branched off into smaller corridors.
Their guides took one of these, and it led to more corridors.
The dimensions of this final one was the standard for the
rest of the kingdom: some ten yards wide and twenty feet
tall. Glowing moss grew on the walls and ceiling, filling the
corridors with a pleasant yellow light. Doorways stood on
the right and the left, and many, many dwarfs passed them
as they moved along the corridor.

Soon they came to the base of great steps that led up hundreds of feet. They climbed them, and arrived at a landing
that connected with several other stairways, all of which
rose up into the mountains of Throal. On the landing were
benches and strange, red-leafed trees, and waterfalls that fell
into a pool from which the dwarfs drank, urging their guests
to drink as well. When he did, J'role found the water de-
lightfully sweet, unlike anything he'd ever tasted. After only
a few minutes of rest on the bench, he felt completely re-

freshed and ready to ascend more stairs. Everyone reacted to the water the same way, and they climbed on.

They came to a corridor where few other dwarfs walked, and their guides led the two young adventurers to some rooms, indicating that one room had been prepared for each one.

Borthum said, "I will have Merrox, Master of the Hall of Records, come and get you on the morn. He can help you find any information you seek about our stonecutting." The dwarf extended his thick, stubby hand to each of them. "Thank you both for your help."

J'role entered his room and found it decorated with glowing flowers and moss. A large, soft bed waited within. On long poles hung clothes in the dwarven fashion—square and heavy—but big enough to fit him. On a table at one end of the room sat a bowl filled with fruit and sweetbread.

But of everything he saw it was the bed that most drew his attention. He shut the door behind him, stripped out of his clothes and walked toward it. The covers were smooth and light, and when he slid between them, the mattress was like drifting on a cloud. He pulled up the covers and their comforting warmth enveloped him.

The magical plants in the room dimmed as he drifted off, and soon J'role was asleep.

The next day he awoke to find his clothes gone and an iron tub filled with warm water waiting for him. It took him a moment to understand what the water was for, then he slipped into it. It smelled of flowers as the suds floated up around him. He bathed and soaked, enjoying the smell of the water and its soothing warmth against his skin.

J'role felt relaxed, but it was not only because he was safe within the heart of the dwarven kingdom. He had successfully pushed thoughts of his father's fate from his mind. It was a tenuous moment of peace, but he would take what he could.

J'role smiled ruefully. Being a thief, what other choice did he have?

When the water cooled he climbed out of the tub and spotted a thick towel resting on the clothes rack. He padded across the smooth stone of the floor and dried himself off. From the rack he then chose a brown tunic with golden spirals, baggy golden pants, and a pair of sandals.

He went over to the bowl containing sweetbread, dates, bananas, and oranges. He ate for a while, and then a knock came at the door. J'role went to open it, and found Releana standing behind an ancient-looking dwarf. Dressed in a robe of blue and silver, the dwarf wore his long silver hair flowing down over his shoulders. Like the other dwarfs he had a neatly trimmed beard.

"Greetings, J'role, the Honorable Thief. I am Merrox, Master of the Hall of Records. If you are ready?"

J'role nodded, and they set off.

Merrox opened the great wooden doors to the Hall of Records, and J'role stepped into an enormous chamber that went on and on. The walls spread out into an enormous valley with a tall dark ceiling. Shelves towered overhead and ran the length of the hall, stacked with scrolls and parchments and books, so thickly packed that in the distance it all seemed a solid mass of paper. Dwarfs sat at heavy tables recording data from one book to another, or sliding tall ladders on wheels along the shelves, climbing up and down them, removing and pulling innumerable records from the shelves.

"We're doomed," said Releana, oddly brief in her summation of the situation.

"Not exactly," said Merrox, with a chuckle that suggested anything from good-natured encouragement to ill-conceived dark humor. "Our codices are quite ordered, and with information from you we should be able to cross-reference the records and find exactly what you are seeking." He paused and cocked his head to one side. "Just exactly what are you looking for?"

Sounding very pessimistic, Releana said, "A forgotten city, hidden from all memory with magic strong enough to blind even the Horrors to its presence; a city no one knows of, no longer marked on any map, and not mentioned for over four hundred years."

Merrox raised an eyebrow. "Well. That *is* a challenge."

J'role had no patience with any of them anymore, for he had worn the ring, and now the longing came full and strong. He had reached the dwarven records. He would persevere. He strode into the hall. Chandeliers with thick wax candles burned overhead. Pools of light flickered on the floor.

He turned back to Merrox, who returned his gaze with one eyebrow lowered and the other raised, "Ah, well," he said. "If you're willing to press on . . ." He led them to an empty table, "Here, we'll use this table as our work area. Now. What information do you have?"

"It's a city to the northeast," said Releana. "Theran, perhaps. Invisible to the eye, but somehow present. There is a magic ring that lets the wearer see the city. However, you can only penetrate as far as the city walls, and no further . . ."

"So you suspect the walls are a key element of the city's wonders."

"Exactly," said Releana. "It's our hope that we can find the designs for the stones of the walls, and thus find the solution to bringing the city back. There might be some clue hidden within the design. Perhaps your people included a secret device to release the city from its hiding place. I don't know for certain. I have only heard of all this from J'role, and our communication is limited . . ."

Merrox listened carefully as Releana spoke, nodding all the while. Then he said, "I find it hard to believe such a city—"

J'role held up his hand, his face set with determination. He nodded.

"Very well then," the dwarf said with a forced smile. "Is there anything known? Perhaps the name of the person or persons who ordered the stones? I expect the name of the city was hidden as well. What about—"

J'role suddenly raised his hand again. The elf queen had spoken the name of the city. What was it again?

Parlainth.

J'role nodded.

"What?" asked the dwarf. "You know something. What?"

"The people that ordered the stones?" suggested Releana. "The name of the city?"

J'role nodded.

They looked at him expectantly. He stared back and shrugged. Were they expecting him to *tell* them the name?

"Yes, yes," said Merrox, "you're mute . . . mute." He turned toward the table, gathering up paper and ink. "But can you write? Could you write the name of the city?"

J'role turned away, shook his head. He blushed; never had he been so ashamed of his inability to communicate. Here he was, possessed of the key bit of information to fulfill their quest, and he could not speak a simple word, nor impart it in any way to the others.

"If we had the name of the city," began Merrox. "There's no guarantee, of course, given the scale of the magic involved ... But it might give us exactly what we're looking for."

"All right then," said Releana. "Let's do it."

J'role looked at her, perplexed.

"Let's sound it out, like we've done for other words. That's how our written language works anyway. I'm sure we can do the same now."

J'role's shame increased. He felt an intense bitterness burning in him. He had killed his father, a weak, gentle man, and here he was, about to play a game! What was the point of anything?

"J'role," Releana said, looking at him carefully, "we need this."

He nodded. He sighed. What else was he to do? Give up? No. He needed something. He needed to long for something just to go on.

"Or kill yourself," the creature said. The image of ragged wrists, blood flowing freely came to him.

He nearly began to cry, but pushed the image from his thoughts and began searching his mind for how to begin.

"How many words?" asked Releana, encouraging him.

He raised a finger.

"All right. Give us the first sound of the word. Give us an object or idea or something that sounds like the first sound."

Parlainth.

Par.

Parchment!

He grabbed a sheet of paper from a dwarf at a nearby table and held it up before them. The dwarf gasped.

"Parchment?" asked Releana. J'role nodded enthusiastically.

"Ment?" Merrox asked. J'role shook his head.

"Parch!" Releana said firmly. J'role pointed to her and nodded.

"Parch. Parch. Parch," the two of them said over and over.

J'role held his hands before him, squeezing the syllable shorter.

"Par," said Releana.

J'role nodded and smiled. He liked this.

"Par, par, par," the two of them said again. Releana said, "The first sound is Par." Dwarfs from neighboring tables had begun to wander over to find out what was going on.

Next sound. *Parlainth.*

Lainth.

He couldn't think of anything so he decided to break it up one more time, saving the *th* for last.

Lain.

What word could he use?

"Pain," said the creature in his thoughts.

He mimed pulling a dagger out of a sheath.

"Dagger," said Merrox.

"Draw," said a dwarf.

"Danger," said Releana.

J'role then pressed the imaginary blade against his wrist and cut himself with it.

A gasp went up from several of the dwarfs who had gathered, but some, along with Merrox and Releana began shouting out guesses.

"Death."

"Suicide."

"Murder."

"Doom."

J'role turned his face into a grimace. Though he kept his mouth shut, he winced his eyes and swayed a bit. He grabbed the wrist and hugged it close.

"Agony."

"Despair."

"Murder."

J'role pointed at the dwarf who had shouted *agony,* then motioned with his hand, encouraging more suggestions along those lines.

"Agony," someone repeated.

"Hurt."

"Torture."

"Sacrifice."

"Wound."

"Pain."

J'role jumped up and down, clapping his hands together.

"Pain?" Releana asked.

J'role remembered he wasn't quite done yet. He spread his fingers an inch apart.

"Close," said Merrox authoritatively to the others. "It's close." He turned to J'role. "It sounds like pain?"

J'role nodded.

"Sane?"

"Plain!"

"Bane?"

"Cane!"

"Gain?"

"Lane!"

J'role threw his hands up and pointed at the dwarf who had said, "Lane." Applause rose up from the gathered dwarfs, and some patted their fellow dwarf on the back. Others nodded sagely to J'role.

A strange good humor began to rise in J'role. He looked around at the happy faces, knowing he had made it happen. Releana was looking at him, smiling a sly smile. She said, "All right. All right. Par-Lane. Yes? Is there more?"

J'role nodded. *Th.*

He thought for a long while, everyone looking at him expectantly. He could think of nothing, and looked around wildly for inspiration . . . seeing only the thousands of records upon the shelves. Thousands, yes.

He waved his hands at the shelves, encompassing the entire Hall of Records in his gesture.

There was a pause, and everyone turned back to him, then a cacophony of suggestions.

"Records!"

"Scrolls!"

"Books!"

"Bills!"

"Blueprints!"

"Designs!"

Realizing the group had taken the wrong tack, he once again waved his arms, trying to get them to understand he was dealing in scope.

"Big!"

"Many!"

J'role pointed at the giver the last suggestion.

"Many!"

"Much!"

"Overwhelming!"

"Hundreds!"

"Hundreds of thousands!"

J'role pointed again.

"Thousands?"

He nodded furiously.

"Thousands!" everyone cried as one.

"Sands," said Merrox.

J'role shook his head.

"Thou!" shouted Releana.

J'role nodded and squeezed his fingers together.

"Th!" everyone tried to say, and the group sounded like a large snake with a lisp. J'role nodded.

"Par-Lane-Th?" Releana asked. "Any more?"

J'role shook his head.

"Parlainth?"

J'role nodded, clapped his hands together. Everyone joined him in applause. "Well," said Merrox. "It's a start. And even if we don't find it, at least we've brought more life into this place than I've seen in years."

The search seemed hopeless. For the rest of the day Merrox and Releana searched the main codices for any mention of Parlainth. The dwarven language of pictures—with symbols added to the illustration of a dragon's head or a sunset to highlight certain syllables of the object presented— allowed countless permutations for representation of the word *Parlainth*. Though most common words or names had well-known, standardized presentations, the hidden city was not well known at all. The search took days.

Meanwhile J'role studied one dwarven map after another, looking for a city located in the area where he had found Parlainth. He found nothing, and a fear began to grow in him that it had all been a dream; a fulfillment of desire created by his confused mind.

When they had completed the search of the maps and main indexes without success, Releana suggested that the group scour the stacks anyway. If the memory and maps of the city had been altered, she reasoned that the indexes could have been transformed as well. So the three of them walked up and down the stacks, climbed up and down ladders, and generally made a nuisance of themselves to the other dwarfs busy at work. Releana had made a list of possible spellings of Parlainth for J'role, and he compared the symbols on the list with those he found on the scrolls and tomes. As the days passed J'role became dizzy from the constant cross-referencing of the titles with this scrap of paper. With each passing day it all seemed more and more hopeless.

After a week had gone by and they had still checked only half the Hall of Record's massive stores, they gathered around their table, slumped dejectedly in their seats.

"Are you sure this is the name of the city?" Merrox asked J'role.

Was he? It was what the elf queen had called it. Did her people have a different name for it. Had she lied to him?

He shrugged.

"Maybe we're going about it all wrong," said Releana. "J'role got the name of the city from the elf queen. But the people of Parlainth probably didn't count on people under the spell's influence meeting with her. J'role found the city, and then deduced that the stones were where the magic was stored. So what matters is the stones, not the name; and because the name itself seems to have been erased from the records, we need a new approach anyway."

"*If* that was the name," Merrox said and shook his head. "It all seems so improbable . . ."

"If the entire population of a massive city—and according to J'role's visions it was massive—invested themselves into the spell it might be possible. Add the tight restrictions that the city put on the spell—they could not bring themselves back, that only a single ring indicated that they even existed, and that the ring itself provided few clues—and such power is definitely possible. The limitations on the spell were enormous. The effects could be enormous as well."

A silence fell over the table, and each of them slipped into deep contemplation. Then Merrox said, "What a horrible decision they made; to hide themselves away like this. To have no power over returning home."

"They must have been terrified of the coming Scourge," agreed Releana.

"Were they more frightened than the elves of Blood Wood?" asked a dwarf who stood nearby and had overheard the conversation. "What they did to themselves . . ."

"No," Merrox said firmly, his voice tight. "I cannot imagine doing what the people of Parlainth did. But to do what the elves of Blood Wood did, and what countless other peoples did for protection, corrupting themselves to stave off the corruption of the Horrors. . . . It is unconscionable."

Another silence came, even deeper than the last. Then Releana said, as if speaking from a terrible distance, a sadness cutting through her words, "The Scourge did things to us that will never truly heal."

J'role found himself nodding, though he had no desire to share his thoughts or feelings. But no one noticed. The truth of the matter weighed on each one. And in that moment they were bound together in a way no words could express. They had all been reminded of the pain that each living person shared in being alive.

"Well, at least we can try to get this city back," Releana said firmly, rousing the group from its deepening despair.

"Yes," said Merrox, shivering, as if shaking off a chill. "You suggested we look at the stones we cut for Parlainth."

"Yes. Let's leave the name behind for now. It might not exist anywhere in this room. But they would have left *something* behind so the city could be brought back. It might well be in the records of your stone quarries ... I don't know. But let's get to it. Let's search through the construction work you did before the Scourge."

"And we can make it more specific because, if it is a huge city, the stone work would be listed under our city records, and would be quite detailed."

"Well, let's look," said Releana.

"But what are we looking for?" asked Merrox with exasperation.

"Anything," said Releana. "Anything at all."

29

In the dream the creature in J'role's thoughts said, "Now, what would be the best thing for a little boy to do if he caused his parents pain?"

J'role did not know. He could not even venture a guess. He was too frightened. Something was in his thoughts. Something flowed and slid around in his mind.

"Come, now. Don't worry so much, little boy. We're going to be together for a while, I think. Now what would be the best thing you could do for your mother and your father?"

At the mention of his father, J'role sensed something, someone, just out beyond the edge of his perceptions—standing behind his mother.

Crying.

They found seven volumes of stonework designs—all without labels. When Releana brought them to Merrox he furrowed his forehead and turned the books around and around searching for a label. "We label everything," he said with whispered astonishment. "I mean, *everything*. I recently found a receipt for the purchase of a ten-foot pole that didn't cost more than a scrap of copper. The date of purchase, the buyer, and the seller were all carefully listed on the scrap."

As Merrox flipped through the pages and pages of designs his brow furrowed even more. "What is it?" Releana asked, a barely contained excitement creeping into her voice.

"These designs. Here. Look." The dwarf turned the open book so she and J'role could see. In the center of the yellowed page was a picture of a stone block. On the block was a symbol from the written language—the foot of a dragon surrounded by three dots, with two dashes beneath the foot.

Because these were the designs for the city's outer walls, J'role assumed they were part of the glyphs used to ward off the Horrors.

Merrox explained that the dwarfs often designed the patterns for the stones ahead of time, making a Master Sheet of the glyphs, and then a grid of these Master Sheets, with one block per square. That way they could be sure all the glyphs would fit on the actual wall or gate. The nameless volumes on the table before them contained the Master Sheets, as well as illustrations of all the blocks that would make up the city's outer wall.

What was odd about this page, Merrox continued, was that in the upper right-hand corner was the picture of another, smaller block. There was another drawing of the dragon's foot, but this time on the left side of the block rather than on the side facing out. On the side facing out was a squiggle of lines and a circle.

"These smaller blocks. . . ," said Merrox, fanning the pages of the thick tome to show the small block in the upper corner of each leaf. "I don't know what they are. I've never seen *anything* like it before."

Releana looked intently at the small blocks as they flipped by. "It looks like the smaller square is the same as the big one, but showing a different side. But why? The purpose of the glyphs is to drive the Horrors away. They have to be able to see them."

J'role understood immediately and excitedly tapped the illustration of one of the smaller blocks. Everyone looked at him, waiting for the explanation. It was so obvious, but he could only keep pointing at the picture of the smaller block and wait for them to see.

Releana got it first. "Yes," she said slowly. "This is how they moved the city to the other plane, and how to bring it back. They didn't face the block out, because they didn't want the Horrors to see it. They hid the glyphs between the stones. The glyphs were used to save themselves. Brilliant."

"All well and good," said Merrox. "But that cannot be so. Look at this." He turned one page after another, and jabbed his short, stubby finger at each of the small stones. "These symbols don't mean anything. They're nonsense."

J'role became furious that Merrox would quash their victory. He turned to Releana, watching her examine each o the blocks. Any moment, he knew, she would solve the last bit of the problem. She was a *magician*.

She nodded to Merrox. "You're right. If it makes sense, it's a sense I can't understand."

J'role snatched the book away from Merrox and flipped through the pages. He stared down at the pictures of the stone blocks, trying to see some sort of order.

But as he stared at each illustration—bits of ink formed into lines and blotches—he saw nothing but confusion. He turned one page after another, and a shame overcame him. He couldn't begin to read at all. What made him think he could read signs that were made to be secret?

He looked up to find them staring at him, concerned. He threw up his hands, turned, and walked toward the door.

"J'role!" Releana called, but he paid no heed.

"Let him be," he heard Merrox say. "We're closer, but we need to rest. It's amazing we've gotten this far. But your friend can only be so useful in these matters. I'll call in several of our kingdom's best magicians . . ."

J'role reached the door and left. Useless, he thought. Useless, useless, useless.

He walked down the corridor and didn't care where he went. What was the point? He'd be dead before they ever found Parlainth. He'd lived out his life with the creature in his thoughts, ever unable to speak.

He thought of his father's death—murder. Remembered the blood, the shocked look on his father's face. His muscles tightened at the memory, and he embraced the thoughts, finding perverse comfort in the shame and agony. This was who he was, a pathetic fool whose only accomplishment was the murder of his father. Despite the terrible nature of the deed, it confirmed everything J'role thought about himself, relieved him of having to move forward or try to change his circumstances.

The dwarfs he passed quickly parted to make a path for the grim-looking boy with his head leaning forward, his quick pace carrying him on toward some unknown destination.

For days Releana and several dwarven magicians hovered around the seven mysterious tomes. They also brought in other tomes from throughout the kingdom, compared the symbols to other arcane references, scribbled notes, and stared thoughtfully at the ceiling.

J'role wandered through the underground kingdom of Throal.

He discovered that most of the dwarfs lived in rooms that led off from the endless corridors, much the way J'role had lived in his kaer. He saw dwarven men and women walking the corridors. He saw craftspeople working forges in wide rooms with magical fires that produced no smoke. He saw jewel-cutters sitting in small alcoves surrounded by another two dozen or so dwarfs all watching intently, their breathing stilled as the jewel-cutter made the final, precise incision. He saw dwarven miners, picks slung over their shoulders, marching down dark tunnels in the morning, and returning dirty but happy each night.

Eventually he stumbled into large construction sites— huge caverns filled with half-finished towers and halls. The dwarfs sang songs in their deep, rich voices as they worked.

A dwarven foreman saw J'role looking quizzically at the construction and said, "Going to be a new city down here. For the newcomers. We've already got Bathebal, but that filled up faster than we expected." He smiled at J'role, expecting some response, but J'role only looked at him, his face set and angry. The foreman hesitated a moment, then walked away.

Time passed, and one day J'role found a series of corridors where no one seemed to go. They were so small that eventually he had to duck down to walk through them. Moving in this fashion for a bit he finally saw that the quality of the light ahead had changed, that the tunnel opened into another cavern. A wind began to sweep around him. Reaching the end of the tunnel, J'role peered out, then took a quick step back.

A path of stone, six feet wide and with thigh-high railings on either side, led out from the corridor. The top of the cavern was ten or fifteen feet above the path, and on either side of the railings dropped an immense gulf of space. The floor of the cavern was far, far below. The echo of the wind filled J'role's ears and the air rushed over his face.

At the base of the cavern stood a large city. Not as huge as Parlainth, but big enough. From J'role's dizzying height the people filling the streets around the spires and halls and buildings looked like tiny children.

The buildings and streets of the metropolis formed a beautiful pattern, as if designed to be seen from above; an elaborate interlocking of squares and circles, with fascinating textures provided by the buildings themselves. He assumed that below him rested Bathebal, the city that the dwarven foreman had mentioned.

The stone path extended out impossibly across thin air, meeting with other paths at the center of the cavern high above the city. Where the paths met was a huge platform covered with plants, like a garden. J'role noticed that glowing moss, more brilliant than any he had yet seen in Throal, grew under the paths and the garden, illuminating the city below.

Intrigued by the garden sitting above the city, J'role cautiously stepped out onto the path. He trembled with fear that his extra weight would make the paths and the garden and himself plunge down and down to the city far below. But the path held, and he walked along it, carefully staying in the middle, keeping his gazed fixed ahead, resting his fingertips on the railing for balance.

The garden was much further than it seemed at first, and was also much bigger. When he finally got there J'role saw that it contained glowing red trees with wide leaves surrounded by a thick underbrush of blue-leaved bushes. The life was even heavier than in Blood Wood, all cramped and pushed together, as if wildly overgrown on a plot of land too small. Half-hidden in the dirt and underbrush were the remains of a path. Picking his way carefully through the brush, he followed it.

The path met up with other paths, and the further he traveled, the clearer the path became. Soon he saw the footprints of those who had come before.

"Halt!" someone said fiercely, and then appeared two dwarfs dressed in bronze armor holding their swords toward him. Though they were shorter than he, J'role doubted they would have trouble killing him.

He remained motionless.

"What is it? Is she coming?" someone from around the bend of the path called out in a distracted tone. From the same direction came another dwarf, this one wearing a scarlet cloak over his gold and brown robes. His hair was white, his face lined with wrinkles. He looked at J'role, first with suspicion, then with a smile. "Ah, and who have we here?"

J'role simply gazed at the three of them.

One of the dwarfs approached, raising his sword. "His Majesty, King Varulus of Throal, has just asked you a question . . ."

"Wait! Wait!" said the king, raising his hand and laughing. He stroked his beard and asked, "You wouldn't be the lad Borthum brought with him? The one who helped capture Garlthik?"

J'role nodded.

"Let him pass."

The guards looked at their king, obviously questioning the wisdom of his orders. But then they stepped aside, and the king waved J'role closer.

When J'role reached him, the king said softly, "You can't speak, eh?"

J'role shook his head.

"Pity," said the king, looking genuinely sad. Then slyly, as if letting J'role in on a secret, he said, "Here, come and take a look at this."

The two of them walked along the path, the guards following close behind. They passed more guards, who watched over the garden's other paths.

They approached a circular railing set into the ground. Coming closer, J'role saw that it surrounded a big hole through which he could see the city below. The king walked up to the railing and looked down. "We call this garden Bathebal's Eye. Used it to study the layout as we built the city." He smiled proudly. "Came out well, don't you think?"

J'role studied the dwarf, not sure what to make of him. He seemed at once imposing and kind.

King Varulus narrowed his eyes at J'role. "I appreciate what you did, you know."

J'role stared back, confused, thinking for a moment that the king referred to the murder of his father.

"Capturing Garlthik. Not an easy task," the dwarf continued. He stepped up to J'role, raising his wrinkled worn hand to J'role's cheek. The fingers felt warm and comforting. "A glum one, aren't you, boy?" The king sighed and turned away, looking down toward the city. "Like so many of us since the Scourge." Suddenly, excitement again. "But look what we're making, eh? New homes for any of the races who wish to live with us. We're building throughout the mountain, sending envoys out to all of Barsaive. We will rebuild the world. We've thought it all out."

The king's words cut through J'role's despair, and he found himself momentarily caught up by the dwarf's enthusiasm. Rebuild the world? Was such a thing possible?

"Your Majesty," said one of the guards.

The king and J'role both turned, and J'role nearly shouted in fear as he saw Queen Alachia of Blood Wood suddenly appear around the bend in the path. She wore a gauzy white dress, punctured with thorns. A few drops of blood hung momentarily on the tips of the thorns, then rolled down her white flesh onto the white dress without leaving a mark. Her long red hair spilled down over her shoulders, curling like thick, writhing vines.

Several elven courtiers followed, wearing chain mail and long swords in jewel-encrusted scabbards. The thorns of the queen's escorts poked through the links in the mail, and again, drops of blood appeared every few minutes.

J'role wanted to turn and run, but he didn't know if the dwarven guards would cut him down on the spot for his hasty actions. Instead he looked at the queen, waiting for her to spot him and demand that King Varulus kill him at once. Had she known he was here? Had she come for the records, as he and Releana had come, to find Parlainth? He waited for her to glance at him, to recognize him . . .

She didn't. Her gaze took in the garden, but passed over J'role as if he were no more than another bush or a tree to her. Her indifference threw J'role completely off balance, for her presence drew him as strongly as it had in Blood Wood. He remembered clearly the pain of her touch, and knew he would gladly feel that pain again. She was still the most beautiful woman he had ever seen.

"Your Majesty," the king said with a tone of forced politeness. "You are looking as lovely as ever." He glanced down at the ground, as if uncomfortable handing out pleasantries of state.

The elf queen dismissed his words with an abrupt question. "Am I not allowed to enter the Hall of Records?"

"No."

"Have our paths diverged so far?"

The king stared at her, his jaw moving silently, slightly, in contemplation. "I don't think I need to speak on the matter."

She stepped closer. The dwarven guards shifted slightly and placed their hands on the pommels of their sheathed blades, which prompted the elven guards to do the same. The king and the queen seemed not to notice. J'role saw that she wore the ring of longing on her finger. He swayed slightly at seeing it, wanting desperately to walk up and take it from her hand. He fought the impulse, succeeding only because he knew he would die if he tried.

Later, he thought. Later.

"Varulus," the queen said and smiled. "Certainly, we have made choices your people would not have made. . . ."

"Did not. We did not make them. As you did not have to make them."

She threw up her hands. "What has this to do with anything?"

"The fact that you cannot see it, your Highness, is enough for me. Will I permit you into the Hall of Records, where you might read secrets, both mechanical and magical, that could lead to the downfall of my kingdom and my allies? No. Certainly not."

"You think me corrupt?"

"Not as we feared four centuries ago when we prepared for the Horrors. No. Not that way." Varulus dropped his eyes, perhaps momentarily unsure. "I do not know. Please. You will not sway me. You and your people made your choice in Blood Wood. You will live with it. And you will live alone."

"Do you think me so powerless?"

"My lady, you and your people are possessed of a power so strong that I would tremble were the same power offered to me. That is what the elves have never understood. The elves of your wood more than any other. Weakness, in degree, is as much a virtue as strength. There are some things one should not be able to do."

Queen Alachia stared at Varulus for a long time, and for just an instant J'role thought he caught a look of sadness in her eyes. She turned and began to walk away.

J'role jumped up. He could not bear to have her completely ignore him, nor could he let her leave with the ring.

He had taken only two bounds toward her when swords came out from all sides, stopping him in place. The moment crackled with uncertainty as both elves and dwarfs wondered whose side the boy was on. They faced off against each other, poised between J'role and the elf queen.

She whirled, facing J'role. A dozen blades flashed through the air between them, framing her face like a garland of silver thorns. Her own thorns cut through the flesh of her face. A single drop of blood slid slowly down her cheek from the tip of a thorn. The tunnel of sword blades seemed to form a pattern of some kind, and J'role found himself trying to make sense of an idea at the edge of his thoughts.

"I know you," the elf queen said coldly. Then she smiled, a smile full of all the kindness and love and passion J'role could ever want. Then the smile vanished, like a gate crashing down. With no more said, she turned once more. Her guards waited to make sure that J'role would remain where he was, then turned and followed the elf queen through the garden and out of sight.

After a long beat King Varulus said, "Lower your blades. He won't follow her anymore. Will you, lad?"

J'role thought of his time in Blood Wood, remembered his father alive beside him as they knelt before her, remembered his father's joy and disappointment at finally encountering the elves.

"Boy? Are you all right?" The king took his hand, held it tight. J'role felt an amazing strength in the hand, but it did not crush like Garlthik's grip.

"What did you see?" the creature hissed in his thoughts. "You saw something in the blades. What?"

The creature's question offered J'role a distraction, and his thoughts leaped for it.

Yes. Something in the blades. The tunnel of blades; silver thorns forming a pattern, and true thorns revealed at the end.

The stones! he realized. He'd solved the mystery of the stones.

He pushed away the feeling of remorse, standing taller now, his mouth firmly closed, but defiant.

He bowed low to the king, who looked at him with surprise. Then J'role strolled casually by the guards, and when he had passed them, he raced down the path, momentarily feeling as if he were flying through the air; on either side nothing but a tremendous drop, in his heart the rising hope of continuing his quest.

He ran through the corridors, leaping left and right to

avoid the numerous dwarfs, who scattered clumsily as he approached. Twice he became lost, but he charged forward anyway, successfully finding landmarks as he pressed on, eventually reaching the Hall of Records. He slammed the heavy wooden doors open, and the crash of the wood against stone reverberated through the hall.

30

The creature whispered, "Here's what I think you should do. I think you should die."

"Die?" J'role asked, suddenly afraid. Already he missed his mother and his father.

"Kill yourself. You really shouldn't be alive, you know. That's what we'll work on for the rest your life. There's nothing I love so much as a suicide that's been stewing for a decade or so."

"Suicide?" J'role thought. He didn't know the meaning of the word.

"It's a big word," the creature said. "Don't worry about it now. You'll come to understand it very well later. But it's the only way you can make up for being such a horrible son."

J'role began to cry.

The person crying in the corner of the room—who was it?—left.

His mother leaned down and picked him up and began to croon.

J'role tried to speak. The noises poured out of his mouth.

His mother thew him back down onto the bed, making his head bang against the stone wall. She leaned down and covered his mouth, forcing him into silence. "Shhh," she said again and again. "Shhh, be silent." He became quiet. "You. . . ," she began, not to him, but to someone else. The creature in his thoughts, J'role realized; the white shadow from the corner of the room. "You didn't tell me about this!"

The creature in J'role's head laughed.

She looked into J'role's eyes. "Speak to no one. No one but me, do you understand?"

He nodded.

* * *

Everyone in the Hall of Records, magicians and researchers, those on ladders and those sitting at tables, turned and looked sharply at J'role. But he paid them no heed. With a swagger and a broad grin he approached the table where Releana and the dwarven magicians worked.

He stepped up onto the table, pointed to the books, then tapped himself on the chest.

"J'role?" Releana asked.

He took one of the books and stood it upright on the table. Several of the magicians moved to stop him, but Releana and Merrox stayed their hands.

He opened the book to the middle, spreading the pages and the covers wide so one page stood very much alone. Then he pointed with one finger at the picture of the small, mysterious block in the upper right-hand corner of the page. He moved his finger perpendicularly to the page, and soon the tip reached the picture of the block. He took the next page in the book and placed it against the open page. Then he raised his finger over the pages, and moved it past the pages.

He repeated the motion of his finger, first moving it toward the page, then bringing up several more pages, then moving it beyond the pages, as if through the illustration of the blocks.

Finally he turned the book so the pages he held faced the magicians. Once more he slowly brought his fingertip toward the first page he held out, touching the illustration of the small block

"What is he doing?" one of the magician's asked, his tone full of annoyance.

For a flickering moment J'role wondered if he was wrong. The image in the garden had seemed so clear: A tunnel of sword blades framing the elf queen. Each one, a flat object, combined to create depth, and in the end, a whole picture.

But once again Releana came to his rescue. She took the book from J'role and said, "Look. Each symbol by itself is meaningless. That's because each illustration is combined with the illustration in the stone behind it. And that bit with the stone behind it. The symbols are not formed by looking at the pictures as if the stones formed a wall, read horizontally, as we're trying to see them. They're made whole by *depth*. We have to imagine standing at one corner of the city, and looking down along the city wall, as if we could see the symbols on one stone after another."

Merrox said, "Each vertical row of stones probably forms one complete symbol."

"When all the stones are in place, we'll have the full picture," Releana finished. "That must be it."

Some of the dwarven magicians nodded sagely, some looked excited, and others looked irritably at J'role. J'role just sighed. He was one step closer to finding the city and getting his voice back.

He spotted Releana looking up at him with a bit of surprise, a bit of pleasure, a bit of awe.

That was good, too.

He waited as the dwarfs and Releana transcribed the symbols on the stones. On fresh parchment they drew one empty square for each vertical row of stones, then went through each page, adding each bit of detail from each of the small squares. Slowly the squares filled, and the magicians nodded and licked their lips, looking at one another with growing excitement.

J'role sat in a chair, watching. He could serve no more purpose now, but he was too excited to leave.

The magicians worked through the night, taking shifts in compiling the symbols, some working while others napped on tables and chairs in the far corners of the hall. Candles were brought in to augment the light of the wall's glowing moss. The dwarfs drew and drew. Food was brought in. Exclamations of "Ah!" pierced the deep silence every now and then, but never with the whole mystery solved, just symbols completed.

Until . . .

"We have it!" Releana shouted suddenly.

J'role nearly tumbled off the chair where he was sleeping, then rushed over to the table. Releana looked down at the two dozen sheets of paper spread out over the table. J'role saw the images of trees and cats and arms and swords and flying chariots, each picture framed and adorned with dots and lines and squiggles, all of which translated the meaning of the word from its basic picture to sounds. The sounds were re-combined to make more words.

"It must be the words spoken to bring the city back," said one dwarf.

When Releana looked up and saw J'role beside her, she put her hand on his shoulder and drew him close. "This is what we say, outside the city walls: 'You are Found. There is a Place for You in the World. Come Home.'"

The expedition—J'role, Releana, and Borthum in the lead, followed by forty dwarfs armed with glittering swords and armor that caught and reflected the sun's light like a pond of clear water—marched north to the Serpent.

The group obtained passage across the river on the *Chakara*, then continued on their way, planning to cut a wide path around Blood Wood and work their way back to where J'role had first seen the city. Though they no longer had the ring, J'role was confident he could find the place again.

They had traveled a full day from the Serpent, and had just made camp, when Borthum raised his head, cocking it to one side, listening carefully. "Animals are approaching." Everyone stopped in their tracks to scan the surrounding area. In all directions small hills rolled up and down like frozen waves, and for a moment nothing was visible in the deepening twilight. Then a long line of blackness swelled up from over a hill.

"Orks," Borthum said, annoyed. "What are they doing this far north?"

"How did they get across the river?" Releana asked.

The dwarf shrugged in reply, then said, "T'skrang riverboat, perhaps? They might have paid to have their animals transported. Or they might have traded their swords for passage." He stared out across the darkening landscape. "There are more of them this time."

"Are they the same—?" one dwarf began to ask.

"I don't know," Borthum said quickly. "Arms!" he shouted.

Everyone scrambled to action, some tossing brands bright with fire out past the camp to widen the circle of light. The dwarfs put on their helmets, drew their swords, and formed two circles, one inside the other.

To J'role the wait for the orks to arrive seemed interminable, but finally came the thunderous beat of hooves. He felt the tension increase around him, saw the firelight slide up and down the swords as the dwarfs heft their weapons in preparation for battle.

But the charge never came. Instead, the ork raiders formed a line about thirty yards away and hailed the dwarfs. They outnumbered the dwarfs two to one, and J'role knew the dwarfs had little hope of winning such a battle.

Borthum sent one of the dwarfs, Noddin, forward as an envoy. Noddin called out to the raiders in a language J'role did not recognize, but that he assumed was the ork tongue.

"He says he wants the children," Noddin said with a glance at J'role and Releana.

J'role felt strangely calm at the words. They seemed to fit in with the pattern and flow of his life.

Borthum furrowed his eyebrows. "Odd. Tell him no . . ."

Before Noddin had a chance to pass this on, the ork leader shouted more of the harsh-sounding words. When he was finished, Noddin said, "He wants Garlthik One-Eye as well. We are to return to Throal and release One-Eye. When One-Eye returns here, they will exchange him for the children."

"He is mad," Borthum said with surprise. "Arms!" Borthum shouted, the matter already settled in his head.

But J'role had other ideas. He was certain the dwarfs would not win a battle, and from what the orks said, he was almost as certain that they meant him no harm.

It was now obvious that Garlthik had spoken to the ork raiders and secured them safe passage to Throal so J'role and the others could find the information to reach Parlainth. Now that they had, Garlthik wanted his freedom, and he needed J'role and Releana to lead him back to Parlainth and use the information they'd gained to enter the city.

A spark of admiration flared in J'role's soul for Garlthik's audacity. His father would never have done such a thing. Garlthik had submitted to capture, had arranged for others to discover the precious secrets he could never have gained on his own.

Brilliant.

A strange excitement came over J'role. It was like being very alive, but also very close to embracing death. The ork could teach him much. Of that J'role was certain. And if Garlthik did mean him harm in the end, then J'role would fight just as fiercely to kill Garlthik.

Yes. It was all becoming clear now, and it excited him to see everything falling into place. Life was made up of all the pain people inflicted on one another. And the thrill of it was to absorb the pain and live off it, to inflict pain and ruin the people who would ruin you. The thoughts made him nervous, but they *seemed* so true.

As the dwarfs prepared to make their stand against the orks, J'role rushed forward, cutting through the dwarven line. A few hands grabbed at his back, but the surprised dwarfs could not catch him.

"J'role!" shouted Releana.

"What's he ... ?" J'role heard Borthum begin to say, but then he was running so hard toward the ork raiders that the only sound he heard was his own heavy breathing.

Ahead of him two ork raiders charged toward him on their beasts. Panic seized J'role as they came along either side of him, and he wondered if, after all, he was going to die at their hands. But as the orks thundered by, a strong hand reached down and grabbed him by the right arm, swinging him up. He landed astride the saddle, sitting behind an ork. The beast's back was wide, and J'role had trouble balancing on it. He instinctively wrapped his hands around the ork's side. The ork laughed and wheeled his six-legged beast back toward the line of raiders.

Noddin was shouting across the night air in the ork tongue. The leader of the orks shouted responses, and prolonged negotiations began. Unable to understand the talk, J'role became distracted by the sensations around him. The fidgeting of the powerful animal on which he sat. The musky odor of both beasts and orks, mingled with the stench of blood. The muscular body of the raider around whom he'd wrapped his arms, the ork's body strong from a life lived under the demands of continual combat.

A cry went up from the dwarven camp, and J'role looked out to see Releana rushing past the ranks of the dwarfs. Again they were surprised, but this time a few gave chase. The ork leader barked some commands and ten of his raiders rushed forward. The dwarfs drew themselves up into a combat formation, ready for an assault. But the orks merely rode up to Releana and scooped her up, then rode back to their own line.

The ork leader shouted a few more words, then raised his fist high in the air. A growl rippled through the ranks of the raiders and they turned their beasts, some pulling their reins up to make their animals' forelegs dance momentarily in the air. Then they raced away into the night. The wind rushed against J'role's face, the beast's muscles moving against his thighs, the thunder of the herd filling his ears. He buried his face against the ork's fur vest, suddenly so happy. How astounding that he should be riding with ork raiders, caught up in deceit and manipulation in a hunt for a hidden city!

Yes. The motion of it all, he thought. If only he could keep moving fast enough, he would never have to feel anything again.

They moved constantly, camping for a few hours to rest the beasts, then continuing on. J'role and Releana remained tied up at all times. The sun was hot, but the orks seemed not to mind.

Releana thought that J'role had run to the orks to prevent the dwarfs from fighting a losing battle, and he only nodded. He felt shame that some part of him was excited to see Garlthik again.

The following day the ork leader came over to talk. He laughed and patted J'role's cheek, then said in broken dwarven, "Garlthik ... told me ... you come ... would come to us all by self. He is wise man ..." The ork tapped his head. "Knows people ..."

The leader walked off. J'role blushed, looked down at the ground. For hours he stared at anything that would keep him from seeing the face of Releana.

On the third day three ork raiders rode into the raider's camp and went directly to the ork leader. A buzz of conversation rushed through the camp. Three more orks went back out with the three who had just returned, and they took a seventh riderless beast with them. An hour later the orks returned, now with a seventh rider. Garlthik One-Eye.

The raiders leaped to the ground even before their beasts stopped moving. Garlthik, obviously not as familiar with riding as the others, waited until his animal came to a complete halt and another ork had taken the reins to hold the beast in place. After finally dismounting he looked around, spotted J'role, and walked briskly toward him. He spread his arms wide and smiled broadly, his odd, ever-present enthusiasm swirling about him like leaves blown in the wind. "J'role, lad!" he cried.

J'role jumped to his feet, though he was still bound to a tree by the cord around his wrists. He looked down and saw

Releana looking at him, pain and suspicion on her face. He felt terribly torn; his shoulders drooped.

Garlthik watched the brief exchange of glances, and stopped. Remaining at a distance, he said, "Good to see you're all right, boy. And you too, girl. I'm glad it all worked out without bloodshed."

"And now you'll release us?" Releana asked. Her face revealed a hostility J'role had not seen since the first time they'd met in the pit of Blood Wood.

Garlthik shook his head seriously. "Not just yet. Not just yet. We've one more errand to run, for you know how to call back the city and I do not." He gestured back at the orks. "I've promised them a big share of the reward, you see. If they don't get it. . . ," he said, then passed his hand over his throat in slitting motion.

"Why should we trust you?"

"Don't. But if you don't do what I say, I'll kill you." His face broke into a grin again. "G'day. We'll be leaving soon." He turned and walked back toward the leader.

Yes, J'role thought with approval. Garlthik had set the choices right out in front. Do it or die. The truth. Not the choices his father had offered, each year slowly withering with promises of "preparations" that would never come. He stared after Garlthik, then sat back down, his thoughts full of the future. Would the citizens of Parlainth be able to remove the creature from his thoughts? Would he get his voice back? Would he and Garlthik go on and have adventure after adventure?

Would Releana ever trust him again?

31

In his nightmares, as in his childhood, his mother makes him speak to her. She tests him almost daily, when no one else is around, to see if he still speaks with the voice of madness.

Slowly she becomes insane. The transformation was slow in life, but speeded up in his nightmare, and he can see each of the subtle transformations on her face and in her eyes, like the shifting of colors during a sunset.

Another day of travel followed, filled with growing apprehension among the ork raiders. J'role noticed that though the leader of the raiders put on a good face for Garlthik, others among them did not. Some of the raiders mimicked his straighter posture, others pointed at his clothes and laughed. It occurred to J'role that Garlthik was not much like his fellow orks, despite being of their race. He spoke dwarven fluently, and dressed in clothing much more like that of J'role's people than the furs and decorative bones of the raiders.

Throughout the day scouts rode off in the same direction the other group had come, returning quickly, their expressions like bad news. At noon, when the raiders had stopped to feed their animals and rest, Garlthik came over to J'role and Releana. "We're being pursued. The scouts are certain of it," he said.

"Dwarfs?" Releana asked with sudden hope.

"Elves, actually. Though I can't imagine what they have to do with any of this."

J'role, however, knew exactly what, but decided not to bother trying to communicate what he knew of the meeting between King Varulus and Queen Alachia.

"The elves number us at least, riding their bone-steeds," said Garlthik after a moment. "If they catch us, it could be bad for us all." Garlthik waited another moment, probably hoping either J'role or Releana would offer some information about the elves. When they didn't, he simply walked away.

"She has the ring of longing, doesn't she?" Releana said. J'role nodded.

"She's after the city. Maybe they know we're heading for it." She paused, then said, "J'role, have you been able to work your bonds free at all?"

He nodded, lying. Though he had been trying, Garlthik had tied the knot all too well. J'role didn't know if he'd ever get out of them.

He lied, but wasn't sure why. Perhaps it was so he could make Releana feel that he was doing well. He told her what he thought she wanted to hear.

He wanted her affection back.

More anxiety filled the afternoon. Scouts were sent off in another direction, in the general direction they had been traveling, and returned with more bad news. Garlthik never came over to explain what it was.

The orks pressed their beasts harder, and J'role recognized landmarks as the raiders followed Garlthik's instructions.

J'role once looked over his shoulder and saw a line of mounted figures rushing after them from the western horizon. The figures were tall and thin, and their steeds looked white but insubstantial. He tried to focus on the mounts as he bounced along, and saw that they were bones—the bones of horses. The sight sent a chill through him, but at the same time there was a stark beauty to the skeletons. As the creatures ran gracefully over the hilly terrain, J'role saw that it was elves from Blood Wood who rode them. But the elf queen among them, and J'role assumed she had sent her servants to finish her work.

Turning forward again, he saw another line of riders approaching from the south. They were closer to the ground than the elves, and J'role recognized them as dwarfs mounted on ponies, their battle armor and swords glinting in the afternoon sun.

Terrible emotions tugged at J'role: Who to please now? He wanted all the choices to go away. He didn't want to hurt anyone else. He just wanted to go adventuring with Garlthik.

"There's a way to make that happen," said the creature.

"I don't want to die anymore."

"But you certainly don't like being alive."

"Why can't you leave me alone?"

"Soon enough. Soon enough."

As they rounded a turn in the gully J'role saw the wide, flat-topped hill. He did not feel the longing with the same intensity as when wearing the ring, but a ghost of the memory returned. He remembered standing on the hillside, looking at the city, wanting so much to enter it.

And now he could call it back.

Garlthik rode up alongside the mount on which J'role sat. "This is it, isn't it, lad?" J'role nodded his head vigorously. The ork leader called a halt, and the beasts stopped awkwardly, breathing heavily, spittle flying from their mouths.

Galthik dismounted, walked over to Releana and grabbed her from behind the ork she had ridden with. He carried her a ways, then set her on the ground, facing the city. "There's something to be said. Say it!"

She stood silent and emotionless.

A panic began to rise up in J'role. Did she really think they could wait until the dwarfs arrived? What if the elves arrived first?

A long, horrible moment passed among the group. The leader of the ork raiders walked up to Releana and drew his sword. He raised it high, threatening her with it, shouting at her in his strange tongue. She did not respond.

He slashed down at her.

J'role scrambled to get off the beast, and fell down to the ground. Lifting his head, he saw Garlthik parrying the leader's blow and then the two men shouting at each other. Garlthik was undoubtedly telling the ork leader that they couldn't afford to kill Releana.

Then the leader of the orks ripped a scarlet jewel from his fur vest, raised it high, and smashed it against a big rock at his feet. J'role pulled back, afraid of the magic it might release. Releana dropped to the ground, as did Garlthik.

A flash cut through the air where the jewel had struck the stone. He heard the roar of hoof beats rushing closer from many sides; within moments the dwarfs and elves would arrive, and the site of the vanished city would become a bloodbath.

When he turned back toward the ork leader, J'role couldn't believe his eyes.

Standing on the spot where the stone had shattered were Mordom, Phlaren, Slinsk, and Gore, all of them smiling upon the gathered crowd.

Mordom looked around at the assembly, moving his raised palm this way and that, the eye in the hand blinking every so often. He turned to Garlthik. "I take it we have reached the site of the city," he said. "This is the arrangement I had with these scorchers."

Garlthik reached for his sword, but the orks around him drew their blades and surrounded him. Garlthik stayed his hand.

"One too many tricks, Garlthik," Slinsk said. "I'm going to kill you, but I'll always admire your style."

The ork leader spoke in his own tongue to Mordom, and Mordom looked out past the crowd, toward the two sets of approaching riders. The smugness washed from his face. He said something to the ork leader, who replied sharply, first sweeping his arm toward the flat hilltop, then pointing at Releana.

Mordom smiled down at her. "My barbaric associate tells me you know the words to bring the city back. Let's have them, quick. I think I've worked hard enough to gather the credit for saving this city." He glanced past J'role and the others again, and this time J'role turned as well. The elves and dwarfs would arrive in mere minutes.

Releana stood defiantly silent. Mordom threw up his hands. "Enough," he said, thrusting his hand into the air and squeezing it into a fist. Suddenly Releana gave out a gasp and clutched her chest. She stood precariously, as if about to fall over yet unable to. J'role started to rush forward, but Garlthik grabbed him with his strong hand and held him in place.

"I can do many things to you, girl. This is just the beginning. If you don't tell me how to call the city back when I let you go, it will all get much worse."

The creature began writhing wildly in J'role's thoughts, as if in a panic. "Do something," it hissed at him over and over. "Do something!"

J'role slipped out of Garlthik's grasp and rushed toward Mordom, his hands still bound. The sudden action startled everyone present. All except for Slinsk, who laughed and slashed his blade at J'role even as J'role raced toward it.

Then Garlthik appeared at J'role's side, parrying the blow at the last instant, the swords clanging against each other right next to J'role's ear. Garlthik gave out a cry as the orks around him cut him with their large blades. Through the cries of pain he shouted, "Speak the words! Damn your pride! The city is our only chance!"

J'role bowled straight into the surprised Mordom. The two of them tumbled to the ground. Over the rising din of approaching hoof beats, J'role heard Releana shout, *"You are Found. There is a Place for You in the World. Come Home."*

With one hand Phlaren grabbed J'role roughly by the neck and raised him high, setting his face just in front of hers. "Do you know, I've wanted to kill you for so very, very long now." J'role remembered the man he'd knocked into the pit back at the kaer, and Phlaren's intense reaction to the news of the death. She had carried that hatred for weeks and weeks. With her free hand Phlaren drew a dagger from her belt.

Suddenly an arrow barbed with thorns sliced through her neck. She held J'role for a moment longer, then collapsed to the ground, dropping him as she did.

J'role whirled and saw the elves riding up, their skeleton steeds galloping wildly, their bowmen firing furiously into the ork raiders. The orks grabbed spears and shields and braced themselves for the elven assault. The dwarfs would arrive any moment.

Then something else caught J'role's attention. A shimmering of star-white walls, the dim shapes forming like fog on a spring evening.

The city was returning, but his view was suddenly cut off as the bleach-white bones of a horse galloped by. An ork leaped forward, driving his spear into the elf who rode the long-dead animal, piercing the elf's chest and knocking him to the ground. Dozens more elves arrived, wielding swords that glowed blue in the dying light of day. While the orks scrambled to reach their steeds, the elves struck them down to the right and the left.

J'role turned back to the city, the battle suddenly forgotten as he remembered his longing to find it, his desire to find the people who might help him. He stood, still and ridiculously placid as the battle swirled around him.

The walls formed.

They weren't new and shiny, as before. They were as

Garlthik had seen them. Huge blocks that had collapsed onto each other decades before. Thick cracks cut through the ruined walls. Within the walls he saw Parlainth's fallen towers, the remains fo the city's great halls, the huge pyramids covered with gnarled gray vines.

Not a living thing stirred within the ruins.

J'role dropped to his knees. Stunned.

The dwarfs arrived, reining in their ponies, shocked by the sight. Even the elves and orks brought their mounts to a stop. The silence descended heavily, broken only by the snorts and whinnies of the many riding beasts in the area. Everyone stared in amazement at the seemingly endless ruins of Parlainth. The city stretched on and on, the once-glorious, astounding metropolis now the scene of fractures, cracks, rocks, and ruined buildings.

None of them had ever seen anything with as much promise of beauty.

The sight before J'role echoed in his thoughts. The arrival of the city had changed everything. Now all gathered here knew exactly what had been lost during the Scourge.

Then suddenly, inexplicably, the fighting began again. Faces filled with fury, the dwarfs, the elves, the orks all raised their arms once more, shouting their battle cries, and rushing at one another. J'role looked around, incredulous. Only those who at any time had worn the ring of longing—Mordom, Slinsk, Garlthik, J'role, and one of the elves in fine clothes of silk and with the ring of longing on his finger—remained too entranced by the city to continue the fight.

An impulse overcame J'role, a sudden urge to rush toward the city walls. He dodged in and out of the fight, just avoiding death by sword, spear, and trampling. The others followed him, desperate to finally reach the city, to be where they had wanted to be for so long. Only Releana, of all those who had never worn the ring, joined the race toward the city, following her J'role.

When he reached Palrainth, J'role staggered once more to his knees, the sight draining him of strength. Shattered skeletons lay everywhere, in some spots become no more than scattered bones. Some of the skeletons had been driven through with swords and spears. Others were no more than rib cages dangling from spires. But over this image J'role could still see clearly the splendor that had once been

Parlainth. The contrast tore at him, and he thought he would die.

Then he spotted a street he recognized, even though he knew that was impossible, and he ran for it. Releana called after him. He ignored her.

Reaching the street, he turned right, and then left, passing ancient bones and ruined buildings, rotted fragments of once-glorious flying chariots. He followed a path he thought he knew, and as he ran J'role began to shake, as if taken by a fever. The sound of his footsteps began to pound loudly in his ears; the air seemed to tear at his flesh. Behind him he heard Releana calling for him. He had lost her, but did not care. What mattered was ahead of him. His "memories" led him forward.

He reached a fallen building. Its wide columns had collapsed and spilled out into the street; the doorways at the top of the steps lay crushed under the roof.

But that didn't matter. He needed to go down. Yes. Down. He ran down the side of the building, toward a door leading down . . .

Motion behind him. He whirled. A huge hand grabbed his bound wrists.

Garlthik One-Eye.

He stared down at J'role, serious. Terrified? Yes, terrified. The ork licked his lips. His voice was dry and cracked. "Not what I expected . . ."

J'role shook his head.

But then Garlthik smiled, a child trying to make things right with a wish. "But you know something, don't you? Don't you?" Garlthik did not wait for an answer, but grabbed J'role by the shoulders and shook him wildly. "You know something!" he whispered harshly. "I saw it in you. You know something."

J'role nodded his head, desperate to please Garlthik so he would stop hurting him.

"Yes, yes," the ork mumbled and with his dagger cut the ropes that bound J'role. "Here," he said indicating the stairs leading down. "Down here?"

J'role nodded. Yes. Something important was down there. "Lead on."

They descended the stairs and came to a heavy stone door. Working together they forced it open, but then had to turn away from the sickly smell that came pouring out, Garlthik raising his cloak before his mouth, J'role using his hands. J'role spotted a torch resting in a sconce. He pointed it out to Garlthik, who grabbed it and lit it with some flint from a sack on his belt.

With Garlthik holding the torch high, the two of them entered the tunnel.

The red torch light flickered gloomily over gray walls. A layer of dust covered the floor, swirling up around their feet as they walked. For the first time since he had rushed into the city, J'role wondered where he was going. He had seen this corridor before, though he had never laid eyes on it. His memories folded back on themselves. Yet something called him forward.

Garlthik looked down at him to see which way to go, and J'role indicated a left turn at an intersection.

They came up to pit in the ground, ten feet long, stretching from wall to wall. They peered over the edge. Below, two giant skeletons rested on spikes—skeletons of things J'role had never seen before. One was wide and long, with a tail that stretched halfway back up the pit, its bones resting against the wall. The other had a long snout and razor teeth.

"Horrors," Garlthik said. "The city's traps killed some of them. But not all."

The Horrors had reached Parlainth after all. Somehow the creatures had found the city, corrupted it. Even after all the elaborate magical machinations, the people sending themselves out of the very world in search of shelter, they had not been safe.

"Do we keep going this way, boy?"

J'role thought for a moment. Yes, though he couldn't remember seeing the pit. He nodded.

"Come on, then." Garlthik tossed the torch across the pit. It skittered across the floor, but remained lit. Garlthik placed his hands against the walls, searching for cracks and studying the nature of the wall. J'role started to do the same on the opposite wall. He slid his fingers between the stone work, and began to inch his way along the pit.

He glanced down once, saw the creatures, and thought again of all that the people of Parlainth had done to keep themselves safe. For nothing.

The thief magic seeped into his body as he moved, and the voices returned, sensations returned: the need to be alone, to trust no one, to put on a pleasing face for all. He tried for a moment to resist, for in the face of Parlainth's failure such warnings seemed futile. Who could ever be safe?

But the sensations washed through his thoughts and muscles. As they took hold, once again J'role wondered how he could have been so naive as to believe he could be happy with other people.

The two reached the other side of the pit and continued on their way. They passed many rooms, some with desks, others with baths. Murals had been painted on the walls, but most of them had been ruined by what seemed to be claw scratchings. Garlthik remained silent, letting J'role lead them on. Neither one made a sound as he walked.

Despite the wisdom of the thief magic, J'role felt comfort walking alongside the ork. Here was his mentor. His . . .

The idea remained stuck for a moment.

Father.

He stopped, looked at Garlthik. The ork returned his gaze, his face startled, perhaps anxious. J'role smiled, and the ork relaxed. "You can sense it, can't you, lad?" Garlthik said. "The treasure nearby. The clues are all here. The pit to keep intruders away, the Horrors who died trying to reach it. Don't know what it is, but there's something of value here."

J'role walked on, and Garlthik followed.

At one point Garlthik put his hand on J'role's shoulder, stopping him. "Wait here," he said, and stepped forward carefully, examining the stones on the floor. Then he stood, withdrew his sword, and poked the tip at the ceiling above.

The ceiling cracked easily—far too easily—and after Garlthik poked a bit more, his work revealed it to be a false ceiling. In the flickering firelight J'role saw the tips of spikes pointing down. "Ahh," said Garlthik. "This is a good one." He leaned forward cautiously and pried at some of the stones in the floor. "The trigger is in the floor stones," he said, softly. "You step on them, and the spikes come down. But it hasn't gone off yet. Which means . . . Ah."

He found a stone that interested him. He took his dagger out and slid it against the stone's edge. After prying the stone loose, he pulled it out. He turned to J'role and handed it to him, then leaned back toward the hole he'd created. "Yes. Yes. The trigger's gone bad. Look here."

He stepped back so J'role could see, leaning carefully over the floor to avoid setting off the trap. The hole revealed a series of chains and pulleys set behind the wall. "See here? That wheel has come off the axle. It's completely jammed. But better to be sure." Garlthik picked up the stone he'd removed from the wall. "Better step back." J'role did so, and Garlthik tossed the stone forward. It clattered across the floor.

Nothing happened.

"All right, then. Lead on."

J'role looked at him, uncertain. Garlthik laughed softly, then stepped forward confidently, willing to show the way. When nothing happened, J'role followed.

Huge cracks ran through the walls, and J'role remembered the collapsed pillars and ruined walls above ground. As they walked on they saw chunks of stone from the ceiling littering the floor. Soon it took great effort to walk over and around the stones. And then they came to a section of corridor completely blocked from floor to ceiling with stones.

Garlthik turned to J'role. "This way?"

J'role nodded. More than that. It was behind the stones, just a few steps away.

Whatever it was.

32

The thing was not in his head yet. He curled up in his bed. The small sounds of his parents' whispers, sometimes soothing, sometimes surprised and harsh, crawled into his ears like spiders.

"It says it can keep us safe," said his mother.

"We can't...," protested his father, then faltered.

"No one need know. It has promised it won't cause J'role harm. It just wants us to give it a place to live."

His father did not answer.

Garlthik set the torch in a sconce and joined J'role in digging through the pile of stones.

For two hours they toiled to remove the upper layer of stones, rested a bit, and then set about their task again. Another two hours passed, and for J'role, the world above no longer mattered. He had no thought of either Releana or the dwarfs or the elves or the orks. All that mattered was getting through the stones to what waited beyond.

His hands became raw with pain, his blood streaking the stones. J'role noticed, but did not stop.

They worked and worked until they could see a door, pressed tightly shut by the weight of the stones, on the other side. Garlthik gave J'role a sly look and re-doubled his efforts.

When they'd finally removed most of the stones, J'role thought he heard something from behind the door. He listened carefully, but heard no other sound. Then he felt the creature sliding about in his mind, and decided he had confused the sensation of the creature with his other senses.

They rolled back the remaining stones, and the door stood naked before them.

"Hold," Garlthik said, and he approached the door, examining it carefully: the handle, the frame, the lock . . . Placing one hand on the doorknob, he drew his sword with the other. "Take the torch," the ork said. J'role did so, holding it high alongside Garlthik.

The ork turned the knob, but the door frame had been bent by the pressure of the stones, and it took several yanks to even loosen it. Garlthik opened it slowly, for the door would not move any faster. As he pried it open with a steady creak, torch light spilled into the room, revealing the shimmer of gold and silver. The light danced across their grinning faces as Garlthik and J'role stepped into the room and saw a treasure trove of jewel-encrusted boxes and silver statues piled high; swords with fiery red blades and buckets stuffed with gold coins.

Seeing something shift from behind the pile of treasure, J'role raised his head and beheld a horrible white shape climbing over the top of the glitter, sending a small avalanche of gold skittering to the floor. The thing's body was broad and fat, something like a giant larvae, except that it had countless human arms, small arms, like the arms of children, growing from its sides. It used the arms to crawl to the top of the treasure, then sat looking down at J'role and Garlthik with large milky-white eyes. Its mouth was a huge mandible that opened and closed, opened and closed, dripping a thick, clear liquid.

When it spoke, it startled J'role and Garlthik, for it seemed impossible that such a thing would be capable of speech.

"J'role, J'role," it said. "I am so happy you have come." And as the thing spoke, J'role felt the same words crawling about in his head.

The creature on top of the pile of treasure said, "You don't know how fortunate I felt when you became a seeker of this city, J'role. I have been trapped here for so, so many years. I thought, 'Here is my chance for freedom.' "

Garlthik looked down at J'role, confused, but said nothing.

J'role could do nothing but stare at the creature. He could not imagine that this bloated monster was the thing in his head.

"Oh, yes. Oh, yes. I've been feeding all this time. Your

pain and the pain you have caused others has been quite tasty." The creature opened and shut its mandibles, and the thick spittle dribbled down onto the treasure. "I have to say, you've lasted longer than the others."

"Others?" J'role thought.

"Others," the creature said sadly. "Usually the child will commit suicide long before now. Then I—my thoughts—wander the world, looking for other suitable parents who will make a deal. You'd be surprised how many there are ... Well, no, I suppose you wouldn't." The creature laughed, and its bloated body quivered. "I kept waiting and waiting for you to finish yourself off and free me ... But then you put the ring on, and I realized you might be able to find me, so I encouraged you when I could. I gave you my memories of the city to goad you on. Then you were so tiresome at times that I decided to make you kill yourself after all and take my chances with someone else. But now I am so proud of you. Of course, I seldom ever get to actually consume my victims."

The creature's small hands scrambled forward over the pile of treasure. When enough of its body hung out over the top, it slid down, pouring toward Garlthik and J'role. The two of them split off to the left and right as the thing slithered across the ground between them. It was as high as J'role, and snapped at his thigh as it rushed by. In his fear, J'role dropped the torch and scrambled up onto a pile of treasure.

Garlthik swung his sword at the creature, but his blade bounced off, leaving no more than a scratch on what seemed to be a chitinous skin. "Grab a blade, boy!" Garlthik called. "We've got to—!" He stopped as the creature turned on him and snapped its mandibles at the ork's arms.

J'role looked about at the many weapons dotting the treasure room. He spotted a sword, grabbed it by the pommel, and drew it out from a pile of gold. The metal was cold and the sword heavy in his hands, but he raised it high and rushed toward the creature. A feverish heat passed through his flesh now. Not only did he want to save Garlthik and prove his worth to the ork, but it was also the chance to kill the thing that had caused him so much torment.

The creature's back was to him, and he felt the thief magic pouring through his body as he rushed forward. Just as he began to swing the blade down, the creature reared up, pulling his head around to face J'role and grabbing J'role's arms with several of the arms growing from its body. The small hands felt moist and rotted, and a foul odor rushed out of the creature's mouth as it spoke, "No surprises from you, J'role. You and I are too close."

The creature laughed, then gave out a horrible shriek. J'role looked past the creature's face and saw Garlthik pulling his sword out of the creature's back; the blade dripped a thick white liquid.

The creature threw J'role away, sending bits of treasure scattering around him. J'role grabbed his blade and rushed back at the creature, who now had Garlthik pressed against the wall. His attack turned the creature, and Garlthik was free.

The two of them kept up this tactic for a long time, attacking from one side and then the other. But the creature seemed to possess limitless energy, and the fight wore much more heavily on Garlthik and J'role.

Finally the creature turned and caught J'role by surprise. Its mandibles snapped down on his arm, snapping the bone in two. For a second J'role saw only a white void, then an incredible pain coursed through his arm, numbing all his ability to take action. He staggered backward, dropping his sword, and fell to the ground.

Garlthik, breathing heavily, looked at J'role, then at the creature. Then he said to the creature, "I leave him to you, if you will let me be."

As he cradled his broken arm against his chest, a sob rose up in J'role's throat.

"I'll have you any way I want," the creature answered. "I have no need to bargain with you."

Garlthik gave out a cry and started swinging his sword wildly, showering the creature with blows, driving it back across the room.

A trick, J'role thought, trying to convince himself. Garlthik had attempted a ruse to throw the creature off guard. But it was to no avail. The creature charged forward into Garlthik, biting at his mid-section. The ork gave a terrible scream as blood sprayed across the walls and the treasure. He dropped his sword and collapsed to the floor. As the creature tossed Garlthik against the wall, J'role saw a huge dark hole in Garlthik's body.

Slowly the thing turned toward J'role. "Alone again," it

said, both in the room and in J'role's thoughts. "Have you ever noticed how alone you are? Even the people you come to depend on leave you in the end." It began to crawl toward him, the arms pushing it along the floor. It moved slowly, wary of any quick motion on J'role's part.

J'role felt the pressure of tears against his eyes as the terrible thing got closer. Hadn't everything been getting better? Wasn't he finally going to be free?

"I want you dead so very, very much. You can understand that, can't you? It's time for you to take your life. Do you understand? After all this time, your death will be the most remarkable . . ." The creature did not finish its words, but purred instead.

J'role was paralyzed with fear, terrified of dying, but wishing it would be all over once and for all. He could not bear the thought of what would happen to him next if he left the chamber. He thought, "I don't want to die."

"Oh, I think you do. Think on these things . . ."

Memories rushed into J'role's thoughts, every horrible thing that had happened since the creature had arrived as a white shadow in the kaer years and years earlier. The whispers at night. The ritual in which his mother had put the thing in him. His mother's insanity. The stoning. His father's drinking.

The memories seared his thoughts. They crashed into his senses, alive as if he were living them all at that moment. He couldn't stand the pain.

"One more memory for you, boy," the creature said. "I kept this one deep, just for this occasion."

J'role is in bed. His mother is performing the ritual, touching her fingertips against his chest.

J'role is frightened. He feels the thing entering his head. His father stands beside the bed.

His father?

"Must we do this?" he asks.

"We've already been through all that," she replies.

"But our son . . ."

"Will be safe. We'll all be safe."

J'role came out of the memory. Gasping for air. He wanted to scream. He wanted to die.

I'm sorry, his father had said all his life.

It wasn't just his mother. His father *knew*. His father did nothing. How could his father have done *nothing*?

All his pity for his father a lie. All his love for his father a lie. How could he have felt remorse for killing such a man?

But the grief swelled in his thoughts, buoyed on the words of the creature. "What have you now? Not even the memories of a kind but failed father. You have nothing."

J'role's hand fell on a jewel-encrusted dagger. He touched it to his wrist, the blade's edge feeling cool and delicious. Over. All over. Please. The torment of living had become too much. No more disappointments. No more betrayal.

The creature sighed.

A noise by the door; footsteps on silver and gold coins.

"Spirits," said Slinsk.

J'role looked up and saw Mordom and his thief companion in the entrance to the room, Slinsk with an expression of horror, Mordom, his palm with the green eye raised, his mouth formed into an amazed smile.

"NOOOO!" screamed the creature and whirled around wildly, its small arms scrambling without control. So swiftly that Slinsk could not react, the creature swung around and drove its mandible into the thief's neck, popping his head off with ease.

Mordom was already gesturing, beginning to cast a spell. J'role remembered that Mordom seemed to have some sort of affinity with the Horrors, and here was the proof. A blue sparkle crackled around his hands and the creature slowed and stared at Mordom.

Distracted from his despair for the moment, J'role pulled the blade away from his wrist. Would he be destroyed by a thing that Mordom could command with a wave of his hands? He jumped up, still holding the blade in his hand, and ran toward the door. He scrambled up the thing's back and jumped off it, flying past Mordom and out the door.

His actions created their own distraction, and he heard Mordom shriek and the creature laugh. "Not again, wizard. I know your tricks now."

J'role ran on, cradling his broken arm. He heard Mordom's footsteps not far behind him, and further back down the corridor the strange scrambling noise of the creature. Its voice stayed with him, taunting J'role as he ran. He lost Mordom somewhere down the passages, but he felt the creature still pursuing him.

J'role raced on and on, no longer knowing where he was or which way was out. But then, ahead, he saw a slice of sunlight making its way down several twists and turns in the corridors. He realized he was near the exit, then came to a dead stop.

The pit was nearby.

He didn't dare run now.

He moved along carefully, poking his foot out.

There it was. He had no brand anymore, but he could feel the edge of the pit.

J'role was too panicked to make it across now; not with his broken arm.

He hesitated, uncertain what to do, when a hand suddenly grabbed at his shoulder.

"Boy," said Mordom. "How do we get out?" His voice was strong and commanding, but J'role also heard the tinge of panic.

Without thought J'role drove the blade in his good hand up into Mordom's belly. The wizard gave out a gasp, and his hands slapped wildly at J'role's face and then found the boy's neck.

J'role tried to slip out of the wizard's grip, but Mordom's hands were strong and J'role screamed in fear.

The words and sounds and babbling ripped from J'role's throat. Mordom staggered back, and in that instant J'role grabbed the wizard and shoved him over the edge of the pit.

A sharp, sudden scream, then the sound of Mordom's body crashing into the bones of the Horrors below as his form was impaled on the many spikes set deep in the pit.

J'role stood breathing heavily now, tears pressing against his eyes. He could never climb across the wall past the pit. Not with his broken arm. Not while he was shaking like this.

He whirled and raced back. "Another way. Another way out. . . ," he thought.

"What makes you think there is another way out? Why torture yourself with life? You have the dagger. Use it."

He ran forward into the darkness, afraid he would run into the creature, but more afraid of moving slowly.

Then he heard it, only a feet ahead, its small arms scuttling like an army of insects along the corridor.

"Ah, here you are." The voice came from his thoughts and from the depths of the dark corridor.

J'role slumped against the wall, too tired to run anymore, too afraid of any more hope. His ranting had stopped now, and the corridor was silent but for the soft, taunting voice of the creature.

"Good. Good. It's time for you to have a rest. You've worked so very, very hard."

The creature came closer and closer. J'role pressed his cheek against the wall, then realized with a start where he was. This was the hole revealing the broken mechanism of the trap that released the spikes from the ceiling.

"What was that?" the creature asked. "What did you just think?"

"I want to die," he thought. "I want to die. I want to die." He let all the misery and despair of his life course through him.

"Of course you do," the creature said. "Who wouldn't, in your position?"

J'role took the dagger and placed it against his wrist. The creature came closer. He dragged the blade across his flesh, lightly. The edge stung and for a moment he thought he might pass out.

"Ahhh," the creature said, its voice rich with ecstasy.

J'role placed his good arm in the hole, his hand searching about for the broken wheel. The pain filled his thoughts, and he could barely concentrate on the task.

"Yes, yes," the creature said. It was only a few steps away now.

J'role found the wheel, took it firmly his hand and began to move it around, searching for the spindle it fit on.

"What are you doing?" The creature was suddenly alert.

J'role took the dagger and once more drew blood from his wrist. Again he felt agony, a horribly pleasant agony, cut through his body. It was tempting to simply finish the job. Why fight anymore? The creature sighed.

J'role found the spindle, slipped the wheel on it.

The creature stopped moving forward. "You're up to something. What?"

"My death," J'role thought softly. And he was. He heard the drops of blood from his wrist plinking against the stone floor. The creature still did not move forward, but from the sound of its voice, J'role thought it might be only a few inches from the stones that would trigger the spikes.

He placed the blade against the cuts already in his wrist, letting the cold metal touch the ragged skin.

"Yes," the creature sighed.

"If I do this, I won't feel any more pain?" J'role asked.

The creature started moving forward.

"Yes. Yes."

J'role felt himself blacking out.

"Do it! Do it!"

He was afraid that if he stopped, the creature would stop moving forward. Slowly he dragged the blade across his wrist. He felt his blood seeping over his flesh.

"YES!" the creature cried. Then, from above, came the sound of stone shattering as the spikes rushed down and drove into the creature's back. J'role rolled back.

The creature screamed a long, long time. When it stopped, it was like the end of a terrible, howling storm.

33

J'role remained on his knees a long time, then, as if in a trance, feeling nothing and thinking nothing, he walked back down the corridors, searching for a way out.

He ended up at the treasure room.

Blood had splattered all over the room's wealth, and the value of the gold and silver jewels seemed slight in comparison to the precious red fluid that stained them.

He saw that Garlthik still breathed. He walked quickly over to him, his feet stumbling on some coins. J'role knelt down beside the ork, and the old thief opened his one good eye. "Ah, lad. Still alive? Good for you. That's the test."

Garlthik began to stand, and J'role tried to push him down. He could wait until help was brought.

"No, no. I want to move. Have to keep moving." He stood and said, "Come."

The two of them wandered down the corridor, using a torch to find a way out of the catacombs. J'role did not speak, for he was afraid of what would happen if he tried. The creature was no longer in his head, and that was good enough. That and walking alongside Garlthik again.

They made their way out into the sunlight and J'role had to cover his eyes with his hands against the sudden brightness. In the distance he heard people calling his name.

Garlthik cocked his head to one side at the sound of the cries. "Ah. I'd best be going. People are coming for you."

J'role took hold of the ork's sleeve.

"No. No," Garlthik said. "It's better if I go on. They want you. I'm just a potential prisoner. Give me some time to get away, will you?"

J'role nodded.

Garlthik touched his hand to J'role's cheek. Then the one-eyed ork ran off through the rotting, ruined streets of Parlainth.

"J'role!" Releana called, and he turned to see her and half a dozen dwarfs walking quickly toward him. The faces and armor of the dwarfs were blood-stained, but they wore smiles.

"Are you all right?" Releana asked as she rushed up to J'role and took his bleeding wrist. His blood flowed over her hand.

Too many ideas and thoughts crowded into J'role's head. Without meaning to, and without understanding what he was doing, he opened his mouth and said, "I . . ."

The voice was like a baby's cry, raspy and painful. He heard his first true utterance in more than half his life and crumpled to his knees, tears swelling in his eyes and running down his cheeks. He thought of his mother and his father and wondered how they could have done such a thing to him. And he wondered how he could have done what he had done to his father. He wanted forgiveness from his father, a forgiveness that would never come. And he wanted to forgive his parents, a forgiveness he thought he could never give.

Releana was kneeling beside him, holding his bloody hand. The others had also gathered around. J'role wanted to speak to her, to show her he had done it. He had gotten his voice back.

But the tears flowed too thick, and his voice cracked with sobs, and his throat was so thick with grief that he could not speak a single word.

ROC

DARING ADVENTURES

☐ **SHADOWRUN #9: SHADOWPLAY by Nigel Findley.** Sly is a veteran who has run more shadows than she cares to remember. Falcon is a kid who thinks he hears the call of magic and the voice of the Great Spirits. Together, they must face deadly confrontation between the world's most powerful corporations—one that could turn to all-out warfare, spilling out of the shadows and onto the streets themselves. (452283—$4.99)

☐ **SHADOWRUN #10: NIGHT'S PAWN by Tom Dowd.** Although Jason Chase was once able to shadowrun with the best, time has dulled his cybernetic edge. Now his past has come back to haunt him—to protect a young girl from the terrorists who want her dead, Chase must rely on his experience and whatever his body has left to give. And he needs everything he's got, as he comes face to face with an old enemy left for dead. (452380—$4.99)

☐ **SHADOWRUN #11: STRIPER ASSASSIN by Nyx Smith.** Death reigns under the full moon on the streets of Philadelphia when the deadly Asian assassin and kick-artist known as Striper descends on the City of Brotherly Love. (452542—$4.99)

Prices slightly higher in Canada.